The Fast Forward MBA in Project Management

SECOND EDITION

ERIC VERZUH

WILEY

John Wiley & Sons, Inc.

Published by John Wiley & Sons, Inc., Hoboken, New Jersey.
Published simultaneously in Canada.

For general information on our other products and services please contact our
Customer Care Department within the United States at (800) 762-2974,
outside the United States at (317) 572-3993 or fax (317) 572-4002.

Wiley also publishes its books in a variety of electronic formats. Some content
that appears in print may not be available in electronic books. For more
information about Wiley products, visit our web site at www.Wiley.com.

Library of Congress Cataloging-in-Publication Data:

Verzuh, Eric.
   The fast foward MBA in project management / Eric Verzuh.—2nd ed.
      p. cm.—(The fast forward MBA series)
   Includes bibliographical references and index.
   ISBN 0-471-69284-0 (pbk.)
1. Project management.   I. Title: MBA in project management.
II. Title.   III. Series.
HD69.P75V475 2005
658.4'04—dc22   2004027080

Printed in the United States of America
10 9 8 7 6 5 4 3 2 1

For Marlene

ACKNOWLEDGMENTS

There are no unimportant jobs on any project, and there are no unimportant people on the project team. From concept through completion, many people have been involved in the development of this book. To each of the people who have shaped this book through their advice, encouragement, and hands-on participation, I offer my thanks.

To Kymberly Actis, for her persistence and commitment as she turned my handwritten drawings into the many figures in this book.

To the professionals who contributed their effort and experience to create the Stellar Performer profiles: Rod Pipinich, Fred Black, J. C. Brummond, Virginia Klamon, John Gaffney, Brian LaMure, Marlene Kissler, and Peggy Jacobson.

To my colleagues and clients for their interest and insights: Steve Weidner, Greg Hutchins, Pen Stout, Karl Hoover, Steve Morris, Peter Wynne, Bill McCampbell, Patrick Bryan, John Spilker, and Kristian Erickson.

To the team at John Wiley & Sons, Inc. who took a risk and saw it through: Henning Gutmann, Renana Meyers, and Sam Case.

To those who put the wheels in motion: Brian Branagan, Linda Villarosa, and Barbara Lowenstein.

I particularly want to thank two top-notch project managers who have taught me much about project management, business, and life, and with whom I've had the privilege to work: Sam Huffman and the late Fred Magness.

Finally, I thank my wife, Marlene, who has played many roles on this project: coach, editor, critic, writer, and partner. Her insight and perspective have been of constant value both as I wrote this book and over the years as I built my business.

ACKNOWLEDGMENTS FOR THE SECOND EDITION

The privilege of updating this book for a second edition was accompanied by some hard work to make sure the result was actually an improvement. My thanks to those who contributed their expertise and energy.

To the professionals who shared their hard-won knowledge: Jim Smith, Donna McEwen, T. J. Filley, Rod Pipinich, and Bill Schafer.

Once again, to my wife, Marlene, whose talents and contributions permeate this work.

ERIC VERZUH

Eric Verzuh is president of The Versatile Company, a project management training and consulting firm based in Seattle, Washington. His company trains thousands of professionals every year in the fundamentals of successful project management including how to get the most out of Microsoft Project. Versatile's consulting practice focuses on helping firms establish consistent, practical methods for managing their projects and implementing Microsoft's enterprise project management solution. The company's client list includes large corporations such as Adobe Systems, Lockheed Martin, and Nordstrom, as well as government agencies and small companies. Verzuh has been certified as a project management professional (PMP) by the Project Management Institute and is a frequent speaker at project management conferences. His other publications include articles, conference papers and The Portable MBA in Project Management (2003), also published by John Wiley & Sons, Inc. Verzuh can be reached via his company's site on the Internet, www.versatilecompany.com.

CONTENTS

"What makes the second edition different?" That's my first question when I see a second edition. Project management hasn't changed too much since the first edition, so this edition is primarily justified with additional content.

- Chapter 10, "Building a High-Performance Project Team," is brand new. It assembles proven team management techniques for transforming a group of people who happen to be assigned to the same project into a cohesive unit committed to a common goal.

- Chapter 13, "Enterprise Project Management," has been significantly revised to incorporate lessons learned in the past five years as firms attempt to institutionalize project management.

- Several chapters have added content. Chapter 5, "Risk Management," includes additional proven risk management techniques. Chapter 4 describes the content for a project proposal. Chapter 12 has more advice on using earned value management techniques.

- Stellar performers—profiles of companies that put project management principles to work—have been added in Chapters 1 and 11. A new feature of this edition is the Fast Foundation for Project Management, a series of templates and checklists designed to make it just a little easier to put the concepts to work on your project. You'll find these tools located at the end of the chapters in which the concepts were presented. The templates are available for download at www. versatilecompany.com/forms, and called out in text with an icon.

It is pretty exciting to have a book that is popular enough to justify a second edition. More than anything, I am proud of how many people have said this book is practical—it makes project management make sense. The book is intended to present a realistic look at the challenges of the project environment and the skills you need to successfully bring a project to fulfillment. On the way, you will learn the tools necessary to achieve each of the five essential success factors. Part 1 lays the groundwork. In addition to simple terminology, it contains global concepts that tie project management to other disciplines, such as quality and product development. Part 1 also includes examples of the organizational changes companies are making to take advantage of project-oriented work.

Parts 2, 3, and 4 present the tools and techniques—the real science—of project management. Because this is a how-to book, the techniques in these chapters are described in detail. These techniques start with simple examples, then progress to tips for managing larger projects. In these sections, you will learn the major responsibilities of a project manager, the definition of a project, and the best ways to plan and control projects. Part 2 deals specifically with setting the goals and constraints of the project. Part 3, "The Planning Process," offers the most effective techniques for managing budgets, monitoring a project's scope, and keeping on schedule. Many of these techniques are features of popular project management software. After reading this section, you will know how to make better use of this software. Part 4 offers methods for controlling a project and keeping it on track. This section focuses on the many tools used to keep a project on track and bring it to successful completion, regardless of whether everything goes as planned. Together, these three sections provide the tool set every project manager needs.

Part 5 describes how the tools presented in this book can be used by organizations and by project managers. We look at the ways in which project management techniques are being adopted by a growing number of organizations. Finally, we look at the kind of problem situations that project managers are likely to face—and how to deal with them using the tools presented in this book.

Eric Verzuh
Seattle
January 2005

Introduction

What are projects, and why are so many businesses reorganizing to include them? Why has project management become such a popular career track? In Part 1 of this book, you will find answers to these questions and more.

Because projects differ from the ongoing operations of a firm, managing them presents a new set of challenges. Over the past 50 years, a number of tools and techniques have evolved to deal with these challenges. Chapters 1 and 2 include an overview of these techniques, along with the five factors that make a project successful.

We live in a world where change—and the rate of change—is constantly increasing. In order to survive and prosper, organizations need to continually modify their products and services. Projects are the means by which these innovations are effected. Greater change = more innovations = more projects.

Project Management in a Changing World

INTRODUCTION

Project managers are changing the world.

- A World Health Organization (WHO) "vaccination army" runs a blitz to attack polio, vaccinating 4.2 million children in a 50,000-square-mile area in three days in southern India.[1]

- A commercial aircraft manufacturer is designing a new model aircraft to be built from lightweight composites, resulting in fuel savings of 20 percent over similar-sized airplanes.

- NASA teams send sophisticated robots and probes to other planets in our solar systems, furthering our understanding of Earth and its origins.

- Nanotechnology researchers manipulate matter at the molecular level, developing materials that hold incredible potential to revolutionize manufactured products, from building bridges to transmitting electricity to the clothes we wear.

Project managers are all around us, too: building a custom home, opening a medical clinic, installing an updated accounting system, or writing a book. Everywhere that people are leading change they are managing projects.

No wonder the project management discipline has leapt from a neglected corner to center stage. Government and industry are embracing the project management discipline as leaders recognize that they are increasingly managing project-driven organizations. But change and projects have been around for thousands of years; what is different now? Just what is project management?

Before we understand the new interest in project management and project-driven organizations, we must first understand the concept of projects. *Projects* are all the work we do *one time.* Whether it's designing an aircraft, building a bakery display case, or creating a business logo, every project produces an outcome and every project has a beginning and an end. Fundamental to understanding the importance of projects is realizing that each one produces something unique. So designing and tooling up to build a new sports car is a project (actually a lot of projects), but manufacturing thousands of them is not. Manufacturing and other repetitive processes are defined as *ongoing operations.*

PROJECT MANAGEMENT IS THE NEW CRITICAL CAREER SKILL

Given this description, we can find projects—and project managers— everywhere. Every graphic artist, systems analyst, carpenter, engineer, attorney, and scientist who is creating a unique product is faced with the challenges of leading a project. As more repetitive jobs are replaced by automation, it is increasingly a necessity to be able to lead change. Economically, the arguments for understanding project management are even stronger. People and companies that innovate, that create and lead change, enjoy higher incomes and profit margins than those that compete based on economies of scale and efficiency.

Project management is not new. The pyramids and aqueducts of antiquity certainly required the coordination and planning skills of a project manager. While supervising the building of Saint Peter's Basilica in Rome, Michelangelo experienced all the torments of a modern-day project manager: incomplete specifications, insufficient labor, unsure funding, and a powerful customer. But only in the twentieth century did the title and the discipline emerge.

Much of modern project management was defined in the 1950s, on the major cold war defense programs. As a result, the discipline grew up within the aerospace and defense industries, but in the 1990s project management broke out of its traditional boundaries. It is now a recognized and valued skill set in organizations across the spectrum, from health care to manufacturing, software to natural resources. The evidence is everywhere:

- As recently as 1990, your search for a college course on project management would have turned up one or two classes within the industrial engineering school. Not so anymore. Project management is a required course in MBA programs, and universities across the country offer advanced degrees in project management.

- By 2004 nearly every Fortune 500 company had attempted to implement a project management office (PMO) in one or more parts of their organization. A PMO is responsible for instilling consistent project management practices. Only a decade earlier, most executives in these companies hadn't even heard of such an entity.

- The use of formal project management cost and schedule reporting techniques—required for decades on Department of Defense programs—is now required of all federal agencies.

- Since 1990, the Project Management Institute, the professional association for project managers, has seen its membership rise from 7,700 to over 100,000 in 2004.[2]

More important, the factors that have driven project management to center stage are not receding.

- Competition from a global economy is so pervasive it has become cliché. That competition is forcing firms to collaborate across organizational and geographic boundaries, introducing the term *virtual teams* to our business vocabulary.

- Evolving technology has put every one of us on ever-faster upgrade cycles. At a personal level, our phones, computers, and cars become out of date faster. For businesses and governments, the upgrade cycles include refineries, chemical plants, medical clinics, and weapons systems.

- The availability of a highly skilled temporary labor force is a perfect match for the projectized economy, providing the ability to rapidly increase or decrease staffing as projects begin and end.

The response to these pressures is reflected in the views of management experts.

- Oren Hararai, professor of management at the University of San Francisco and the author of two books on the changing business environment, sees the project-oriented employment trend growing. "The future of business is fluid networks of unaffiliated organizations, multiple careers simultaneously, work revolving around projects, as fluid as the external environment. Routine work can be automated or outsourced—the real value of an organization will be based on how quickly people can come together and focus on problems and solutions and then disband.[3]

- Tom Stewart, writing in *Fortune* magazine, says companies "have redrawn their boundaries, making them both tight (as they focus on core competencies) and porous (as they outsource noncore work).[4]

- Pen Stout, author, instructor, and project management consultant, sees a symbiotic relationship between the independent worker and the major corporations. "There will be strong 'big big' companies, strong 'small small' companies, not much in the middle. Project management works because it's a way for the bigs to use the strengths of the smalls."[5]

- Best-selling authors Ram Charan and Larry Bossidy make the connection between strategy and success by emphasizing the "discipline of getting things done." "If your business has to survive difficult times, if it has to make an important shift in response to change—and these days just about every business does—it's far, far more likely to succeed if it's executing well."[6]

Projects are all around us. Project management skills transcend corporate and industry boundaries, enabling us to do the same. The people who lead projects—who turn visions of what might be into tangible products and services—stand out. Further, the biggest driver of the growth in project management is getting even bigger. As we will see in the next section, change is everywhere, and change means projects.

KEY CONCEPT — THE INCREASING PACE OF CHANGE

The most irrepressible trend favoring project management is the increasing pace of change. We embrace change as it gives us increased quality of life, as with advances in medical technology or fuel economy. We may resist or resent change, particularly when it is forced upon us in the form of new regulations or new competition. But change cannot be denied and its pace is faster than ever.

New products and services are exploding onto the scene overnight, while current products are becoming obsolete faster than ever. The recent Internet boom and bust showed in dramatic fashion how rapidly the world economy can assimilate and adapt. Technology is not the only evidence of change. Pressure to increase the quality, availability, and affordability of health care keeps medical professionals and administrators restructuring their organizations. Corporate mergers in banking, insurance, telecommunications, computers, and media bring the challenges of integrating cultures and systems.

As businesses scramble to keep up with fast-moving competitors, riding the tsunami of change becomes critical to success. This emphasis on change increases the importance of project management, because a rapid rate of change brings a greater need for projects. In response to a rapidly changing marketplace, a company might reengineer itself, develop new products, or form alliances with other firms. Each of these innovations is brought about by one or more projects. Greater change = more innovations = more projects.

At a personal level, the pace of change carries the same significance. What career can we expect in 10 or 20 years, when the careers that existed 10 or 20 years ago have so often disappeared? What skills will maintain our personal and corporate ability to thrive? Among the many skills that will help us thrive in this changing world, project management stands out as the discipline originally designed to drive change.

EVERYONE BENEFITS FROM UNDERSTANDING PROJECT MANAGEMENT

The trend toward more projects has produced an ever-increasing need for people who understand how to run them effectively. Every project participant, from part-time team member to executive sponsor, becomes more effective once he or she understands the basics of project management. Learning these basics is especially important for managers at all levels, because every manager will be involved in many projects—and their authority will give them a major impact on each one.

Project management has gone beyond being merely a personal skill set. It is now considered an organizational competency. Whether you are charged with increasing your firm's total project management capability or you are playing a role on a project, you contribute to the firm's ability to effectively complete projects. Executives who select and sponsor projects may spend only an hour or two a week directly involved in a project, but their ability to speak the language of project management will dramatically affect the team's perception of management support. Likewise, functional managers—whose primary contribution to projects is to assign personnel—make more effective decisions and enable their people to perform more efficiently when they know and use the tools of project management. Of course, project team members and project managers directly affect their productivity through the use of the discipline.

This book is written for people who need to understand the time-tested techniques of project management and how those methods are being put to use in the twenty-first century. It is for people who need a complete foundation in the discipline, whether they are recent graduates, experienced executives, midlevel managers, or team members wanting to be team leaders. This book is primarily about *how:* how to get agreement on goals and how to reach them, how to enlist team members and project sponsors, how to negotiate schedules and budgets, and how to reduce risk and increase the odds of success.

DOWNLOADABLE FORMS FOR PROJECT MANAGEMENT

To make this book even more practical, this edition includes downloadable checklists, forms, and templates you can use for managing your own projects. These tools are intended to get you started quickly. Download these forms from www.versatilecompany.com/forms. Look for these at the end of Chapters 4, 5, 7, 8, and 11.

PROJECT MANAGEMENT: ART INFORMED BY SCIENCE

Project management has been called both an art and a science. In these pages, you will see how mastering the science of project management provides a foundation for the art of leadership. The necessary skills are common to both. There is no question that the best project managers are also outstanding leaders. They have vision, they motivate, they bring people together, and, most of all, they accomplish great things.

As an author, speaker, and consultant on project management, it has been my privilege to meet many of these great project managers over the years. They exist in all organizations, and they are known by management as the ones to turn to for tough projects. More important, these are the people others want to work for. I seek out these acknowledged leaders because they live and thrive in the project environment every day—the true proving ground. Amid their varied experiences is a constant theme, the basis for their success: They rigorously apply the project management discipline. For all their intangible leadership qualities, the roots of their strength are the proven techniques described in this book. That's important for all of us, because it means that success in leading projects is not reserved for the lucky few born with the skills; rather, it is a discipline that can be taught and learned. That has been my job for well over a decade, to teach new project managers tangible tools: systematic processes that can be learned in class on Tuesday and applied on the job on Wednesday.

From these great project managers and my work with thousands of professionals who have attended my classes, I've learned that certain characteristics are consistently found on successful projects in every industry. Boiled down, they consist of these five project success factors:

1. *Agreement among the project team, customers, and management on the goals of the project.* "Clear goals—now there's a yawner!" you might say. The importance of having clear goals seems so obvious that it's almost embarrassing to bring it up. Yet thousands of projects, at this very moment, do not have clear goals, and the results of this fuzziness can be devastating. In this book, you will find at least half a dozen techniques that clarify goals, and you will discover how to make these techniques work together. This means you'll employ at least six different methods to make sure that all the stakeholders want the same thing. Far from being a yawner, you'll find that this process of arriving at clear goals together can be invigorating and powerful.

2. *A plan that shows an overall path and clear responsibilities and will be used to measure progress during the project.* Since every project is unique, the only way to understand and execute it efficiently is with a plan. Not only does a good plan show *who* is responsible for what and when, but it also demonstrates *what* is possible. It contains the details for estimating the people, money, equipment, and materials necessary to get the job done. And because the plan is the basis for measuring progress, it can also act as an early warning system for tasks that are late or over budget. In Chapters 5 through 8, you'll find a systematic planning model that integrates the traditional planning techniques. This model presents a logical, step-by-step approach to creating and executing a detailed plan.

3. *Constant, effective communication among everyone involved in the project.* People—not plans or software—complete projects. A successful project is a result of people agreeing on goals and then meeting them. From concept through implementation, success depends on the ability to come to agreement, coordinate action, recognize and solve problems, and react to changes. All of these things require that people communicate well. Every technique in this book is a communication technique, designed to improve the formal and informal ways we communicate critical project information.

4. *A controlled scope.* Success is in the eye of the beholder. This is why, from the very start, the successful project manager will ensure that everyone involved understands exactly what can be accomplished within a given time frame and budget. This is called "managing stakeholder expectations," and it is an important, ongoing task throughout the project, especially if changes are introduced. Stakeholders must not only agree to the original scope of the project, but also understand any changes in scope. This book contains a systematic method for establishing realistic goals for cost, schedule, and quality, as well as techniques for keeping the goals consistent throughout the project.

5. *Management support.* Project managers rarely have enough formal authority to make all the decisions it takes to complete a project. They rely on people in traditional management roles to supply people and equipment, make policy decisions, and remove organizational obstacles. Even the most enthusiastic, creative, motivational project leaders will stumble if they do not enlist the people with authority to act on their behalf. The good news is that many of the techniques in this book can be used to "manage upward," that is, to guide the people with power toward timely decisions that keep the project moving.

Far from being mysterious, these five essential factors can be achieved through the diligent, persistent use of the science of project management. That is not to say that success comes without art—on the contrary, art is immensely important. Art encompasses political and interpersonal skills, making creative decisions when complete information is lacking, knowing intuitively when to delegate work, and more. But learning the basic science is requisite to practicing this art. Stirring up the team with a fiery speech will be a waste of energy if the project lacks goals and a basic plan.

The art of leadership embodies skills that are gained through experience, sensitivity, and a thorough knowledge of the basic science of management. Learning the basics of project management can be your first step on the road to becoming a skilled and inspiring leader. While developing all these skills may take time, the basic science can be learned fairly quickly; able students can read and practice the lessons in this book on their very next project.

 ## PROJECT MANAGEMENT MAGNIFIES OTHER STRENGTHS

Project management is a discipline designed to facilitate change, and its value grows when used with other leading business practices. Consider the relationship between project management and these other disciplines that improve efficiency and effectiveness.

- New Product Development (NPD) is a framework for identifying the need for a new product, as Robert Cooper says, "from idea to launch."[7] Cooper has developed and branded the StageGate™ process, which includes the key activities and decision points necessary to bring a new product to market and to have the market embrace the product. Within NPD many projects exist. To successfully work the NPD process, every project must be managed effectively.

- Six Sigma is an offshoot of the quality management discipline that enables organizations to increase efficiency and quality—in other words, to produce more and/or better products for less time or money. It relies on structured problem solving, statistical analysis, and process management methods. Since every Six Sigma project solves a different problem, the same five project success factors apply.

- Portfolio management is an emerging method of linking the firm's strategic goals to tactical plans. In this sense, the portfolio represents all the assets of the organization, including the projects. Portfolio management requires executives to understand where the people and assets of the firm are being deployed, and what return these assets are generating. A key challenge in this oversight is to know how many projects are under way, what the forecasted budgets for those projects are, and whether active projects are expected to be completed as planned. Effective project management practices are required to provide correct information to the executives managing the portfolio.

There are other examples. Every chapter of this book will provide further examples of the ways that project management techniques leverage other disciplines.

END POINT

Our global civilization is changing rapidly—and that change is accomplished through projects and is being led by project managers.

Projects are defined as work that happens one time only and has both a clear beginning and end. This kind of work may be contrasted with the ongoing operations of an organization that involve repetitive work—such as manufacturing—with no defined end.

Projects enable us to adapt to changing conditions. Reengineering an organization, assessing a company's direction in a new market, bringing out a new product, or adapting new technology are all necessary changes accomplished through projects. In this increasingly projectized workplace, project management has become a critical job skill and a viable career path. Professionals at every level of the organization become more valuable when they understand and apply the discipline of project management.

The purpose of this book is to help you gain these skills. Learn them and you will have every chance of steering a project from its planning stages through to its successful conclusion. While employing art and creativity are also important, the tools put forth in this book—the science of project management—provide the foundation for the success of any project.

Stellar Performer: OrthoSpot
Entrepreneurs Leverage Project Management

March 2000 was the beginning of the end for many Internet companies as the so-called dot-com bubble burst on Wall Street. Amid this gloomy backdrop, four entrepreneurs put their ideas on the line and started OrthoSpot, offering an Internet-based inventory management solution to orthopedic surgeons. By 2004 they had survived the launch years, with hundreds of orthopedic practices across 44 states relying on OrthoSpot's distribution network to supply over 60,000 products.

CEO Bill Schafer attributes the company's survival and continued growth to using fundamental project management techniques from the start. "We didn't have any idea how to start a business—how to get funding or bring our product to market." So the prelaunch months were spent in planning, building a detailed picture of the work ahead of them.

They started with a fundamental question: "What do we have to do to make money?" They built an answer from the top down. "We needed a product, business infrastructure, and sales and marketing distribution structure. Our first three major tasks became: Get a business model, raise money and set up an office." Shari Cohen, vice president of customer relations, had offered her home's basement as the original offices. "The wall's were covered with sticky notes and string, showing all the tasks and what had to be done before what."

Venture capital became difficult to find in 2000, limiting the number of employees OrthoSpot could bring on board. Schafer relied on the detailed plan to accomplish a lot with a small team. "The early-stage mentality of overcoming obstacles by intensity can lead you astray if you don't have focus and keep your eye on the objective and allocate resources appropriately."

Schafer also relied on the plan when making strategic decisions. He found that the new thinking OrthoSpot was bringing to orthopedic practices attracted other opportunities. "When you're changing the way business is done and you're making headway, a lot of opportunities present themselves—for example, do this for cardiologists. But we don't have enough people and hours to do it all, so a focus on the plan keeps energy directed. The payoff is that the team stayed incredibly energized. When they are focused they can do incredible things."

The early focus on executing against a plan has seeped into every operation at the firm. New product development efforts and system implementations for customers are driven from detailed work-breakdown structures. "It's in our DNA—project planning and accountability," says Schafer. As a result, he believes OrthoSpot is positioned to be incredibly competitive. "We compete and win against companies that have a hundred times our capital."

Orthopedic practices across the United States rely on OrthoSpot to bring efficiency and lower costs, enabling them to offer better value to their patients. OrthoSpot relies on fundamental project planning and execution to serve its growing customer base and enable the OrthoSpot founders to enjoy the fruits of their vision and hard work.

Source: Interview with Bill Schafer, June 26, 2004.

The Project Environment

INTRODUCTION

Understanding project management begins with understanding the project environment. This environment is different from that of a traditional organizational environment. This chapter looks at the ways in which managing projects differs from managing ongoing operations and shows how the discipline of project management has evolved to address the challenges that are unique to projects. In addition, this chapter establishes the terminology used throughout the book, describes the project management process, and investigates the organizational challenges posed by projects.

KEY CONCEPT — PROJECTS REQUIRE PROJECT MANAGEMENT

Why do we need a different discipline for managing projects? To answer this, we have to consider that the range of activities in any workplace can be broken down into two groups: projects and ongoing operations. To put it simply, *projects* are all the work that's done one time, and *ongoing operations* represent the work we perform over and over. By looking at each one separately, we'll see how they present different management challenges.

How a Project Is Defined

All projects have two essential characteristics:

1. *Every project has a beginning and an end.* The date of the beginning may be somewhat fuzzy, as an idea evolves into a project. The

end, however, must be clearly defined so that all project participants agree on what it means to be complete.

2. *Every project produces a unique product.* The outcome could be tangible, such as a building or a software product, or it could be intangible, such as new hiring guidelines. Part of the recent interest in project management stems from the realization that firms that deliver services have plenty of projects and can manage them with the same tools that have been used successfully in companies that produce tangible goods.

Projects abound in every industry. Here are a few examples, drawn from a variety of industries:

- Engineers redesign controls on an automobile dashboard.
- An advertising firm produces print and television ads to promote a new razor.
- Hospital administrators restructure responsibilities for nurses in their maternity ward.
- Manufacturing engineers document their processes to gain ISO certification.

Notice that each of these projects is plowing new ground, and each will be finished when it reaches the goal. Projects are unique and temporary.

Notice also that some of these projects produce tangible products, such as new software or a redesigned dashboard, while others, such as the restructuring of responsibilities for nurses, are intangible. Project results may be tangible or intangible.

Definition of Ongoing Operations

Ongoing operations have the opposite characteristics of projects in that they have no end and they produce similar, often identical, products. Ongoing operations are often the primary purpose of a firm or a department. Let's look at a few examples:

- An insurance company processes thousands of claims every day.
- A bank teller serves over 100 customers daily, providing a few dozen specific services.
- Power companies operate hydroelectric dams, controlling the energy produced and the water flowing through, day after day, for decades.

Ongoing operations produce similar products and have no defined end. Traditional management theory has focused almost exclusively on ongoing operations like the ones in the preceding list. Experts in accounting practices, process improvement strategies, inventory management, staffing, and human relations have all viewed the organization as an ongoing set of activities. The focus on managing ongoing operations continues to be relevant in the twenty-first century, but now these experts must also master the techniques necessary to manage work that is temporary and unique.

KEY CONCEPT The Challenge of Managing Projects

Work that is unique and temporary requires different management disciplines. Because projects have different characteristics than ongoing operations, they pose a brand-new set of challenges. Here are some of the challenges that face project managers:

- *Personnel.* Every project has different personnel needs. The number of people needed—and their different skill sets—is different for each project. Where do these people come from? Where do they go, once they are no longer needed? These staffing problems may be compounded if several projects are running simultaneously. If all projects hit their resource peak at the same time, it could place an impossible burden on an organization. And if all the projects should end around the same time, the company may be forced into layoffs.

- *Estimating.* In order to evaluate potential projects, organizations need accurate estimates of costs and schedules. But because each project is different, estimates may contain more assumptions than facts.

- *Authority.* Organization charts define authority within a firm, but they usually represent the ongoing operations of the firm. When projects cross organizational boundaries it is no longer clear who has authority for many decisions. This can lead to political maneuvering and a gridlock that blocks progress.

- *Controls.* Normal accounting practices match operational budgets to operational costs on a quarterly or annual basis. But these time frames are not sufficient to keep a project on track. By the time quarterly accounting reports show a project over budget, it may be so far out of control that it's beyond recovery.

This list of difficulties and challenges could go on, but it should be clear by now that managing projects is not the same as managing ongoing operations. Notice that this does not mean project management is more difficult than managing ongoing operations—only that managing projects presents a different set of challenges.

The project management techniques within this book have evolved to meet these challenges. As you progress through this book, you can review this list of problems to see just how the tools and techniques you are learning address each one.

Clearly, projects and ongoing operations overlap and interact. Projects initiate or change ongoing operations. At times, projects exist within an ongoing operation, while at other times the reverse is true. Both may be funded out of the same budget process and use many of the same people. Both require a wide range of the same management skills: written and oral communication, conflict resolution, motivation, accounting, and negotiating, to name just a few.

But these similarities can obscure the real differences between projects and ongoing operations. Recognizing these differences leads to a better understanding of their different challenges. Projects, as we have seen in the preceding section, have unique problems that require different management disciplines. Project managers must learn these disciplines to become effective leaders.

THE EVOLUTION OF A DISCIPLINE

> If one of you decides to build a tower, will he not first sit down and calculate the outlay to see if he has enough money to complete the project? He will do that for fear of laying the foundation and then not being able to complete the work.
>
> —Luke 14:28–29

From the time humans first worked together to build a shelter or cultivate a crop, there have been projects and project management. Yet it has been only since World War II that a formal project management discipline has emerged. During and immediately after the war, the U.S. government was engaged in enormous weapons development projects. The Manhattan Project, in which the first atomic bomb was designed and built, is generally recognized as the first project to use modern project management techniques.

Subsequent government initiatives to build nuclear-powered submarines and warships required so much innovation and invention, and were so hugely expensive, that they could not be governed by existing management techniques. The first modern project management methods were constructed to deal with these enormous projects. Their names—*program evaluation and review technique* (PERT) and *critical path method* (CPM)—are still well known today.

Understanding the development of project management as a discipline can lend insight into its role in the world today. Before World War II, project management was considered a subset of technical knowledge. For example, John Roebling, who conceived and led the building of the Brooklyn Bridge with his son, Washington, was a civil engineer who pioneered the building of suspension bridges with steel cables. But even though Roebling was known as a great civil engineer, his triumphs building this and other bridges were due at least as much to his management skills. Similarly, Michelangelo, the architect of Saint Peter's Basilica in Rome, also managed the project, which included tasks such as wrangling with the popes over finances. Even today, as project management gains recognition as an independent discipline, it is still common to view it as the rightful domain of the lead technician, whether this individual is an engineer, an accountant, or a physician.

The experience of the U.S. government with the aforementioned atomic and nuclear projects began to change this notion. Because there were so many facets to these giant projects, no one person could be responsible for all the technical decisions. Bottlenecks involving coordination and communication began to restrict progress. In addition, Congress demanded some accounting of the enormous amounts of money pouring into these programs. This crucible of change forged the first formal management procedures for planning and managing projects. Even though expert knowledge of nuclear physics or submarine warfare was still necessary, the managers of these projects were no longer required to be the leading experts in their field.

Since then, the U.S. government has been a leader in developing and promoting project management techniques, for the very good reason that these techniques continue to be necessary to manage its huge defense, space, and civil projects.

During the last half of the twentieth century, project management evolved from an unacknowledged skill set into a recognized profession, complete with academic degrees and certifications. But one key question remains: Is project management a set of knowledge and techniques that can be understood and applied independent of a technical specialty? To what degree is technical knowledge required to effectively lead a project? Could John Roebling have designed the Brooklyn Bridge and then employed a project manager with no engineering skills to complete it?

 Project Management Is Industry-Independent—Project Managers Are Not

The popularity of project management in recent years owes much to its ability to transcend boundaries. The techniques put forth in this book can be applied to projects in any industry. From Silicon Valley to Broadway, projects of every size are becoming more efficient, and their products are improving in quality, thanks to the use of solid project management methods.

This industry independence has been a major factor in the development of project management as a discipline, but that independence doesn't extend to the people practicing the discipline. Project managers must not only know how to operate in business and project environments, they must also be well acquainted with the focus of the project. Specifically, project managers require skills in three different areas:

1. *Project management.* This is the pure discipline described in this book.

2. *Business management.* Negotiating, finance, customer recruitment, organizational development, communication, and motivation are skills that any good manager should have, whether managing projects or operations.

3. *Technical.* Nearly every company that has developed a career path for project managers begins the path with technical competence. Whether it's accounting, advertising, computer chips, or oil pipelines, the person leading the work needs to know it thoroughly. These same career paths, however, don't require candidates for project lead roles to be the best technicians in the group.

Project managers are more likely to be involved in technical decisions on small projects, but even on large programs, managers need to understand the work being performed. If they don't, they might be able to act as facilitator, catalyst, motivator, and cheerleader, but they won't be able to understand or participate in technical problem solving. "Good," you might be thinking. "I don't want to be involved in the detail work." But project managers who don't understand the technology they are managing can lose the confidence of their teams, particularly teams that are proud of their technical ability.

It makes sense that the best project managers bring a mix of skills to their job, and that the larger the project, the more project management skills are required. But even the leader of a one-person project needs to be able to organize work and communicate clearly with customers and management. (Figure 2.1 uses a three-axis graph to illustrate how the project environment dictates different skill requirements for project managers.)

Perhaps the best proof that management theory is portable comes from the companies that work with the discipline the most, that is, the project management consulting firms. These firms work effectively in all industries—not by having all the right answers, but by having all the right questions. Bring them in to kick off a project and they'll focus your team on the key issues, help you to perform risk assessments, and build project plans. Throughout this process, however, they will be acting as a catalyst and facilitator—not as a decision maker. The decisions will be made by the project manager with the help of his or her team, because they are the ones who possess the technical skills demanded by the specific project.

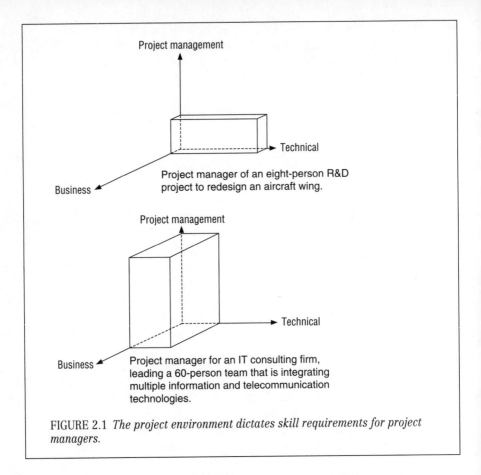

FIGURE 2.1 *The project environment dictates skill requirements for project managers.*

Project management is industry-independent—the theory works in all kinds of industries. But project managers are not industry-independent—they must have good technical skills in their field.

KEY CONCEPT — THE DEFINITION OF SUCCESS

This section focuses on the framework of project management. Just what are the components that go into building a successful project? How is this success defined? Here are a few answers to these questions:

On time. The product is delivered according to schedule. Some projects are essentially worthless if they aren't on time. For example, the IT infrastructure required to operate an Olympic Games is no good after the games are complete.

On budget. The project meets forecasted cost estimates. Projects are investments, and those that run over budget can end up costing the organization more than they bring in.

High quality. The product must be of a high quality. Quality is often difficult to define. According to Philip Crosby, quality is "conformance to requirements."[1] In the project management context, quality refers to the outcome of the project. This outcome has two components:

1. *Functionality.* What the product is supposed to do. How fast will it go? How many people will it carry?

2. *Performance.* How well the functionality works. Software can have all the right features, but if the features don't work, it is considered poor quality.

Both functionality and performance can and should be specified early in the project. How they are specified will depend on what's being built or delivered. Process requirements for a hospital reengineering project, for instance, will be documented differently than requirements for a new model of a commercial aircraft.

KEY CONCEPT

THE COST-SCHEDULE-QUALITY EQUILIBRIUM

Cost, schedule, and quality are the three primary variables of a project. Change one or more of these variables, and the ones remaining will also be changed. For example, if the amounts of time and money available for a project are reduced, this will almost certainly limit the quality of the product. Similarly, to deliver the same quality in a shorter period will cost more. Your challenge, as a project manager, is to balance these variables to create the optimal cost-schedule-quality equilibrium.

KEY CONCEPT

Managing Expectations

Unfortunately, delivering a project on time, on budget, with high quality doesn't always mean you are successful. Why not? Because your definition of the cost-schedule-quality equilibrium may not have been the same as your customer's or manager's definition. Even if their expectations of cost and speed are unrealistic, nevertheless, they are the final judges of your project, and in their eyes it may be late, over budget, or poor quality.

This may seem unfair, but it does happen. This kind of disagreement, however, is preventable. Recognizing that our project's success is defined by the perceptions of others is a powerful incentive to make sure that all parties involved in the project agree on the basics. This leads us to a new success formula for project managers:

1. Set realistic expectations about the cost-schedule-quality equilibrium with all the project's stakeholders.
2. Manage expectations throughout the project. If the equilibrium changes, make sure everybody knows and accepts the new equilibrium.
3. Deliver the promised product, on time and within budget.

THE ULTIMATE CHALLENGE: NO DAMAGE

In an environment where the focus is delivering high quality on time and under budget, project managers can be tempted to meet impossible goals by sacrificing the people on the team. It happens in every industry, and always for the same reason: Meeting the project goals outweighs the needs of the individual team members. And this attitude isn't reserved just for the project team; vendors and even customers are often put through the wringer to satisfy the project goals. But asking people to give 120 percent, project after project, just doesn't work. They get worn out, demoralized, and just plain angry. The ultimate challenge for project managers is to meet the cost, schedule, and quality goals of the project without damage to the people. That means the project ends with high morale, great relationships with customers, and vendors that can't wait to work with you on the next project.

PROJECT MANAGEMENT FUNCTIONS

Setting realistic expectations, fostering agreement among all parties, and then delivering the product is frequently challenging and always requires a wide array of techniques (see Figure 2.2). From a high level these techniques can be grouped into the three project management functions.

1. *Project definition* lays out the foundation for a project. There are two activities involved in this groundwork.
   - The project manager must determine the purpose, goals, and constraints of the project. He or she must answer questions like, "Why are we doing this?" and "What does it mean to be successful?" The answers become the foundation for making all project decisions because they describe the cost-schedule-quality equilibrium and connect the project to the mission of the organization.
   - The manager must establish basic project management controls. He or she must get agreement on which people and orga-

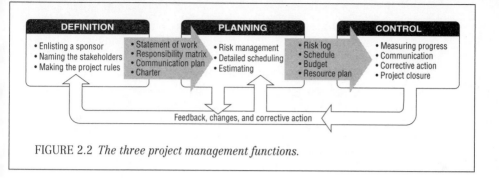

FIGURE 2.2 *The three project management functions.*

nizations are involved in the project and what their roles will be. The manager also needs to clarify the chain of command, communication strategy, and change control process. The documented acceptance of these decisions and strategies communicates expectations about the way the project will be managed. It also becomes an agreement to which you can refer to keep everyone accountable to their responsibilities in the project. The written document that comes out of this process of definition can be defined as the *project rules* because, like the rules to any game, they outline how to play and what it takes to win.

2. *Project planning* puts together the details of how to meet the project's goals, given the constraints. Common estimating and scheduling techniques will lay out just how much work the project entails, who will do the work, when it will be accomplished, and how much it will cost. Along the way, risk management activities will identify the areas of greatest uncertainty and create strategies to manage them. The detailed strategy laid out in the plan becomes a reality check for the cost-schedule-quality equilibrium developed during project definition.

3. *Project control* includes all the activities that keep the project moving toward the goal. These activities include:
   - *Progress measurement.* Measuring progress frequently identifies any problems early, making them easier to solve. Progress measurement is also a feedback mechanism, validating the estimates in the plan and the cost-schedule-quality equilibrium.
   - *Communication.* Communication is critical in controlling a project, because it keeps all the participants coordinated and aware of project progress and changes.
   - *Corrective action.* This consists of the day-to-day responses to all the obstacles and problems a project may encounter.

These functions sum up the responsibilities of the project manager. The functions are sequential: A project must begin with definition, then proceed to planning, and finally to control. And the functions must be repeated time and again, because planning will inevitably lead to modifications in the definition, and controlling actions will require constant changes to the plan and, occasionally, changes to the definition. During an ongoing project, a manager may spend time every day defining, planning, and controlling the project.

Parts 2, 3, and 4 of this book correspond to these three functions of the project manager: project definition, project planning, and project control. Each part deals in detail with the techniques necessary to perform each of these functions.

PROJECT LIFE CYCLE

A project life cycle represents the linear progression of a project, from defining the project through making a plan, executing the work, and closing out the project (see Figure 2.3). At first glance, it might seem that this life cycle is the same as the project management functions. Define, plan, and execute seem to map directly to definition, planning, and control. The difference is that the life cycle is linear and the phase boundaries represent decision points. Let's look more closely at these four decision points:

1. *Define.* The phase begins when a project and a project manager are named in a *project charter,* and it is completed when the project rules are approved. Approving this written document means that all interested parties agree on the project goals, approach, and cost-schedule-quality equilibrium.

2. *Plan.* After the rules are approved, the project manager begins building the project plan. Of course, as the details of how to execute the project are worked out, it's likely that some of the decisions in the project rules will change. At the end of the planning phase, all parties must not only approve the plan, but also any necessary changes to the project rules.

   Defining and planning can be short phases, particularly for short projects. Since planning often changes the project rules, some companies use a single phase, called *initiation,* to describe both of these activities (see Figure 2.3). The best argument for keeping the

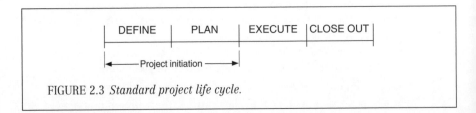

FIGURE 2.3 *Standard project life cycle.*

phases separate is that a number of questions need to be answered in the definition phase before a detailed plan can be produced. The basic assumptions and agreements worked out during definition make the planning activities more focused and productive.

3. *Execute.* We are now at the stage of performing the actual work as approved in the plan. This phase probably takes 90 percent or more of the project's effort. The execution phase is complete when the goal of the project is reached.

4. *Close out.* This is the smallest phase of the project, but no less important than the others. Closeout activities perform three important functions: (1) making the transition to the next phase, whether that is operations or another product development phase; (2) establishing formal closure of the project in the eyes of the customer; and (3) reviewing project successes and failures with a view to improving future projects.

The importance of the first two phases in the project life cycle cannot be overemphasized. Even though these two phases—define and plan—usually represent 10 percent or less of the total effort, they are essential in preparing the team for efficient performance during the execution phase.

 **A Product Development Life Cycle**
May Contain Many Projects

One of the reasons project management techniques are increasing in popularity is due to their role in new product development. Whether the effort is a new drug, a new software product, a new model car, or a new baseball stadium, it is done one time and produces a unique product. Since product development has the same characteristics as a project, creating these new products provides excellent opportunities for applying project management. The four steps necessary to create a new product are known as the *product development life cycle:*

1. *Requirements.* This step defines the function and performance requirements for the product. Whether you're building a house, an airplane, or an information system, requirements describe how the product will meet the needs of the customer.

2. *Design.* Design conceives a product that will meet the requirements and describes it in detail. For instance, a blueprint is a detailed description of a house.

3. *Construct.* Next, the product is built, and any documentation necessary for its operation is written. If a building is being constructed, this is where they dig the holes and pound the nails. In the case of

REQUIREMENTS	DESIGN	CONSTRUCT	OPERATE

FIGURE 2.4 *Product development life cycle.*

a new model of an aircraft, construction might encompass a wide range of activities, including the creation of new manufacturing processes. (In this case, the product isn't exactly a new airplane, but rather a new process for building airplanes.)

4. *Operate.* After the product is developed, it has a life span in which it is actually used. Projects then turn into ongoing operations: A baseball stadium holds games, a manufacturing process turns out new automobiles, or a software product company supports its users. The operation phase can last for years and may contain many projects.

There are two important points to understand about the product development life cycle. First, this is a simplified life cycle model. Any firm that has documented its development process will have a far more detailed model, including not only more phases, but a number of subphases or steps. For instance, a detailed development life cycle for producing information systems can contain 50 to 100 discrete steps. The process for bringing a new drug from initial research all the way through FDA approval could have 1,000 steps.

Second, even though it is simplified, the development life cycle model (as portrayed in Figure 2.4) can probably apply to your industry and environment (even a service industry). This model will be used in examples throughout the book, because, while it is simple enough to apply to most cases, it still shows the basic differences between product development life cycles and a project life cycle.

KEY CONCEPT Product Life Cycle versus Project Life Cycle

Although new product development, like a project, has a beginning and an end and produces a unique product, *it may consist of more than a single project* (see Figure 2.5). Anyone wishing to apply project management to new product development must understand the differences between a product life cycle and a project life cycle. These differences are easily defined. A *product development life cycle* will be industry-specific. The specific steps for reengineering an emergency room admissions process are different from the steps for building a refinery. The *project life cycle* is industry-independent, because project management theory is industry-independent. Defining these differences further:

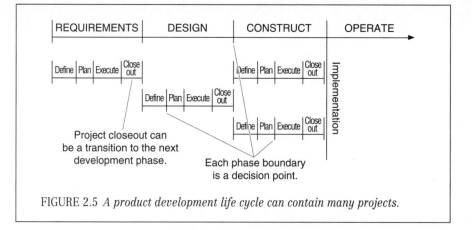

FIGURE 2.5 *A product development life cycle can contain many projects.*

- The product development life cycle describes the work required to create the product. The project life cycle focuses on managing the work.
- A product development life cycle may contain many projects, each of which must go through the full project life cycle.

Understanding that any development effort can contain multiple projects and that each one needs to be managed as a complete project is one of the keys to success in project management.

ORGANIZING FOR PROJECTS

Certain firms perform nothing but project work; large construction companies fit this model. The majority of their organization is devoted to specific projects. On the other end of the spectrum, utilities are operations-oriented. The majority of companies, however, conduct ongoing operations *and* projects.

Creating an organizational structure that supports projects has never been easy. After all, if a project happens only one time, requires a unique mix of people, and has a unique reporting structure, how can any firm create an organization chart that will last beyond the end of the next project? While projects can play havoc with organization charts, over the years there have been some classic organizational responses to the project environment (see Figure 2.6). The following spectrum of organizational styles favors ongoing operations on the one end and projects on the other.

Function-driven firms are organized around primary functions such as advertising, engineering, information systems, manufacturing, and human resources (see Figure 2.7). Workers have one manager who both assigns and monitors their work and handles administrative

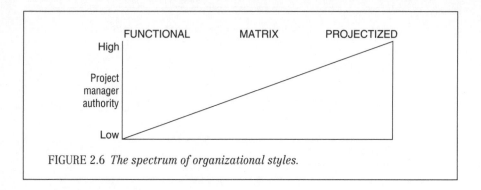

FIGURE 2.6 *The spectrum of organizational styles.*

tasks, such as compensation. Projects *within* functional groups pose no organizational problems, but projects that *span* functional groups are arduous to manage because project managers have no functional authority and must work through the functional managers to assign, monitor, and coordinate work.

Matrix organizations are required when many projects span functional boundaries. This structure gives authority to both project managers and functional managers by having both of them report to the same executive (see Figure 2.8). Functional managers will be involved in deciding who will work on project teams and will maintain respon-

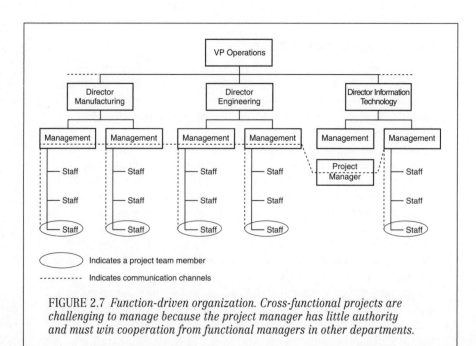

FIGURE 2.7 *Function-driven organization. Cross-functional projects are challenging to manage because the project manager has little authority and must win cooperation from functional managers in other departments.*

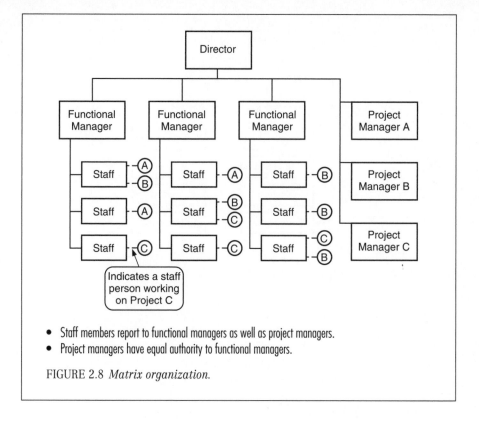

- Staff members report to functional managers as well as project managers.
- Project managers have equal authority to functional managers.

FIGURE 2.8 *Matrix organization.*

sibility for long-term administration issues. Project managers assign, monitor, and coordinate work among the project team. The main problem with the matrix organization is that every person working on a project has two bosses—and if these people work on more than one project they will have even more.

Project-oriented organization is appropriate for firms that work on large, long-term projects. Rather than finding projects within and among functional departments, functional departments exist within the project (Figure 2.9). Project-oriented firms (also called *projectized firms*) may have redundant operations among multiple projects, but they're willing to put up with that organizational inefficiency in order to maximize management effectiveness on the project. For example, in the heavy construction industry, such firms set up an entire organization for managing every aspect of their enormous projects.

Another style of project-oriented organization is the *program.* Programs consist of many related projects, but unlike a single project, they have no specific completion date expected. For example, when Boeing develops a new model aircraft, the company establishes a program that is responsible for everything from selling the aircraft to

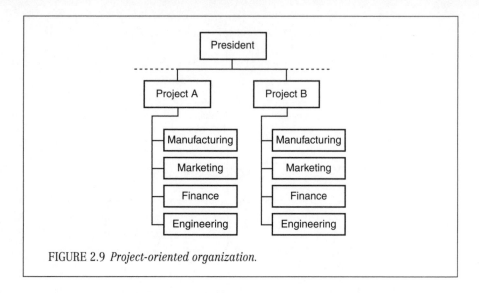

FIGURE 2.9 *Project-oriented organization.*

developing customer service processes—a wide variety of separate but related projects. A variation of the program is a *product-oriented structure,* which uses the firm's products as the driving organizational factor. Product-oriented organizations replicate functional disciplines such as marketing and product development for each product organization. An example is a software company that has marketing, development, and testing personnel assigned to specific product groups, such as word processing and spreadsheet groups.

KEY CONCEPT   Surviving Your Organizational Structure

Understanding organizational styles is more than an academic exercise because choosing the right structure could provide a competitive advantage for a firm. But how does the structure affect you as a project manager? Consider the following five issues:

1. *Authority.* Clearly, the difference between the organizational styles is that some favor projects while others favor ongoing operations (Figure 2.6). In the function-driven organization, the project manager has almost no authority, and in the project-oriented firm, the project manager has total authority. Less authority requires more effort to get decisions made and implemented.

2. *Communication.* Communication is a primary project success factor no matter what the organizational style. Most organizational structures facilitate vertical (top-down and bottom-up) communication patterns, but your communication requirements may run counter to the prevailing patterns. Crossing organizational bound-

aries always takes more effort, but you must do whatever is necessary to keep all the stakeholders informed and coordinated.

3. *Priority.* Multiple projects often compete for limited quantities of people, equipment, and funding, especially in firms with the traditional, function-driven management style. Project managers in a function-driven structure often have their teams and resources raided to handle a problem with ongoing operations or to work on a new project.

4. *Focus.* If a firm is project-oriented, you can be certain that projects are the center of its attention and the reason for its existence. Everyone has a unifying purpose that drives all decisions and helps to increase productivity. This compares favorably with matrix and function-driven organizations, where project team members are often working on projects less than half their time. In these companies, the diffused focus and increased span of responsibilities tend to lower emotional commitment and productivity.

5. *Chain of command.* If the chain of command for a project runs counter to the organizational structure, it takes more effort to bring a problem to the attention of the proper manager. As the project breaks through functional boundaries, more and more functional managers are required to approve decisions. And, if certain functional groups have competing interests, clashes over authority can bring progress to a standstill.

Project-oriented firms make it easy to run projects because their entire structure is set up for that purpose. In most organizations, however, project managers may have difficulties in dealing with the authority structure. In these cases, they will have to rely more on the authority of their own expertise—and on the project management tools presented in this book.

PROJECT MANAGERS ARE LEADERS

The discipline of project management can be compared to a set of woodworking tools. Both are designed for specific purposes, and both are capable of amazing results in the hands of a master.

Every project needs someone who, regardless of his or her title, performs the functions of project management. It is a role that can be fulfilled in a few hours a week on small projects or spread among many people on very large projects. But this role cannot be defined purely in terms of the functions of project management or the project management tool set. It must also be understood that the primary responsibility of a project manager is to lead all the stakeholders—the customers, management, vendors, and project team—and encourage them to work together during the course of the project.

Bringing a project to a successful conclusion may require every technique in this book, but none of these techniques will be enough unless the manager wants to lead. The project manager is the catalyst—the initiator who lifts the entire project and puts it into motion. As you learn the techniques presented here, never forget that it is your energy and attitude that gives them power!

END POINT

Projects differ from the ongoing operations of a firm in that they are temporary and unique. These qualities mean that factors like personnel management, lines of authority, budgeting, accounting controls, and communication need to be handled differently in the project environment. The project management techniques discussed in this book have evolved to meet these challenges.

Modern project management evolved from the giant defense projects during and after World War II. These endeavors were so enormous that normal management techniques proved inadequate. In addition to technical knowledge, managers of projects came to need business skills and the new skills related to managing temporary and unique projects. Project management techniques have now become industry-independent, even though each project manager must have skills specific to his or her industry.

Successful projects deliver a high-quality product on time and on budget. Project managers, however, need to be aware that everyone involved in a project—all the stakeholders—must agree on what success means. Managing expectations is one of the main jobs of a project manager. Success depends on the manager guiding the project through four stages in its life cycle: definition, planning, execution, and closeout.

One of the reasons for the present popularity of projects is the growing number of new products. Product development employs a process roughly similar to that of projects; the differences are that a *product development life cycle* describes the work required to create the product, while a *project life cycle* focuses on managing the work. This need for new projects has brought about the creation of companies organized around doing projects—project-oriented organizations.

Stellar Performer: Seattle Children's Hospital and Regional Medical Center
Hospital-wide Process Redesign

Virginia Klamon

The growth in project management is powered by the speed of change in every sector of the American economy. The techniques traditionally applied to the manufacturing or aerospace industries are proving equally valuable in the services sector, particularly when applied to process redesign or improvement efforts.

In 1996, Children's Hospital of Seattle, Washington, a regional leader in pediatric medical services, realized it needed to dramatically improve its patient management process. Customer complaints were mounting and employee morale was suffering.

The hospital organized a team to undertake the effort of redesigning patient management systems and named the project "Encounters." The new system would streamline and standardize processes such as admitting, registration, scheduling, and insurance verification. The goal was to make things easier and more efficient at Children's, from the initial call from a family or doctor, to the visit or stay, and following discharge.

STAGE ONE: DIAGNOSTIC ASSESSMENT

From August to November the project team performed a diagnostic assessment as stage one of the effort. The team gathered customer feedback data, interviewed key organization stakeholders, created a process map of the current system, and identified external business needs driving current industry changes. The primary deliverable from this stage was the project charter. This document included a scope definition, process goals and objectives, project approach, resource requirements, cost-benefit assessment, and risk matrix. The project scope definition included the boundaries of the organizational change and the work required to accomplish it.

STAGE TWO: PRELIMINARY DESIGN

The project team quickly moved to the second stage—preliminary design—once the project charter was drafted and approved.

Using creative thinking and proven process modeling tools, the team was ready to move forward to design a new patient management system. During this stage each new process link was painstakingly identified and documented. An iterative approach allowed successive design ideas to be layered in on top of the ever-developing process model. Patient scenarios were used to test the evolving design, allowing the team to walk through each step patients would encounter as they were admitted or treated.

(Continued)

(Continued)

Stakeholder involvement is critical to organizational redesign, particularly during the development of the preliminary design, the new conceptual process model. To promote involvement and stakeholder input, a display room was open 24 hours a day, seven days a week. From March through July 1997, employees, patients, and physicians were invited to view the new preliminary design. Feedback was encouraged and received, creating repeated design adjustments throughout the phase.

STAGE THREE: DETAILED DESIGN

From July through December the team drilled the new processes down to the lowest level of detail as part of the third stage, detailed design. The new designs were rigorously tested through hours of computer-based process simulation. Using simulation, the project team was able to model system performance, running what-if scenarios to determine how long patients would have to wait to check in for a clinic visit and what it would cost if they added additional staff during specified shifts.

It's important to realize that redesigning the process meant redesigning all aspects of the patient management system, including work flows, process performance measures, information systems, facilities and space, roles and job descriptions, and organizational culture. Computers don't simulate the social system components, so stakeholder involvement was designed into the process every step of the way. The communication plan consciously chose a variety of mediums to keep the information flowing, including a newsletter, all-hospital forums, and presentations to the Hospital Steering Committee.

STAGE FOUR: IMPLEMENTATION

In January 1998 the team began to prepare for stage four of the project: implementation. Significant changes were required for the hospital computer systems. New software was selected to meet the requirements of the new system design. New services were planned for rollout. Detailed comparisons of the current process were made against the new design so that changes would be identified and documented. Sequencing of dependent activities was determined and tracked on a master project plan.

With implementation under way, the hospital has already begun to reap the benefits of its new Encounters patient management system. A more streamlined admissions process, including patient/family valet parking, is producing increased customer satisfaction. The segments of referral processing installed so far are already producing enhanced efficiencies during the patient check-in process.

(Continued)

(Continued)

STAGE FIVE: CONTINUOUS IMPROVEMENT

Children's Hospital, like many organizations today, faced the formidable challenge of redefining the organizational culture. It endeavored to develop new norms for promoting continuous learning and continuous improvement. While continuous improvement is defined as the final stage of the redesign life cycle, it represents much more than the completion of the hospital's redesign project. It represents the cyclical nature of an improvement process.

Encounters is changing both the processes and the culture of Children's Hospital. The team attributes its successes to many factors, including some of the universal best practices of project management.

Sponsorship

The Hospital Steering Committee (HSC), led by the hospital's chief operating officer (COO) and medical director, was visibly involved in the project. The members publicly supported the project by attending project functions, feedback sessions, and design review sessions and by representing Encounters to the greater hospital organization, including the board of trustees. The COO acted as the primary contact point and was the most visible member of the HSC to the project and the hospital staff.

Early Stakeholder Identification and Involvement

During stage one, the team developed a comprehensive system map defining all process areas impacted and the extent of the interrelationships. Most areas of the hospital were impacted in some way. While the Hospital Steering Committee acted as the representative body for all stakeholders, other stakeholders were clearly recognized and represented, including patients and families, physicians, insurers, and employees.

Communication Plan

A communication plan supported the project from start to finish, identifying the different stakeholder groups, their information needs, and the channels for reaching them. The channels ended up covering the spectrum: visibility rooms, all-hospital forums, project e-mail, intranet updates, a newsletter, and a 24-hour voice-mail hot line open for project-related questions and comments.

Team Building

The project team was carefully selected based on members' functional or technical knowledge and prior experience working on similar projects. Initially, there were just a handful of individuals working together, but during the preliminary design and detailed design phases the team eventually grew to more than 50 to 60 and edged up close to 100 at times. Experiential team-building exercises and creative problem-solving training prepared them to think beyond the status quo and endure the challenges of organizational and cultural change.

(Continued)

(Continued)

Risk Management

A consistent obstacle to organizational change is the fear and resistance people have to leaving old ways behind. Encounters consciously addressed this risk by bringing in resources to assist the team in defining behavioral and cultural change requirements that would support the new processes going forward. Workshop sessions had also been held prior to this effort, which provided information and practical tips for understanding the human side of change. These activities helped to make employees aware of the dynamics of dealing with change and to understand how people move through the change curve, thus helping them respond constructively.

Detailed Planning

Each stage of Encounters was progressively more complex and forced the team into areas beyond its experience. To keep the project controlled and to support the team members who were learning while performing, the project plans were broken into great detail, often listing task assignments day by day. At times the amount of planning and oversight activity and project work grew so much that several outside project management specialists were temporarily brought on to the project.

Scope Management

Organizational change projects are particularly susceptible to scope creep because they have so many dimensions and touch so many parts of the firm. To fight this tendency, all the process design deliverables were subject to rigorous change control, beginning with the project charter in stage one. All requests for changes were logged and addressed weekly by a project oversight team consisting of two process managers, the information systems director, members of the project team, and the project manager.

SUMMARY

Health care is changing more rapidly than nearly any other industry. Children's Hospital and Regional Medical Center shows that dramatic change can take place and improve the service provided to its young patients. Its success is testimony to the potential for the industry, the commitment required from every level of the hospital's staff, and the need for a structured, disciplined approach to organizational change.

Virginia Klamon is a process engineering consultant.

PART 2

Defining the Project

Who is responsible for what? Who has authority? What are our goals? How do we communicate? In most organizations, these questions were answered long ago; the unique nature of projects, however, means that all of these questions have to be addressed each time a project begins. How they are answered will constitute the rules of the game, and all those involved in the project—the stakeholders—have to agree on these project rules.

The rules define the project, and this structure of rules then provides the foundation for the next two stages of the project: planning and control. Chapters 3 and 4 look at the roles played by the various stakeholders and the steps necessary to bring all of them to agreement on the definition and direction of the project.

Project Stakeholders

INTRODUCTION

At times, it seems as though technology does all the heavy lifting in our economy. A closer look, however, reveals that it is always *people* who make the technology produce. On projects, we call these movers and shakers *stakeholders,* because they have a stake in the project. The first task of a project manager is to identify these stakeholders.

Customers, decision makers, vendors, and employees obviously belong in this group, but, in a larger sense, anyone who participates in the project or is impacted by its result is a stakeholder.

Identifying stakeholders is a primary task because all the important decisions during the definition and planning stages of the project are made by these stakeholders. These are the people who, under the guidance of the project manager, establish agreements on the goals and constraints of the project, construct the strategies and schedules, and approve the budget.

This identification is an ongoing task. Throughout the initial stages of the project, the project manager must continue to clarify who the stakeholders are and what roles they will play. This chapter describes the roles of the five primary stakeholders—*project manager, project team, functional management, sponsor,* and *customer—* and the impact each has on the success of the project. It's important to keep in mind that these are all *roles.* They can, therefore, be filled by one or more people, and an individual can play more than one role.

STAKEHOLDERS ARE THE HEART OF A SUCCESSFUL PROJECT

The customer may always be right, but project managers have a different mantra: "Satisfy stakeholders!" It's not enough to deliver on the customer's demands; successful projects have to meet all stakeholder expectations. Remember that the first project success factor states that the project team, customer, and management must all agree on the goals of the project. Satisfying all stakeholders is a tough target, particularly if they pop up later in the project with new demands and requirements (this can happen!). This is why it's critical for project managers to know from the start exactly who the stakeholders are and what they want. Only then can they fulfill their primary task of satisfying the stakeholders.

Project managers may have to satisfy each stakeholder, but they will also receive valuable contributions from each one. All parties involved in a project have a vital interest in the project's success—and each has an essential contribution to make. Whether it's authority, funding, or expertise in product requirements, all contributions are needed to ensure success. Projects that lack one of the key stakeholders are likely to come to an abrupt halt or career off course.

How to Identify Stakeholders

Sometimes identifying stakeholders is easy; other times you have to go out and find them. When searching for stakeholders, rather than asking, "Who is the customer?" or "Who is the project team?" ask, "Who will make a contribution?"

STAKEHOLDER ROLES: PROJECT MANAGER

What does a project manager contribute to the project? Magic, or, more precisely, practical magic. Just as a symphony conductor directs the orchestra to bring out the magic in the music, the project manager must keep all the disparate groups in a project moving in harmony. Whether he or she is planning the project, identifying the stakeholders, watching for cost overruns, or refereeing disputes, the project manager has the primary role in any project. And, while balancing all the various tasks can make project managers appear like magicians, the skills that form the basis of this magic can be learned.

Because this book is mostly about the contribution project managers make to projects, the description here is brief; however, one point needs to be made. Once selected, the project manager should clearly identify the stakeholder roles on the project, *including his or her own.*

The project manager must ask questions like: "What is my authority?" "Who do I report to?" "Does this mean I'll be relieved of other responsibilities?" "What are my expectations?" If you are a project manager, you are an important stakeholder, too. Don't forget to satisfy yourself!

STAKEHOLDER ROLES: PROJECT TEAM

KEY CONCEPT

Who will do the work? The answer is the project team, in tandem with the project manager. All groups and individuals who contribute time, skills, and effort to the project are considered team members. In addition to the people from the company assigned to the project, these can include contractors, vendors, and even customers.

The concept of customers as team members might seem confusing, because they are the ones being served by the project. But it is not unusual for customers to have specific project tasks to perform. For example, on information systems projects, customers are often active participants in the system definition and design phases. Or, when the project involves switching to a new office complex, the customer might take responsibility for organizing the training associated with operating the new facility.

Determining who will be part of the team happens at the start of the project, during definition and planning. This process is complete when the team members have agreed to their responsibilities and roles on the project. Let's look at the steps in this process, from start to finish:

- Tasks are broken down until the different skill requirements emerge.
- The project manager and sponsor then begin recruiting people and organizations with the necessary skills.
- The project manager negotiates the involvement of these new team members.
- The manager clarifies the plan and ensures that all members understand it.
- Team member responsibilities are documented in both the statement of work and the project plan.

It's often easy to identify the essential players on small projects, but much more difficult and time-consuming on large projects. However, this time is well spent because the makeup of the project team is critical to project success.

Keep Team Members with Minor Roles Informed

Many team members play essential, but minor, roles. You, as manager, will need to distinguish between these part-time or temporary members and the core team, because communication strategies will be different for each. For example, people from another department may contribute less than 10 percent of the effort to your project and be involved for only a few weeks. You will need to communicate any progress related to their work before they actually get involved, but they won't need to participate in every weekly status meeting. In addition, some people with very specialized skills may make a very limited, but essential, contribution to your project. You will not only want to keep them aware of progress related to their tasks, but you will have to consult with them concerning their availability to your project.

KEY CONCEPT · STAKEHOLDER ROLES: MANAGEMENT

Working productively with company management is important to the success of any project. *Management,* in this case, refers to *functional management,* also known as *line management.* These can be department managers, first-level supervisors, or executive vice presidents. With the exception of a project-oriented organization, functional managers are responsible for an organizational unit, such as "Engineering" or "Internal Audit" rather than for a specific project. These are the people with long-term control over employees and other resources in the firm. They are also involved in setting company policies—policies that may impact the project. Figure 2.8 shows a typical matrix organization.

Chapter 1 identified "management support" as one of the commonly stated characteristics of successful projects. When asked to expand on what kind of management support is most helpful, most project managers describe help in "getting the right people at the right time" and "timely decisions based on the facts presented by the project team." These perceptions highlight the contributions that functional management makes to the project team. They can also guide the project manager in identifying which functional managers might be stakeholders on a specific project.

The project manager must work closely with functional managers in getting the best people for the job. After management has initiated a project and described its scope, the project manager designs a work plan that details what skills are required for the project and which departments the workers possessing these skills will come from. Armed with this information, the project manager is now ready to identify the managers of those departments; these are the managers who will have control over the workers assigned to the project team and will decide when they are available. These managers must approve the statement of work (as described in Chapter 4) and the project plan, because the potential team members identified in these documents will come from their department. Throughout the life of the project, these functional managers can be extremely helpful in solving personnel or performance problems.

"Making timely decisions based on the facts provided by the team" is the other major responsibility of management. Identifying the managers who will make decisions can be tricky. Start with the obvious ones:

- Managers whose operations will be affected by the outcome of the project
- Managers representing other stakeholders, such as the customer
- The manager to whom the project manager reports

For each of these managers, remember to keep in mind why they will be interested in your project and which decisions they will influence.

After identifying the obvious decision makers, the project manager needs to identify the less obvious ones, such as those with veto authority. As an example of the importance of this task, consider the story of a training department in a large company that decided to create a project management curriculum. The training specialist responsible for the curriculum proposed a progression of courses, from basic topics, such as scheduling, through advanced topics, such as negotiating and program management. It was a very thorough curriculum, based on requirements gathered from organizations throughout the company and available courses from respected vendors. But the proposal wasn't implemented. The manager responsible for purchasing and administering this curriculum looked at the number of students projected annually for the intermediate and advanced topics, and he decided there was not enough demand to warrant the overhead associated with these courses. It was difficult to dispute his decision because this manager was applying sound, stated company policy.

The training specialist had not considered this stakeholder or his veto power, and the result was a dramatically scaled-down curriculum with a far smaller scope. The question that wasn't asked soon enough was, "Who will be involved in approving this curriculum?" (Miller and Heiman describe this decision maker in their book, *Strategic Selling*. While this is primarily a book about selling, any project manager promoting organizational change will benefit from understanding the decision-making processes outlined in the book.[1])

Ask the Right Questions about Managers

Which managers will make decisions? Who has veto power? Who is indirectly affected by these decisions? These are the kinds of questions a project manager needs to ask when considering who the stakeholders in management are. The responsibility matrix described in Chapter 4 is an excellent tool for distinguishing between the different types of stakeholder involvement.

KEY CONCEPT — STAKEHOLDER ROLES: SPONSOR

Many projects are organizational anomalies. They cross department and corporate boundaries; they staff up for short periods, then disband; they may span a portion of a budget cycle while drawing funding from multiple groups within a company. The temporary, ad hoc nature of projects can create major problems for project managers because their authority is typically insufficient to cope with these organizational challenges. The sponsor is the solution to these problems.

The sponsor is the person with formal authority who is ultimately responsible for the project. A sponsor may be a senior executive or a junior manager. The sponsor's position and authority in the organization are independent of any project, which enables the sponsor to act as a connection between a project and the normal decision-making process. The sponsor might use his or her power on behalf of the project manager, provide advice, or influence project priority. The sponsor provides the authority that the project manager often lacks.

There are two basic concepts in understanding the importance of sponsors to the project. First, sponsors are ultimately responsible for the success of the project. The real, formal authority that comes from their title and position in the organization endows them with this responsibility. Second, the sponsor's primary task is to help the project team be successful. The best sponsors know they aren't sponsoring a project, they are sponsoring the *project manager* and the *project team.* The sponsor's job is to help these people be successful. That's why another term for sponsor is *champion,* as in "I am championing this project team and I will not let anything stand in their way!"

Duties of a Sponsor

A sponsor's primary contribution to a project is his or her authority. There are many tangible ways sponsors lend their authority to projects. A sponsor may:

- Prominently support the project manager by issuing a *project charter.* The charter is an announcement that names a new project, the purpose of the project, and the project manager. (For more on charters, see Chapter 4.)

- Assist in developing a *responsibility matrix.* The responsibility matrix shows how different stakeholder groups will be involved in the project.

- Review and approve the *statement of work* (SOW). The SOW describes the goals, constraints, and project management guidelines of a project.

- Review and approve the *project plan*. The sponsor must endorse the cost-schedule-quality equilibrium represented in the plan.

- Advise the project manager, and discuss the status of the project with this manager on a regular basis. Sponsors must involve themselves in a project before problems arise so that they're able to join in the problem solving. Uninformed sponsors—sponsors in name only—are of little help to a project manager when obstacles arise.

- Monitor and maintain the priority of the project relative to other projects. Because an organization has limited resources, there are always more valid projects proposed than time, money, and people can deliver. To execute projects efficiently, an organization must be clear about the priorities of its various projects, including the amount of funding and other resources assigned to each. In spite of stated intentions to prioritize, however, the reality is that people are often pulled from one project to fight fires on another. This robbery may continue until the original project falls so far behind that people are thrown back at that one. The sponsor's job is to keep this unproductive staffing practice from affecting the project. He or she must keep the size of the project team and the size of the budget as constant as possible.

- Assist the project manager in overcoming organizational obstacles. When the project manager lacks the authority to overcome bureaucracy, the sponsor will have to step in on behalf of the project. Proof of the value of this type of intervention comes from a study by an information systems department in a Fortune 500 firm. This study determined that having a known and active sponsor was the *number one reason* for a project's success, because problems were given timely attention by a manager who had authority to effect a solution.

In most corporate environments, enlisting a powerful, interested sponsor is critical to the success of a project. This manager will promote and protect the project and provide the formal authority in the organization that a project manager often lacks. We have discussed the qualities to look for in a sponsor. Now we turn to the last in our list of the five project stakeholders.

STAKEHOLDER ROLES: THE CUSTOMER

Whenever a project exists, somebody will be paying for it. And whoever pays usually gets the first and last word on product description, budget, and the criteria by which success will be measured. Although other stakeholders may try to squeeze in extra requirements, the final say on the product will come from the customer, because this customer is paying the bills.

This sounds simple enough—the customer is the one who pays the bills—but in reality, identifying the customer is not always that simple. Consider a project manager who is given the task of installing the latest Microsoft operating system on all the desktop computers in her company. Since there are a number of possible options when installing this operating system, the question arises: Who should decide which options will be installed? Should this decision come from the 335 employees using the computers? Is this group the customer? Or is the president of the company, who is funding the project, the logical choice? In this case, the project manager must go beyond the question, "Who is the customer?" and instead ask, "What process should I use in determining the installation requirements, and who should be involved in making the cost-benefit trade-off decisions?"

As this example demonstrates, accurately identifying the customer on a project can be difficult. In a large and diverse customer group, it can be unclear exactly who has the authority to represent the group. Here are some guidelines for dealing with different customer groups:

- The project manager must distinguish between the people with final authority over product requirements, those who must be consulted as the requirements are developed, and those who simply need to be informed what the requirements are. Where there is a known customer, such as on defense, construction, professional service, or information system projects, it might seem easy to identify this stakeholder. But problems arise from the fact that so many people in the customer organization are anxious to offer product requirements, while so few of them will actually be paying the bills. (The responsibility matrix, described in Chapter 4, is a good tool for managing this challenge.)

- In the case of industries whose products have many customers (automobiles, software, appliances, etc.), the project manager must ascertain which departments should be included as stakeholders. In companies like these, there are so many ultimate customers that the project must develop alternate "customer representatives." Marketing departments often fill this role by performing market research on what the next product should be, but problems may arise when other departments also want to be included.

- In public sector projects, project managers need to follow the customs and laws governing public works projects. These municipal projects present special challenges, because the customer group is composed of all the citizens who will use the utility, road, or other service built by the project. Citizens also fund the project. "Do I need to listen to *all* my stakeholders?" lamented a project manager for a major municipal government. "There are over 200,000 people who'll be affected by the sewage treatment system we're installing!"

Fortunately, his answer existed in the laws describing the public comment process used in his municipality. These laws lay out an orderly process for including the citizen stakeholders in public hearings on the proposed project. Despite this legitimate process, however, it's important to note that public works projects are very often contentious; they can be held up by lawsuits from citizen groups or become political footballs. A project manager can only put out information on the project, follow the rules, and hope for the best.

Customers contribute funding and product requirements. Determining who fills the role of customer can present real challenges to a project manager. In making this determination, a manager must be guided by two basic questions: Who is authorized to make decisions about the product? Who will pay for this project?

KEY CONCEPT

LEAD THE STAKEHOLDERS

This chapter started by emphasizing the importance of defining the stakeholders, because not only is project success judged by stakeholder satisfaction, but every stakeholder makes an essential contribution to the project. As the project manager, you not only need to know who your stakeholders are, you also need to exercise leadership with this diverse group. Since no one knows more about your project than you, it is up to you to lead the project in the right direction. Here are a couple of ways to exercise this leadership:

- *Control who becomes a stakeholder.* As noted, among functional managers and customers there are always plenty of people anxious to influence your project. However, if you feel that certain people don't have the right to this influence, you need to push back. You can get the support of your sponsor or other stakeholders in this endeavor, but you need to use whatever persuasive skills you have to control who is allowed to influence the project.

- *Manage upward.* Many of the stakeholders, including your sponsor, functional managers, and some of your customers, will have more formal authority than you do as the project manager. But they need you to lead them. They need you to ask the hard questions, provide reasonable alternatives, confront them with facts, and continually motivate them toward action by your own persistence and enthusiasm.

END POINT

Because they include everyone with a vital interest in a project, stakeholders are the heart of a successful project—and the heart of successful project management involves satisfying the expectations of these stakeholders. The first step in this process is gaining agreement: The project manager, the project team, functional management, the sponsor, and the customer must all agree on the goals of the project. The project manager must then coordinate all these stakeholders in the process of guiding the project through its various stages. This includes not just leading the project team, but also managing upward, that is, using your expertise and knowledge of the project to guide the functional managers, sponsor, and customer.

Making the Rules

INTRODUCTION

Every project is different. Different schedules, different products, and different people are involved. And, on any given project, the various stakeholders may have differing ideas about what the project is about. Your job, as project manager, is to make sure that everyone involved understands the project and agrees on what success will look like. The term *project rules* is not in any project management text or glossary. But clarifying the rules of the game for a new project is exactly what skilled managers need to do. And before they can communicate these rules to the players, they must be absolutely sure of them themselves. As in any new game, a project manager might ask: Who is on my side? How will we keep score? What is the reward? Seasoned project managers know that a new project can be as different from its predecessor as ice hockey is from gymnastics.

The need for project rules is part of the challenge of each new project. Since each one is different, you have to re-create the basic roles and processes of management every time a project begins. A close parallel is what happens in a reorganization of a company. After a reorg, the typical questions are: Who is responsible for what? How will we communicate? Who has authority? If these questions are not answered, the organization will fall apart; the same holds true for projects.

KEY CONCEPT   PROJECT RULES ARE THE FOUNDATION

Remember the five rules for the success of a project? These were defined in Chapter 1 and include agreement on goals, a plan, good communication, scope control, and management support. No less than three of these crucial factors are dependent on a careful writing of the project rules:

1. *Agreement on the goals of the project among all parties involved*

2. *Control over the scope of the project*

3. *Management support*

This chapter looks at how to create project rules that will address these three factors. All project management activities flow from and depend on these rules, which is why there must be general acceptance of the project rules before the project begins. All the stakeholders—project team, management, and customer—must agree on the goals and guidelines of the project. Without these documented agreements, project goals and constraints might change every day. They are the guidelines that orchestrate all aspects of the project. Let's take a closer look at how a careful writing of the project rules can influence our three success factors:

1. *Agreement on the goals.* Getting agreement on project rules is rarely easy. This is because the views of all the stakeholders must be heard and considered. This give-and-take may be so time-consuming that some may push for moving on and "getting to the real work." This haste would be counterproductive, however. If the stakeholders can't come to agreement on the basic parameters of the project before the work begins, there is even less chance they will agree after the money begins to be spent. The time to resolve different assumptions and expectations is during this initial period before the pressure is turned up. One of the definitions of a successful project is that it meets stakeholder expectations. It's the job of the project manager to manage these expectations, and this job begins by writing them down and getting agreement. Project rules document stakeholders' expectations.

    Project rules also set up a means by which the project may be changed in midstream, if necessary. This *change management* stipulates that the same stakeholders who agreed to the original rules must approve any change in the rules. (For more on change management, see Chapter 11.) The possibility of change emphasizes once again the necessity of having everything down on paper before the project begins. With this material in hand, the project manager will be well equipped to detail any effects that the changes might have on cost, quality, or schedule in an ongoing project.

2. *Controlled scope.* Because each project is different, each is an unknown quantity when it is started. This uniqueness adds to the challenge and fun of projects, but it can also lead to dramatic over-

runs in budgets and schedules. Later in the chapter, we'll look at several ways of avoiding these overruns by keeping the scope of a project clearly defined. A careful writing of the project rules is key in keeping the project team focused and productive.

3. *Management support.* It is a rare project manager who has sufficient authority to impose his or her will on other stakeholders. This is why a sponsor from senior management (as defined in Chapter 3) is a crucial factor in the success of a project. We will discuss how this management support may be written into the project rules. There are four methods to ensure that everyone understands, and agrees to, the project rules. The first, the *project charter,* is an announcement that the project exists. The following three, the *statement of work,* the *responsibility matrix,* and the *communication plan,* are developed concurrently and constitute the actual written documents containing the project rules.

Note: As you read this chapter it will be helpful to refer to the downloadable forms found at the end of the chapter.

KEY CONCEPT — PUBLISH A PROJECT CHARTER

In the early 1970s a television show began each episode with Jim Phelps, ably played by Peter Graves, accepting a dangerous, secret assignment for his team of espionage agents. Sometimes on an airplane, other times in a restaurant or at a newspaper stand, Phelps received a plain manila envelope containing photographs and a cassette tape. After describing the mission, the voice on the cassette always ended with the famous line, "This tape will self-destruct in five seconds." We knew the extent of their risk because week after week the message was consistent: Phelps and his agents were working alone and, if caught, would not be assisted or recognized by the government of the United States. Dangerous, mysterious, and always successful, *Mission: Impossible* brought a new cold war victory every week.

With his committed team and detailed plans, Jim Phelps is a study in successful project management, with one exception—the *Mission: Impossible* team required complete secrecy and anonymity. No one could know who they were or what they were doing. Most corporate and government projects are exactly the opposite. Project managers don't need secrecy, they need recognition.

Because projects are unique and temporary, a project manager's position and authority are temporary. When a project begins, most of the people and organizations necessary for its success don't even know it exists. Without formal recognition, the project manager operates much like Jim Phelps, mysteriously and without supervision, but with far less spectacular results. That's why a project charter is so important; it brings the key players out into the open where everyone can see them.

A project charter announces that a new project has begun. The purpose of the charter is to demonstrate management support for the project and the project manager. It is a simple, powerful tool. Consider the following example.

During a major software product release, Sam, the project manager responsible for training over 1,000 help desk workers, selected a printer to produce the custom training materials required for the project. This large printing order was worth more than $500,000. After authorizing the printing, he was challenged by a functional manager who asked, "Who are you to authorize these kinds of expenditures?" (Sam is not a functional manager.) Sam responded by simply producing a charter and the statement of work for his project, signed by the program manager responsible for the entire release of the new product. "Any other questions?" he asked. "No. Sorry to have bothered you, Sam."

The charter clearly establishes the project manager's right to make decisions and lead the project.

The Content and Audience of a Project Charter

A charter is powerful, but it is not necessarily complex. As an announcement, it can take the form of an e-mail or a physical, signed document. It contains the name and purpose of the project, the project manager's name, and a statement of support from the issuer. The charter is sent to everyone who may be associated with the project, reaching as wide an audience as practical because its intent is to give notice of the new project and new project manager. The simplicity of the charter can be seen in the downloadable charter form found at the end of this chapter.

Establishing Authority

From their positions of temporary authority, project managers rely on both expert authority and legitimate authority. *Expert authority* stems from their performance on the job; the better they perform their job and the more knowledge and ability they display, the greater authority they will be granted by the other stakeholders. *Legitimate authority* is the authority conferred by the organization. The project charter establishes legitimate authority for the project manager by referencing the legitimate authority of the sponsor. In the second of the preceding examples, Sam received authority from the program manager for his specific project. The charter said, in effect, "If you challenge Sam within the scope of this project, you are also challenging a powerful program manager."

Project Managers Need Expert Authority

 Don't be misled by the power of the charter. Legitimate authority is important, but it is not sufficient. Project managers, like all leaders, lead best when they have established expert authority.

Getting the Right People to Sign the Charter

 The charter establishes legitimate authority, so the more authority the signature has, the better, right? Not necessarily. If every project charter had the signature of the company president, it would soon become meaningless. The sponsor is the best person to sign the charter, because he or she is the one who will be actively supporting the project. The customer is another good choice for signing the charter. Every project manager would benefit greatly by a show of confidence from the sponsor and the customer.

Project Charter Can Have Two Meanings

There are two ways most firms use the term *project charter*. One is the way it is described here: as a formal recognition of authority. This is the way the Project Management Institute recognizes the term.[1] The other refers to the project definition document described in this chapter as a statement of work. Both uses will probably continue to be widespread.

The Charter Comes First

This chapter describes three techniques that document the project rules: the statement of work, the responsibility matrix, and the communication plan. All of these are agreements among the stakeholders. The charter, on the other hand, is an announcement, which makes it different in two ways. First, it should precede the other documents, because formal recognition of the project manager is necessary to get the agreements written. Second, it is not meant to manage changes that occur later in the project. The charter is a one-time announcement. If a change occurs that is significant enough to make the charter out of date, a new charter should be issued rather than amending the original.

WRITE A STATEMENT OF WORK

Clearly documented and accepted expectations begin with the statement of work (SOW). It lists the goals, constraints, and success criteria for the project—the rules of the game. The statement of work, once written, is then subject to negotiation and modification by the various stakeholders. Once they formally agree to its content, it becomes the rules for the project.

The Statement of Work May Be Called by Different Names

This is one project management technique that, though widely used, is called by many names. At least half the firms using the term *statement of work* use it as it is defined in this book. Watch for these different terminologies:

- Contracts between separate legal entities that include one or more statements of work will use the SOWs to define product requirements or subprojects within the contract.

- Some firms use the term *charter* instead of *statement of work*. This can be confusing because, as we have seen, this term has another common use in the project management vocabulary.

The term that an organization may use to describe the statement of work is ultimately unimportant. It is the content that matters, and this content must establish clear expectations among all stakeholders.

Audience

The statement of work is similar to a contract in that each is a tool that clarifies responsibilities and actions in a relationship. The difference is in the audience each one is aimed at. While a contract is a formal agreement between two legal entities, an SOW is directed solely at stakeholders from the same legal entity. To clarify:

- When the customer and the project team belong to the same business, the SOW is the only project agreement required.

- When the project team and the customer are different legal entities, there will be a formal contract between the two. If this contract is very large and is broken into several subprojects, the project manager may use an SOW for breaking the project into even smaller pieces and assigning them within the firm.

The Statement of Work Is Not a Contract

Although it is used to manage expectations and establish agreements, much like a contract, the statement of work as it is described here is not meant as a substitute for a contract.

STATEMENT OF WORK: MINIMUM CONTENT

Many different topics may be included in a statement of work, but certain contents *must* be included. The downloadable form at the end of this chapter will help you create your own SOW.

1. Purpose Statement

Why are we doing this project? This is the question that the purpose statement attempts to answer. *Why* is always a useful question, particularly when significant amounts of time and money are involved. Knowing the answers will allow the project team to make more informed decisions throughout the project—and will clarify the purpose for the customer.

There may be many *whys* involved here, but the purpose statement doesn't attempt to answer them all. Neither the purpose statement nor the statement of work builds a complete business case for a project. That should be contained in a different document, typically called either a *business case* or a *cost-benefit analysis.* If there is a business case, reference it or even copy its summary into the SOW.

Purpose Statements Need to Be Clear

Avoid purpose statements like the following: "The purpose is to build the product as described in the specification document XYZ." "The purpose is to deliver the product that the client has requested." Neither of these statements explains why the project is being done, so they are useless as guides for decision making.

Here is an example of a good purpose statement from an information systems project:

> *The purpose of this project is to gather revenue data about our subsidiary. During the spin-off of the subsidiary, the finance group needs this information about the subsidiary's business in order to make projections about its future revenue. This data will come from the four months beginning June 1 and ending September 30. The finance group will be finished analyzing the data October 31, and won't need it afterward.*

Notice that this purpose statement doesn't describe in detail what data is needed. That belongs in another document called the *analysis docu-*

ment. Because the purpose statement was so clear, the team was able to make other decisions, such as producing minimal system documentation. The project team knew that the life of the product was so limited that it wouldn't require lengthy documentation meant for future maintenance programmers.

2. Scope Statement

The scope statement puts some boundaries on the project. *Scope creep* is one of the most common project afflictions. It means adding work, little by little, until all original cost and schedule estimates are completely unachievable. The scope statement should describe the major activities of the project in such a way that it will be absolutely clear if extra work is added later on. Consider the scope statement for a training project in Table 4.1. It's not as detailed as a project plan, but the

---

TABLE 4.1 SAMPLE SCOPE STATEMENT

Project Management Training Rollout

This project is responsible for all training development and delivery. Specifically, this project will:

- Provide a detailed statement of training objectives for approval by the Project Office, VP of Operations, and Director of Human Resources.
- Purchase the necessary equipment and outfit training rooms at each division office.
- Acquire the rights to use and modify training materials previously developed by training suppliers.
- Modify or oversee modification of the training materials to be consistent with company standards for project management.
- Produce or contract out the production of training materials.
- Train and certify instructors.
- Promote the training to the management team at all divisions.
- Oversee the scheduling of classes, instructors, and shipments of course materials.
- Oversee and authorize travel requirements.

The following activities are critical to the success of the project, but beyond the scope of the project:

- Standardize the company's project management practices across divisions.
- Recruit trainers with subject-matter expertise.
- Identify the people who will attend the training.
- Schedule the classes at the individual sites at times that accommodate the people who will be attending.
- Administer training logistics for each site.

This scope statement is only one section within the project's statement of work.

---

major activities are named clearly enough to define what the project will and won't do.

Clarifying scope is more than just a fancy way of saying, "It isn't my job." All the cost, schedule, and resource projections are based on assumptions about scope. In fact, defining the limits of a project is so important that you will find boundaries being set in several different places besides the scope statement. The deliverables section of the statement of work and the work breakdown structure also set boundaries that can be used later to determine if more work is being added to the project. Even a product description such as a blueprint can be a source for defining scope and setting limits on scope creep.

Use the scope statement to define a project's place in a larger scenario. For instance, a project to design a new part for an aircraft will be a subset of the life cycle of the total product (i.e., the entire aircraft; see the discussion of projects versus products in Chapter 2). The scope statement is the correct place to emphasize the relationship of this project to other projects and to the total product development effort.

Specify What Is Beyond the Project's Scope

Be sure to specify what the project will *not* deliver, particularly when it is something that might be assumed into the project. Some activities may be out of the scope of the project but nonetheless important to successful completion. For example, in Table 4.1, "Recruit trainers with subject-matter expertise" is obviously a necessary part of training development and delivery, but it is specifically excluded from the project by placing it in the list of activities "beyond the scope of the project."

Product Scope versus Project Scope

Product scope can remain constant at the same time that project scope expands. If an electrical contractor estimates the work on a job with the assumption that he or she will be installing a special type of wiring, the contractor would do well to clarify who is responsible for ordering and delivering the materials. Taking on that responsibility doesn't change the *product* scope, but it adds work for the contractor, so the *project* scope is expanded.

3. Deliverables

What is the project supposed to produce? A new service? A new design? Will it fix a product defect? Tell a team what it's supposed to produce. This helps to define the boundaries of the project and focuses the team's efforts on producing an outcome. *Deliverable* is a frequently used term in project management because it focuses on output. When

naming deliverables, refer to any product descriptions that apply—
a blueprint, for instance. Once again, don't try to put the product
description in the statement of work; just reference it.

Realize that there can be both intermediate and end deliverables.
Most homeowners don't have a blueprint for their house, but they get
along fine without it. At the same time, no home buyers would want
their contractor to build without a blueprint. The distinction lies in
whether the deliverable is the final product that fulfills the purpose of
the project—in this case, the house—or whether it is used to manage
the project or development process, like a blueprint. Here are some
other examples:

- A document specifying the requirements of a new piece of software
  is an intermediate deliverable, while the finished software product
  is an end deliverable.

- A description of a target market is an intermediate deliverable,
  while an advertising campaign using magazine ads and television
  commercials is an end deliverable.

- A study of a new emergency room admissions policy is an intermediate deliverable. The actual new emergency room admissions
  process is an end deliverable.

It's important to note that project management itself has deliverables (as in the deliverables associated with each phase of a project
life cycle, as discussed in Chapter 2). The statement of work can call
for deliverables such as status reports and change logs, specifying frequency and audience.

Always Start with a Detailed Product Description

If there is no detailed product description, then creating one should
be the *only* deliverable for a project. Trying to nail down all the important parameters, such as cost, schedule, resource projections, and
material requirements, is futile if the product specification isn't complete, because the project team doesn't really know what they are
building. Software product and information system projects are
famous for committing this crime against common sense. It is premature to give an estimate for building a house before the design is complete, and it doesn't work any better in other disciplines. (For more on
this problem see "Phased Estimating" in Chapter 8, and "Product Life
Cycle versus Project Life Cycle" in Chapter 2.)

4. Cost and Schedule Estimates

Every project has a budget and a deadline. But the rules should state
more than just a dollar amount and a date. They should also answer

questions like: How fixed is the budget? How was the deadline arrived at? How far over budget or how late can we be and still be successful? Do we really know enough to produce reliable estimates? In addition, because cost and schedule goals have to be practical, it makes sense to ask other questions, such as: Why is the budget set at $2.5 million? Why does the project need to be finished December 31? Since one of the goals of making the rules is to set realistic expectations for project stakeholders, these figures must be realistic and accurate. (Any reasonable cost or schedule estimate requires using the techniques laid out in Part 3, "The Planning Process.")

Write It All Down!

Someone once observed that, when given a range of possible dates and costs, the customer remembers only the lowest cost and the earliest date. (How nice that the customer is such an optimist and has such great confidence in the project manager and his or her team!) That is exactly why it is so important to get all assumptions and agreements written down and formally accepted. The written statement of work is a much better tool for managing stakeholders than is memory.

5. Objectives

What are the measures for success? If we produce the deliverables on time and on budget, what else does it take to be successful? Often, some important additional objectives are included in a statement of work. For example, on a project to replace a section of an oil pipeline, a stated objective was "No measurable oil spills," because the pipeline was in an environmentally sensitive area. When a department store chain installed a major upgrade to its nationwide inventory system, the stated objective was "Installation will not interrupt any customer interactions at the retail stores."

Objectives should be specific and measurable, so that they can provide the basis for agreement on the project. If the oil pipeline project had simply said, "The project will be executed in an environmentally sensitive manner," a project team would have no measurable guidelines. Instead it stated clearly, "No measurable oil spills," thus providing guidance for important decisions during the project.

Objectives can also measure outcomes. Measuring the success of an advertising campaign is not based solely on cost and schedule performance in developing it, but on the impact it makes on the target market. A stated objective might read:

Retail sales of our product will increase by 5 percent among 25- to 40-year-old females living in the San Francisco Bay area within three months of the beginning of the campaign, and by 10 percent after one year.

This objective won't be measured by the ad agency when the magazine ads and television spots are completed, but the customer will certainly be aware of it for the year after the campaign is initiated.

6. Stakeholders

In any statement of work, the project manager should identify anyone who will influence the project—that is, all the stakeholders. There are five key stakeholder roles that exist in any project: project manager, project team, sponsor, management, and customer. (Stakeholders are the subject of Chapter 3.) Each one is necessary for success. List the major stakeholders and their role, describing their contribution to the project.

7. Chain of Command

Who reports to whom on this project? A statement of work must make this clear. A common way to illustrate the chain of command is with an organization chart. The need for a defined chain of command becomes increasingly important as the project crosses organizational boundaries. Figure 4.1 is an organization chart for an internal project in which all the stakeholders report to the same person. It spells out who will make decisions and which superior to refer a problem to. Since customers also make decisions, it is often useful to include their reporting structure in the SOW as well.

Go Beyond the Minimum

After including all the necessary content listed here, be sure to add any other assumptions or agreements that are unique to this project. But be careful. Putting "everything you can think of" into the SOW will make it unmanageable. Remember that its purpose is as a tool to manage stakeholders.

Write the Statement of Work First

You, as project manager, need to write out the statement of work and then present it to the stakeholders. Even though you may not know all the answers, it is easier for a group to work with an existing document than to formulate it by committee. The stakeholders will have plenty of chances to give their input and make changes once the SOW is presented to them. (Experience has shown that after all the storm and

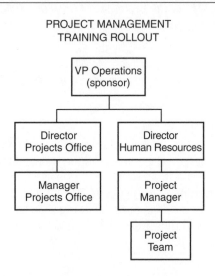

- The project manager and project team report to human resources because training is an HR function.
- The projects office acts as a subject matter expert.
- This chart complements the responsibility matrix in Table 4.2.

FIGURE 4.1 *Example: Organization chart.*

fury of group discussion is over, you may find that as much as 80 percent of your document remains as you wrote it.)

Dealing with Change

The statement of work is a tool for managing expectations and dealing with change. Should there be disagreements once the project has started, these can often be solved by simply reviewing the original SOW. It is also true that the original agreements and assumptions may change during the course of a project. In this case, all stakeholders must understand and agree to these changes, and the project manager must write them into the SOW. The SOW that remains at the end of the project may be very different from the original document. The amount of this difference is not important; what is important is that everyone has been kept up-to-date and has agreed to the changes.

KEY CONCEPT   **RESPONSIBILITY MATRIX**

A statement of work answers many questions about a project, including the purpose, scope, deliverables, and chain of command. There is, however, a need for another document that precisely details the responsibilities of each group involved in a project. This is called a *responsibility matrix*. The importance of this document is growing as corporations reengineer themselves and form partnerships and virtual companies. In these kinds of environments, many groups that otherwise might have nothing to do with each other are brought together to work on projects.

A responsibility matrix is ideal for showing cross-organizational interaction. For example, when a truck manufacturer creates a new cab style, it requires changes in tooling for the supplier as well as on the assembly line. The inevitable questions then arise: Who will make design decisions? Will the supplier have a voice in these decisions? When does each group need to get involved? Who is responsible for each part of the project? The responsibility matrix is designed to answer questions like these.

Setting Up a Responsibility Matrix

A responsibility matrix lays out the major activities in the project and the key stakeholder groups. Using this matrix can help avoid communication breakdowns between departments and organizations because everyone involved can see clearly who to contact for each activity. Let's look at the steps involved in setting up a responsibility matrix:

1. *List the major activities of the project.* As shown in Table 4.2, only the major project activities are listed on the vertical axis; detailed task assignments will be made in the project plan. (Table 4.2 is a sample responsibility matrix for the training project described in Table 4.1.) Because the responsibility matrix shows interaction between organizations, it needs to emphasize the different roles required for each task. In highlighting the roles of the various stakeholders involved in the project's major activities, the matrix in Table 4.2 uses the same level of detail as the scope statement in Table 4.1.

   On very large projects it can be useful to develop multiple responsibility matrixes with differing levels of detail. These matrixes will define subprojects within the larger project.

2. *List the stakeholder groups.* Stakeholder groups are listed on the horizontal axis of the matrix. Notice how groups such as project team and user council are named rather than individual team members; these individual team assignments are documented in the project plan. It is appropriate, however, to put individual names on the matrix whenever a single person will be making decisions or has complete responsibility for a significant part of the project.

3. *Code the responsibility matrix.* The codes indicate the involvement level, authority role, and responsibility of each stakeholder. While

TABLE 4.2 RESPONSIBILITY MATRIX FOR PROJECT MANAGEMENT TRAINING ROLLOUT

Activity	Training Team Project Manager	Project Office	VP Operations (Sponsor)	Site Coordinators	HR Director
Develop training objectives	E	C/A	A	A	A
Outfit training rooms	E		A	E	A
Acquire the rights to use/modify training materials	E	C	A		C
Modify training materials	E	I			
Establish materials production process	E		A		C
Recruit qualified trainers	I	C/A	A		E
Train and certify instructors	E				I
Promote training to divisions	E	E	E	E	E
Schedule classes, instructors	E	I	I	E	
Administer travel	E		I		
Standardize project management practices	I	E	A	I	I
Identify training participants			E	E	
Administer site training logistics	I			E	

Legend: E = responsible for execution; A = final approval authority; C = must be consulted; I = must be informed.
- *The training team and project manager report to the director of human resources.*
- *The project office is not managing the project; they are the subject matter experts.*
- *Notice how this responsibility matrix defines major tasks in much the same way as the scope statement in Table 4.1.*
- *The task level emphasizes the interaction among these stakeholders during the project.*

there are no limits to the codes that can be used, here are the most common ones:

E—Execution responsibility. This group will get the work done.

C—Must be consulted. This group must be consulted as the activity is performed. The group's opinion counts, but it doesn't rule.

I—Must be informed. This group just wants to know what decisions are being made.

A—Approval authority (usually an individual). This person has the final word on decisions or on acceptance of the work performed for each activity.

Notice how decisions can be controlled using I, C, and A. Specifying clearly these different levels of authority is especially useful when there are different stakeholders who all want to provide requirements to the project. For example, in Table 4.2, the project office has a say in selecting the basic course materials and instructors, but is left out of modifying the training or certifying the instructors. By using the responsibility matrix to specify these responsibilities, the project manager (in the training department) has successfully managed the role of the project office.

4. *Incorporate the responsibility matrix into the project rules.* The matrix becomes part of the project rules, which means that once it is accepted, all changes must be approved by those who approved the original version. The advantage to this formal change management process is that the project manager is always left with a written document to refer to in the event of a dispute. There is a downloadable form for creating a responsibility matrix at the end of this chapter.

Clarify Authority

When writing out the responsibility matrix you need to leave no doubt about who must be consulted and which stakeholder has final authority. This will have the effect of bringing out any disagreements early in the project. It's important to make all these distinctions about authority and responsibilities early, when people are still calm. It's much more difficult to develop a responsibility matrix during the heat of battle, because people have already been acting on their assumptions and won't want to back down. Disagreements on these issues later in the project can escalate into contentious, schedule-eating conflicts.

CREATING A COMMUNICATION PLAN

People make projects happen. They solve problems, make decisions, lay bricks, draw models, and so on. It is the job of the project manager to make other people more productive. Through agreements, plans, recommendations, status reports, and other means, a project manager coordinates and influences all the stakeholders while giving them the information they need to be more productive. He or she also manages customer expectations. But no matter what the task, every action of a project manager includes communication. Careful planning reduces the risk of a communication breakdown.

Let's look at what can happen when such a breakdown occurs. Dirk, a project manager for a consulting firm, tells this story:

> *We were assisting one of the biggest pharmaceutical companies in the United States with FDA approval for a new production facility they were building. Like most of our projects, the client requested a lot of changes as we proceeded. I followed the normal change management process outlined in our contract, getting the client project manager to sign off on any changes that would cause a cost or schedule variance with the original bid. Although the changes caused a 50 percent increase over the original budget, the client approved each one, and I thought I was doing my job right.*
>
> *When we finished the project and sent the bill for the changes, our customer's president saw it and went ballistic. He came down to my office and chewed me out. He'd never heard of any changes to the original bid, and he sure didn't expect a 50 percent cost overrun. The president of my company flew out to meet with the customer's president. I spent two weeks putting together all the documentation to support our billing, including the signed change orders. We did get paid, but you can bet I didn't get an apology from their president. And we didn't bill them for the two weeks I spent justifying the bill.*
>
> *I made the mistake of assuming the client's project manager was passing on the cost overrun information to his superiors. I don't make that mistake any more.*

This story illustrates the dangers of letting communication take care of itself. The answers to questions like, "Who needs information?" "What information do they need?" "When and how will they get it?" vary on every project.

A communication plan is the written strategy for getting the right information to the right people at the right time. The stakeholders identified on the statement of work, the organization chart, and the responsibility matrix are the audience for most project communication. But on every project, stakeholders participate in different ways, so each has different requirements for information. Following are the key questions you need to ask, with tips for avoiding common pitfalls:

1. *Who needs information?*

   Sponsor. The sponsor is supposed to be actively involved in the project. There shouldn't be a question about who the sponsor is after writing the statement of work.

   Functional management. Many people may represent functional management. Their two basic responsibilities of providing resources and representing policy will dictate the information they need. Each functional manager's name or title must appear on the communication plan, though it may be appropriate to list several together as having the same information needs.

   Customers. Customers make decisions about the business case— what the product should be, when it is required, and how much it can cost. There are likely to be many different levels of customer involvement, so individual names or titles must be listed.

   Project team. The project team can be a particularly complex communication audience. It will be relatively straightforward to communicate with the core team, because they'll be tightly involved in the project. Other project team members, such as vendors, subcontractors, and staff in other departments, may have a variety of communication barriers to overcome, so each will need to be evaluated separately.

   Project manager. While the project manager is the source of much information, he or she will often be on the receiving end as well.

2. *What information is needed?* In addition to the obvious cost and schedule status reports, several other types of information are distributed during the project. Basically, three categories classify how information is managed:

   Authorizations. Project plans, the statement of work, budgets, and product specifications must all be authorized. Any document that represents an agreement must have an approval process, including steps for reviewing and modifying the proposal. Be specific about who will make the decision.

   Status changes. Reports with cost and schedule progress fall into this category. So do problem logs. It is common to issue status reports, but the content of each report should be specific to the audience receiving it.

   Coordination. The project plan helps to coordinate all the players on a project. It contains the tasks and responsibilities, defines the relationships between groups, and specifies other details necessary to work efficiently. When change occurs during the course of a project, coordination among teams or locations is often required on a daily basis. The communication plan should record the process for keeping everyone up-to-date on the next steps.

Keep the Status Report Short

A common mistake is to include in the status report everything about the project that anyone might want to know. Instead of having the intended effect of informing everyone, these obese reports are over-whelming for a busy audience. When developing the report content, keep it practical. A department manager responsible for 250 projects made the point this way, "Some of our project leaders have 10 projects. If they have to spend two hours a week writing status updates, there won't be any time left for them to do work. They report to supervisors overseeing up to 80 projects. We need a way to identify and communicate the key information quickly so project leaders and supervisors can spend time solving problems and moving the projects ahead!"

Set Up an Escalation Procedure

Some problems get out of hand because they must be passed up several layers of authority before they can be resolved. The project manager must set up a procedure for communicating with higher management—called an *escalation procedure*—when a project begins to run over cost or schedule. This escalation procedure will determine which level of management to contact, depending on the degree of variance from the plan. (See Chapter 12 for further discussion of escalation thresholds.)

Make Information Timely

For information to be useful, it has to be timely. As part of the communication plan, the project manager needs to decide how often to contact each stakeholder and with what information. In fact, stakeholder response to the communication plan is a way of discerning the involvement level of each stakeholder. For example, a sponsor who won't sign up for frequent status meetings or reports is signaling his or her intention to support this project from afar. Table 4.3 uses a matrix to map which information needs to be communicated to each stakeholder and how often. Notice that a time for response is designated in Table 4.3; unless the stakeholder agrees to respond within this required time, his or her commitment to the project remains in question. The downloadable form for building this type of communication plan is included at the end of this chapter.

Include Regular Meetings in the Communication Plan

It's best to have regularly scheduled progress meetings written into the communication plan. While everyone says they would rather be proactive than reactive, many sponsors or supporting managers want to

TABLE 4.3 COMMUNICATION PLAN

Stakeholder	What Information Do They Need?	Frequency	Medium	Response
Sponsor	• High-level cost, schedule, quality performance • Problems and proposed actions	Monthly	Written report and meeting	Required in 3 days
PM's supervising management	• Detailed cost, schedule, quality performance • Problems, proposed actions, assistance required	Weekly	Written report and meeting	
Customer executive	• High level cost, schedule, quality performance • Problems and proposed actions • Required action by customer	Monthly	Meeting with project sponsor Published meeting minutes	Required in 5 days
Customer contact	• Detailed cost, schedule, quality performance • Problems and proposed actions • Required actions by customers • Coordination information for customer action	Weekly	Written report and meeting Include in project team meeting	Required in 3 days
Project team	• Detailed cost, schedule, quality performance • Problems and proposed actions • Coordination information for next two weeks • News from customer and sponsor	Weekly	Project team meeting Published meeting minutes	

Even a simple plan makes communication more deliberate and represents stakeholder commitment to attending meetings and responding in a timely manner.

have status meetings only as needed—meaning only when there is a big problem. They are willing to let the project manager handle everything as long as it is going smoothly (they call this type of uninvolvement "empowering the project manager"). In reality, when troubles occur, by the time these higher-level managers get involved, it is often too late for them to help. This is why scheduled meetings are important. If things are going smoothly, the meetings won't take long, but if a problem does arise, these meetings will give management the background information they need to be effective.

How Will Communication Take Place?

There are now myriad ways to stay in constant communication. Internet and intranet technologies allow more people to share information simultaneously. Status reports are now posted on project web sites, and videoconferencing enables project teams to be spread around the world and still meet face to face. But with all these options, the question still remains the same: What is the best way to get the information delivered? One thing is certain: Technology doesn't have all the answers. Putting a project's status on a web site, for instance, doesn't ensure that the right people will see it. You need to consider the audience and its specific communication needs. For example, because high-level executives are usually very busy, trying to meet with them weekly—or sending them a lengthy report—may not be realistic.

Consider the communication breakdown described earlier in this chapter. After Dirk's client contact failed to report budget overruns, he learned the hard way how to manage communication with a customer: "After that project, I always plan for my president to meet with a client executive at least quarterly. It goes into our contract. The client likes to see our president on-site, too, because it shows we take them seriously." In this case, the medium isn't just a meeting—it is a *meeting with the president.* (This is also an example of the company president being a good sponsor for the project manager.)

Dirk has learned to get his customers to commit to regular project status meetings. He includes this commitment in the contract, and, because the commitment is clear and formal, the customer is likely to pay attention to it.

Not all projects, however, need that level of formality. In the case of small projects with few stakeholders, you might find that discussing communication expectations early in the project is sufficient. A project manager might build a communication plan solely for his or her own benefit and use it as a strategy and a self-assessment checklist during the project without ever publishing it. In either case, whether a communication plan is formally accepted as part of the project rules or is just a guide for the project manager, the important thing is that communication has been thoughtfully planned, not left to chance.

Take a Tip from Madison Avenue

If you want to communicate effectively, why not take a lesson from the folks on Madison Avenue? Whether they are running ad campaigns for cars or computers, movies, milk, or sunscreen, they use both repetition and multiple media channels. You can mimic this by providing hard-copy reports at status meetings and then following up with minutes of the meeting. In the case of a video- or teleconference, providing hard-copy supporting materials becomes even more important.

Don't Miss Out on Informal Communication

While it is important to plan for communication, it is also true that some of the best communication takes place informally and unexpectedly. You can nurture the opportunities for informal communication. Be available. Get into the places where the work is being done or the team members are eating their lunch. Listen. Watch for the nonverbal, unofficial signs of excitement, confusion, accomplishment, or burnout.

THE PROJECT PROPOSAL LAUNCHES THE PROJECT

Project managers deliver projects, but do they deliver the right projects? If it is on time, within budget, and has the specified quality, how could it be anything but a success? The activities described previously in this chapter build a strong foundation for successful project execution—whether the project is worthwhile or not! As a project manager, you may not be responsible for deciding which projects to pursue, but you might participate in developing a project *proposal,* the basis for project selection.

Should we launch a new product? Invest in a new wing at the R&D facility? Implement the latest supply chain management software? These potential projects could provide big payoffs or produce huge disappointment. The sophisticated analysis necessary to make these decisions is beyond the scope of this book, but we can understand the fundamental factors that contribute to any business case and thereby improve our ability to manage the project to achieve the maximum benefit.

The Foundation of the Statement of Work

The basic content of the project proposal overlaps the content found in the statement of work. That makes sense, because both are used to move a project from an inspiration to a tangible, achievable goal. Since the proposal is written first, any overlap with the statement of work represents an opportunity to either verify an earlier assumption or to develop that topic in greater detail.

A Mini-Analysis Phase

As we'll see next, the content of the project proposal covers many topics that will be investigated in greater detail further along in the project. For example, articulating business requirements and predicting the tangible benefits are often performed in detail once a project is approved. It helps to understand the time spent developing the business case as a *mini-analysis phase*—knowing we won't take the time to thoroughly investigate every option and check up on every assumption, but instead will assemble enough information to make the decision to formally launch the project. We know that we will continue to evaluate the worth of the project as it progresses through subsequent phases. This iterative approach to project selection is consistent with phased estimating, which is presented in Chapter 8.

Basic Project Proposal Content

The information and analysis required to select a project will vary dramatically depending on your industry and the size of your projects. The content described here addresses the minimum topics most project selection boards require. You may find it useful to reference the downloadable forms at the end of this chapter as we explore each section of the proposal.

1. Project Goal

State the specific desired results from the project over a specified time period. For example, the goal of a training project could be: "This project will improve our ability to plan projects with accuracy and manage them to meet cost, schedule, and quality goals."

2. Problem/Opportunity Definition

Describe the problem/opportunity without suggesting a solution. The people approving the project must understand the fundamental reason the project is being undertaken. This problem/opportunity statement should address these elements:

- Describe the problem/opportunity. If possible, supply factual evidence of the problem, taking care to avoid assumptions.

- Describe the problem/opportunity in the context of where it appears in the organization and what operations or functions it affects.

- List one or more ways to measure the size of the problem. Qualitative as well as quantitative measures can be applied.

3. Proposed Solution

Describe what the project will do to address the problem/opportunity. Be as specific as possible about the boundaries of the solution such as what organizations, business processes, information systems, and so on will be affected. If necessary, also describe the boundaries in terms of related problems, systems, or operations that are beyond the scope of this initiative.

4. Project Selection and Ranking Criteria

Ideally, your firm has specific selection or ranking criteria that is addressed here. The example categories here might assist a selection board in ranking one project against another.

Project benefit category. Projects typically fall into one of the following categories:
- *Compliance/regulatory.* Laws or regulations dictate the requirements for the project.
- *Efficiency/cost reduction.* The result of the project will be lower operating costs.
- *Increased revenue.* For example, increased market share, increased customer loyalty, or a new product could all produce increased revenue.

Portfolio fit and interdependencies. How does this project align with other projects the organization is pursuing and with the overall organization strategy?

Project urgency. How quickly must the organization attempt this project? Why?

5. Cost-Benefit Analysis

This section summarizes the financial reasons for taking on the project. It consists of an analysis of the expected benefits in comparison to the costs with an attempt to quantify the return on investment.

Tangible benefits. Tangible benefits are measureable and will correspond to the problem/opportunity described in item 2. For each benefit, describe it and quantify it, including a translation of the benefit into financial terms such as dollars saved or gained. Include any assumptions you used in calculating this benefit. Forecast benefits are usually not certain, so describe the probability of achieving the result.

Intangible benefits. Intangible benefits are difficult to measure, but are still important. For example, reducing complexity in a task may increase employee job satisfaction, a worthwhile benefit but a difficult one to measure. Again, describe the benefit, the assumptions used to predict the magnitude of this benefit, and the probability the benefit will be realized.

Required resources (cost). What labor and other resources will be required? Include a comment about the accuracy of these figures. Typical cost categories include internal (employee) labor hours, external labor, capital investment, and the ongoing cost to support the result of the project.

Financial return. There are many financial methods that compare the tangible up-front cost of the project with the expected tangible benefits achieved over time. These are beyond the scope of this book, but your project selection committee should describe which of these financial measures to use.

6. Business Requirements

Describe the primary success criteria for the project in terms of what the business or customer will be able to do as a result of the project's successful completion. Many completed projects are a disappointment to the customer because they don't really address the core business/functional need that the customer had. It takes skill to uncover and document business requirements, because they usually lurk beneath the surface—below the symptoms of the problem or the customer's perception of what solution should be implemented. Remember that these requirements will be elaborated on during subsequent phases of the project, so the goal in the proposal is to understand the primary results to be achieved at a high level.

Requirements Record the Customer's View

If you describe a requirement using one of the following phrases, you are more likely to be accurately describing the true end state desired by the customer.

The project will be judged successful when . . .

We know _____

We have _____

We can _____

We are _____

You can substitute the names of specific users or customers in these statements, such as "Project sponsors know the cost and schedule status of all projects for which they have responsibility."

7. Scope

List and describe the major accomplishments required to meet the project goal. These may include process or policy changes, training, information system upgrades, facility changes, and so forth. Clearly an overlap to the statement of work, the scope description in the proposal is likely to be less detailed than the one developed for that document.

8. Obstacles and Risks

Describe the primary obstacles to success and the known risks (threats) that could cause disruption or failure. The difference between obstacles and risks is that risks *might* occur, but obstacles are *certain* to occur. Chapter 5 describes how the risk management process works continuously throughout the project to help identify potential threats and either avoid them or reduce their negative impact.

9. Schedule Overview

At a high level, describe the expected duration of the project (planned start and finish), significant milestones, and the major phases. This is an initial schedule estimate that will be refined during project definition and planning, but it is always useful to manage expectations by commenting on the accuracy of this schedule prediction.

Increase Your Value

For the purposes of this book, it is assumed that project managers are typically assigned to projects that have already been selected. In that case, the project manager uses the project proposal as the starting point for writing the project rules and creating a detailed plan. However, a proposal is far more than a starting point: It is the reason the project exists. Understanding every aspect of a project proposal makes a project manager much more valuable to the project's owner, because that means the project manager will make all decisions in the context of the ultimate goals for the project. Further, project managers looking for greater responsibility in the firm should realize that projects achieve goals—and that those who can select the right goals for a firm ultimately make a far larger impact than those who simply carry out orders.

END POINT

Each project is a new beginning, with new opportunities and new pitfalls. Making the project rules will put it on a firm footing and point it toward three of the five project success factors.

1. *The project team, customer, and management must all agree on the goals of the project.* Write down the goals and constraints in the statement of work and let the stakeholders demonstrate their agreement by signing it.

2. *The size (scope) of the project must be controlled.* Listing the deliverables and writing the scope statement are the first steps for controlling scope. Once the statement of work is signed, it can be used as a tool to refocus all the stakeholders on the legitimate responsibilities of the project.

3. *Management support.* Tangible support from management starts with issuing the project charter and signing the statement of work.

The project definition activities in Chapters 3 and 4 are the foundation of project management. The activities in the next two stages—planning and control—rely on the agreements made in the project rules. The project plan will depend heavily on the responsibilities, scope, and deliverables defined during this stage. Communication strategies will form a structure for project control.

Making the project rules is also the first opportunity for the project manager to exercise leadership. Successfully bringing the stakeholders to an agreement about the fundamental direction of the project will establish your role as the leader.

FAST FOUNDATION IN PROJECT MANAGEMENT

Start the project with a strong foundation. The templates and checklist you find on the next several pages address the key actions required to initiate the project with clear goals, effective communication, and management support.

1. The *project proposal* assembles the information necessary for a sponsor or project selection board.

2. A project sponsor can use the *charter* template to formally authorize the project and project manager.

3. The *statement of work* represents the formal agreement between project stakeholders about the goals and constraints of the project.

4. The *responsibility matrix* clarifies the role and authority of each project stakeholder.

5. Effective communication is no accident. Use the *communication planning matrix* to identify who needs what information and how you'll be sure to get it to them. Remember that having more mediums of communication increases the likelihood your message will get through.

6. As you initiate the project, use the *definition checklist* to guide the team.

Every one of these templates is available for download at www.versatilecompany.com/forms. Use these documents as the foundation of your own project management standards.

Downloadable Project Proposal*

Project name: **Sponsor:**

Project Manager: **Prepared by:**

Revision History

Revision date	Revised by	Approved by	Description of change

Project Goal

Problem/Opportunity Definition

Proposed Solution

Project Selection and Ranking Criteria

Project benefit category:

❑ Compliance/regulatory   ❑ Efficiency/cost reduction

❑ Revenue increase

Portfolio fit and interdependencies

Project urgency

Cost-Benefit Analysis

Tangible Benefits

Benefit

Value and probability

Assumptions driving value

Downloadable Project Proposal*

Intangible Benefits
- Benefit
- Value and probability
- Assumptions driving value

Cost Categories
- Internal labor hours
- External costs
    - Labor (consultants, contract labor)
    - Equipment, hardware, or software
    - List other costs such as travel and training

Financial Return

Business Requirements

Scope

Major project activities

Out of scope activities that are critical to the success of the project

Major Obstacles

Risks

Schedule Overview   *Estimated Project Completion Date:*

Major Milestones

External Milestones Affecting the Project

Impact of Late Delivery

Downloadable Project Charter*

Project name: **Sponsor:**

Project Manager: **Date:**

This charter serves to announce the initiation of the [project name] project. We are undertaking this project [*describe project background and purpose*].

[*Project manager name*] has been selected to lead this project.

Please provide your complete cooperation to the project and to [*project manager name*].

Thank you.

This charter formally authorizes the project manager and is sent out from the sponsor or project selection board.

Downloadable Statement of Work*

Project Manager:

Sponsor: **Date:**

Revision History

Revision date	Revised by	Approved by	Description of change

Purpose

Scope

Major project activities

Out of scope activities that are critical to the success of the project

Deliverables

Cost Estimates

Cost Type

Internal labor hours

External costs

    Labor (consultants, contract labor)

    Equipment, hardware or software

    List other costs such as travel & training

Schedule Overview   *Estimated Project Completion Date:*

Major Milestones

External Milestones Affecting the Project

Impact of Late Delivery

Objectives

Stakeholder Analysis

Name and Role	Major Responsibility or Contribution

Chain of Command

Project Team

Customer Approval Chain

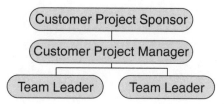

Assumptions

Assumption:

Impact if assumption is incorrect:

Downloadable Responsibility Matrix*

Project Name:

Project Manager:

This matrix describes the level of participation and authority for project stake-holders on major project activities.

Stakeholders

Activity

E *Execution responsibility.* Stakeholder responsible for getting the work done. Not necessarily a decision maker, but drives the group to make decisions in a timely manner.

A *Approval authority.* Final approval on accepting the outcome of this activity. Makes decisions.

C *Must be consulted.* As work is performed this stakeholder contributes information. Does not make decisions, but is asked for input prior to decisions.

I *Informed after a decision is made.* Wants to stay updated on progress of this activity.

Downloadable Communication Plan*

Project Name:

Project Manager:

This communication plan describes our strategy for keeping the project's stakeholders sufficiently informed to avoid any disappointment regarding cost, schedule, or quality goals.

Stakeholder	Information needs	Frequency*	Medium	Response

*Daily, weekly, monthly

Downloadable Definition Checklist*

Project Name:

Project Manager:

Stakeholder Analysis

❏ The project sponsor is known and actively involved in supporting the project.

❏ The project sponsor has sufficient authority within the project environment to effectively champion the project team.

❏ Functional managers supplying personnel or other resources to the project have been identified and are ready to supply the required resources.

❏ The people who will approve requirements and specifications, changes to requirements and specifications, and who will accept the final product are identified and have agreed to the process for these approvals.

❏ The people who will approve funding and changes to funding are known and a process exists for approving changes to funding.

❏ Stakeholders inside and outside the firm that will have veto power over any decision in the project are known and are identified in the responsibility matrix and communication plan.

❏ All contributors necessary to complete the project have been identified and understand their role on the project.

❏ The stakeholders that will receive and operate the outcome of the project are included in the responsibility matrix.

❏ Stakeholders who will be affected by the outcomes of the project are known, their stake is understood, and there is a strategy for managing them to benefit the project.

❏ A project charter that clearly identifies and shows management support for the project manager has been published.

Project Proposal

❑ A project proposal has been prepared and approved.

❑ The project manager has received and understands the proposal.

❑ Any future milestones requiring an updated proposal and renewed approval have been identified.

Documenting the Rules

❑ A statement of work has been accepted in writing by the primary stake-holders.

❑ The assumptions used to write the statement of work, particularly the cost and schedule estimates, are identified as assumptions and are realistic.

❑ There is a clear chain of authority for escalating issues and making timely decisions.

❑ A communication plan exists to identify the strategies for keeping all project stakeholders appropriately informed.

❑ A responsibility matrix has documented the roles of the various stake-holders as they relate to the major decisions and activities within the project. The stakeholders represented on the responsibility matrix have agreed that it accurately represents their involvement.

❑ A process has been established for evaluating and approving changes to the statement of work, specifications, requirements, and other control documents.

PART 3

The Planning Process

I keep six honest serving men,
(They taught me all I knew)
Their names are What and Why and When
And How and Where and Who.
                        —Rudyard Kipling

Was Kipling talking about project management? Maybe not, but his rhyme makes a good case for planning. Developing realistic cost and schedule commitments—and actually meeting them—requires detailed planning.*

The ultimate challenge in project management is *doing it right the first time*. But how can we be expected to produce accurate estimates when we're producing a unique product, one that hasn't been built before? How can we gain control over team members who don't really report to us? How can we manage stakeholder expectations so they get what they want *and* want what they get?

Accurate, organized information is the foundation of our ability to overcome these seemingly impossible obstacles. There are certain planning techniques that organize information in ways that enable us to make good decisions. There are a few ways that a project plan helps to organize a project:

*My thanks to Walter Derlacki, an experienced project manager and instructor, who introduced me to this project management rhyme.

ID	Task Name	Labor	Resource Names	Jun 15							Jun 22				
				S	M	T	W	T	F	S	S	M	T	W	T	F
1	Acquire lawn materials	32 hrs.	Homeowner												
2	Remove debris	256 hrs.	Teens, youth group												
3	Prepare soil	32 hrs.	Teens, rototiller												
4	Plant lawn seed	64 hrs.	Teens												
5	Plant shrubs	32 hrs.	Teens												

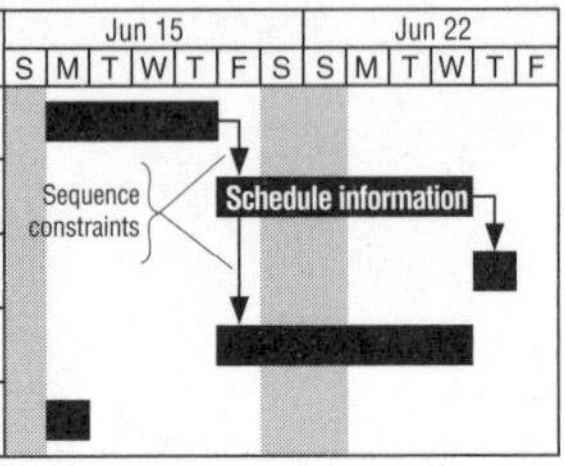

FIGURE P.1 *Essential project plan information.*

- A plan analyzes in detail how to balance costs, schedule, and quality, providing data that the project manager uses to manage stakeholder expectations.

- A plan becomes the basis for evaluating progress during the project.

- A plan includes comparisons between possible strategies for executing the project, allowing the team to choose the approach with the best chance of success.

- The resource projections contained in the plan for each project can be combined to create resource projections for the entire department or company.

Like Kipling's honest serving men, the plan contains the *what, who,* and *when* of the project. Remember the five project success factors identified in Chapter 1: *clear goals, strong communication, management support, scope control,* and *a plan used to measure progress.* Every one of these relies on the kind of information found in the basic project plan, as described in Figure P.1. In Chapters 5 through 9 you will discover the tools for building the plan and the process for balancing it against reality.

The planning techniques in the next five chapters are the tools that seasoned project managers have used for decades to organize information to make better decisions. Like the rudder of a ship, information alone is not enough; but without it, the vessel and the project both recklessly wander out of control.

Risk Management

INTRODUCTION

Life is full of uncertainty. Project managers call that *risk*. Consider the following scenarios:

- A Silicon Valley software company subcontracts part of a product development effort to a software shop in Los Angeles. How will the project manager in San Jose make sure the subcontractor produces the right product on time?

- To reduce administration costs and streamline admissions, a hospital is considering reengineering its process for creating and storing patient records. How can hospital administrators accurately estimate the cost of the change when they aren't even sure what the change will entail?

- In the design to build a completely new fighter aircraft, a defense contractor specifies lightweight composite materials. How can the contractor be sure the new materials will hold up under the pressures a fighter jet endures?

In these projects, there is uncertainty about the schedule, the costs, and the quality of the end product. How can this uncertainty be managed?

Risk management is the means by which uncertainty is systematically managed to increase the likelihood of meeting project objectives. The key word is *systematic,* because the more disciplined the approach, the more we are able to control and reduce the risks. This chapter presents a framework for transforming the uncertainty inherent in projects into specific risks and developing strategies for managing them.

 ## THE RISK MANAGEMENT ADVANTAGE

All projects experience the unexpected; but some project managers are ready for it. Impossible? The language of project risk management explains this phenomenon:

- *Known unknowns* represent identified potential problems, such as the possibility of a strike when a labor contract expires, or enough rain to stall a construction project during winter in Seattle. We don't know *exactly* what will happen, but we do know it has a potential to damage our project and we can prepare for it.

- *Unknown unknowns* are the problems that arrive unexpectedly. These are the ones you honestly couldn't have seen coming. But seasoned project managers do expect them, because they know something unexpected always happens.

The risk management advantage is that fewer problems catch the project team off guard. For every surprise thunder shower the project manager just happens to have an umbrella handy.

The ability to prepare for and reduce uncertainty is well illustrated within the insurance industry, where risk management has become a sophisticated science. Actuaries are constantly researching the probabilities of various calamities, and this research helps them set insurance premiums. Not only do insurance companies charge us for assuming risks, they actively try to avoid risks by encouraging their policyholders to avoid risky behavior. Premiums are reduced for non-smokers and for automobile owners with good driving records. The insurers even send representatives into businesses to advise them how to avoid accidents—and reduce the clients' premiums when they follow the advice.

ALL PROJECT MANAGEMENT IS RISK MANAGEMENT

Insurance companies understand and practice risk management better than most project managers because they realize that it is their primary business. Not many project managers realize that it is also *their* primary task, but those who do have an edge: They are constantly on the outlook for uncertainty that could lead to project failure.

Risk management is the primary job of a project manager? Yes, it's true, especially if you look at it this way: Every technique in every chapter of this book is really a risk management technique. Some techniques reduce the risk of being late. Others reduce the chances of overrunning the budget. A few address the process for ensuring the quality of the end product. And all techniques try to increase the satisfaction of every stakeholder and improve the chances of success.

All project management activities can be construed as managing risk, but the risk management process is a specific set of activities you'll consciously perform to identify and manage risks on the project. Like project definition, these are outcomes of the risk management process (see Figure 5.1). Let's consider the ways in which risk management activities relate to *project definition, project planning,* and *project control.*

Definition

The first risks surface as the project is conceived, the business case is constructed, and the goals for cost, schedule, and product scope are developed. Initially, these risks may be listed as assumptions, but as it becomes clear that they represent specific threats, they become the first documented risks.

Planning

Figure 5.1 shows the function of planning as having two major components: *risk management* and *schedule and budget development.* Schedule and budget development are the detailed plans required for day-to-day management of the project. Techniques for creating these detailed plans are described in the next three chapters. Risk planning

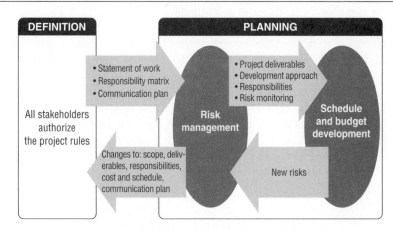

FIGURE 5.1 *Risk management influences the project plan and changes assumptions in the project rules.*

represents the formal, conscious activities of the project manager and team to identify risks and to formulate strategies for managing the risks. *It cannot be overemphasized that risk planning happens repeatedly throughout the project.* Risk planning analyzes the project's deliverables, environment, and stakeholders from a critical perspective to find any weaknesses. The project team identifies risks and develops strategies for neutralizing the risks. Those strategies, in turn, will affect the detailed action plan and may require changes to the statement of work, responsibility matrix, or communication plan.

Risk management and detailed planning have a symbiotic relationship and are iterated two to four times before project execution begins. With each iteration, the assumptions are more fully exposed and the risk management plan and the detailed schedule and budget become a more accurate reflection of reality.

Control

As the project is monitored for progress, known risks are watched and new risks are identified. Risks that don't materialize are removed from the risk plan, new risks are added, and the process of risk planning is repeated. All of these activities result in updates to the statement of work, budget reserves, progress reports, work breakdown structure, and the many other project management deliverables.

KEY CONCEPT   Business Risk versus Project Risk

The City of Seattle acquired a beautiful new office tower in the early 1990s after the lender foreclosed on the original developers. The city government was able to buy the building at a huge discount because so much of it was vacant. The developers had taken a risk in building the tower, and when the downtown office market hit a slump, they began to lose money. There was no evidence of cost overruns during construction; demand for office space simply didn't materialize.

This is an example of a successful project (a beautiful building, on time and on budget) that turned out to be an unsuccessful business venture. Business risk is inherent in all business activities, but it is seldom the project manager's job to manage it; that responsibility lies with the owner of the project. *Selecting the right project is business risk. Managing uncertainty to meet the stakeholders' objectives is project risk.*

KEY CONCEPT   THE RISK MANAGEMENT FRAMEWORK

Figure 5.2 describes a risk management process that is repeated throughout the project:

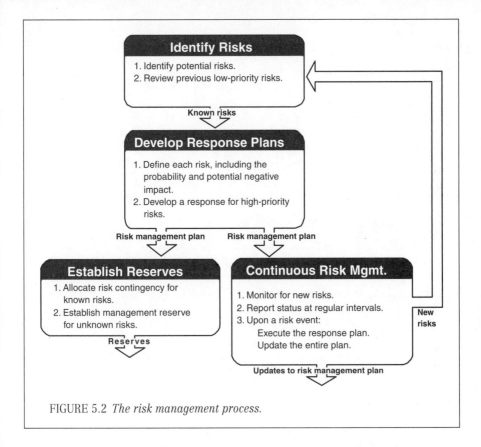

FIGURE 5.2 *The risk management process.*

- *Identify risks.* Systematically find all the factors that threaten project objectives.

- *Develop a response.* Identify each risk in terms of its possible damage and degree of likelihood and develop strategies for reducing risk in each case. Most projects have an enormous number of potential risks. Quantifying the potential damage and the probability that a risk will occur enables the team to prioritize the risks, focusing their attention where it does the most good.

- *Establish reserves.* Set aside additional funding for the project that will be used in case specific risks occur—the known risks—as well funding for the unknown risks.

- *Continuous risk management.* Implement the strategies and monitor the effects of these changes on the project. Risk strategies may require fine-tuning as they are put into effect. Communicate with the stakeholders as new risks are found, known risks are avoided, and risk reserves are spent.

Plan for Ongoing Risk Control

If it is smart to proactively plan for risk at the beginning of a project, it is even smarter to continuously plan for risk *during* the project. In the process of working through a project, new risks—both large and small—will usually emerge. Risk management is successful only if its steps are consciously repeated and applied to all risks throughout the life of the project. Planning for ongoing risk management is part of risk control and is usually documented either in the communication plan or in a specific risk management plan (to be discussed later).

STEP ONE: IDENTIFY THE RISKS

One of the scenarios at the beginning of this chapter involved defense contractors concerned about the strength of the new material they were building into fighter planes. In this example, the first critical step of risk management was performed: The risk was identified. Identifying risk involves skill, experience, and a thorough knowledge of project management techniques—both the art and science of project management. There are four techniques for identifying risk: asking the stakeholders; making a list of possible risks (a risk profile); learning from past, similar projects; and focusing on the risks in the schedule and budget. We will look at these four techniques in detail, along with tips for making them work better.

Getting Information about Risk from Stakeholders

If you want to know what could possibly go wrong on a project, just ask the people on the team—they've probably been making their own lists since they were assigned to the project. Here are two ways to involve the team in identifying project risks.

1. *Brainstorming sessions.* Everyone's favorite method for generating ideas works well for identifying risks. Gather the stakeholders and any others involved in the project and follow basic brainstorming rules:
   - Generate as big a list of potential risks as possible. Don't try to evaluate the risks as they are named; let the creativity of the group flow.
   - After generating a list of potential risks, combine similar risks and order them all by magnitude and probability. Risks that have little chance of affecting the project can be crossed off.
   Don't try to solve all the risks at the meeting. If there are easy answers, be sure to capture them, but keep the session focused on *risk identification, not response development.*

2. *Interviewing.* Interviewing individuals about risk requires a more structured approach than brainstorming. Using a risk profile with specific questions will help stimulate the person being interviewed to think about all aspects of the project.

Murphy's Risk Management Law

The art of identifying risk begins with a critical attitude. Because we're trying to find problems before they emerge, it's appropriate at first to adopt the attitude that "anything that *can* go wrong *will* go wrong." Later, after we've developed solid strategies for managing the risks, we can be optimistic again. There is, however, a big difference between a critical examination of the project to identify risks and plain old griping. It's up to the project manager to set the tone.

Include All Perspectives

People bring different perspectives to the project depending on their project role. Be sure to include customers, sponsors, team members, subcontractors, functional management, and people who have worked on similar projects. They all have a stake in the project and they'll gladly take this chance to help ensure its success.

Using a Risk Profile

One of the best ways to ensure the success of a project is to apply the lessons learned from past projects. This is done by using a risk profile. A risk profile is a list of questions that address traditional areas of uncertainty on projects (see Table 5.1). These questions have been gathered and refined from previous, similar projects. Creating a risk profile is an ongoing process: At the end of this project, what has been learned will be incorporated into the profile.

Good risk profiles follow these basic guidelines:

- *They are industry-specific.* For example, building an information system is different from building a shopping mall.

- *They are organization-specific.* While industry-specific profiles are a good place to start, the profiles are even better when they address risks specific to a company or department.

- *They address both product and management risks.* Risks associated with using or developing new technology are *product risks. Management risk* addresses project management issues, such as whether the team is geographically dispersed. Table 5.1 has examples of both product and management risks.

- *They predict the magnitude of each risk.* Even simple, subjective indicators of risk such as "high–medium–low" contribute to a clearer assessment of specific risk factors. More specific quantitative indicators offer the opportunity for greater refinement and accuracy over many projects.

Risk profiles are generated and maintained by a person or group independent of individual projects. (See discussion of the project office in Chapter 13.) The keeper of the risk profile participates in postproject reviews to learn how well the risk profile worked and to identify new

---

TABLE 5.1 EXAMPLE: RISK PROFILE QUESTIONS

Project Team

1. How many people are on the team?
2. What percent of the team is fully dedicated to the project?
3. Which team members will spend 20 percent or less of their time working on this project?
4. What is the experience level of the team?
5. Have team members worked together before?
6. Is the team spread out geographically?

Customer

1. Will the customer change current processes to use the product? (No) (Minor changes) (Major changes)
2. Will the project require the customer to reorganize? (No) (Minor changes) (Major changes)
3. Are the customers in different departments? Companies?

Technology

1. Will there be technology that is new to the development team?
2. Will there be technology that is new to the users or customers?
3. Is there any new or leading-edge technology in the project?
4. Are the product requirements clearly documented and signed by all necessary stakeholders?
5. Are the product requirements stable?

Executive Support

1. Is there a known project sponsor who is actively involved in the project?
2. Is there sufficient recognition, support and involvement from all the senior management required for the success of the project?
3. Is senior mangement setting deadlines or budget limitations independent of the project manager's schedule and budget estimations? If so, are these constraints realistic?

- Develop categories of risk, then list several questions for each category.
- Each question probes at a possible weakness.
- Add new categories and questions over time.

risks that need to be added to the profile. These profiles, when kept up-to-date, become a powerful predictor of project success. The combined experience of the firm's past projects lives in their questions.

It is even possible to buy good risk profiles. Consulting firms will sell them as part of their project management services. The Software Engineering Institute offers a detailed list of questions for evaluating risk on software projects in its *Continuous Risk Management Guidebook.*[1]

Historical Records

History continues to be the best predictor of the future. In addition to the history incorporated in the risk profile, a project manager can investigate what happened on similar projects in the past. There may be useful risk-related information already written down that you can tap into, such as:

- Planned and actual performance records that indicate the accuracy of the cost and schedule estimates.

- Problem logs that portray the unexpected challenges and relate how they were overcome.

- Postproject reviews that generate the lessons learned from the project; while these lessons are often ignored, they may be critical to the success of your project.

- Customer satisfaction records. Records like these are increasingly available in our service-oriented economy. You can mine them for the pitfalls or triumphs of your predecessors, particularly when a previous project generated either glowing praise or mountains of complaints from the customer.

Be Your Own Historian

You can be your own source of historical records in the future. Organize project documentation in such a way that it will be easy to reference long after the project has been finished.

Estimating Schedules and Budgets

Risk management contributes to detailed planning, but detailed planning is also an opportunity to discover risks (see Figure 5.1). As part of the plan, each low-level task will require a cost and schedule estimate. When you are involved in this process, watch for those tasks that are difficult to estimate; this usually means that there is some uncertainty associated with them. Treat these individual tasks the same way you would any other risk: Identify the reason for the uncertainty and create a strategy for managing it. (Chapter 8 deals in detail with estimating.)

The risks identified during scheduling and budgeting usually affect smaller parts of the project, but they are important just the same. Managing the small risks as well as the big ones means that little things are less likely to trip you up.

Recognizing detailed planning as a risk management opportunity further emphasizes the iterative and unbreakable relationship between risk planning and schedule development.

Prioritize the Risks

If performed energetically, these risk identification activities will have created a long list of potential risks. However, many of these risks won't be worth managing—they'll have a low impact, a low probability, or both. Even without performing detailed analysis of these risks, the project manager and team will nonetheless be able to use their intuition to quickly sort through and winnow out the risks it doesn't pay to worry about. That means the outcome of the risk identification process is a list of known risks that are worth studying and planning for.

STEP TWO: DEVELOPING A RESPONSE STRATEGY

Not every risk will jeopardize a project. Some are no more than pebbles in a pond; they cause a ripple that quickly subsides. But others resemble an underwater earthquake that causes a tidal wave. Project managers must recognize the difference between the two. They must know how to discern the magnitude of the risk *and* how to develop an appropriate strategy to deal with it. This strategy is called *response development,* and it has three components:

1. Defining the risk, including the severity of the negative impact.
2. Assigning a probability to the risk. How likely is it that this problem will occur?
3. Developing a strategy to reduce possible damage. This strategy will be based on the severity and probability of the risk.

Defining the Risk

Being able to concisely describe the risk is essential to understanding it. The Software Engineering Institute offers this simple but effective format for recording a risk.[2]

Condition: A brief statement describing the situation that is causing concern or uncertainty.

Consequence: A brief statement describing the possible negative outcomes that may be caused by the condition.

The more clearly the condition can be described, the more accurately the impact can be predicted—and the better chance there will be of effectively managing the risk. Here's an example of a poorly defined risk:

The project requires the use of technology that is new to the project team.

This statement doesn't give any clues to how badly the cost and schedule might be affected. The new technology should be named, and why it is causing uncertainty should be explained.

Here's a statement that does it better:

The state agency requires that all diagrams be developed using a software tool that our technical writers have not used before. In addition, the only boring machine that can handle the soil conditions is a complex product that has been used only a few times by our company.

Now that's getting more specific. In fact, we see that there are two separate risks associated with new technology. Each should be addressed separately. That will also make it easier to assess the impact, or consequences, that attempting to use the new technologies could have on the project.

After you have successfully defined the risks, you need to record the consequence of these risks in terms of cost, schedule, and possible damage to the project. Cost and schedule effects are tangible and can be matched against the original cost-benefit analysis, while damage refers to the intangible negative affect of a risk. Tables 5.2 and 5.3 are examples of risk statements in which the condition and the consequence have been clearly defined. At the end of the chapter you'll find a downloadable form that can be used to document a risk in this way.

Just as the first rule of problem solving is to thoroughly understand the problem, the first rule of risk analysis is to thoroughly describe the risk.

Using Probability Theory in Risk Management

What are the chances of getting a six when rolling a single die? The math is pretty simple: There are six sides and all have an equal chance of being on top, so the probability is one out of six, or 0.167. How many houses in a specific area are likely to have flood damage in a year? An insurance company will count the number of houses in the area that have had flood damage in the past to predict flood damage

TABLE 5.2 RISK ANALYSIS EXAMPLE 1

Definition

Condition: The soil conditions in the area where the pipeline crosses the river require a complex boring machine with which we have little experience.

Consequence: Incorrectly operating the machine will damage it and/or the riverbank. Damage to the machine could cost from $50,000 to $250,000 in repairs and 2 to 4 weeks in lost time. Damaging the riverbank may result in landowners or environmental groups trying to prevent us from obtaining permits for future pipelines.

Probability

Probability of $75K equipment damage—20%
Probability of $200K equipment damage—20%
Probability of no equipment damage—60%
Probable cost of equipment damage—$55K
Probability of riverbank damage—25%

Strategy

The equipment provider will supply an operator for an estimated cost of $10,000. Using their operator reduces the chance of equipment damage to less than 5% and they will bear the cost of repair. The probability of riverbank damage is also reduced to 5%.

- The probability was determined from the experience of this company and interviews with two other companies who use the product.
- Probable cost of damage = (75K × 20%) + (200K × 20%)
- The strategy adds $10,000 to the project cost, but reduces the risk of cost damage to zero and the schedule risk to less than 5%. The risk of intangible cost due to riverbank damage is also reduced.
- The strategy is described in two project management tools:
  1. Communication plan—includes increased monitoring and coordination activities with the equipment vendor.
  2. Project plan—Shows the equipment vendor as the resource on the task and the additional $10,000 in labor.
- This risk strategy is referred to as "risk transfer," because the project paid the equipment operator to take the risk.

in the future. What are the chances of falling behind on your project because a subcontractor doesn't come through? That's a little bit harder to quantify, but it's part of our job when we're analyzing risk.

Predicting the likelihood that a problem will occur contains the same difficulties as making any estimate. Many of the same rules apply to both. (See the golden rules of estimating in Chapter 8.) Looking at historical data will generally give the best indication of possible problems. But even when experienced project managers use all the

TABLE 5.3 RISK ANALYSIS EXAMPLE 2

Definition	**Condition:** The state agency requires that all diagrams be developed using a software tool that our technical writers have not used before. **Consequence:** All diagram generation and document management tasks will take longer. Limitations of the tool will cause rework.
Probability	On average, the slower work and the rework will add up to 25% more effort on documentation tasks. Probable labor cost: $1.25 \times 20 = 25$ Probable schedule: 1.25×4 months $= 5$ months
Strategy	Send all the technical writers to a 2-day course on the new tool. The training cost is $2,200. This will reduce the productivity factor to 1.1. Make one of the technical writers the tool expert. It will be his or her job to spend an average of 1 day each week to exercise the tool to find its limitations and to create standards and templates to build on its strengths. This will bring the productivity factor down to 1.0. The tool expert will spend 5 labor days to create document management strategies that ensure a smooth production process and eliminate rework.

- The probability is a subjective estimate based on the average normal productivity of a junior technical writer versus a senior technical writer. Since all writers will be new to the tool, all are assigned the junior productivity factor.
- The normal cost for the required documentation is 20 labor months and the normal duration is 4 months.
- The strategy is to shorten the learning curve. It will cost 2 days of training (duration) and the time spent by the tool expert on experimentation adds a cost of 21 days (1 day a week for four months plus 5 days). So the new tool's duration consequence is cut to 5 days and the cost consequence is 21 days labor plus the cost of training.
- The strategy is shown in the project plan, which shows the cost and duration of training and who will attend. Tasks are added for experimenting with the tool and developing tool standards. These additional tasks result in increased labor costs.

tools at their disposal, assigning probabilities to a risk remains as much an art as a science. The sheer number of possible problems, including those that are intangible and impossible to quantify, requires that a project manager use creativity and intuition as well as knowledge and experience in assessing risks.

There is a temptation to flee from the hard work of developing a probability estimate for each risk. Oftentimes the hard data that makes statistical analysis possible just doesn't exist. Why worry about the infinite number of possible problems your project could encounter? That is exactly the point: Because there are an infinite number of possible risks to your project, it is necessary to quantify the known risks in order to prioritize them and establish a budget for managing them.

Assigning a probability to the risk helps to assess the consequences of the risk. If you multiply the probability of a risk by the negative consequences, you will begin to see how bad the risk really is. This is often referred to as the *expected value* of the risk:

$$\text{Probability} \times \text{Impact} = \text{Expected Value}$$

The example in Table 5.2 defines probability in terms of percentages to predict the probable cost of the damages. That means the expected value of the risk is $55,000. Understanding the expected value will influence the amount spent reducing the risk.

Even when there is absolutely no hard data available about a risk, the project manager can distill the intuition of the team to provide useful assessments of probability and impact. A common method (illustrated in Figure 5.3) is to use a consistent probability and impact matrix throughout the project. It uses subjective assessments to place risks in one of nine quadrants. Key components of using this subjective assessment are:

- The same matrix must be used throughout the project since the method relies on subjective judgment. This allows team members to adjust their thinking to a consistent reference point.

- It is okay to make a larger matrix. Again, make sure the same matrix is used throughout the project.

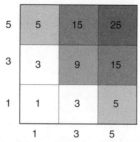

Team members can assign a ranking of 1, 3, or 5 to both probability and negative impact. Any risk whose total score is 5 or above should be analyzed further.

FIGURE 5.3 *Assign probability and impact to known risks.*

- Continue to use objective data to quantify both probability and impact whenever possible, then place that risk in one of the quadrants. Using objective data for reference points makes the subjective judgments more consistent.

- Have a diverse group of project stakeholders assess the risks then merge their assessments. If only the project manager is rating probability and impact, the ratings will be skewed by his or her unique perspective and risk tolerance.

Some risks have less to do with a specific event and more to do with the project's environment and its effect on productivity. For instance, the entire risk profile developed by the Software Engineering Institute addresses environmental risk factors such as the possible changes in requirements for a project, how skilled the project team may be, and the diversity of the user community.[3]

Assigning a probability to risks from the project's environment relies on intuition and experience. You need to ask the right questions: How good are the team's skills, and how much faster or slower will this make them? How strong is the business case for the project, and how many major changes in requirements will happen? Because these factors are intangible, they are hard to assess, but if risk management is practiced systematically on all projects, at least there will be a record of how skillfully a manager used his or her intuition. This feedback will aid in making future risk assignments more accurate.

Finally, realize that assigning probabilities to risks is done for a very practical reason: You need to be sure that the size of the solution matches the size of the problem. The combination of subjective and objective assessments of known risks enables the team to rank the risks. The risks at the top will receive attention first, and the risks at the bottom of the list will be addressed later.

How to Reduce Risk

Up to now, we've concentrated on assessing and quantifying the risks to a project's success. The time has come to develop strategies for dealing with these risks. This is the hard part, because there are as many ways to reduce risks as there are potential risks.

What is the best way to reduce a risk? The answer lies in the method we have discussed for assessing a risk: Reduce the impact, the probability, or both. For instance:

- If an event is out of my control but I can prepare for that event, then I have reduced the impact. That is why I take a first aid kit on a camping trip.

- In the risk example shown in Table 5.2, hiring an expert to operate a complex machine reduces the probability of an accident.

There are basically five categories of classic risk response strategies: *accepting, avoiding, monitoring, transferring,* and *mitigating the risk.* Let's look at these in detail.

1. Accepting the Risk

Accepting the risk means you understand the risk, its consequences, and probability, and you choose to do nothing about it. If the risk occurs, the project team will react. This is a common strategy when the consequences or probability that a problem will occur are minimal. As long as the consequences are cheaper than the cure, this strategy makes sense.

2. Avoid the Risk

You can avoid a risk by choosing not to do part of the project. This deletion of part of the project could affect more than the project—the business risk could also be affected. Changing the scope of the project

---

TABLE 5.4 RISK BEYOND THE PROJECT'S CONTROL

Definition	**Condition:** The product design calls for a computer operating system that is yet to be released and the manufacturer has a reputation for releasing unreliable products late. **Consequence:** If the product doesn't meet specifications, custom software will have to be written. If the product is late, the entire project will be delayed.
Probability	Probability of the product having defects that affect the project is 15%. Probability of the product being one month late (enough to negatively impact our project) is 30%.
Strategy	1. **Avoid.** Choose a new design that relies on stable technology. 2. **Monitor.** Get on the beta test team to have early access to the software and thoroughly test the features that affect the project. Two months prior to the planned project release, assess the probability of the risk and have an alternate design ready.

Two possible strategies are listed. Each results in changes to project documentation.
1. Avoid
- Project plan—Shows the new design and development tasks and the associated increase in cost and schedule.
- Product requirements—Document any changes in the product's capability.
2. Monitor
- Communication plan—Includes monitoring the beta test results and reporting them.
- Project plan—Shows the additional activities for the beta test and development of the contingency design.

---

might change the business case as well, because a scaled-down product could have smaller revenue or cost-saving opportunities (see Table 5.4). *Risk/return* is a popular expression in finance—if you want a high return on an investment, you'll probably have to take more risk. Avoiding risks on projects can have the same effect—low risk, low return.

3. Monitor the Risk and Prepare Contingency Plans

Monitor a risk by choosing some predictive indicator to watch as the project nears the risk point. For example, if you are concerned about a subcontractor's performance, set frequent status update points early in the project and inspect his or her progress. The risk strategy in Table 5.4 is to monitor the risk by being part of the test team.

Contingency plans are alternative courses of action prepared before the risk event occurs. The most common contingency plan is to set aside extra money, a *contingency fund,* to draw on in the event of unforeseen cost overruns. It's important to make sure that this fund is used only for unforeseen cost overruns—not to make up for underestimating or substandard performance. Table 5.4 contains an example of a contingency—the project team is betting on a new technology, but they are also creating an alternative design that uses more stable technology. If it looks like the new technology isn't going to be workable, the team will have an alternative in place. It's important to note here that creating the alternative design probably costs a substantial amount. Contingency plans can be looked on as a kind of insurance and, like insurance policies, they can be expensive.

When using this "monitor and be prepared to act" strategy, two factors should be included in the risk response plan: *detectability* and *trigger events.*

1. A tricky factor in monitoring a risk is the ability to detect the risk in time to respond. For example, hurricane response procedures rely on the fact that most hurricanes can be tracked for several days as they develop over the ocean. Knowing the speed and intensity of the storm gives authorities time to broadcast instructions to local residents. Conversely, a tornado can form, touch down, and wreak havoc virtually without notice. For a known risk within the project, the team should assess the detectability using a subjective scale (such as 1–5, where 5 is "very difficult to detect"). The effort invested in monitoring the risk will reflect the probability, impact, and ability to detect. If a risk is particularly difficult to detect and the impact and probability is large, it probably justifies plenty of mitigation as well as contingency preparation.

2. Trigger events define the line we cross between monitoring the risk and implementing the contingency plan. Trigger events are described as objectively as possible, so it is clear when we've arrived at one. The reason for trigger events is illustrated in a well-known story: If a frog jumps into a pan of boiling water, it will immediately jump out. But if a frog is sitting in a cool pan of water that is placed on a stove it will stay in the water until it is boiled to death. Trigger events help us recognize when the water in our project is 'too hot' and we need to take action. The monitoring strategy in Table 5.4 has a trigger date set to monitor the risk and make a decision about whether to implement the contingency.

4. Transfer the Risk

Even though paying for insurance may be expensive, assuming all the risks yourself could cost a great deal more. Many large projects purchase insurance for a variety of risks, ranging from theft to fire. By doing this, they have effectively *transferred risk* to the insurance company in that, if a disaster should occur, the insurance company will pay for it.

While purchasing insurance is the most direct method of transferring risk, there are others. For example, hiring an expert to do the work can also transfer risk. In one example (see Table 5.2), the project manager was concerned that a piece of heavy equipment operated by the project team would be damaged—or would damage the job site. Her solution was to hire an operator from the company leasing the equipment. Because this operator works for the equipment leasing company, the leasing company would pay for any damage to the equipment or to the site.

Another way to transfer risk is to use a contract for service, in this case, a *fixed-price contract*. A fixed-price contract states that the work will be done for an amount specified before the work begins. Fixed schedules may also be added to such a contract, with penalties for overruns. With fixed-price contracts, project managers know exactly what the cost of this part of a project will be. They have effectively transferred the cost and schedule risks from the project to the subcontracting firm; any overruns will be the responsibility of the subcontractor. (The only downside to this scenario is that the subcontractor, knowing it will be held to the original bid, will probably make the bid higher to make up for the risk it is assuming.)

Another type of contract for service is called a *reimbursable,* or *cost-plus,* contract. Reimbursable contracts pay subcontractors based on the labor, equipment, and materials they use on a project.[4] The risk of cost and schedule overruns is borne completely by the project on these contracts. The project is not able to transfer risk with this kind of contract, but when the work to be performed is poorly defined, or the type of service is open-ended, a reimbursable contract is the only type a subcontractor will sign.

Clearly, transferring risk to another party has advantages, but it also introduces new risks. A major component of this strategy is effective contracting and subcontractor management—topics beyond the scope of this chapter.

5. Mitigate the Risk

Mitigate is jargon for "work hard at reducing the risk." The risk strategy in Table 5.3 includes several ways to mitigate, or reduce, the productivity loss associated with using a new software tool. Mitigation covers nearly all the actions the project team can take to overcome risks from the project environment.

Identify Which Risks You Can Control

The first step in determining a response to a possible problem is to identify those risks that are within the control of the project team—and those that are not. Here a few examples of each kind of risk:

- Federal laws and regulations that affect your project are beyond your control. Labor disputes that cause some or all of your team to walk off the job are up to the company to handle. Who controls the weather? When the risk is beyond your control you generally have two options: Avoid it or monitor it and prepare a contingency plan.

- The behavior of the project team is within the team's control. For example, a breakdown in communication can be solved by changing the way the team communicates. Other challenges such as design or staffing problems can also be overcome by changing the way the team works.

Record Risk Management Strategies

The insights gained during risk planning must be documented. Complete risk response planning by summarizing your risk analysis in a risk log and updating other project management documents.

The previous examples demonstrate how individual risks may be analyzed. Keep this analysis organized so you can review it later. Summarize the risks using a risk log. Table 5.5 is an example of a risk log that's updated weekly. (To create your own, see the downloadable risk log at the end of this chapter.) When you update such a log, do the following:

TABLE 5.5 MONITOR RISKS USING A RISK LOG

Risk ID	Priority	Date Found	WBS	Responsible Person	Description	Strategy	Current Status (As of 6/12)
7	1	5/12	3.2	J. Daniels	The product design calls for a computer operating system that is yet to be released, and the manufacturer has a reputation for releasing unreliable products late.	1. Get on the beta test team. Test features affecting the project. 2. Assess the probability of the risk on 7/14. 3. Have an alternate design ready.	1. Beta versions are very unpredictable. New beta due 6/15. **Risk: High.** 2. Meeting scheduled. 3. Have identified alternative software. Design will be ready on 7/14.
2	2	5/7	4.6.3	F. Oak	The state agency requires that all diagrams be developed using a software tool that our technical writers have not used before.	1. Send all tech. writers to training. 2. F. Oak is creating standards and templates to build on its strengths. 3. F. Oak will create document management strategies.	1. Completed 6/2. Improving learning curve. 2. Completed 6/10. Templates and standards are effective. 3. Having trouble with document merging. Working with product rep. to solve. **Risk: Medium.**
12	3	7/7	2.1	J. Barnes	Soil conditions require a complex boring machine we are likely to damage.	The equipment provider will supply an operator for an estimated cost of $10,000.	Operator and equipment are contracted and scheduled. **Risk: Low.**

- Make sure there is someone responsible for every risk.
- Rank risks by severity and probability. Life doesn't give us time to expunge every risk from the project, so keep the most important ones at the top of the list where they won't be ignored.

Consider Risk Strategies Carefully

Sometimes it seems that, for every risk problem solved, a new risk appears. For instance, if you contract out specialized work, this can reduce risk by transferring it to the subcontractor. But subcontracting can reduce control over the project and increase communication difficulties. In addition, you will need to develop a strategy for managing the subcontractor. What all this means is that you need to weigh the advantages and disadvantages of each proposed risk strategy very carefully.

STEP THREE: ESTABLISH CONTINGENCY AND RESERVE

The notion of a rainy-day fund is an old one. On a regular basis we set aside money—usually a small amount—in a sugar bowl or bank account, earmarked for that rainy day when things go wrong. When the car suddenly needs a new transmission, the refrigerator dies, or some other unpredictable malady strikes, we have the funds available to handle it. Some consider it the act of a cautious person; others maintain it is just common sense—something any responsible person would do. In project risk management terms these are called *contingency* and *reserve funds,* and it is absolutely the responsibility of the project manager and the sponsor to establish these accounts.

We have established that the risks recorded in our risk log are known unknowns; we know about them but we can't predict with certainty what will happen to them. To prepare for these risks we have several strategies available, some of which call for preparing a contingency plan—a plan that we will execute if the risk materializes. It makes sense that these contingency plans must be funded in advance, but it is not clear how much money should be set aside—after all, it is statistically unlikely that every contingency plan will be executed. Here are four steps you can follow to produce a reasonable contingency budget:

1. Identify all the risks in the risk log, where your strategy is to monitor the risk and prepare a contingency plan.
2. For each of these risks, estimate the additional cost of executing the contingency plan. If you total the cost of all the contingency plans,

that is the amount you'd set aside if the probability for each of these risks is 100 percent. But the probability for each risk isn't 100 percent, so derive an expected value of the contingency for each risk by multiplying the probability the risk will occur times the cost of the contingency plan (expected value of contingency = cost of contingency × probability of risk event).

3. Sum the expected value of contingency for each of these risks. That will produce a number that executive management will choke on because nobody could conceive of so many things going wrong on a project. This is where the negotiation begins.

4. There is no "good guy" or "bad guy" in this negotiation. Set aside too much money and you are denying funds to other legitimate projects from which the firm could benefit. Set aside too little money and when known risks materialize you won't be able to fund a response. All parties to this negotiation should have the same goal in mind—to prepare for the known risks. All parties face the same challenge—forecasting the future.

Contingency reserves account for identified risks, *known unknowns*. Management reserve accounts for the *unknown unknowns*. As we've said before, the unknown unknowns are the events that we didn't see coming. No project, no matter how diligent the risk identification actions, will avoid the unknown unknowns. Therefore, like our rainy-day fund, we set aside a specific amount, earmarked to be spent on reacting to unforeseeable obstacles that arise during the project. How much do you budget for the unknown? Firms that consistently establish a management reserve for projects will tell you that, over time, a certain percentage of the performance budget (the budget based on the work breakdown structure) emerges as the right amount. High-risk industries such as software development may add as much as 30 percent to the budget. More predictable projects will use an amount closer to 5 percent of the performance budget. The key to establishing management reserve is to do it consistently for every project and at the end of the project to determine how much was spent. Over multiple similar projects, an acceptable range will appear.

STEP FOUR: CONTINUOUS RISK MANAGEMENT

No matter how rigorous, thorough, and diligent the initial risk planning activities, it is the ongoing risk management activities that produce results.

Our risk plan is based on the best information available when the project begins. As the project is performed, new information emerges—some favorable and some unfavorable. From a risk management perspective, we want to know how that affects our known risks and whether any new risks emerge. Stay ahead of the risks by scheduling the following activities on a regular basis:

- Monitor known risks with a risk log. Each risk in the risk log can be updated before every project status meeting to reflect the most recent information—even if that means "no change."

- Check for new risks at regular status meetings. This activity won't have the same level of thoroughness that the first risk identification activities had, but by routinely asking for new risks the project develops a climate of risk awareness. When team members do sense a risk, they'll know where to report it.

- Repeat the major risk identification activities at preplanned milestones within the project. These can be temporal, such as every six to nine weeks, or at the beginning of a new phase. The key is that these be planned in advance and that they are actually performed; otherwise it isn't likely to happen. If there is reluctance on the part of project team members to repeat these activities during the project, remember that investing in risk identification is the "ounce of prevention."

- When new risks are identified, prepare response plans and check whether sufficient contingency or management reserve exists.

- Some risks don't materialize. When that happens, retire them from the risk log, but be sure to record why they didn't materialize—was it good luck or good risk management?

Continuous risk management is essentially the practice of repeating the major risk management processes throughout the life of the project. Through constant vigilance, we continuously root out risks before they become problems.

END POINT

Projects, like life, are full of uncertainty. The risk management techniques in this chapter attempt to manage that uncertainty. From one perspective, everything a project manager does involves a type of risk management.

Risk management begins and ends with attitude. Skepticism and critical analysis expose lurking dangers. Then rational assessment, balanced by historical data, judges the probability and severity of the risk. Next, positive, creative problem solving forms a strategy to remove the hazard, and vigorous, energetic execution overcomes the obstacle. Finally, persistent, systematic vigilance reveals new perils, and the cycle begins again. Throughout this contest, we are confident and relentless.

FAST FOUNDATION IN PROJECT MANAGEMENT

Continuous, systematic risk management uncovers problems before they damage the project. The templates on the next pages provide a starting point for your own systematic risk management process.

1. The *risk assessment* template should be completed for every risk that has a reasonable chance of threatening the project.

2. The *risk log* offers a simple, systematic method for tracking active risks. Once the risk has been retired it can be moved to the bottom of the list.

Both of these templates are available for download at www.versatilecompany.com/forms. Use them to form the foundation of your own risk management process.

Stellar Performer: The Software Engineering Institute
A Model for Risk Profiles

One of the world's leading resources for project management expertise is the Software Engineering Institute (SEI). Sponsored by the U.S. Department of Defense and operated by Carnegie Mellon University in Pittsburgh, Pennsylvania, SEI has been researching and documenting best practices in software development since 1986. One of its most recent contributions is the *Continuous Risk Management Guidebook,* released in 1996.* Among the many tools and techniques included in its 552 pages is the Taxonomy Based Questionnaire (TBQ), otherwise known as a *risk profile,* an excellent model for any firm developing a rigorous risk assessment process.

The TBQ's structure is designed to systematically probe all aspects of a software project. Its core is the Software Development Risk Taxonomy, which separates potential risk categories common to software projects. The taxonomy is broken into three levels: *class, element,* and *attribute* (see Figure 5.4).

Each element has from three to seven attributes, for a total of 64 different risk attributes for a software project to judge. This detailed framework allows a series of questions about each attribute—the questionnaire included in SEI's guidebook has 194!

Not only has SEI produced a model others can imitate, but the institute has also answered the most common objection to detailed risk analysis: "194 questions about risk is too many for my

Class	Product Engineering	Development Environment	Program Constraints
Element (within a class)	1. Requirements 2. Design 3. Code and Unit Test 4. Integration and Test 5. Engineering Specialties	1. Development Process 2. Development System 3. Management Process 4. Management Methods 5. Work Environment	1. Resources 2. Contract 3. Program Interfaces
Attribute (within an element)	*Multiple attributes for each element*	*Multiple attributes for each element*	*Multiple attributes for each element*

FIGURE 5.4 *Software Development Risk Taxonomy*

(Continued)

(Continued)

project!" While Chapters A-32 through A-34 in the guidebook present the complete taxonomy, questionnaire, and guidelines for their use, Chapter A-25 has a short set of questions to indicate which, if any, of the TBQ questions to skip.

Consistently using the Software Development Risk Taxonomy to identify and categorize risks has two benefits:

1. Risk identification becomes more systematic, leading to better identification of potential risks and more accurate assessment of their probability and impact.

2. Risk mitigation strategies become associated with particular risk categories. Over time, this leads to a better understanding of the effectiveness of a particular mitigation strategy on a specific risk.

Project managers in the software development and information technology worlds can pick up the taxonomy and questionnaire and start using them right away. Project managers in other industries can use the taxonomy and questions as a model for developing their own risk identification process.

Source: Software Engineering Institute, *Continuous Risk Management Guidebook* (Pittsburgh, PA: SEI, 1996), pp. 439–442, 471–509.

*Special permission to reproduce *Continuous Risk Management Guidebook,* © 1996 by Carnegie Mellon University, is granted by the Software Engineering Institute.

Downloadable Risk Analysis Template:
Fill Out for a Specific Risk*

Project name:

Risk ID #   **Responsible person**   **Risk identification date**

Condition

Trigger event

Consequence/impact description

Consequence/impact value

Probability

Expected value

Response strategy

Known cost of response

Contingency for response

WBS relationship (tasks associated with condition or response strategy)

Downloadable Risk Log*

Project name

Last updated

Risk ID	WBS	Rank	Date found	Assigned To	Description	Strategy	Status	Closeout date

Description of fields:

Risk ID: A unique identifier.

WBS: WBS number of the task(s) related to this risk.

Rank: How important is this risk relative to others? Rank with 1 = highest. No risks have the same rank.

Date found: Date risk became known. mm/dd/yy.

Assigned to: Person who is assigned to manage this risk.

Description: High-level description of risk event, impact, and probability.

Strategy: What will be done to reduce the probability, impact, or both?

Status: Ongoing log of changes to risk, in order from most recent to oldest. Format: mm/dd/yy—action/update.

Closeout date: When did the risk probability go to zero? Describe in the final status. Remove any rank from this risk.

Work Breakdown Structure

INTRODUCTION

If you take a car trip to a town less than 100 miles away, it may not take much planning. Just hop in the car, check the gas gauge, and go. But if you were going to drive from the Florida Keys to Anchorage, Alaska, you'd probably spend some time looking at maps and researching your route. Somehow you'd break the big trip down into pieces. Maybe you would do this with geographic borders, such as states. Or you could plan it by how far you might go each day. But whatever approach you use, the only way to accurately plan a trip of this size is to break it down.

The same is true for projects. At a high level, you may understand a project well enough to balance its cost-schedule-quality equilibrium, but you also need to be able to break it down—to understand the whole project by understanding its parts. The *work breakdown structure* (WBS) is the tool for breaking down a project into its component parts. It is the foundation of project planning and one of the most important techniques used in project management. If done well, it can become the secret to successful project management. The WBS is perhaps the most powerful technique in this book.

DEFINING THE WORK BREAKDOWN STRUCTURE

The work breakdown structure identifies all the tasks in a project; in fact, a WBS is sometimes referred to simply as a *task list*. It turns one large, unique, perhaps mystifying, piece of work—the project—into many small, manageable tasks. The WBS uses outputs from project definition and risk management and identifies the tasks that are the foundation for all subsequent planning (see Figure 6.1)

Work breakdown structures can be set up in either graphic or outline form (see Figures 6.2 and 6.3). Either way, they list the various tasks involved. For example, designing and putting in a new lawn with a sprinkler system, surrounded by a new fence, involves a number of different tasks. The graphic WBS paints a picture that makes it easy to understand all the parts of a project, but the outlined WBS is more practical because you can list hundreds of tasks on it—far more than can be listed using the graphic approach.

The WBS clarifies and provides necessary details for a number of project management activities. Building a WBS helps to:

- *Provide a detailed illustration of project scope.* Though the statement of work defines scope at the conceptual level, a comprehensive look at a project's scope can be accomplished only with a WBS.

- *Monitor progress.* The tasks on the WBS become the basis for monitoring progress because each is a measurable unit of work.

- *Create accurate cost and schedule estimates.* The WBS will detail costs for equipment, labor, and materials on each task.

- *Build project teams.* Every team member wants clear work assignments and a sense of how his or her work fits into the overall effort. A good WBS does both. You can also increase the team's commitment to the plan by having them participate in building the WBS.

KEY CONCEPT   Understanding the WBS

The WBS breaks all the work in the project into separate tasks (tasks may also be referred to as *activities*). There are two kinds of tasks on a WBS: *summary tasks* and *work packages.*

"Install the sprinkler system" for a lawn is a summary task, because it includes several subordinate tasks. Installing a sprinkler system might include several of these distinct, subordinate tasks, such as digging trenches or installing pipes. Each of these separate tasks is called a *work package.* By performing all these simple work packages, you accomplish a summary task (see Figure 6.3).

Note that a summary task is not actually executed; it is, rather, a *summarization* of the subordinate work packages. The work packages are the ones that are actually executed. Understanding the relationship between summary tasks and work packages is fundamental to building a good WBS.

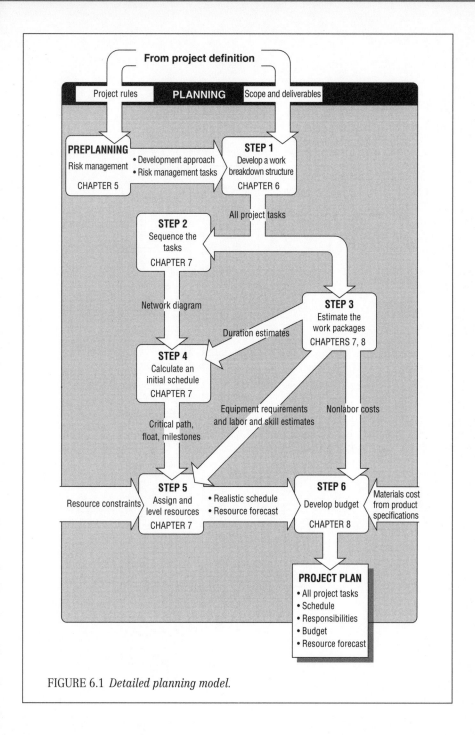

FIGURE 6.1 *Detailed planning model.*

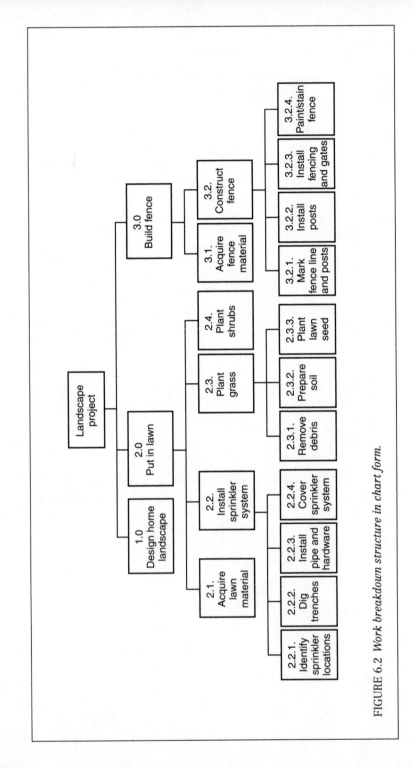

FIGURE 6.2 *Work breakdown structure in chart form.*

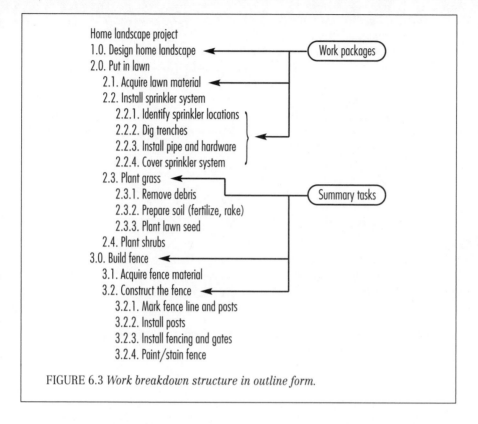

Home landscape project
1.0. Design home landscape ← Work packages
2.0. Put in lawn
    2.1. Acquire lawn material ←
    2.2. Install sprinkler system
        2.2.1. Identify sprinkler locations
        2.2.2. Dig trenches
        2.2.3. Install pipe and hardware
        2.2.4. Cover sprinkler system
    2.3. Plant grass ←
        2.3.1. Remove debris ← Summary tasks
        2.3.2. Prepare soil (fertilize, rake)
        2.3.3. Plant lawn seed
    2.4. Plant shrubs
3.0. Build fence ←
    3.1. Acquire fence material
    3.2. Construct the fence ←
        3.2.1. Mark fence line and posts
        3.2.2. Install posts
        3.2.3. Install fencing and gates
        3.2.4. Paint/stain fence

FIGURE 6.3 *Work breakdown structure in outline form.*

BUILDING A WORK BREAKDOWN STRUCTURE

A good WBS makes it easy for everyone on the project to understand his or her role—and it makes managing the project much easier, too. But don't be fooled; it isn't always easy to build a good WBS. There are three steps that provide a guideline to developing a useful WBS.

WBS Step One: Begin at the Top

A WBS breaks down a project into descending levels of details, naming all the tasks required to create the deliverables named in the statement of work (SOW). You can begin the breakdown process by listing either the major deliverables or the high-level tasks from the scope statement on the first tier.

Figure 6.3 demonstrates listing the major deliverables, or products, as the first step in making a WBS. The three major deliverables—design, lawn, and fence—are on tier one. Notice that the landscape design is listed as a major deliverable, even though it isn't an end product, like the lawn and fence. The statement of work can list many intermediate deliverables as well as end deliverables. All deliverables from the SOW appear on the WBS.

The other approach to getting started is to use the high-level tasks described in the scope statement as the tier-one tasks. Since the WBS shows all project work, it is essentially a detailed illustration of the processes involved in the project. Therefore, tier one can be set up as a view of these processes, representing the major phases or stages of a development life cycle. But even when using this approach, tier one still shows a deliverable for each phase. Either way, your WBS will be linked to the statement of work.

Getting Started on the WBS

 Sometimes the hardest part of making a work breakdown structure is getting started. The WBS includes so much that it can appear overwhelming. A good way to begin is to review the work you've already done during project definition and risk management.

WBS Step Two: Name All the Tasks Required to Produce Deliverables

A task name describes an activity that produces a product. For example, if a WBS in a landscaping project lists "lawn" or "shrubs," you will need to add verbs to each task name: "lawn" becomes "put in lawn," "shrubs" becomes "plant shrubs," and so on. The next step is to break down each task into the lower-level, detailed tasks required to produce the product. Figures 6.2 and 6.3 illustrate how the WBS looks with multiple task levels.

This sounds easy, doesn't it? Don't be deceived. Breaking down the WBS can be the most difficult step in the planning process, because it's where the detailed process for building the product is defined. For example, a high-level task may seem easy to understand, but upon breaking it down, the project manager may find that he or she is unable to list all the detailed tasks required to complete it. At this point, it's time to invite more team members, with diverse skills, into the planning process.

In fact, when planning a large, multidisciplinary project, it makes sense to get a small team to create the top two tiers of the WBS, then give each task to an expert in the subject to break it down into work packages. When these experts are through, they can be brought together with the core team to construct the entire WBS. This kind of participative planning not only creates more accurately detailed work breakdowns, it can also encourage higher levels of commitment to the project.

A WBS may be especially difficult to create if the project covers new ground. Here's an example: Tom, a human resources manager for a company of about 10,000 people, was leading a project to create a new process for forecasting the firm's workforce requirements over a three-year time span. When he began to put together his WBS, he quickly realized that he wasn't sure what steps to follow in developing the new process. Because there was no precedent for this kind of project in his company, Tom and his team had to spend time devising a new strategy.

The resulting plan was presented to the customers, which, on this project, were the high-level managers who would use the system to forecast their personnel needs. This management group approved the plan, but in this case they weren't just approving the schedule or budget, they were also approving the new strategy that Tom and his team had devised. And, since much of the plan outlined how this management group would participate in designing the new system, they were also accepting their roles as defined in the plan.

When Tom's team had completed its plan, he commented, "We spent at least two weeks planning this project and most of that time was spent on the WBS. That was about two weeks longer than I originally intended. But by spending the time to get a detailed strategy worked out, I can see we actually saved a lot of time. If it took us two weeks to figure out how to handle this project, imagine how many blind alleys we would have run down without this plan."

WBS Step Three: How to Organize the WBS

Once all the work packages are identified, it is possible to rearrange them in different ways. For example, it can be useful to place work packages under different summary task headings; in this case, the overall project will remain the same even though the work packages are grouped differently. Figure 6.4 demonstrates how it's possible to have two different breakdowns of the same project tasks. The same work packages are reorganized under different summary tasks.

Different ways of organizing work packages may emphasize different aspects of a project. For example, one grouping of work packages might highlight the various components of a new product, while another arrangement might emphasize the major phases of the product's release. This kind of difference is illustrated in Figure 6.4, where the first WBS provides high-level visibility on the widget's two main components. By contrast, the second WBS provides high-level visibility on the major phases of the new release. Both may be useful when communicating with the various groups involved in the project, because the focus of each arrangement may speak to the concerns of individual stakeholders.

Be Sure That Summary Tasks Are Meaningful

When organizing the work breakdown structure, remember that the sole purpose of summary tasks on the WBS is for communication, or visibility. (Recall that summary tasks aren't actually executed, they are just a summarization of work packages.) So every summary task should be meaningful to some stakeholder (including the project manager). If there are summary tasks that have no audience, erase them. As long as the work packages remain, the scope of the project is the same (compare Figure 6.5 to Figure 6.4).

CRITERIA FOR A SUCCESSFUL WORK BREAKDOWN STRUCTURE

Because a good WBS is easy to read, people often assume that it's also easy to write. This, however, is a false assumption; there are large numbers of inaccurate and poorly developed work breakdown structures produced every year. However, if your WBS meets the the following evaluation criteria, you can be sure it will be useful in planning, communicating, and tracking your project. Here are three criteria for a successful WBS.

1. *The WBS must be broken down starting at the top.* It is a top-down decomposition. You need to make sure your work packages are subsets of your summary tasks. The test is simple: Start with any work package and work your way up the hierarchy, asking, "Is this task a subset of the task above it?" (Figure 6.6 illustrates this rule.) Following this rule allows you to:
   * *Use standard project management software.* Do it any other way and the software will give you nothing but nonsense at the summary level.
   * *Present meaningful project information at the summary task level.* For example, costs for summary tasks are derived simply by adding up the costs of all subordinate tasks. This enables you to track the project at the work package level, yet present the status of the project to your sponsor using more meaningful information from the summary tasks.

2. *Work packages must add up to the summary task.* One of the most frustrating planning mistakes is to omit necessary tasks. You can avoid this problem by taking extra care when adding up the products of all the work packages below any summary task. Altogether, these subordinate tasks should produce the outcome named by the summary task. See Figure 6.7 for a further illustration of this point.

3. *Each summary task and work package must be named as an activity that produces a product.* This means giving each task a descriptive name that includes a strong verb—the *activity*—and a

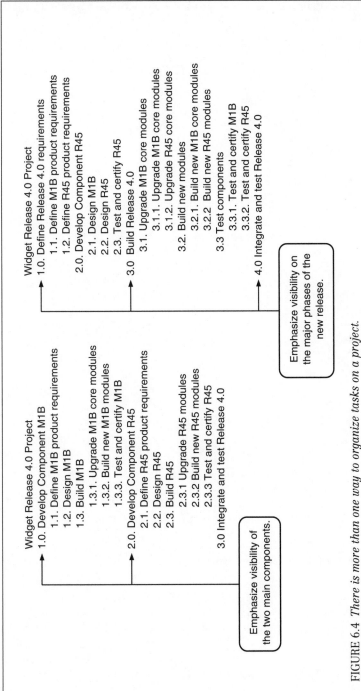

Widget Release 4.0 Project
1.0. Develop Component M1B
    1.1. Define M1B product requirements
    1.2. Design M1B
    1.3. Build M1B
        1.3.1. Upgrade M1B core modules
        1.3.2. Build new M1B modules
        1.3.3. Test and certify M1B
2.0. Develop Component R45
    2.1. Define R45 product requirements
    2.2. Design R45
    2.3. Build R45
        2.3.1 Upgrade R45 modules
        2.3.2 Build new R45 modules
        2.3.3 Test and certify R45
3.0 Integrate and test Release 4.0

Emphasize visibility of the two main components.

Widget Release 4.0 Project
1.0. Define Release 4.0 requirements
    1.1. Define M1B product requirements
    1.2. Define R45 product requirements
2.0. Develop Component R45
    2.1. Design M1B
    2.2. Design R45
    2.3. Test and certify R45
3.0 Build Release 4.0
    3.1. Upgrade M1B core modules
        3.1.1. Upgrade M1B core modules
        3.1.2. Upgrade R45 core modules
    3.2. Build new modules
        3.2.1. Build new M1B core modules
        3.2.2 Build new R45 modules
    3.3 Test components
        3.3.1. Test and certify M1B
        3.3.2. Test and certify R45
4.0 Integrate and test Release 4.0

Emphasize visibility on the major phases of the new release.

FIGURE 6.4 *There is more than one way to organize tasks on a project.*

Widget Release 4.0 Project
1.0.   Define M1B product requirements
2.0.   Define R45 product requirements
3.0.   Design M1B
4.0.   Design R45
5.0.   Upgrade M1B core modules
6.0.   Upgrade R45 core modules
7.0.   Build new M1B modules
8.0.   Build new R45 modules
9.0.   Test and certify M1B
10.0.   Test and certify R45
11.0.   Integrate and test Release 4.0

FIGURE 6.5 *WBS with no summary tasks. The widget release 4.0 project has the same amount of work required even though the summary tasks are removed.*

strong noun—the *product*. Without these, the task becomes ambiguous. Two cases in point:

- *Open-ended tasks.* "Perform analysis" or "Research" are activities we understand, but since there is no hard product being produced, they are activities that could go on indefinitely. Better task names include the products of the analysis or research, such as "Define hardware requirements," "Write a problem statement," or "List candidate vendors." The focus on producing a product gives the task—and the team—a clear ending, which makes it easier both to estimate and to track the task.

- *Open-ended activities.* "Database" is a task that will show up in thousands of projects this year, but what is the action required? It could be many things, from design to load to test. That's the point—it is unclear what is meant by this task. Clarify the task by including an activity, as in, "Test the database."

WBS: The Key to Success

Apply the following rule to any work breakdown structure and you will find yourself in absolute control of your project. This is the secret of successful project management: *Break the project into small, meaningful, manageable units of work.*

WORK PACKAGE SIZE

The most common problem with projects that extend dramatically beyond their schedule is that work packages are so large

Landscape Project

1.0. Design home landscape
2.0. Put in lawn   *2.0 is a subset of the project.*
  2.1. Purchase lawn material
  2.2. Install sprinkler system   *2.2 is a subset of 2.0.*
    2.2.1. Identify sprinkler location
    2.2.2. Dig trenches   *2.2.2 is a subset of 2.2.*
    2.2.3. Install pipe and hardware
    2.2.4. Cover sprinkler system   *2.2.4 is a subset of 2.2.*
  2.3. Plant Grass
    2.3.1. Remove debris
    2.3.2. Prepare soil
    2.3.3. Plant lawn seed
  2.4. Plant shrubs
3.0. Build fence   *3.0 is a subset of the project.*
  3.1. Acquire fence material
  3.2. Construct the fence   *3.2 is a subset of 3.0.*
    3.2.1. Mark fence line
    3.2.2. Install posts
    3.2.3. Install fencing and gates   *3.2.3 is a subset of 3.2.*
    3.2.4. Paint/stain fence

FIGURE 6.6 *Evaluation rule 1: The WBS must be a top-down decomposition.*

that they can spin out of control. If a task is estimated to be eight months long and 3,800 labor hours (i.e., three people working full-time on the task), it's not a task, it's a subproject! This is the kind of task that is right on schedule for 7 months, suddenly hits a rough spot in the eighth month—and ends up taking 12 months. The size of this task has made it unmanageable. If the entire project were to be planned in the same manner the trouble would be multiplied many times over. To ensure that the work packages are the correct size, follow these common rules of thumb.

- *The 8/80 rule.* No task should be smaller than 8 labor hours or larger than 80. This translates into keeping your work packages between 1 and 10 days long. (Obviously, this is a guideline and not an iron-clad law.)

- *The reporting period rule.* No task should be longer than the distance between two status points. In other words, if you hold weekly status meetings, then no task should be longer than one week. This rule is especially useful when it is time to report schedule status, because you will no longer have to hear about task statuses that are 25, 40, or 68 percent complete. If you've followed a weekly report-

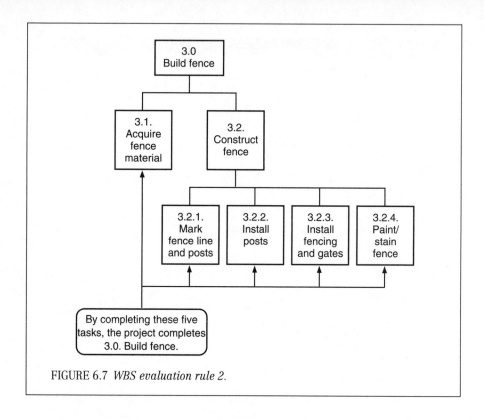

FIGURE 6.7 *WBS evaluation rule 2.*

ing rule, tasks will be reported as either complete (100 percent), started (50 percent), or not started (0 percent). No task should be at 50 percent for two consecutive status meetings.

- *The "if it's useful" rule.* As you consider whether to break tasks down further, remember that there are three reasons to do so:
  1. *The task is easier to estimate.* Smaller tasks tend to have less uncertainty, leading to more accurate estimates.
  2. *The task is easier to assign.* Large tasks assigned to many people lose accountability. Breaking down the task can help to clarify who is responsible. Another potential benefit is that having smaller tasks assigned to fewer people can give you greater flexibility in scheduling the task and the resource.
  3. *The task is easier to track.* The same logic applies as in the reporting period rule. Because smaller tasks create more tangible status points, you will have more accurate progress reports.

If breaking down a task in a certain way is not useful—that is, if it doesn't make it easier to estimate, assign, or track—then don't break it down!

When Very Small Tasks Make Sense

Is it possible that tasks broken down into one-hour increments could be useful? Talk about micromanagement! While projects spanning months probably wouldn't benefit from such small tasks, it is common to plan to this level for complex projects of short duration. Preventive maintenance for manufacturing plants can require the entire operation to be shut down for a day or a week. In order to minimize the time the plant is down, these projects are often planned out in hourly increments, which allows close coordination among many people and quick identification of any behind-schedule work that could delay reopening the plant.

While many managers might balk at having to reduce a large project into relatively small increments, the results can be rewarding. Consider these examples:

- An upgrade to a municipal wastewater treatment plant had a project budget of more than $500 million. In spite of the size of this project, contractors were required to plan and report work packages in units of no more than two weeks or $50,000. By requiring this detailed level of information, the municipal government's project office could identify any problems within a matter of weeks—no small feat for a project of this size. The project finished on time and under budget.

- In an article in *Sloan Management Review* on Microsoft, Michael Cusumano observed, "Managers generally allow team members to set their own schedules but only after the developers have analyzed tasks in detail (half-day to three-day chunks, for example) and have agreed to commit personally to the schedules." Yet, in a company the size of Microsoft, hundreds of people may be required to develop a new product. While working with these small increments will produce an enormous amount of detail, it dramatically increases the accuracy of estimating and tracking a project.[1]

Put Project Management into the WBS

You can benefit by putting project management activities into the work breakdown structure. List them under a summary task called "Project management" (as shown in Figure 6.8). Though some of the tasks will be finite, such as hiring a subcontractor, the majority will consist of everyday work, such as communication and problem resolution. These everyday duties may be grouped under a heading called "Managing the project." Now you have a place to assign all the time spent on project management duties.

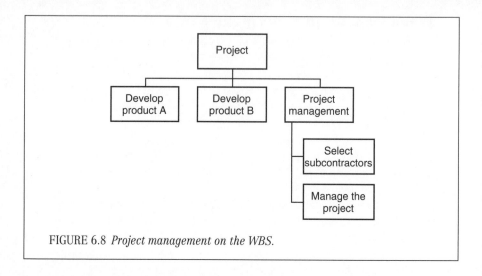

FIGURE 6.8 *Project management on the WBS.*

PLANNING FOR QUALITY

KEY CONCEPT

Common sense tells us that it is cheaper to design a product correctly than to fix it after it is built. Whether it is an airplane, an ad campaign, or a piece of software, the earlier an error is detected in the development life cycle, the cheaper it is to fix. In his excellent book, *Rapid Development,* Steve McConnell develops some general conclusions about the cost of fixing mistakes, in this case, on software projects.[2]

> *If a defect caused by incorrect requirements is fixed in the construction or maintenance phase, it can cost 50 to 200 times as much to fix as it would have in the requirements phase.*
>
> *Each hour spent on quality assurance activities such as design reviews saves 3 to 10 hours on downstream costs.*

How do we make sure that we catch problems early in the development life cycle? The answer is different for every industry. Aircraft designers use different techniques than software developers. Architects use different techniques than manufacturing engineers. But what does project management have to offer in this search for possible problems? It offers the risk management techniques we have already discussed; it also offers a process for setting standards for completion of the product. These standards, called *completion criteria,* form our next topic.

Completion Criteria

Completion criteria answer these two critical questions about each work package: (1) What does it mean to be complete with this task?

(2) How will we know it was done correctly? As McConnell's statistics illustrate, the time to ask these questions is early in the development life cycle. Yet these may be the tasks with the most intangible results. How do you test a problem statement or a business case? It may not be easy, but it is important. Determining completion criteria demands that the project manager and team look to the best practices in their industry. Here are some examples of completion criteria:

- *Peer reviews.* These are common in many industries in the early part of a product development life cycle when there is nothing tangible to test. Peer reviews, also known as *walk-throughs,* are based on the premise that three to six heads are better than one. Passing the review doesn't guarantee the product will be perfect, but experience has shown that subjecting tasks to peer reviews results in dramatically better results in the front end of the development life cycle—and this leads to more cost-effective work in the construction phase.

- *Checklists.* For instance, an engineering group at an aerospace company has developed checklists for evaluating new drawings. The checklists cover the standard tests each drawing must pass, and a lead engineer will use the checklist to evaluate another engineer's drawing. In this case, completion criteria for a drawing involve "passing the checklist."

- *Systematic testing.* There are almost always tests to run later in a product's life cycle. For example, airplane manufacturers have extensive test labs that simulate the stresses experienced by aircraft in flight. Passing rigorous, systematic testing can be defined as completion criteria.

In addition to improving quality, completion criteria improve our understanding of each task, which results in more accurate estimates and higher rates of success.

The Acceptance Process: Begin with the End in Mind

One of Stephen Covey's seven habits of effective people is to "begin with the end in mind."[3] This is particularly good advice for project managers, who need to consider early on the process for delivering the final product. This process is called the *acceptance process.* Considering the acceptance process might add a few tasks to the WBS, such as turnover tasks at the end of the project. These might include training, initial start-up of the new product, or a postimplementation assessment.

BREAKING DOWN LARGE PROGRAMS

A program manager responsible for a billion-dollar contract will not immediately break the program down into one-week increments. He or she will break the contract into projects, which in turn will be broken down into subprojects. Eventually, the work will be broken into small work packages, requiring between 8 and 80 hours in labor. This project within a project within a program approach is based on the top-down nature of the work breakdown structure.

WATCH FOR DIFFERENT TERMINOLOGY

WBS versus PBS versus BOM. Occasionally, what is really a *product breakdown structure* (PBS)—also known as a *bill of materials* (BOM)—will be called a *work breakdown structure* (WBS). Defense programs commonly refer to "work breakdown structures," but instead of breaking down the program, this type of WBS breaks down the product. (Figure 6.9 shows a partial WBS for a jet fighter program.) The defense industry has used this format for many years and probably will continue to use it.

The defense industry's WBS is useful for breaking down all the components of an aircraft, but it does not break down all the tasks

---

Airframe
    Airframe analysis and integration
    Midfuselage
    Empennage (tail)
    Edges
    Wings
    Forward fuselage
    Aft fuselage
Avionics
    Avionics analysis and integration
    Electronic warfare
    Core processing
    Radar
Utilities and subsystems
    Armament
    Hydraulics
    Fuel
    Electrical
    Landing gear

FIGURE 6.9 *Partial WBS from a fighter aircraft program.*

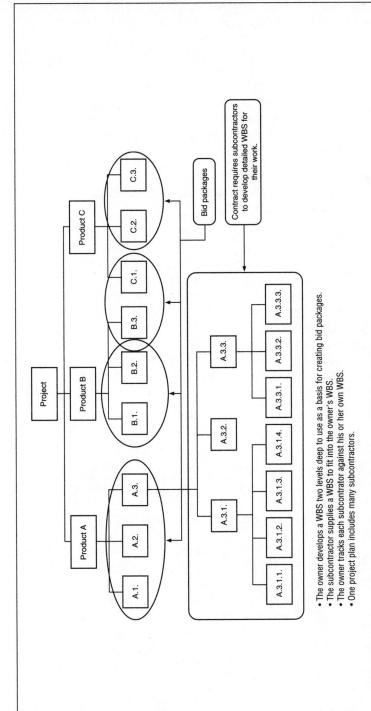

FIGURE 6.10 *Subcontractors can supply their own part of the WBS.*

- The owner develops a WBS two levels deep to use as a basis for creating bid packages.
- The subcontractor supplies a WBS to fit into the owner's WBS.
- The owner tracks each subcontrator against his or her own WBS.
- One project plan includes many subcontractors.

required to develop those components. In fact, multi-billion-dollar programs are commonly broken down into only five or six levels, so the bottom tier—which is still referred to as *work packages*—might contain millions of dollars worth of subprojects. In this case, *work package* has a radically different meaning.

Because most of us will work on projects of less than $10 million, the difference between the product WBS and the project WBS will not usually concern us. It is important, however, for project managers to recognize that some industries ascribe different meanings to the terms used in this chapter.

 CONTRACTORS OR VENDORS CAN
CONCEPT **PROVIDE A WBS**

If your project employs contractors or vendors to do some of the work, you can make a WBS part of the bid requirement. (You can also make it a reporting requirement for the winning bidder.) This can be a good tool for evaluating bids, particularly if there are wide variations in the cost and schedule estimates of the bidders; tying the bid to a WBS will show clearly when one contractor is making different scope assumptions than another.

When managing vendors, it is useful to require them to manage and report against a detailed WBS; this will often reduce the likelihood of unpleasant surprises later in the project. (Figure 6.10 shows how requiring a WBS as part of a bid can be used on a large project requiring multiple subcontractors.)

END POINT

A project can best be understood by a thorough understanding of its parts. The work breakdown structure breaks the project down into many small, manageable tasks called *work packages*. The process of deciding who will perform these tasks and how they will be arranged provides the structure for the actual work of the project.

Most books on project management devote between one-half to two pages to work breakdown structures. "What's the big deal?" people say. "It's just a task list." It's a big deal because so much of a project manager's job relies on the WBS. Estimating, scope management, subcontracting work, tracking progress, and giving clear work assignments all depend on a well-defined breakdown of the tasks that make up a project. For every problem a project manager encounters, there is probably some way that he or she can use the WBS and its work packages to help solve it.

Realistic Scheduling

INTRODUCTION

If you ask people what makes a project successful, "a realistic schedule" usually tops the list. But ask them to be more specific, and several characteristics of a realistic schedule emerge. A realistic schedule:

- Includes a detailed knowledge of the work to be done
- Has task sequences in the correct order
- Accounts for external constraints beyond the control of the team
- Can be accomplished on time, given the availability of skilled people and enough equipment

Finally, a realistic schedule takes into consideration all the objectives of the project. For example, a schedule may be just right for the project team, but if it misses the customer's completion date by a mile, then it's clear that the whole project will need reassessment. Building a project plan that includes all the necessary parts and achieves a realistic balance between cost, scheduling, and quality requires a careful, step-by-step process.

Chapter 6 dealt with the first step in planning the project: the work breakdown structure. This chapter explains planning steps two through five. Each planning step relies on the one preceding it, and each adds a new element to the plan. You can use the diagram in Figure 6.1 (see page 115) as a guide in this chapter.

PLANNING OVERVIEW

Here is a quick recap of the steps involved in planning a project. The first two actions prepare the groundwork for planning and so can be considered preplanning activities. The remaining five steps develop the detailed plan.

- *Create the project definition.* The project manager and the project team develop the statement of work, which identifies the purpose, scope, and deliverables for the project and defines the responsibilities of the project team (Chapters 3 and 4).

- *Develop a risk management strategy.* The project team evaluates the likely obstacles and creates a strategy for balancing costs, schedule, and quality (Chapter 5).

- *Build a work breakdown structure.* The team identifies all the tasks required to build the specified deliverables. The scope statement and project purpose help to define the boundaries of the project.

- *Identify task relationships.* The detailed tasks, known as *work packages,* are placed in the proper sequence.

- *Estimate work packages.* Each of these detailed tasks has an estimate developed that includes the amount of labor and equipment needed and the duration of the task.

- *Calculate initial schedule.* After estimating the duration of each work package and figuring in the sequence of tasks, the team calculates the total duration of the project. (This initial schedule, while useful for planning, will probably need to be revised further down the line.)

- *Assign and level resources.* The team adjusts the schedule to account for resource constraints. Tasks are rescheduled in order to optimize the use of people and equipment used on the project.

These steps generate all the information required to understand how a project will be executed. The steps are systematic, but they don't necessarily come up with the "right answer." It may take several iterations of these steps to find this answer, which is the optimal balance between cost, schedule, and quality. Chapter 9 will address the challenge of finding the optimal cost-schedule-quality equilibrium for a project, but right now, we will look at the step-by-step instructions for creating a project plan. Step one is the creation of a work breakdown structure, which was covered in the previous chapter. We start here with step two, which involves identifying the relationships between the different tasks.

PLANNING STEP TWO: IDENTIFY TASK RELATIONSHIPS

The sequence in which detailed tasks—work packages—are performed is determined by the relationship between the tasks. To illustrate this point, consider the following five tasks from the landscaping project described earlier. These tasks constitute a subset of that project:

1. Acquire lawn materials
2. Remove debris
3. Prepare soil
4. Plant lawn seed
5. Plant shrubs

As the homeowner and the teenage children who will be working on this project contemplate these tasks, the question arises: What is the proper sequence? Any time a series of tasks is performed, there will be *sequence constraints*—that is, certain tasks that must be performed before others. Sequence constraints are governed by the relationships of different tasks. For instance, rocks, weeds, and other debris must be removed before the lawn seed can be planted. Performing these tasks in the reverse order doesn't make sense because the seed would be lost when the weeds were removed. Figure 7.1 shows both a predecessor table and a network diagram, two different ways of recording sequence constraints. A predecessor table is a common way to display task relationships. (In fact, this is exactly the way most project management software records the relationships.)

Notice that tasks 1 and 2 have no predecessors. Either one can be done first, or, if there are enough people, they could be done at the same time. Tasks that can be performed at the same time are known as *concurrent tasks*.

There are just two basic rules when graphing task relationships with a network diagram:

1. *Define task relationships only between work packages.* Even though a project might have hundreds of work packages and several levels of summary tasks, keep the sequence constraints at the work package level. Summary tasks, remember, are simply groups of work packages, so it wouldn't make sense to put a task relationship between a summary task and its work package. (The only exception to this rule occurs, occasionally, on very large projects, where networks can be created to illustrate project relationships at the summary level.)

2. *Task relationships should reflect only sequence constraints between work packages, not resource constraints.* Changing a net-

work diagram because of resource constraints is the most common error in building network diagrams. The fact that there aren't enough people or other resources to work on multiple tasks at the same time is irrelevant here. Regardless of resources, the tasks will still have to be performed in the same order. (Figure 7.1 demonstrates the mistake of rearranging the network because the same resource, in this case, the teenagers, are working on tasks 1 and 2.)

PREDECESSOR TABLE

	Task	Predecessor	Resources
1	Acquire lawn materials		Homeowner
2	Remove debris		Teens and youth groups
3	Prepare soil	1, 2	Teens
4	Plant lawn seed	3	Teens
5	Plant shrubs	2	Teens

Correct

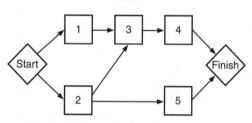

- Network diagram with milestones at the start and finish.
- This network has two *concurrent* paths.

Incorrect

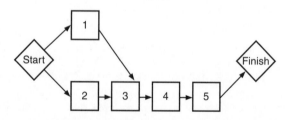

- The most common network diagram mistake is removing all concurrent tasks for the same resource.
- Resource constraints may prevent tasks 4 and 5 from being performed at the same time, but that shouldn't change the network. The network only represents task sequence constraints.

FIGURE 7.1 *Network diagram developed from a predecessor table.*

Milestones Are Useful Markers

In setting up the sequence of events, many project managers find it useful to mark significant events in the life of a project. These markers—called *milestones*—are often used in work breakdown structures and network diagrams (see Figure 7.2). Milestones have zero duration, so adding them to a project doesn't affect the schedule at all. There are three great reasons to use milestones:

1. *Project start and finish milestones are useful anchors for the network.* The milestones don't change anything on the project, but many people find it easier to read.

2. *Milestones can be used to mark input from one party to another.* Many projects are dependent on inputs from certain external sources (they have *external dependencies*). For example, a government agency might release an environmental impact report for an electric utility on a certain date. A project in that electric utility can use that release date as a milestone. Figure 7.2 shows a milestone representing an external dependency.

3. *A milestone can represent significant events that aren't already represented by a work package or summary task.* For example, if a firm receives progress payments based on work accomplished, these payment points could be shown with milestones.

Milestones are useful to show major progress points, but the real progress indicators remain the detailed work packages. Every work package has specific completion criteria and a tangible result—which is the ultimate progress indicator.

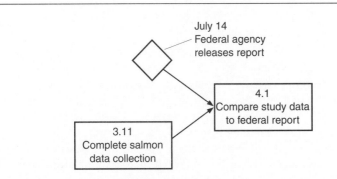

- During an environmental impact study, the project uses data from a federal agency.
- Task 4.1 will not be able to start until at least July 14, the day the federal report is released.

FIGURE 7.2 *Milestones can show external dependencies.*

Finish-to-Start Relationships

The finish-to-start relationship states that one task must be completed before its successor task can begin. The network diagrams in this chapter all follow this simple assumption because it is the most common, but there are other types of relationships. Tasks with start-to-start (SS) relationships allow the successor task to begin when the predecessor begins. Finish-to-finish (FF) tasks can start independently of each other, but the successor cannot finish until the predecessor finishes. Figure 7.3 shows the value of using these other types of task relationships.

PLANNING STEP THREE: ESTIMATE WORK PACKAGES

In order to determine the cost and duration of an entire project, it's necessary to build a cost and schedule estimate for each work package; this is called *bottom-up estimating*. A lot of information is generated in the estimating process, so it is critical to record it in a systematic manner. (Table 7.1 shows the work package estimates for the home landscape project. Tables 7.2 to 7.5 illustrate some of the variables that affect work package estimates.)

The schedule estimate for a task measures the time from initiation to completion. This estimate is usually referred to as *duration* of a task. When building a schedule estimate, it's important to include *all* the time the task will span. For instance, it may take only 1 day to order materials, but if it takes 10 days for delivery, the total duration of the task will be 11 days. Similarly, while a certain decision might take only two hours to make, it might be more realistic to estimate duration at 5 days if the decision maker is likely to be busy at that time.

Cost estimates come from four sources:

1. *Labor estimates.* These project how much human effort will be put into a task. If three people work 8 hours a day for three days, the total labor estimate will be 72 hours. On small work packages, labor is estimated in hours. (At the project level, labor can be such a large item that it is sometimes expressed in years.) In addition to recording the labor estimate, you will need to record the skill requirement. For example, a task might specifically require an electrician eight hours a day for three days. If more than one skill type is required, list them all.

2. *Equipment estimates.* Equipment requirements need to be identified at the work package level. These estimates then become the basis for estimating the total equipment cost for the project. Equipment, in this case, includes the tools necessary to perform the task,

Finish-to-start The most common task relationships on the network are *finish-to-start*. The first task must *finish* before the next one can *start*.

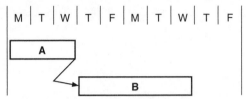

Task A must finish before Task B can start.

Start-to-start The successor task can *start* as soon as the predecessor task *starts*. The example shows a painting company, painting all the rooms on one floor of an office building. After the first room is prepared, both the prep crew and the paint crew can be working at the same time. Overlapping the tasks reduces the total duration of the project.

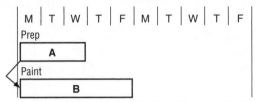

Task A must start before Task B can start.

Finish-to-finish The successor task can *finish* only when the predecessor task is *finished*. The example shows the last two tasks of a design phase. Planning for the construction phase can begin before the final design approval, but it cannot finish until design is complete.

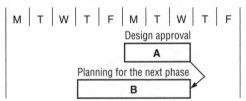

Task A must finish before Task B can finish.

FIGURE 7.3 *Task relationships.*

from cranes to specialized software. (Don't bother to list common tools such as word processors, copy machines, or hammers.) Like labor, equipment use should be estimated in hours.

3. *Materials estimates.* Materials for the project can be a major source of project cost—or virtually nonexistent. While a construction project may have a significant portion of its total cost represented by raw materials, a project to institute new hiring guidelines

TABLE 7.1 HOME LANDSCAPE PROJECT WORK PACKAGE ESTIMATES

ID	Task Name	Duration	Labor Hours	Resource Names
1	Design home landscape	5 days	80 hrs.	Homeowner [0.5], Teens [1.5]*
2	Put in lawn			
3	Acquire lawn materials	2 days	64 hrs.	Homeowner, Teens [3]
4	Install sprinkler system			
5	Identify sprinkler locations	1 day	Fixed fee, 8 hrs.	Contractor homeowner
6	Dig trenches	2 days	Fixed fee	Contractor
7	Install pipe and hardware	3 days	Fixed fee	Contractor
8	Cover sprinkler system	1 day	Fixed fee	Contractor
9	Plant grass			
10	Remove debris	4 days	256 hrs.	Teens [3], Youth group [5]
11	Prepare soil	4 days	96 hrs.	Teens [3], rototiller
12	Plant lawn seed	1 day	16 hrs.	Teens [2]
13	Plant shrubs	6 days	96 hrs.	Teens [2]
14	Build fence			
15	Acquire fence material	2 days	16 hrs.	Homeowner
16	Install fence			
17	Mark fence line	1 day	32 hrs.	Homeowner, Teens [3]
18	Install posts	5 days	80 hrs.	Teens [2]
19	Install fencing and gates	6 days	144 hrs.	Teens [3]
20	Paint/stain fence and gates	3 days	72 hrs.	Teens [3]

*On task 1, both the homeowner and teens are working 4 hours per day.

will have no raw materials. Software development projects have no raw materials, but an information system project to install commercial off-the-shelf (COTS) software will have to include the cost of the software. *Even though materials costs can be a major portion of the project's cost, total materials cost should be estimated from the product specifications—not estimated from the bottom up using the work breakdown structure.* (Chapter 8 covers project budget

TABLE 7.2 WORK PACKAGE ESTIMATE: EXAMPLE 1

Task description: During an environmental study, a power company counts salmon during a 40-day salmon run.

Assumption: The federal agency overseeing the power company dictates the length of the study.

Duration: 40 days

Materials: None

Labor and Equipment Table

Type	Average Use	Total
Salmon specialist	1 @ 10 hrs./day	400 hrs.
Field technician	2 @ 10 hrs./day	800 hrs.
Truck	1 all day	40 days

Increasing the number of people on this task does not change the duration, but it could increase the accuracy of the study.

development in greater detail.) Including materials in the work package estimate helps to identify exactly when each of the materials will be needed; these schedule requirements, in turn, will determine order and delivery dates.

4. *Fixed-price bids.* Fixed-estimate costs can replace the three previous cost sources. For example, a vendor or subcontractor might make a fixed-price bid that includes labor, equipment, and materials. Fixed-price bids mean that the vendor takes responsibility for costs; should there be overruns, the cost to the project will not change. (The landscape project in Table 7.1 includes fixed-price bids by the sprinkler contractor.)

Is it really necessary to concentrate on costs when trying to build a realistic schedule? It is, because each cost represents a resource constraint. Costs such as hiring subcontractors and purchasing materials will constrain the schedule. Later on, the schedule will be adjusted to account for these resource constraints (this is the fifth step of planning), but before adjusting the schedule we need to identify all the resource requirements, one work package at a time.

How the Amount of Labor Relates to Duration

How long it takes to perform a task usually depends on how many people are assigned to do it. When you estimate the duration of a task,

TABLE 7.3 WORK PACKAGE ESTIMATES: EXAMPLE 2

Task description: During a training project, software is upgraded on 20 workstations in a training room.

Assumption: The average time to install the software is 2 hours per workstation. Testing is 1 hour per workstation. Only 1 person can work on one workstation at a time.

First Estimate

Duration: 5 days   *Materials:* 20 copies of the new software

Labor and Equipment Table

Type	Average Use	Total
Computer technician	1 @ 8 hrs./day	40 hrs.
Tester (user or technician)	1 @ 4 hrs./day	20 hrs.
Software test kit	1 per tester	1 test kit

The training manager did not want the training room out of use for a whole week. In fact, he wanted the upgrade done over a weekend so the training room didn't lose any availability.

Revised Estimate

Duration: 2 days   *Materials:* 20 copies of the new software

Labor and Equipment Table

Type	Average Use	Total
Computer technician	2 @ 10 hrs./day	40 hrs.
Tester (user or technician)	1 @ 10 hrs./day	20 hrs.
Software test kit	1 per tester	1 test kit

By adding 1 computer technician and working longer days, the duration was cut from 5 days to 2.

you will normally figure in the amount of available labor. In the example in Table 7.3, when a training manager added one more technician to a task involving a software upgrade, this addition, plus longer working days, cut the duration of the task from five days to two.

The work package estimates for the home landscape project in Table 7.1 include an example of using extra people to reduce the duration of a task. When the project team (the homeowner and the family's three teenagers) estimated task 10, "Remove debris," they agreed it would be a long, unpleasant task if they worked on it alone. So they recruited some of the members of their local youth group to help them for a few days. With eight people working on the task, it can be accomplished in four days.

TABLE 7.4 WORK PACKAGE ESTIMATES: EXAMPLE 3

Task description: A government agency is mapping a forest. Aerial photography of the entire area is the first step in creating the maps.

Assumption: An aerial photography subcontractor rents airplanes (complete with pilots and photographers). The agency has one scientist ride with every airplane. The forest is broken into 60 squares. They can photograph one square per day. During the flight, a ground technician stays in radio contact with the scientist to answer mapping questions.

First Estimate
Duration: 60 days
Materials: None

Labor and Equipment Table

Type	Average Use	Total
Scientist (in plane)	1 @ 8 hrs./day	480 hrs.
Airplane	1 @ 8 hrs./day	480 hrs.
Ground technician	1 @ 8 hrs./day	480 hrs.

The forest area traditionally has so much cloudy weather that the agency estimates there will be only one clear day out of every three, but the photography needs to take place during the three months of summer when there is no snow.

Given this requirement, they decide to fly two airplanes every clear day. On days they can't fly there is no airplane cost and the scientist and ground technician can work on other things. A single ground technician can stay in contact with both airplanes.

Revised Estimate
Duration: 90 days
Materials: None

Labor and Equipment Table

Type	Average Use	Total
Scientist (in plane)	2 @ 2.7 hrs./day	480 hrs.
Airplane	2 @ 2.7 hrs./day	480 hrs.
Ground technician	1 @ 2.7 hrs./day	240 hrs.

Since one ground technician can talk to both airplanes, the total labor for that person is cut in half. The expected hours for the scientist and the airplanes stay the same.

The average use estimates are used during the resource-leveling step to indicate the average amount of time the scientists and ground technician will have available to work on other projects during this 90-day period.

TABLE 7.5 WORK PACKAGE ESTIMATES: EXAMPLE 4

Task description: A systems analyst is working on three projects at the same time. One of her project managers asked her to estimate the design of a subsystem.

Assumption: She will continue to work on all three projects simultaneously.

First Estimate
Duration: 40 days
Materials: None

Labor and Equipment Table

Type	Average Use	Total
System analyst	1 @ 2.5 hrs./day	100

Her project manager needed the design performed much faster and suggested he could get another analyst to work with her part-time.

Revised Estimate
Duration: 30 days
Materials: None

Labor and Equipment Table

Type	Average Use	Total
System analyst	2 @ 2.5 hrs./day	150

Adding people to a design task can speed up some of the work, but much of it will be done together so it results in an increase in the total labor cost. It is possible the resulting design will be better, but that is another assumption.

Then the project manager asked her what it would take to get it done the fastest. "Talk to my other project managers and arrange to get me completely off those projects for a few weeks so I can concentrate 100 percent on yours."

Revised Estimate
Duration: 10 days
Materials: None

Labor and Equipment

Type	Average Use	Total
System analyst	1 @ 8 hrs./day	80

Not only was she able to spend more time per day on this task, but she knew if she was able to concentrate on it 100 percent she would be more productive.

How Productivity Relates to Duration

When estimating the number of people needed for a task, you will need to consider their productivity. Adding people to simple tasks always reduces the duration. Productivity is said to be constant when the total labor hours do not change as the number of people assigned to the task changes. (The productivity of the technicians in Table 7.3 was constant; so was the "Remove debris" task in Table 7.1.)

However, in the case of tasks involving knowledge workers, adding more workers does not always result in greater productivity and a shorter duration of a task. For example, if two engineers are working on a complex problem, adding three more may actually slow the task and produce no recognizable change in product quality. The result is a measurable decrease in productivity because the cost for labor increased while the product stayed the same. (The estimate in Table 7.5 is another example of this factor.)

Another point to consider when measuring productivity is that people who spend all their time on one project are usually more productive than people who spread their time across multiple projects (again, see Table 7.5). The analyst estimated that the most productive way for her to work—requiring the fewest hours and fewest days—was to be able to devote her attention 100 percent to one project.

When calculating hours for your part-time project workers, it is usually unnecessary to figure out exactly what hour of which day they'll be working on your project. By assigning an availability assumption, such as "two hours per day," to all their tasks, the estimates for the duration of the task are proportionally increased. This approach allows each individual team member to decide for him- or herself when to actually work on the task. It doesn't matter whether they get started on it as soon as it's scheduled or work on it the last day. All you need to do to prepare a detailed plan is to give them a start time and a completion time.

As you can see, there is much to be considered when estimating the costs and duration of work packages. Chapter 8 will discuss the subject further, with many more tips and techniques.

PLANNING STEP FOUR: CALCULATE AN INITIAL SCHEDULE

Calculating a schedule may be one of the most well known, but unappreciated, of all project management techniques. It can be particularly tedious and time-consuming when done by hand for large projects. Yet it is the key to establishing realistic schedules and meeting them. (The tedium involved is a compelling reason to use project management software.)

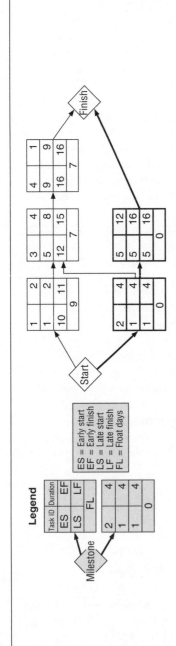

Legend

Task ID	Duration
ES	EF
LS	LF
FL	

ES = Early start
EF = Early finish
LS = Late start
LF = Late finish
FL = Float days

Task ID	Duration
1	2 days
2	4 days
3	4 days
4	1 day
5	12 days

Step one: Forward pass—Work forward from the start to calculate all early start and early finish dates.

Forward pass steps:

1. The early start of task 2 is assumed to be the first day of the project. (Task 1 also has an ES of day 1.)
2. The early finish of task 2 is determined by counting forward the duration of the task. Since it is a four-day task that begins on day 1, the earliest it can finish is day 4.
3. The early start of task 5 is one day after task 2 finishes. That's because the start of a task is assumed to be 8 A.M. and the finish is 5 P.M. If task 2 ends at 5 P.M. on day 4, task 5 can begin at 8 A.M. on day 5.
4. Again, determine the EF of 5 by counting forward the duration of the task. It begins on day 5 and is 12 days long; therefore, it will finish on day 16.

Repeat these steps along each path of the network. Notice that task 3 has two predecessors. The predecessor that finishes latest will dictate the ES of 3. In this case, that is task 2.

FIGURE 7.4 *Calculating a schedule.*

Step two: Backward pass—Work backward from the finish to calculate all late start and late finish dates.

Backward pass steps:

1. Set the project finish date. The project's finish date can come from two places: It can be the EF of the last task on the project, or it can be an externally imposed finish date, such as April 15 for filing income tax. (An "externally imposed finish date" means that the finish date is set by someone outside the project team.) The project finish date becomes the late finish (LF) for the last task on the project, in this case, task 5.

2. Count backward the duration of the task to determine the late start (LS) for 5. The finish is day 16, so the LS is 5. That means if task 5 does not start by day 5, it will cause the project to miss the final completion deadline.

3. Work the network backward. Task 2 must be finished no later than 4 in order for task 5 to begin by day 5.

4. Repeat these steps along all paths of the network. When a task has multiple successors, its late finish must be early enough for all the successors to meet their late start time. Task 2 has multiple successor tasks. It must be finished no later than day 4 to allow task 5 to begin on time.

Step three: Calculate float and identify the critical path.

Calculating float:

Looking at the set of schedule dates for each work package, (in this figure and Figures 7.6 and 7.7), it is obvious that some have the same early start and late start. Practically speaking, that means those tasks have no schedule flexibility. Float is calculated by subtracting ES from LS. Float is really the measure of schedule flexibility for a task. Notice how tasks 3 and 4 in figure 7.4 have 7 days of float. These tasks have a lot of flexibility as to when they will actually be performed—task 3 can start as early as day 5 or as late as day 12.

FIGURE 7.4 *(Continued)*

As discussed earlier, the initial schedule is calculated by using the network diagram and the duration of each work package to determine the start and finish dates for each task, and for the entire project. Figure 7.4 shows how the network and task duration can work together to produce an initial schedule. Schedule calculation provides a set of detailed schedule data for every work package, as shown in the following:

Early start—The earliest date a task can begin, given the tasks preceding it.

Early finish—The earliest date a task can finish, given the tasks preceding it.

Late start—The latest date a task can begin without delaying the finish date of the project.

Late finish—The latest date a task can finish without delaying the finish date of the project.

Calculating the schedule to determine these four dates is a three-step process. Referring to Figure 7.4 will help to clarify this process.

Step One: Forward Pass

The forward pass will help you determine the early start (ES) and early finish (EF) for each task. It is so named because it involves working through a network diagram from start to finish. (The next step will involve the reverse—a backward pass.) In Figure 7.4, we follow a forward pass through the diagram, step by step.

Figure 7.5 shows another way of displaying this information. It's called a *time-scaled network* because it uses a time scale across the top and each task is laid out across the calendar. Notice that all the early start dates are the same in Figures 7.4 and 7.5.

Step Two: Backward Pass

The backward pass determines the late start and late finish dates. All of us have made this calculation hundreds of times—whenever we set an alarm clock. The goal of the backward pass is literally to work backward from the project finish date to determine how late any task can begin or end. The late start (LS) and late finish (LF) are calculated in Figure 7.4.

Step Three: Calculate Float

Some tasks have flexibility in when they can be performed in the schedule and others have no flexibility. The term for this schedule flexibility is *float*. (Another common term is *slack*.) Float is calculated by

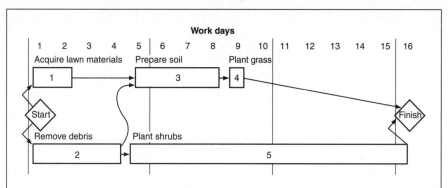

FIGURE 7.5 *Time-scaled network. This contains the same network information as Figure 7.4, but the format is different.*

subtracting early start from late start. (How to calculate float is demonstrated graphically in Figures 7.4, 7.6 and 7.7.)

KEY CONCEPT   Critical Path

When the initial schedule has been calculated, the project schedule begins to take shape. One of the key features of the initial schedule is the critical path. The term *critical path* is one of the most widely used—and most widely misunderstood—of all project management terms. But the concept is simple: The critical path is defined as all of the tasks with zero or negative float. When outlined on a network diagram, the critical path is the longest path through the network. (The critical path is boldly outlined in Figures 7.4 and 7.6.)

The tasks that have zero float must be completed at their early finish date or the project finish will be delayed. Making sure that all critical path tasks begin and end on time is the surest way of making the project end on time. That's why you'll hear a project manager motivating someone to complete a task by telling the person, "It's on the critical path!"

Since it is the longest path through the network (the *longest path* means the longest duration, not necessarily the most tasks), the critical path is one measure of schedule viability. This is because it demonstrates the *minimum* time the project will take. Sometimes it takes a network diagram with the critical path outlined to show stakeholders that their optimistic schedule estimate is unrealistic.

These are just two of the ways that the project manager might use the critical path. Several more are described later in this chapter and in Chapters 9 and 14.

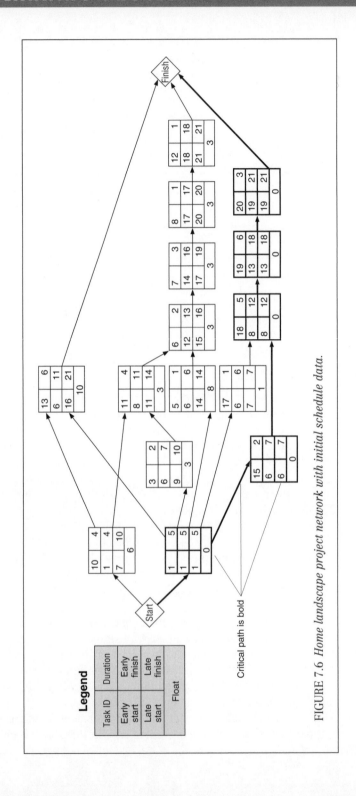

FIGURE 7.6 *Home landscape project network with initial schedule data.*

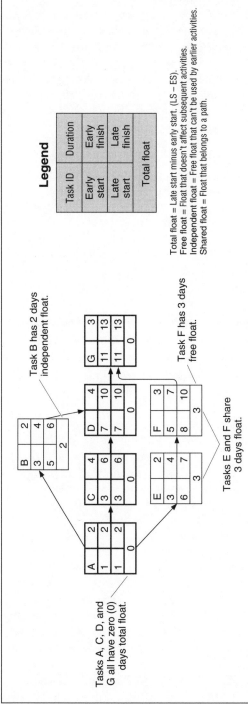

Tasks A, C, D, and G all have zero (0) days total float.

Task B has 2 days independent float.

Task F has 3 days free float.

Tasks E and F share 3 days float.

Total float = Late start minus early start. (LS − ES).
Free float = Float that doesn't affect subsequent activities.
Independent float = Free float that can't be used by earlier activities.
Shared float = Float that belongs to a path.

Legend

Task ID	Duration
Early start	Early finish
Late start	Late finish
Total float	

- Task B has independent float, so you can assign it to be complete by its late finish date. Whether it finishes on day 4 (EF) or day 6 (LF), won't affect the start of successor tasks.
- Task E has total float of 3 days, but zero days free float because every day of delay for E delays F. That means if you allow Task E to finish on day 7 (LF), Task F becomes critical.
- If tasks have shared float, don't let the first tasks in the path use up the entire float and make remaining ones critical.

FIGURE 7.7 *Managing float.*

Shop Early and Avoid Negative Float

Not every project has a critical path. If a project has an externally imposed finish date that allows more than enough time to complete the project, all tasks will have float. A simple example is Christmas shopping. December 25 is the externally imposed finish date. Early in the year, when there are 200 shopping days until Christmas, nobody is stressed because there is still plenty of float. Like Christmas shopping, most projects with no critical path are put off until all the float is used up.

When all the float has been used up, a new term emerges to describe the situation: *negative float.* Negative float results when externally imposed finish dates are impossible to meet (such as 10 presents to buy at 6 P.M. on December 24). Figure 7.8, for example, shows a network diagram with a critical path that is longer than the allotted schedule. When there is negative float, it means that adjustments will have to be made to bring the schedule in line with the critical path. This is the kind of information you will need when you renegotiate the cost-schedule-quality equilibrium.

Gantt Charts and Time-Scaled Networks

A picture is worth a thousand words. The network diagram is essential in calculating the schedule, but it can be terribly difficult to decipher on a large project. Thankfully, there are two very good alternatives, which display both the schedule information and the task relationships.

Gantt charts, named after Henry Gantt, who developed them in the early 1900s, have become the most common method for displaying a project schedule. Figure 7.9 is a Gantt chart for the home landscape project. It has the same schedule dates as the network in Figure 7.6. Notice that all the tasks are currently scheduled at their early start date—you can tell that because all noncritical tasks display float. The great advantage of the Gantt chart is its clarity: The horizontal axis shows the schedule and the vertical axis lists the work breakdown structure.

Another excellent graphic for displaying a schedule is the time-scaled network (as shown in Figures 7.5 and 7.10). One advantage that this diagram has, compared to the Gantt chart, is the ability to condense the network onto less paper. On large projects, the Gantt charts can grow too large to print, whereas the time-scaled network, because it combines many tasks on one line, can be made one-half to one-tenth the height of the Gantt.

The initial schedule represents the combination of task sequence and task duration, but it's called an *initial schedule* because it hasn't

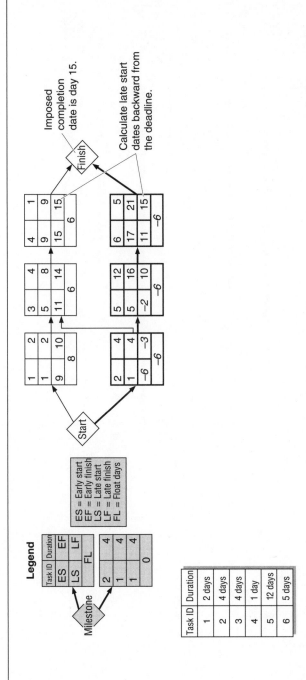

FIGURE 7.8 *Negative float. When imposed deadlines result in negative float, that is a warning the project is out of equilibrium. The cost, schedule, or quality objectives must be revised.*

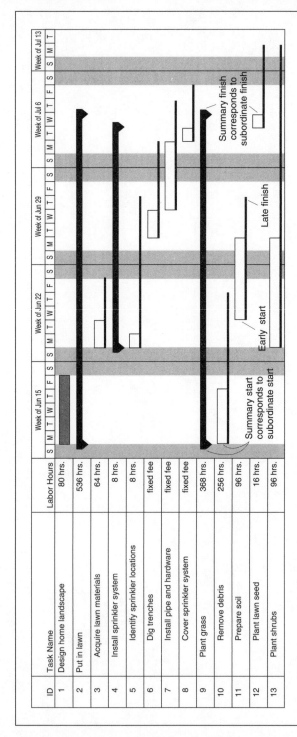

FIGURE 7.9 *Gantt chart for home landscape project.*

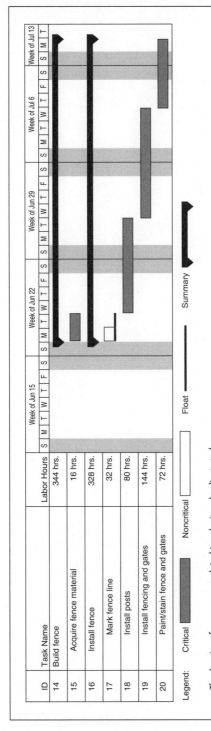

ID	Task Name	Labor Hours
14	Build fence	344 hrs.
15	Acquire fence material	16 hrs.
16	Install fence	328 hrs.
17	Mark fence line	32 hrs.
18	Install posts	80 hrs.
19	Install fencing and gates	144 hrs.
20	Paint/stain fence and gates	72 hrs.

Legend: Critical ▨   Noncritical ▭   Float ▭   Summary ▬

• The duration of a summary task is driven by its subordinate tasks.
• The float for a noncritical task begins at its early start and ends at its late finish.
• This chart shows an early start schedule—all tasks are currently scheduled to begin on their early start date.

FIGURE 7.9 *(Continued)*

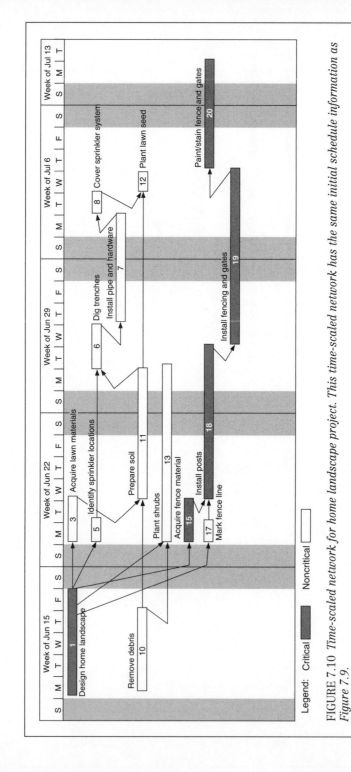

FIGURE 7.10 *Time-scaled network for home landscape project. This time-scaled network has the same initial schedule information as Figure 7.9.*

taken into account people and equipment limitations. The next planning step uses the initial schedule as a starting point and balances it against the resources available to the project.

PLANNING STEP FIVE: ASSIGN AND LEVEL RESOURCES

The goal of resource leveling is to optimize the use of people and equipment assigned to the project. It begins with the assumption that, whenever possible, it is most productive to have consistent, continuous use of the fewest resources possible. In other words, it seeks to avoid repeatedly adding and removing resources time and again throughout the project. Resource leveling is the last step in creating a realistic schedule. It confronts the reality of limited people and equipment and adjusts the schedule to compensate.

Using the home landscape project as an example, we can see how resource leveling makes a project schedule more realistic. The network (Figure 7.6) shows, in terms of task scheduling, that it's possible to put in the lawn and build the fence at the same time. But when we consider that the family has only the three teenagers available to work on the project, that means they have just a total of 24 labor hours available per day (3 teens × 8 hours a day). Trying to put in the lawn and build the fence concurrently is unrealistic because it would require each teen to work far more than eight hours a day for more than half the project. (The resource spreadsheet on the Gantt chart in Figure 7.11 indicates clearly how unrealistic the schedule is.) Resource leveling will adjust the schedule to keep the teens busy at a consistent, reasonable rate. (Figure 7.12 on page 158 shows the same project as Figure 7.11, but with the resources leveled.) Not only does resource leveling take unreasonable overtime out of their project, but it keeps the teens employed for a longer time at a steady rate. That's usually an advantage for any project team.

Let's consider a few of the problems faced by project managers in this process of leveling resources.

Every project faces the reality of limited people and equipment. The idea is to avoid both over- and underallocation. As the home landscape project demonstrates, too many concurrent tasks can call for more resources than are available. For example, as discussed, the initial schedule had the teens working on the fence and the lawn during the same period, and this resulted in the teens being overallocated during the first half of the project (they would have had to work more than eight hours a day to meet this schedule).

Project managers need to remember that whether it's teenagers planting the lawn, bulldozers, or programmers, there are rarely a bunch of spares sitting on the shelf. This overallocation problem can

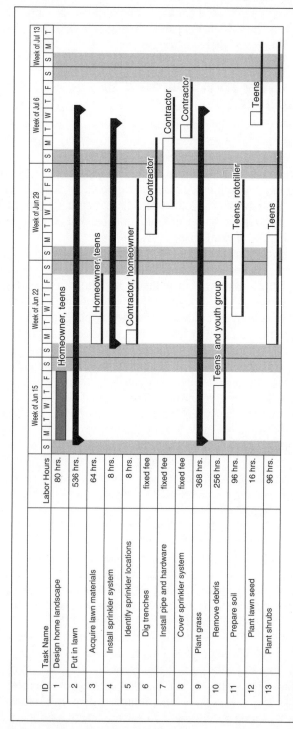

FIGURE 7.11 *Gantt chart with resource spreadsheet for home landscape project.*

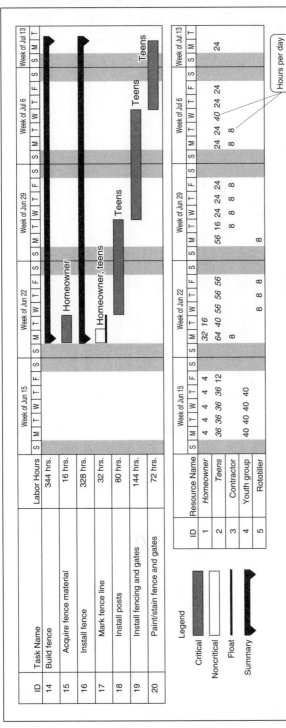

The following data tables are shown in the figure:

ID	Task Name	Labor Hours
14	Build fence	344 hrs.
15	Acquire fence material	16 hrs.
16	Install fence	328 hrs.
17	Mark fence line	32 hrs.
18	Install posts	80 hrs.
19	Install fencing and gates	144 hrs.
20	Paint/stain fence and gates	72 hrs.

Legend

- Critical
- Noncritical
- Float
- Summary

ID	Resource Name	Week of Jun 15 S M T W T F S	Week of Jun 22 S M T W T F S	Week of Jun 29 S M T W T F S	Week of Jul 6 S M T W T F S	Week of Jul 13 S M T
1	Homeowner	4 4 4 4 4	32 16			
2	Teens	36 36 36 36 12	64 40 56 56 56	56 16 24 24 24	24 24 40 24 24	24
3	Contractor		8	8 8 8 8	8 8	
4	Youth group	40 40 40 40				
5	Rototiller		8 8 8	8		

Hours per day

- The resource spreadsheet shows the labor hours per day for each resource. Overallocated resources are in italics.
- The family has three teenagers working on the project, for a total of 24 hours each day. (3 teens @ 8 hours).
- There is only one homeowner, who is available for 8 hours a day.
- Given this initial schedule, with all tasks beginning on their early start dates, both the homeowner and teens are overscheduled during much of the project.

FIGURE 7.11 *(Continued)*

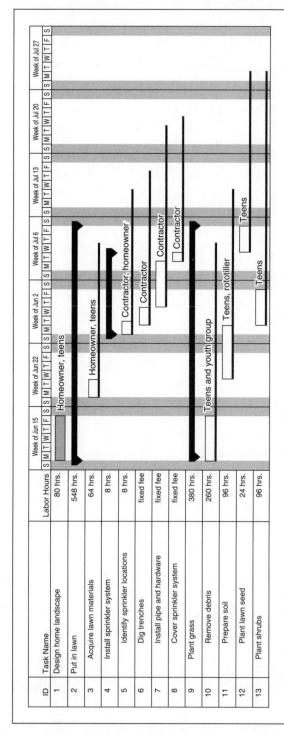

FIGURE 7.12 *Gantt chart with resource-leveled schedule for home landscape project.*

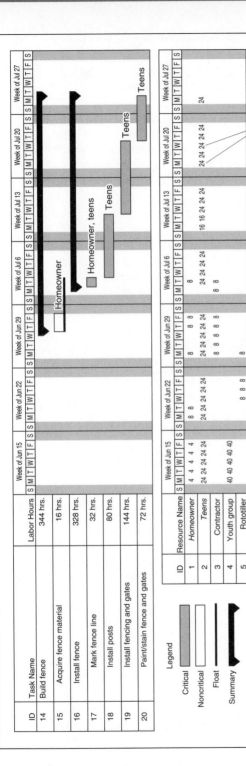

The leveled schedule has eliminated the task overlaps, which caused unrealistic work hours for the teens and homeowner.

- *Task 5*—Delayed 5 days to level homeowner while keeping the sprinkler contractor on schedule.
- *Task 10*—Reduced teens to 4 hours per day (each) so they can participate in design home landscape at the same time. (Design home landscape also calls for each teen to work 4 hours per day.) Added an additional day for the youth group to work on the task. This changed the task duration from 4 to 5 days and the total labor from 256 hours to 260 hours.
- *Task 12*—Changed the task from two teens for one day (16 hours labor) to one teen for 3 days (24 hours labor). One teen working on the task alone won't be as efficient, but now the other two teens can work on task 18 at the same time.
- Tasks 13, 15, and 17—Delayed these tasks to level the project and their successor tasks were delayed as well.
- The new schedule is 10 workdays longer, but neither the teens nor the homeowner are overallocated on any day.

FIGURE 7.12 (*Continued*)

become especially acute if project managers imagine that they have a large supply of a rare resource, such as the unlimited time of the only subject expert in the company. In this case, not only has the schedule become unrealistic, but the manager may have overloaded a key resource.

The other side of the problem is underallocation. If the project team isn't busy on your project, it will likely be reassigned to other projects and be unavailable when the next peak comes. In the worst case, during lulls in the project some of the unassigned people may get laid off, becoming permanently unavailable and taking valuable knowledge about your project with them.

A further problem arises if people working on this project are also working on several others at the same time. If every project in the firm has wild swings in its resource requirements, it is almost impossible to move people smoothly between projects. Instead, people are yanked off one project to help another catch up, only to be thrown at yet another that is even further behind.

The Process of Resource Leveling

It is important to remember how we are defining the term *resources*. Resources are the people, equipment, and raw materials that go into the project. Resource leveling focuses only on the people and equipment; the materials needed for the project are dictated by the specifications.

Resource leveling begins with the initial schedule and work package resource requirements (see Table 7.1). The leveling follows a four-step process:

1. *Forecast the resource requirements throughout the project for the initial schedule.* The best tool for this process is a resource spreadsheet such as the one portrayed in Figure 7.11. This spreadsheet, correlated to the schedule, can forecast all the people and equipment needed on each day of the project. The initial schedule is sometimes called an *early start schedule.* At first, this might seem like good project management, that is, getting as early a start on everything as possible. But an early start schedule usually has a lot of uneconomical resource peaks and valleys. For example, the overallocation of the teens during the first half of the home landscape project is the kind of misallocation common to early start schedules.

2. *Identify the resource peaks.* Use the resource spreadsheet (Figure 7.11) and the resources histogram (Figure 7.13) to find the periods in the project where there are unrealistic or uneconomical resource amounts.

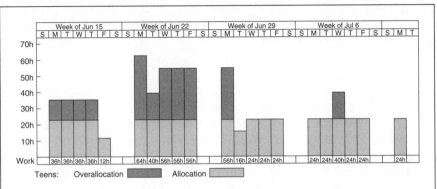

- There are three teenagers assigned to the project. Together, they have a total of 24 hours available each day.
- The initial schedule in Figure 7.11 is not realistic because the teenagers are overallocated during the first half of the project.

FIGURE 7.13 *Resource histogram.*

3. *At each peak, delay noncritical tasks within their float.* Remember that float is schedule flexibility. Tasks with float can be delayed without changing the project deadline. By delaying these tasks, you'll also be filling in the valleys of the resource histogram, that is, moving tasks from periods of too much work to periods when there is too little work. This means that you will need fewer people, and they will be more productive, but the deadline will stay the same. (A comparison of the initial schedule in Figure 7.11 with the leveled schedule in Figure 7.12 demonstrates how task 5 was delayed within its float, thus removing a resource peak for the homeowner on June 24.)

4. *Eliminate the remaining peaks by reevaluating the work package estimates.* Using the project float in step 3 may not be enough to eliminate all the peaks and valleys. For example, instead of having two or three people working together on a task, consider whether just one person could do the work over a longer period of time. (Task 12 in Figure 7.12 was changed from two teenagers for one day to one teen for three days.) Alternatively, available people might be added to a task to shorten its duration. When performing these changes, take note that each change to a work package estimate is going to change the amount of float, or time flexibility, for that task. In other words, after changing a work package estimate, you will need to return to step 4 and recalculate the initial schedule. Then you will also need to repeat the first three steps of resource leveling. (This kind of recalculation is made much easier by using project management software.)

What to Do If the Resource-Leveled Plan Is Still Unrealistic

Reestimating work packages and delaying tasks within their float can remove the worst resource peaks and valleys, but the plan might still contain unrealistic or uneconomic resource peaks. At that point, your next option is accepting a later project completion date.

On the home landscape project, the schedule had to be extended by two weeks to balance the available labor with the amount of work. This can be a difficult decision, but that's what it means to create a realistic cost-schedule-quality equilibrium. In Chapter 9, there will be further discussion of the factors that balance the schedule against cost and quality.

 ## Computers Will Not Do Everything

Some of the tedious calculations described here are easily performed by project management software, but don't be fooled. Computers really perform only two tasks: data storage and calculations. Even if you employ a good software package, you will still have to understand each one of the steps in this chapter. (The appendix summarizes the planning steps using the home landscape example.)

END POINT

The detailed planning techniques presented in this chapter are often downplayed as mere scheduling techniques. But not only do they build a realistic schedule, these techniques form the foundation of the science of project management.

The planning model in this chapter portrays the step-by-step method of building a detailed plan. Laying out a detailed plan may not solve all the problems you'll face as a project manager, but it does provide a tool set for solving many of them. Every one of these planning techniques will be referred to again in later chapters. They are the entry point to the science of project management; without them it's impossible to practice the art.

 ## FAST FOUNDATION IN PROJECT MANAGEMENT

Large or complex projects can follow the advice in Part 3 together with project management software to build detailed action plans. Simpler projects may call for a simpler format.

The *action plan* template is simply a spreadsheet formatted with standard headings for recording the basic information of a plan and tracking actual performance. Fill in the calendar portion by shading the cells to create a Gantt chart. This template is available for download at www.versatilecompany.com/forms.

Home Landscape Action Plan

Project Manager: Home Owner   Last Updated: 6/27

Task ID	Task Name	Assigned to*	Baseline Start	Actual Start	Baseline Finish	Actual Finish	Baseline Labor	Actual Labor	Labor Remaining	Comments
1	Design home landscape	HO, Tn	16-Jun	16-Jun	20-Jun	20-Jun	80	72	0	
2	Put in lawn									
2.1	Acquire lawn material	HO, Tn	23-Jun	24-Jun	24-Jun	25-Jun	64	64	0	
2.2	Install sprinkler system	Cn	30-Jun		8-Jul		fixed	na	na	
2.3	Plant grass									
2.3.1	Remove debris	Tn, YG	16-Jun	16-Jun	20-Jun	23-Jun	260	350	0	
2.3.2	Prepare soil	Tn, Rt	25-Jun	26-Jun	30-Jun		96	60	40	work weekend
2.3.3	Plant lawn seed	Tn	9-Jul		11-Jul		16		16	
2.4	Plant shrubs	Tn	1-Jul		4-Jul		96		96	Call 6/30 - shrub dlvry
3	Build fence									
3.1	Acquire fence material	HO, Tn	3-Jul		4-Jul		16		16	
3.2	Install fence	Tn	8-Jul		28-Jul		328		328	

*Assigned to' Initials
HO = Homeowner   Tn = Teens   Cn = Contractor
YG = Youth Group   Rt = Rototiller

Home Landscape Action Plan

Task ID	Task Name	Assigned to	Gantt Schedule (week beginning)						
			15-Jun	22-Jun	29-Jun	6-Jul	13-Jul	20-Jul	27-Jul
1	Design home landscape	HO, Tn	MTWTF						
2	Put in lawn								
2.1	Acquire lawn material	HO, Tn		MT					
2.2	Install sprinkler system	Cn			TWTF	MT			
2.3	Plant grass								
2.3.1	Remove debris	Tn, YG	MTWTF						
2.3.2	Prepare soil	Tn, Rt		WTF	M				
2.3.3	Plant lawn seed	Tn				WTF			
2.4	Plant shrubs	Tn			TWTF				
3	Build fence								
3.1	Acquire fence material	HO, Tn			TF				
3.2	Install fence	Tn				TWTF	MTWTF	MTWTF	M

'Assigned to' Initials
HO = Homeowner   Tn = Teens   Cn = Contractor
YG = Youth Group   Rt = Rototiller

The Dynamics of Accurate Estimating

INTRODUCTION

"Kris, how long will it take to implement this new design?"

"If you mean how long until we produce a product with the new design feature, I'd guess eight months."

"You guess? Come on, we need something firm."

"All right. I *estimate* it will take eight months."

"Great. Let's do it."

This kind of dialogue is exchanged on thousands of projects every year. Simple as it is, it points up some of the key issues in accurate estimating. First, notice how Kris tried to clarify what was being requested before venturing a guess. Second, note that guessing wasn't acceptable; it was only when he changed his guess to an estimate that it was taken seriously.

Estimating is forecasting the future, trying to predict the time and money necessary to produce a result. Because forecasting the future is an uncertain business, it should come as no surprise when an estimate turns out to be wrong. But a wrong estimate isn't good enough for most project stakeholders; customers, especially, want the product on time and within the promised budget. This means that we need to focus on estimating accurately; we need to be able to predict the future in an uncertain world.

Professional estimators—those people who make their living by developing cost and schedule estimates—have developed many methods of predicting the future. When you consider how many formulas and calculations these professionals work with, it would seem reasonable to define estimating as a science. We shall see, however, that art plays a critical role in estimating. (It may be that those with extremely accurate methods for predicting the future have left the pedestrian field of project management and are applying their expertise in locales where the fruits of their labor are more quick and tangible, such as Wall Street or Monte Carlo.) This chapter confronts the difficulty of forecasting the future. We will examine the factors that make our estimates wrong and suggest techniques that can make them more accurate. At the end of the chapter you'll find a downloadable checklist you can use as you complete your project plan to ensure you've covered all the bases described in this chapter and the other chapters in Part 3.

ESTIMATING FUNDAMENTALS

As we've observed many times, projects are unique. In fact, the more unique they are, the more difficult they are to estimate; the less unique, the easier. Research and development (R&D) projects, for instance, are extremely difficult to estimate, because they are attempting to solve new problems. But every project will produce a unique product, which means that a different combination of tasks will be employed. In addition, there are usually a number of other unique or unpredictable factors on any project:

- The people on the project team may be unknown to the manager. However, their particular skills and knowledge will affect their productivity, and the more complex the tasks are, the more this productivity factor counts.

- Projects that rely on new technology face questions about the reliability of the new technology and the learning curve of the team.

- Since estimates are used to coordinate activities and forecast resources, incorrect timing predictions will cost money. If the project is behind schedule when a subcontractor arrives, you may have to pay the subcontractor to sit around and wait. If it is so far behind schedule that the vendor must be sent away, then this vendor may not be available when needed.

KEY CONCEPT **Avoid the Classic Mistakes**

Common sense is not all that common. There are certain mistakes that many of us seem to fall into, even though common sense may warn us to avoid them. Following are the most common.

Making "Ballparks in Elevators"

Maybe it's their authority, or maybe it's that you're off guard, but whenever a high-level manager or customer catches you in an elevator, hallway, or break room and asks for an estimate, you inevitably respond with an optimistic, seat-of-the-pants guess that you regret the moment it escapes from your mouth. The problem is compounded if that manager happens to be on the way to a meeting where your "estimate" will be the topic of discussion. The trouble here is obvious: It's impossible to consider all the details required for an accurate estimate when you're riding between the fourth and tenth floors. But the question is how to avoid this optimistic guessing. Here are a few suggestions:

- Assume a thoughtful, concerned expression and respond to the manager, "There are a lot of factors that will impact the effort required. . . ." Then list a few of these factors and add, "I wouldn't want to mislead you by offering a guess on that."

- Offer to get a sheet of paper and write down exactly what the manager is requesting. At the same time, start listing the questions that need to be answered before a useful estimate can be produced. If the manager has a hard time being specific about what he or she wants—and you can produce several questions he or she can't answer—this should help the manager to understand that there are too many unknowns to make a responsible estimate.

- If all this maneuvering fails and the manager or customer continues to press you, it's time for the art of "ballparking." There can be three possible responses when using this technique: (1) Respond with the best guess you've got, while trying to factor in everything that could make it wrong. This response is appropriate for people who can be trusted not to use this figure against you later on. (2) Take your very best guess and double it. Then double it again. This is obviously not a rational way to make estimates, but then again, they are hardly being rational by asking you for an estimate in the elevator. (3) Refuse to give an estimate without further specifications and planning time.

Estimating without Complete Specifications

This is the type of mistake that a contractor might make if asked to estimate a construction project without a blueprint. In actuality, developers and contractors rarely make this mistake more than once. On the other hand, software developers and managers of information systems (IS) projects seem to make this mistake constantly. Someone has an idea, the idea gets approved with a budget and a deadline, and off they go! They don't seem concerned that the specifics of implementing the idea won't be known until they are halfway through the project. The allure of this mistake is that it seems as if team members are adopting good business practices; after all, they do have a budget and schedule attached to the new initiative. But without complete specifications, it isn't clear what the project will be producing, so there is no basis for an accurate estimate.

Confusing an Estimate with a Bid

Bids and estimates are not the same thing. An *estimate* is a projection of how much and how long a project will take, while a *bid* is the schedule and budget a subcontractor offers to deliver the project. The bid will quite likely be made up of estimates, but it will also include *profit margins* for the subcontractor. The important distinction is that a bid is calculated to be both attractive to the customer and profitable to the bidder, while an estimate is a prediction of what it will really take to deliver. The best bidders—the ones who make both themselves and their customers happy—are also good estimators.

Padding the Estimate

There are many legitimate reasons for adding time or money to an estimate. Contingency funds may be added for risks identified during the risk management process. Extra time is usually added to allow for inevitable delays like illness or vacations. But padding the estimate is different. Adding time and money to the estimate solely for the purpose of bringing the project in early and under budget is neither legitimate nor productive. The best strategy is to offer honest, detailed estimates. Then, if they get cut, you can use the actual performance data during the project to fight for acceptance of the original estimate. Eventually, this kind of straight dealing will gain you a reputation as an honest estimator who delivers on promises.

Table 8.1 shows how adding to the cost and schedule just to be safe is counterproductive in two ways. First, a valuable project may not get approved because the artificially high estimate makes it look like a bad investment. Second, if the project is approved with an inflated budget, this means it is taking money away from other potentially valuable projects.

KEY CONCEPT   Follow the Golden Rules

Just as there are classic estimating mistakes to avoid, there are certain golden rules that apply at all times to all projects. These rules emphasize the appropriate attitude toward estimating.

Have the Right People Make the Estimates

Three factors define who the right people are:

1. The estimators must be experienced with the work they are estimating. No matter which techniques are used, estimating is always based on an understanding of the work to be done.
2. The people who will actually perform the work should also be involved in estimating it. They will have the best grasp of their own limitations. They will know, for example, just how much time their

TABLE 8.1 ARTIFICIALLY INFLATING PROJECT ESTIMATES CAN HURT THE BOTTOM LINE

Project	Priority	Best Estimate	Inflated 20%	Revenue Year 1
Blue	1	300,000	360,000	1,000,000
Red	2	150,000	180,000	750,000
Orange	3	200,000	240,000	750,000
Green	4	200,000	240,000	600,000
Black	5	150,000	180,000	500,000
Total		1,000,000	1,200,000	

- The total budget for projects in a year is $1,000,000.
- Projects are prioritized by their return on investment over five years. The table contains the return in the first year.
- The best estimate is the project manager's most accurate estimate based on detailed specifications.
- Because every project manager inflated the best-cost estimate by 20% "just to be safe," the Black project was delayed a year.
- If all projects perform to their best estimate, 150,000 will not be invested, which reduces revenue the following year by $500,000.

schedule will allow them to work on this project; they will also know whether they will need a steep learning curve before they are productive. Most important, when people make an estimate for their own work, they are usually more motivated to achieve it than when the estimate comes from the outside.

3. The estimators must understand the goals and techniques of estimating. Even when people understand the task at hand, they should not be allowed to estimate their own work until they learn both *how* to estimate and the *goal* of estimating, which is producing accurate estimates that will come true, not optimistic projections of the best possible performance.

Base the Estimate on Experience

Even though no two projects are alike, there are often enough similarities that performance data from past projects are useful in estimating future ones. Professional estimators constantly use new performance data to refine their estimating models. Building this type of database is beyond the scope of the individual project manager; the organization must take responsibility for it. With this kind of database, project estimates can become more and more accurate. Without it, every project team must start from scratch and rely solely on each member's memories and gut feelings. Past performance data will make every estimating technique in this chapter more accurate.

Don't Negotiate the Estimate—Negotiate the Equilibrium

There are effective ways of countering attempts to meddle with an estimate. Consider the following scenario.

A project estimate has been developed by experienced estimators using past performance data from similar projects and employing sound estimating techniques. The project manager brings the estimate to management or customers and they begin to whittle away at the schedule and budget. (Or perhaps they may even take out a cleaver and whack away a big part of both.) At first the project manager stands her ground, but under continuing pressure, begins to give up cost and schedule, slowly letting the finish date move earlier and the budget get smaller.

Stop! This estimate was built from the product specifications, and it represents a realistic balance of cost, schedule, and quality. Dickering over cost or schedule alone throws the entire estimate out of equilibrium. While no estimate will go unchallenged, the proper defense is to demonstrate how the estimate is tied to the product specification and work breakdown structure. When estimates are developed correctly, they can be reduced only by changing the product or the productivity of the workers.

Three Levels of Accuracy

Everyone wants accurate estimates, but accuracy costs money. It makes sense, therefore, to use different estimating techniques for the different decision points in a project. For example, initial evaluation of a project idea shouldn't take as much time and effort (or money) as the detailed planning necessary for formal project approval. Let's look at three levels of accuracy at different stages in a project.

Idea Evaluation or "Ballpark Estimate"

This is the estimate we all try to avoid giving. Ballpark estimates can be off by as much as 90 percent, yet they are still useful for initial sizing. Ballparks take almost no time—they are the result of a gut feeling from an expert. Their accuracy relies on the estimator's knowledge. *The only function of a ballpark estimate should be to evaluate whether it would be useful to get a more accurate estimate.*

Project Selection or Order of Magnitude

Also known as ROM for "rough order of magnitude," this estimate also has a wide variance, but is based on extrapolations from other projects instead of the gut feelings of the ballpark estimates.[1] The main difference between a ballpark estimate and an order-of-magnitude estimate is represented by a few hours of effort comparing the proposed project to past projects. For example, a builder may find that a proposed building is about twice the size of a similar one he has built and will therefore estimate the new one at twice the cost. If he decides that the proposed site for the new building will be more challenging, he might add another 10 to 20 percent. If an order-of-magnitude estimate is acceptable, several actions may result: A project may be formally initiated, a project manager identified, account codes set up, and the work begun on defining and planning the project. This planning is where the real work of creating an accurate estimate will take place.

Detailed Estimates

Detailed estimates are sometimes referred to as *bottom-up estimates,* because they are based on all the various steps involved in project planning. A detailed estimate includes all the schedule and resource information (as discussed in Chapter 7) and a forecast of a project budget and cash flow (described later in this chapter). This is the estimate that will be used to manage the project and evaluate its success.

There is a huge difference in accuracy between an order-of-magnitude estimate and a detailed estimate, because the latter assumes a detailed understanding of the product and is based on the availability of key resources. Enormous amounts of work specifying product requirements and design work take place between the order-of-magnitude estimate, when there are no specifications, and the detailed estimate, which is based on specifications. This work required large expenditures of time and money, but this money was not spent until the inexpensive ballpark and the order-of-magnitude estimates had determined that the project was feasible.

ESTIMATING TECHNIQUES

Good project managers realize that it takes time and effort to produce accurate estimates, so they choose among a variety of estimating methods to get the accuracy they need. There is no shortage of information in this field. A number of books have been written on estimating alone. Computer-based estimating models with proprietary algorithms cost thousands of dollars. There are entire seminars taught on estimating software projects, construction projects, and pharmaceutical development projects. This book cannot make an exhaustive presentation of all these estimating methods; instead, our purpose is to help you understand the dynamics of accurate estimating by presenting a variety of established estimating techniques—the basic building blocks used by all skilled estimators.

Phased Estimating

Phased estimating is a favorite among project managers because it requires cost and schedule commitments for only one phase of the project at a time. The phased estimating approach recognizes that it is impractical to demand a complete estimate at the beginning of the product life cycle. Instead, it breaks down the full product life cycle into phases, each of which is considered a project (see Figure 8.1). If you recall from Chapter 2, the product development life cycle describes the work required to create a new product, while the project life cycle focuses on managing the work. There can be a number of projects involved in the development of a new product.

The term most commonly applied to blending project life cycles and product development life cycles is *phase gate development,* which specifically calls out both the product development and project management deliverables and decision points in each development phase (see Figure 2.5). The term *phase gate* refers to decision points for evaluating whether the development should continue. Each phase gate

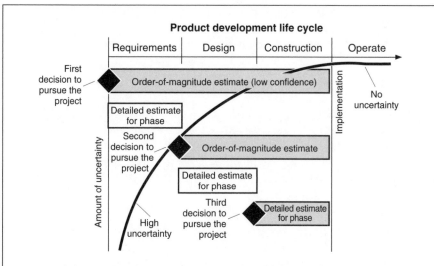

- At each decision point make two estimates: A cost and schedule commitment for the next phase, and an order-of-magnitude estimate for the remainder of the project.
- This example shows three decision points, but a product development life cycle could use 2 or 10 decision points—however many make sense to reduce the risk of overcommitting based on too little information.
- The amount of uncertainty is high at the beginning of the development life cycle—too high to make accurate estimates.

FIGURE 8.1 *Phased estimating.*

is clearly defined so the project team knows what they need to produce to reach the gate and what criteria will be used for getting approval to move to the next development phase.

There is an enormous amount of uncertainty at the beginning of every development life cycle, but this uncertainty is reduced as the project progresses and more information is gathered. This presents a dilemma, because the customer, more than any other stakeholder, wants an accurate time and cost estimate for the complete development life cycle. This demand is easy to understand because the customer is trying to make an investment decision. The problem is that there is so much uncertainty when the product development effort is first considered that an accurate cost and schedule projection is impossible to produce.

The phased estimating approach recognizes this impossibility and instead breaks down the full product life cycle into phases, each of which is considered a project. Here is what this process looks like:

- The first phase is initiated with an order-of-magnitude estimate for the full development life cycle combined with a detailed estimate for the first phase. This detailed estimate is considered a commitment by the project team; this commitment signals an end to the uncertainty that surrounds a new project. By agreeing to a detailed plan with a fixed completion date, the team becomes more focused and productive.

- At the end of the first phase, a new authorization for the second phase starts this cycle once more. A new order-of-magnitude estimate is developed for the remainder of the product life cycle together with a detailed estimate for the second phase. The new order-of-magnitude estimate will be much more accurate than the previous one because so much has been learned from the first development phase. This cycle of phase authorization will be repeated at each phase gate, and each time the order-of-magnitude estimate will become more accurate.

The reason project managers and teams like phased estimating should be clear by now: It is because they are required to make cost and schedule commitments for just one phase at a time; they have to look only as far as what can be called a "realistic planning horizon." The people who are funding the effort, however, don't always understand this benefit. To them it appears that the project team is not accountable to any overall budget, but simply keeps coming back for more money at every phase of the project.

What this customer group needs to realize, however, is that phased estimating is a risk-reduction technique that also works in their favor. If the project team is required to commit to a cost and schedule estimate for the full product development life cycle before it has enough information about the product, this will place everyone at risk. This is because the team is likely to come up with an inaccurate estimate at this early phase.

Customers often believe that getting a firm commitment from the project team is their safeguard against runaway budgets, but, in this case, they are mistaken. Without a realistic budget, unforeseen costs are likely to crop up as the project progresses—and the customer will be the one to pay for them. This will be true even if the project team is an external firm with a fixed-price contract. If these overruns become too extreme, this team may simply leave, preferring damage to its reputation to bankruptcy. At this point, the customer will have lost money, and the project will still be incomplete. Without the accurate estimate, both sides will lose.

On the other hand, if the customer and project team work for the same organization—as many product development projects do—then it is obvious who will pay for cost overruns: the company that both work for. If the original estimate was too low, no amount of pressure from above will get the project team to meet it. Again, both sides lose.

Customers will embrace phased estimating when they understand that every new phase gives them an opportunity to completely reevaluate the effort, or even cancel it if it looks too expensive. If they like the product but don't like the project team, then this is the obvious time to choose another. While it's true that canceling will mean that they have no end product to show for their money, at least they will have canceled an unrealistic project before it cost them even more.

Phased estimating is always used on construction projects. If you planned to build a house, no contractor would commit to a bid until you knew the location and had a blueprint. After the design was complete, you might find that the cost of the house was too high and decide not to pursue the project. This realization didn't come without cost, because you had to spend time and effort to find the location and pay for the design of the house. But it was smart to do your homework before you started digging a hole for a house you couldn't afford!

Now consider this true example: A software company decided to relocate its offices. Company officials spent a year determining whether to build or move to an existing building. After deciding to build, they announced the location and said the move would take place in "12 to 18 months." Once the building design was complete, they set schedules for the actual construction and for moving.

But at the same time they were using this phased estimating model for their new building, they continued to set hard delivery dates for software products that were barely more than ideas (this is common practice in the software industry). Although it was obvious to them that phased estimating applied to their office building project, they never considered applying it to their software projects.

Successful project managers treat every phase of the development life cycle as a project. They use the phased estimate approach to formally review the cost-schedule-quality equilibrium several times during the product development life cycle. The great advantage to this method is that it allows the project to be directed by many small, informed decisions rather than one large, premature decision.

KEY CONCEPT — Apportioning

Also known as *top-down estimating,* apportioning begins with a total project estimate, then assigns a percentage of that total to each of the phases and tasks of the project. The work breakdown structure provides the framework for top-down estimating (as shown in Figure 8.2). Making useful top-down estimates relies on some big assumptions, among them:

- Since apportioning is based on a formula derived from historical data of other, similar projects, the historic projects must be very similar to the project at hand for the formula to be accurate.

- Since apportioning divides a total project estimate into smaller pieces, it will be accurate only if the overall estimate is accurate.

Although apportioning is rarely as accurate as a bottom-up estimate, it is an appropriate technique for selecting which projects to pursue. Despite its wide accuracy variance, it allows a project selection

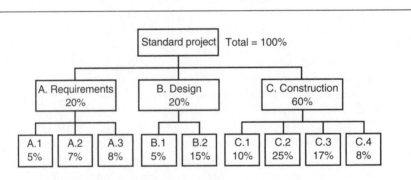

- Some types of projects break into consistent proportions.
- Firms that have developed standard work breakdown structure templates use past projects to create the apportioning formula.
- With a good high-level estimate, the formula shows how big each of the project phases and tasks should be.
- For example, if the total budget estimate is $40,000, that leaves $8,000 for requirements, $8,000 for design, and $24,000 for construction.

FIGURE 8.2 *Work breakdown structure as a basis for apportioning.*

committee to approximate the length of project phases; this information then helps the committee decide which projects can be initiated and executed during a given budget period (see Table 8.2).

Apportioning is a valuable technique when used in conjunction with phased estimating. During phase reviews, the formula for apportioning can use the figures from the actual cost/effort of completed phases to increase the accuracy of the order-of-magnitude estimate (see Figure 8.3). For instance, if the original top-down estimate dictated a phase-one cost of $75,000, and the actual phase-one cost was $60,000, this means that the overall project estimate should be reduced by 20 percent. Again, notice the need for an accurate apportioning formula.

KEY CONCEPT Parametric Estimates

As the name implies, the parametric technique seeks a basic unit of work to act as a multiplier to size the entire project. The golden rules of estimating really apply with this technique: It is always based on historical data, and the estimator must develop a solid parametric formula. To see how parametric estimating works, consider the following examples:

- A cycling group in Dallas, Texas, was planning a cross-country bicycle trip, starting in Seattle, Washington, and ending in Miami, Florida. Based on their experience riding together every Saturday for two months, they figured they could average 80 miles per day comfortably. A road atlas put the total trip distance at 3,334 miles. Dividing 3,334 by 80, they estimated the total trip would last 42 days. At this point, the only parameter was this normal daily rate of 80 miles. But when one of the riders pointed out that all their practice rides had been on relatively flat terrain in dry weather, they made changes to their model. They reduced their average daily mileage to 30 for the mountainous parts of their route (the route had about 200 miles of mountain crossing), and they added 10 percent for weather delays. This changed the formula from one to three parameters: normal daily rate, mountain rate, and weather factor. The new parametric formula looked like this:

Trip duration

$$= \left(\frac{\text{total miles} - \text{mountain miles}}{\text{normal daily rate}} + \frac{\text{mountain miles}}{\text{mountain rate}} \right) \times \text{weather factor}$$

$$\text{Trip duration} = \left(\frac{3{,}334 - 200}{80} + \frac{200}{30} \right) \times 1.10$$

$$\text{Trip duration} = 50 \text{ days}$$

TABLE 8.2 APPORTIONING SUPPORTS ANNUAL BUDGET DEVELOPMENT

Project	Total Schedule	Total Cost	Description	Requirements	Design	Construction	Total Cost Year 1
A	2 years	$500,000	% schedule completion in 1 year	100%	66%	0%	
			Phase budget	$100K	$100K	$300K	
			Amount of phase budget spent in 1 year	$100K	$66K	$0	$166K
B	2 years	$300,000	% schedule completion in 1 year	100%	66%	0%	
			Phase budget	$60K	$60K	$180K	
			Amount of phase budget spent in 1 year	$60K	$39.6K	$0	$99.6K
C	4 years	$400,000	% schedule completion in 1 year	83%	0%	0%	
			Phase budget	$80K	$80K	$240K	
			Amount of phase budget spent in 1 year	$66.4K	$0	$0	$66.4K
D	6 months	$100,000	% schedule completion in 1 year	100%	100%	100%	
			Phase budget	$20K	$20K	$60K	
			Amount of phase budget spent in 1 year	$20K	$20K	$60K	$100K
E	1 year	$300,000	% schedule completion in 1 year	100%	100%	100%	
			Phase budget	$60K	$60K	$180K	
			Amount of phase budget spent in 1 year	$60K	$60K	$180K	$300K
				Total project budget required for fiscal year			$732K

A company has five projects that will begin in its next fiscal year. Based on past experience, it has developed apportioning ratios for its standard projects.

- The requirements phase uses 20% of the total budget and 30% of the total schedule.
- The design phase uses 20% of the total budget and 30% of the total schedule.
- The construction phase uses 60% of the total budget and 40% of the total schedule.

Based on order-of-magnitude cost and schedule estimates and the apportioning formula, the company was able to estimate the total project budget required for the next fiscal year.

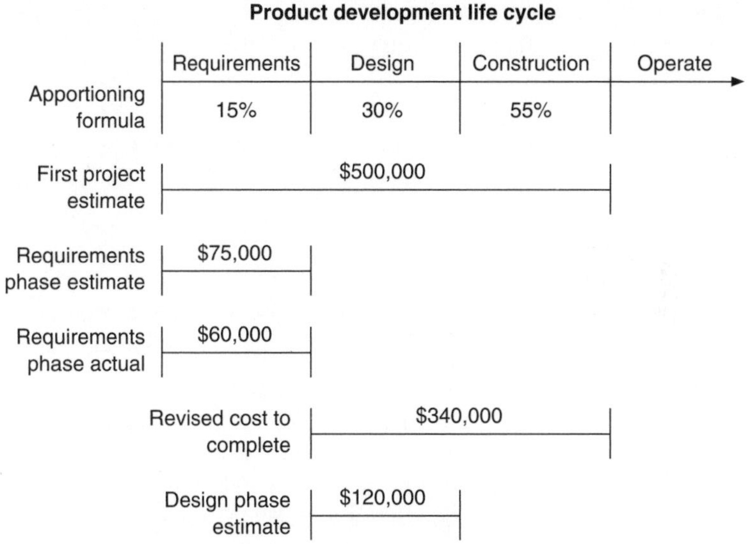

Product development life cycle

	Requirements	Design	Construction	Operate
Apportioning formula	15%	30%	55%	
First project estimate	$500,000			
Requirements phase estimate	$75,000			
Requirements phase actual	$60,000			
Revised cost to complete		$340,000		
Design phase estimate		$120,000		

Prior to initiating the first phase, the total development estimate was $500,000. The actual cost to complete the first phase was lower than estimated. To develop the second-phase estimate, the apportioning formula was used with the first phase actuals to reestimate the remaining budget for the project.

$$\text{Revised total budget} = \frac{\text{actual cost of first phase}}{\text{apportioning ratio of first phase}}$$

$$\text{Example: } \$400,000 = \frac{\$60,000}{.15}$$

Remaining cost to complete = revised total budget − first-phase actual cost

Example: $340,000 = $400,000 − $60,000

Design phase estimate = revised total budget × apportioning ratio

Example: $120,000 = $400,000 × .3

Clearly, this entire example requires a proven apportioning formula.

FIGURE 8.3 *Apportioning works with phased estimating.*

- A manufacturing company needs to have its 340-page user manual translated into several languages. Based on past translation projects, they have created a parametric estimating model. The basic unit of work is a page. On average, 15 pages per day can be translated into the target languages. This parameter assumes two people working together on every target language. If the number of people is increased or decreased, the parameter changes. But if they add a new language and therefore new members to the team, the parameter of 15 pages a day is probably too optimistic for the first document.

$$\text{Translation project duration (per language)} = 23 \text{ days} = \frac{340}{15}$$

- To estimate the carpet allowance on a house remodel, the project manager figured a cost of $5 per yard for purchasing the carpet and $4 per yard to install it, or $9 total cost. Then he measured the length and width of all the rooms, calculated the area in square yards, and multiplied by $9. Construction projects are full of parametric estimates of this kind.

- On a defense program to build a new jet fighter, the total number of engineering drawings required was estimated from a conceptual model of the proposed aircraft. Thousands of drawings would be created from this model, and, based on past experience, they estimated that the average drawing would take 200 engineering hours. With the drawing as the basic unit of work, this simple parametric model allowed them to estimate the total engineering effort. By dividing the total number of hours by the number of engineers they assigned to the project, they set the high-level schedule. Obviously, this was not sufficient detail for managing all the work, but because their parametric model allowed them to accurately estimate both the number of drawings and the average time per drawing, at least the engineering phase was accurately sized.

Certain lessons can be distilled from these three examples:

1. While it's possible to use parametric models to create either project-level or task-level estimates, the estimates will be more accurate at the lower level. Nevertheless, high-level parametric estimates make excellent order-of-magnitude estimates and are accurate enough for the process of project selection.

2. When building detailed estimates, greater accuracy is achieved by first estimating the low-level tasks (work packages) using parametric models, then combining all these work package estimates to build the project or phase estimate. It is useful to employ parametric modeling at all decision points (phase gates) in the phased estimating approach, both to create the high-level estimate and to ensure the next phase commitment.

3. The variables in the parametric formula almost always require detailed product specifications. The more accurate the specifications, the more accurate the model. For example, the translation

project required a completed user guide in the original language. Construction projects require blueprints. Both of these examples make one important point: Parametric estimating is usually applied to the *construction phase* of a product life cycle.

Bottom-up Estimating

Bottom-up estimating requires the most effort, but it is also the most accurate. As the name implies, all the detailed tasks are estimated and then combined, or "rolled up" (see Figure 8.4). Bottom-up estimating is another name for the planning model presented in Chapters 6 and 7 (see Figure 6.1). The final component of that model, building a project budget and cash flow, is described at the end of this chapter.

Within the planning model, step three calls for estimating work packages. (Recall that work packages are the lowest-level tasks on the project.) The accuracy of the entire model is dependent on the accuracy of these work package estimates. (Recall from Chapter 6 the rules for work package size and from Chapter 7 the many variables that affect work package estimates.)

If bottom-up estimating is so accurate, why isn't it always used? It would seem the accuracy justifies the additional time to build the schedule. The answer is that at the very beginning of a product devel-

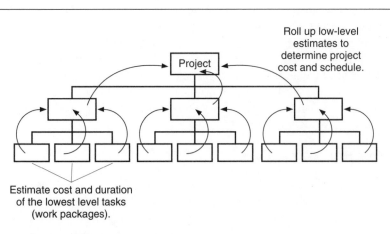

- The work breakdown structure provides the framework for a bottom-up estimate.
- The planning model in Figure 6.1 is a complete description of a bottom-up estimating technique.

FIGURE 8.4 *Bottom-up estimating.*

opment life cycle, there just isn't enough information to develop a detailed bottom-up estimate for the entire life cycle. So bottom-up estimating works only to build the detailed phase estimates.

K E Y CONCEPT   **BUILDING THE DETAILED BUDGET ESTIMATE**

Project budget estimates can be ballparked, calculated with parametric formulas, and determined through apportioning. While these high-level estimates are useful in the process of selecting projects, they are not accurate enough for managing a project. Once the project is approved, there is a need for a detailed, accurate cost estimate.

The detailed cost estimate becomes the standard for keeping costs in line. Everyone—customer, management, project manager, and team—is better served when a cost target is realistically calculated from a detailed plan. The team understands how the goal was created and customers and management can be more confident that the project will stay within budget. Forecasting cash flow enables the project's funding to be planned and available when needed. And finally, during the course of the project, this detailed cost information will help in controlling the project, monitoring the progress, identifying problems, and finding solutions.

Sources of Data for the Detailed Budget

The actual calculation of a budget is pretty straightforward; it simply involves adding up figures. Just about any spreadsheet program is a good tool for the total budget calculation. What isn't easy is creating the numbers that go into the overall calculation. The following categories are the basis for the budget calculation. (Keep in mind that these are high-level categories. Depending on the size and nature of any project, some categories may be eliminated or may need to be broken down to be more specific.)

Internal Labor Cost
Internal labor costs represent the effort of people employed by the firm. The planning model discussed in Chapters 6 and 7 forms the basis for estimating the total labor costs (see Figure 6.1).

The detailed source for all labor estimates comes from estimating the individual tasks. Including the sequence constraints and leveling the resources presents a realistic view of how many people are required. The resource projection represents the total effort. All that remains is to multiply each resource by its hourly (or daily, weekly, monthly) rate to derive the total internal labor cost for the project. Figure 8.5 shows the total resource projection derived from the detailed schedule, the labor rates, and the total project labor cost.

Use the Burdened Labor Rate

The actual hourly pay of salaried employees varies from person to person, often for no discernible reason. But it is rare to have to worry about actual pay when estimating labor costs. Instead, look to the finance department to establish a standard burdened labor rate for each labor type. A *burdened rate* is the average cost of an employee to the firm. It includes wages, benefits, and overhead. Overhead represents the many fixed costs that are spread over all projects, such as functional management, workplace facilities and equipment, and nonproject costs like training. It's not necessary for a project manager to figure out this rate; nearly every company has an established burdened labor rate on record.

Don't Leave Out the Cost of Staffing the Project

A big mistake—which, unfortunately, is made on a routine basis—is leaving out the cost of internal staff in the project budget. The usual justification for this folly is that "these workers are free to the project because their salary is a constant." But this statement would be true only if salaried employees had infinite hours available to work on projects. Including internal labor cost in a project budget is necessary to build the kind of realistic budget that will allow management to choose among multiple project opportunities.

Internal Equipment Cost

Internal equipment costs apply to special equipment that is not routinely available. They do not apply to the kind of equipment that is standard or assumed for all workers. Technical writers, for example, are assumed to have computers with word processing software; street repair crews are assumed to have shovels. But if that street repair crew needs a backhoe, the cost for this special equipment needs to be estimated separately. This separate estimate allows the purchase and maintenance costs of the internal equipment to be passed on to the customer.

These internal equipment costs can be estimated using the same steps used in estimating internal labor costs. Figure 8.6 shows equipment use on the resource plan.

Estimating Equipment That Will Be Used Up

If equipment will be purchased and used up on a single project, then all you will need to do is add up the pieces of equipment and the cost

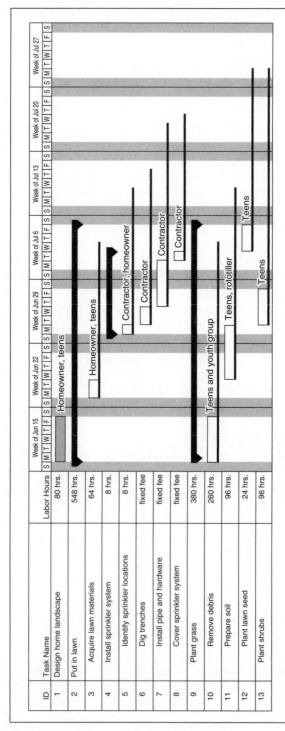

ID	Task Name	Labor Hours
1	Design home landscape	80 hrs.
2	Put in lawn	548 hrs.
3	Acquire lawn materials	64 hrs.
4	Install sprinkler system	8 hrs.
5	Identify sprinkler locations	8 hrs.
6	Dig trenches	fixed fee
7	Install pipe and hardware	fixed fee
8	Cover sprinkler system	fixed fee
9	Plant grass	380 hrs.
10	Remove debris	260 hrs.
11	Prepare soil	96 hrs.
12	Plant lawn seed	24 hrs.
13	Plant shrubs	96 hrs.

FIGURE 8.5 *Calculated labor and equipment costs using the project plan with resource spreadsheet.*

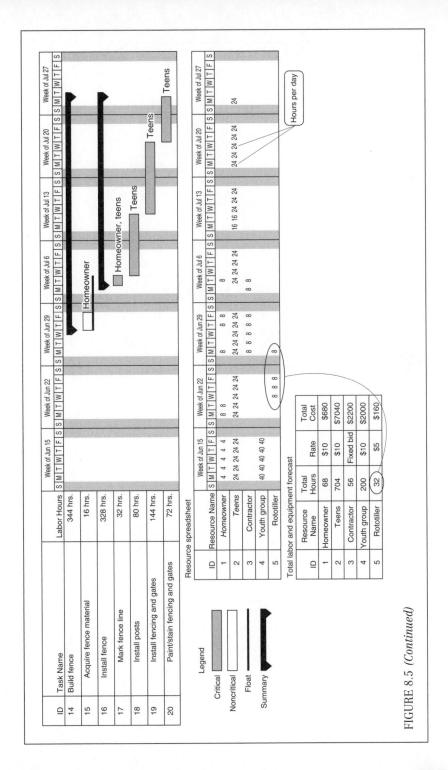

FIGURE 8.5 *(Continued)*

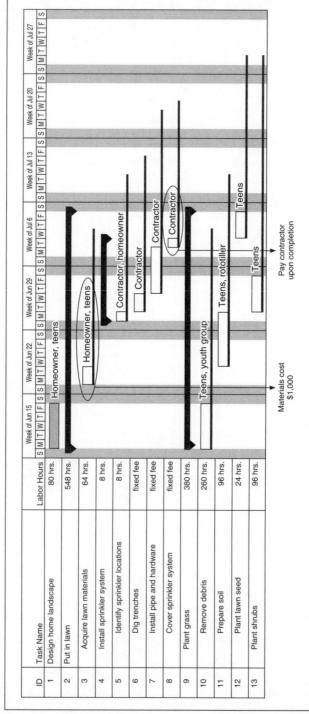

FIGURE 8.6 *Calculate a cash flow schedule using the project plan with resource spreadsheet.*

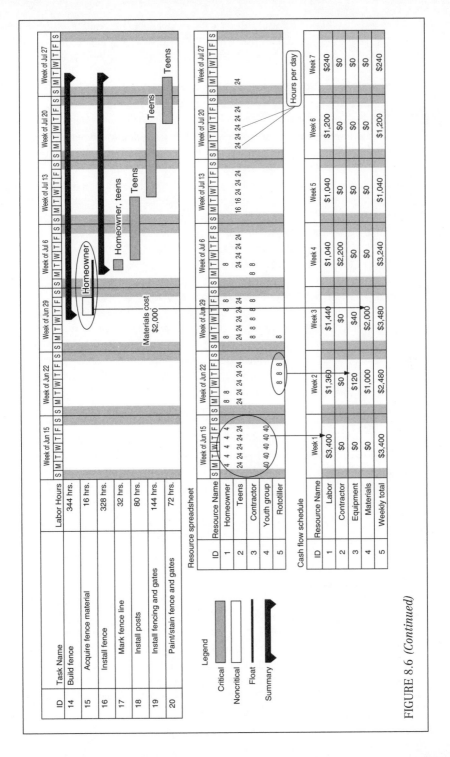

FIGURE 8.6 (Continued)

of each (a parametric estimate). For example, a boring machine used to dig utility tunnels uses up drill bits at the rate of 1 every 50 feet. So a 1,300-foot tunnel will require 26 drill bits (1,300 divided by 50).

Estimating Equipment Used on Multiple Projects

Use a unit cost approach to estimate equipment purchased for one project but expected to be used on many others. Here's an example.

R&D engineers for an aerospace company needed an expensive computer to run complex tests. At $50,000, the computer would double the project budget, and this extra cost would probably prevent the project from being approved. But since they could identify five other potential projects that would use the machine in the immediate future, they were able to justify the cost of the new computer by spreading its cost over the expected use for the next two years. The formula used to spread the cost across several projects gave them a unit cost (hourly rate) that they could apply to their project estimate.

External Labor and Equipment Costs

It's possible to use the same approach in estimating external labor and equipment costs as in estimating internal labor and equipment. The only differences will stem from the type of contract negotiated with the external contractor or vendor. Under a cost-plus contract, the labor and equipment rates are written into the contract, and the vendor bills the project for the amount of labor, equipment, and materials supplied to the project. In this case, either the project manager or the vendor can estimate the work and arrive at the total cost by using the same bottom-up method described for internal costs. In the case of a fixed bid, however, the vendor will estimate the total cost of labor and equipment for their part of the project and will be held to this figure (that's why it's called a *fixed bid*). In this latter case, the vendor has performed the necessary estimating; all that's needed is to add this estimate into the total labor and equipment costs. (See Chapter 5 for more on the difference between fixed bids and cost-plus contracts and their impact on estimating accuracy.)

Materials Costs

Materials are the "things" that go into a finished product. For some projects, materials represent half or more of the total costs, while for others, materials costs are inconsequential. A software development project, for example, may produce millions of lines of code, but no tangible materials are required. Materials can be raw, such as plywood, concrete, or welding rod, or materials can be subcomponents of your product, such as computer hardware, telephone switches, or air-conditioning units.

Until now, we've stressed the value of the work breakdown structure as the basis for identifying all costs. When it comes to materials costs, however, the WBS is relegated to second place. The first place to look is the product specification. For example, the blueprint for a building is the basis for calculating how much concrete, plywood, plumbing, or flooring to purchase. It shows the number of sinks, doors, windows, and elevators to order. Similarly, the network design will determine the number of workstations, routers, hosts, and telephone switches required for a computer network.

The work breakdown structure can be used to ensure that every task that requires materials will have them. This is done by planning order and delivery tasks. Include the payment dates as tasks, and you'll have all the information you need to build a cash flow schedule for the project.

KEY CONCEPT — GENERATING THE CASH FLOW SCHEDULE

Knowing *when* money will be spent is almost as important as knowing *how much* will be spent. Companies that depend on operations to generate the cash to fund projects need to control the rate at which money goes into the project. Let's look at a couple of operations that depend on cash flow schedules:

- A small housing developer plans to build five houses, sell them, and build five more. By keeping his rate of production constant, he intends to keep all of his employees busy at a steady rate. By staggering the starting dates of all the houses, he can move crews from one house to the next and, he hopes, sell house number one before it's time to start house number six. Timing is everything in his plan. If there are too many people on a framing crew, the job will get done too fast and the next house may not have the foundation ready for the crew. If the completed houses don't sell within his planned time frame, he won't be able to fund new houses and will have to lay off workers.

- A municipal engineering department spreads all street maintenance projects across its fiscal year in order to keep its use of people and equipment steady. Large engineering projects that span fiscal years are also carefully timed. The department heads make sure that they spend only the amount of budget allotted per year, but they need to stretch out this budget to the very end of the year so a project doesn't have to stop and wait for the new fiscal year to begin.

Once the project's schedule and costs have been estimated, generating a cash flow projection is pretty simple. Figure 8.6 shows the information from the project schedule that determines the cash flow. It's easy to see how project management software can readily calculate cash flow from all the other data that's been entered.

END POINT

Estimating will never be a science that produces 100 percent accurate results. Complete accuracy requires the project manager to forecast the future and to be in control of all project variables—two requirements that will never be met. But estimates can be sufficiently accurate to support good business decisions. In all the estimating techniques presented in this chapter there are consistent lessons:

- It takes time and costs money to develop accurate estimates.
- Every technique gives better results when it is used consistently. The lessons of the past improve the forecasts of the future.
- Comparing actual performance to estimates is essential to refining the estimating model. Without this comparison there is no science in the process, only gut feelings.
- Many of the techniques work together. The art of estimating is knowing when to use which technique and knowing how much accuracy is required for the business decision at hand.
- The variables that make estimates wrong are often beyond the control of the project team. Variables such as changing specifications, failed technology, bad weather, and team turnover can't be accurately predicted, and yet they result in a variance from the plan.
- It's apparent that project managers working independently never create accurate, useful estimation processes. It takes a conscious effort by the firm to establish estimating practices and make sure they are used on every project and updated over time to increase accuracy.

Perhaps the most important lesson we can learn about estimating is that all the stakeholders are responsible for accurate estimates. Customers, sponsors, and management, for example, have more control than the project team over factors such as the stability of the specifications, the availability of personnel, and the deadline pressures. A cooperative approach between these stakeholders will yield positive results. When estimating becomes an adversarial game between the project team and the customer, there will always be a loser. On the other hand, if all stakeholders understand the dynamics of estimating and work honestly to reduce the uncertainty of the project, everyone will win.

FAST FOUNDATION IN PROJECT MANAGEMENT

A thorough project plan is the foundation of a strong project. Use the planning checklist on pages 201–202 to guide your team and yourself to ensure you've covered all the bases.

The planning checklist is available for download at www .versatilecompany.com/forms. As you and your colleagues use this checklist you'll find new items to add, customizing it to better fit your projects.

Stellar Performer: Tynet, Inc.
Tynet, Inc., Uses Project Management to Increase Customer Satisfaction

Installing computer networks is a high-risk, competitive business. Thousands of companies, large and small, offer the services to tie together local area networks, telephone equipment, and Internet service providers. Profit margins are thin, especially for reselling computer hardware and network software. Bids for the service required to put the networks together need to be accurate, because any underestimated labor quickly eats up profits for the job. Tynet, Inc., which has been installing networks since 1989, identifies project management as its competitive edge.

Brian LaMure is the director of network services for Tynet and a certified project management professional. He credits dramatic increases in revenue and profitability to Tynet's emphasis on project management. "We began using the project life cycle as the basis for our entire network services business, from initial sales through implementation and follow-up. Before that time, nearly 80 percent of our projects were late and/or over budget, meaning we lost money. By focusing on some of the basics, we've reduced failed projects to almost zero." In Tynet's case, the basics include using a phased estimating model, parametric estimating, more customer involvement in managing the project, and more detailed project planning.

PHASED ESTIMATING

One of the reasons Tynet had so many late or overbudget projects in the past was the way it bid them. A Tynet sales representative would visit a prospective client to understand the problem and develop a proposal. Since there were often technical issues that the sales representative didn't understand completely, it was easy for the representative to underestimate a project. "Now we use a phased estimating model based on a standard project life cycle," explains LaMure. "The previous model was a no-win scenario for the sales reps, because they couldn't be expected to understand all the components of a job, but they were under pressure to get the business."

Tynet's phased estimating model follows six phases. (See Figure 8.7.)

1. *Business analysis.* This is where a sales representative spends time most productively. The sales reps qualify clients to make sure the client and Tynet are a good fit, and if they aren't, they'll refer the client to someone else. If it looks like Tynet could help the customer solve a problem, the sales representative sets a time for a design engineer to evaluate the project.

2. *Concept.* Together, the design engineer and sales representative spend between 4 and 12 hours learning the client's business objectives for the network and developing a detailed estimate. This is work the client doesn't pay for, but it builds their confidence that Tynet will be able to deliver the right solution. The bid for time and materials will vary up to 25 percent

(Continued)

(Continued)

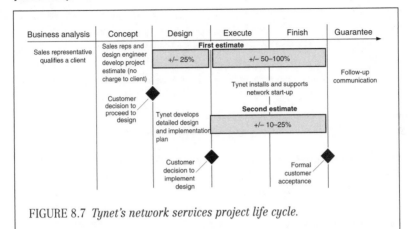

FIGURE 8.7 *Tynet's network services project life cycle.*

for the design phase and up to 50 to 100 percent for the actual implementation of the entire project. If the customer accepts the bid, the design phase begins.

3. *Design.* During design, the design engineer works with a project manager and, if necessary, a lead engineer to develop a complete network design and detailed project plan for the remainder of the project. They also reestimate the project based on this additional information and submit a new bid to complete the project. This bid is accurate within 10 to 25 percent. If the customer accepts the bid, the hardware and software is ordered and the service is scheduled. If the client company doesn't like the bid or the design work, it pays Tynet for the design phase and the contract is over. If the bid is more than the customer wants to pay, even though they realize it is realistic, the detailed project plan can be used as a tool for finding work the client can do in-house, thus decreasing the hours Tynet puts into the project.

4. *Execute.* The system solution is installed. The project manager uses the detailed plan to make sure everything stays on track.

5. *Finish.* The project manager and the original design engineer meet with the client to make sure the system is operating effectively. All of Tynet's work is unconditionally guaranteed, so they want to make sure the client is completely satisfied.

6. *Guarantee.* Sales representatives continue to stay in touch with clients after the project is over so that any problems can be quickly resolved. The reps also help clients recognize new opportunities for improving their business based on their new network capabilities. These activities are Tynet's way of supporting a customer to grow both their business and their network capacity over the long term.

(Continued)

(Continued)

The increased time and expertise Tynet spends on developing proposals still sometimes result in estimates that are off by as much as 100 percent; it is easy to see, therefore, why the previous bidding process often produced proposals that were impossible to deliver. By offering bids at both the concept and design phases, both Tynet and its clients reduce their risks. Tynet is less likely to dramatically underestimate a job, and the client has two opportunities to evaluate the bid.

PARAMETRIC ESTIMATING

When the project manager and design engineer build their detailed estimates in the design phase, they use a parametric model that has been refined over many projects. Each component of the system, whether it's installing hardware, software, or delivering training to the client, is estimated separately. Since a network project is typically composed of a unique set of known components, LaMure and his team have created a list of all the components they've used on past projects and an estimate for each. By continually comparing their project performance to the parametric estimating tables, they refine the estimates, making future project bids more accurate.

DETAILED PROJECT PLANS

The detailed parametric estimating model lends itself to detailed planning and control. Every task has a person and a schedule assigned, so accountability is clear and tracking more effective. LaMure estimates that overall delivery time has decreased by 50 percent through more effective execution, which is a result of better plans. Another cost benefit to the client is that breaking the tasks down into smaller increments makes it easier to put the person with the right skill on each job. That means a senior technician isn't working on jobs that a more junior team member could accomplish at a lower billing rate.

CUSTOMERS INVOLVED IN PROJECT MANAGEMENT

Before instituting the phased life cycle model, Tynet bid work on a fixed-price basis; this meant that if Tynet was wrong, it paid the price. By giving the customers two opportunities to accept its bid, and by using detailed project plans and parametric estimates, Tynet has increased the customer's involvement in managing the project. This has enabled Tynet to change its bids to a time-and-materials basis, reducing its risk. "With more detailed information, the customer gains more control of the project and has better cost-schedule-quality results," explains LaMure. "They can see that they're better off than forcing us to add contingency factors into a fixed-price bid."

(Continued)

(Continued)

Not only are the customers getting more for less these days, but Tynet's vertical partners are happier as well. Vertical partners are the other vendors that are often involved in networking projects. For instance, if an accounting software vendor needs network upgrades to install its product at a client site, they would rather recommend a company that can be relied on to deliver on time and on budget. Increased referrals are one of the reasons the network services division has tripled its revenues within two years of implementing these project management fundamentals.

Tynet is proof that project management isn't just a discipline that improves efficiency. The company has used it to restructure their entire network delivery process, and the results speak for themselves.

Source: Interview with Brian LaMure, June 1998.

Stellar Performer: Adobe Systems
Developing a Calibrated Model for Estimating Project Time

John Gaffney

Today, Adobe Systems is known for sophisticated desktop software products such as Adobe Photoshop, but in fact the company got its start in 1982 by developing PostScript, the first device-independent page description language. I joined Adobe as a software developer in 1984 when Adobe was developing the Apple LaserWriter, the first PostScript printer.

After Apple introduced the LaserWriter in 1985, many new customers signed up with Adobe to license PostScript software for their products. Adobe grew quickly; by 1990 it had developed many PostScript printers, but had an admittedly marginal track record in accurately estimating its project times. In an attempt to improve that track record, I developed a simple estimating formula based on actual development time of completed projects. The formula predicted total projected time, given the printer complexity and the assumption that only one software developer would work on the project—which was the norm. The formula soon became known inside Adobe printer engineering as the "Gaffney Meter," a name invented by my colleagues. This model proved to be reasonably reliable, so I later modified it for estimating multiple-developer project time.

CREATING THE SINGLE-DEVELOPER MODEL

A half a dozen or so completed printer projects were analyzed for clues. It was no surprise that the more complex projects took longer, so it seemed appropriate to use a simple count of product features and custom development tasks to measure the project's complexity. This complexity count accounted for special printer features such as color printing, duplex (two-sided) printing, and Japanese fonts.

One completed project was a relatively simple printer whose development tasks were in common with all other projects; it had taken five months from the time the developer received the hardware until the printer was certified. This project was used as the baseline, or *zero-complexity*, project against which more complex projects were compared.

A simple plot of all the complexity counts against their project times showed an expected exponential growth in time as the number of complexities increased. The project time T as a function of its complexity count C behaved something like this:

$$T = 5 \text{ months} \times G^C$$

where G was some uncalibrated *time growth factor*. For a zero-complexity ($C = 0$) project, this model yielded the expected five-month development time for the "simple" printer. A couple of

(Continued)

(Continued)

trial-and-error calculations showed that $G = 1.2$ matched the plot of completed projects fairly well.

Single-Developer Time Estimation Model

Refer to Figure 8.8. The single-developer project time T (in months) for a project with a complexity count C is:

$$T = 5 \text{ months} \times 1.2^C$$

One way of looking at this model is that *every complexity added to a project increases the project time by 20 percent*. This compounding effect is not surprising. Adding another product feature to an already complex product takes longer to develop and contributes more uncertainty than adding it to a simpler product.

Some Nuances of the Model

Applying the model to a new project is more of an art than a science, especially in determining the project's complexity count. For example, some product features are more complex than others; the easy ones are sometimes counted as 0.5 and difficult ones as 1.5 or 2. In reality, the

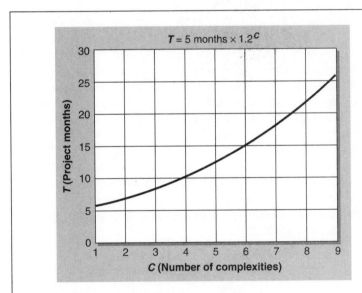

FIGURE 8.8 *Single-developer estimating model.*

(Continued)

(Continued)

average complexity weight is 1, especially for highly complex projects, so it does not matter too much how the complexities are weighted.

Some projects, such as maintenance releases or upgrades, reuse much of the code developed for earlier versions of the product, so a simplification that has a complexity value of -1 is sometimes used. Another simplification involves assigning an especially skilled developer to the project.

In spite of these subtleties, analyzing a project's complexities and calculating the estimated project time is a valuable tool for meeting customer expectations. If the model indicates that a project is going to be too late to hit a market window, negotiating with the customer to simplify the project sometimes enables the product to ship on time.

CREATING THE MULTIPLE-DEVELOPER MODEL

Eventually, more and more printer projects at Adobe became so complex that assigning only one software developer was not appropriate. The complexity/time relationship of the single-developer model appeared to be correct, so it seemed reasonable to analyze how the overall project complexity changes when multiple developers are assigned. Adding developers helps reduce the task-related complexity, simply because more developers share the task load; however, adding developers also adds a complexity of its own.

For example, Figure 8.9 shows the effect of adding developers to a complexity 9 project: For one developer, a complexity 9 project would take roughly two years, due mostly to the fact that the lone developer must work serially on the project tasks. Assigning a second developer significantly reduces the project time to about 13 months, thanks mostly to sharing the task load. In other words, the task-related complexity has been reduced by half while adding a comparatively small people-related complexity. Adding a third developer does not reduce the project time as much because there are fewer tasks to share. In addition, with three developers assigned, the people-related complexity becomes more significant. Notice from the graph that the project time increases if you add too many developers.

Using fewer developers than optimal may be cost-justified. Project managers need to evaluate this by comparing the estimated lost revenue from a later product introduction with the cost of additional developers, who could perhaps be assigned to other, higher-priority projects. In this example, maybe that third developer could be assigned to a different project where one more person would shorten the schedule much more.

MULTIPLE-DEVELOPER TIME ESTIMATION MODEL

The model for estimating the project time T (in months) for a project of complexity C with multiple developers D is:

(Continued)

(Continued)

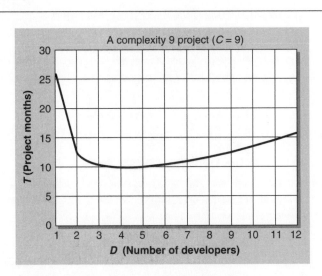

FIGURE 8.9 *Multiple-developer estimating model.*

$$T = 5 \text{ months} \times 1.2^{C/D + 0.5 \times (D-1)}$$

The C/D term says that the task-related complexities C are divided among the number of developers D, and the $0.5 \times (D-1)$ term adds one-half complexity for each additional developer. Note that this model becomes the single-developer model when $D = 1$.

HOW WELL DID THE MODEL REALLY WORK?

In general, the model had a good track record. Some critics said that it was too easy to adjust the complexities during the project to make the end date come out right, but the model was usually accurate to within a month or two for projects lasting about a year. One engineering manager quoted a 15 percent variance, but no one has done any rigorous model verification.

Some customers did not like the model because there was no way of expressing the notion that working harder would bring in the project completion date. They missed the point that the model was calibrated against projects whose developers worked very hard, often including nights and weekends. Such is the nature of printer development.

Today, the model is rarely used in Adobe printer engineering because most printer development takes place at customer sites with software kits delivered by Adobe.

(Continued)

(Continued)

MAKING YOUR OWN TIME ESTIMATION MODEL

The ability to devise your own model relies on these factors:

- You can define a "simple" project which has development tasks in common with all others.
- There are past project records to use for calibration, including the "simple" project described here.
- Your projects are similar to one another, yet vary in complexity.
- There are countable tasks or features that represent the complexity of the projects.

Step 1: Establish a Baseline Project

Find a completed simple project whose tasks or features are in common with all other projects. This project can have one or more developers. Use its project time to set T_0, the duration, and D_0, number of developers, of a zero-complexity project.

Step 2: Calibrate the Time Growth Factor

In your project records, find 6 to 10 other projects that have the same team size as the simple project but have more complexity and took longer.

For each of these projects, identify and count the complexities, such as product features or custom work. Make a plot of complexity count against project time and compute a value for G, the growth factor, which most accurately describes how your project times increase with increasing complexity.

Step 3: Calibrate the People Penalty Factor

If you can, find 6 to 10 projects that have the same moderate complexity but a different number of developers. Plot the number of developers against the project times for these same-complexity projects and compute a value for P, the people penalty, which will probably be somewhere in the range of 0.4 to 0.6.

Step 4: Validate Your New Model

Once you calibrate the model, you should validate it by applying it to new projects or other completed projects. If the model is not working, feel free to recalibrate it with different completed projects, or invent your own model from scratch.

John Gaffney is a Senior Engineering Director for Adobe Systems.

Downloadable Planning Checklist*

Project Manager

Risk Management
- ❑ The project team has invested time and energy into identifying all project risks.
- ❑ A risk response strategy has been developed for all risks that have a significant impact or probability.
- ❑ Contingency funds or time have been allocated by management.
- ❑ Funds to account for unexpected problems have been set aside as Management Reserve.
- ❑ A risk log has been developed to manage known risks and is accessible to all project team members.
- ❑ Every risk in the log has someone responsible for managing it.
- ❑ There is a plan in place for continuously identifying and responding to new risks.

Work Breakdown Structure
- ❑ Tasks have been identified to produce every deliverable in the statement of work.
- ❑ The work breakdown structure for the project is consistent with standard WBS guidelines and/or templates for similar projects.
- ❑ The project team participated in building the WBS or has reviewed and approved it.
- ❑ Every task on the WBS has a strong, descriptive name that includes a noun and a verb.
- ❑ Every task on the WBS has a beginning, an end, and clear completion criteria.
- ❑ Project management tasks are included on the WBS.
- ❑ Tasks have been broken down to a level that enables clear responsibility to be assigned.
- ❑ The WBS follows the rules for creating a top-down decomposition.
- ❑ The structure of the WBS has been evaluated to ensure the summary tasks are meaningful to stakeholders that require high-level understanding of the project.

Task Sequence
- All work packages have predecessor tasks identified and task relationships are illustrated using a network diagram.
- The team has reviewed all predecessor-successor relationships to ensure there are none missing and that none of the relationships are unnecessary.
- Only work packages have predecessor-successor relationships defined. These relationships are not defined for summary tasks.
- External schedule constraints are represented by milestones.

Estimating
- Wherever possible, historical data has been used as the basis for estimating.
- Ball park estimates have only been used for initial screening and are not the basis for setting any project baselines.
- Estimates have been prepared by people who understand how to perform the work and who understand the constraints of the people who will perform the work.
- Work package estimates include both the duration and the estimated labor.

Scheduling
- Critical path analysis has been performed to identify critical path tasks and schedule float.
- Resource leveling has been applied to ensure the schedule represents a realistic allocation of personnel and other resources.
- The schedule is based on realistic assumptions about the availability of project personnel.
- Portions of the schedule that contain many concurrent tasks have been evaluated for risk.
- The cost-schedule-quality equilibrium is realistic and acceptable to the customer.

Vendors and Subcontractors
- Vendors and subcontractors have signed contracts with specific scopes of work.
- The work to be performed by vendors and subcontractors is integrated into the WBS and schedule.
- There are specific milestones and activities planned for monitoring vendors and sub-contractors.

Approvals
- The detailed action plan has been presented and approved.

Balancing the Project

INTRODUCTION

As I prepared to write this chapter I received an e-mail that ended this way:

> *I have recently changed job focus. I work part-time from home while caring for my six-week-old girl. Parenthood has consumed more of my personal resources than I budgeted. Consequently, I am behind schedule on this project.*

This new father is not only learning about the demands of parenthood, he has aptly summed up a dilemma of life: limited resources. Whatever we do, we are faced with limited time, limited money, and a shortage of the people, equipment, and materials we need to complete our job. This problem of limited resources goes beyond issues of efficiency or productivity. No matter how efficient they may be, new fathers and projects alike must realize their limits and make choices.

But doesn't good project management mean we get more done, in less time, for less money? This is a valid question. Good project management *does* deliver more for less (particularly when compared to bad project management). But there are still limits. The best predictor of project success remains realistic stakeholder expectations. The project manager needs to rein in any unreasonable demands by the customer, as well as any unreasonable hopes of the project team. If these hopes and demands are allowed to drive a project, the result will almost certainly be cost and schedule overruns—and painful disappointment later in the project. Instead, project managers must establish realistic expectations through rational analysis of the facts. They must employ the definition and planning techniques described in previous chapters to balance the project scope against these three most common project constraints:

1. *Time.* The project, as defined, won't get done in the time originally envisioned in the project rules.
2. *Money.* The project can deliver the desired outcome on schedule, but the cost is too high.
3. *Resources.* The projected cost is acceptable, but the schedule calls for people, equipment, or materials that aren't available. You could afford them, but there aren't any to hire.

If one or more of these constraints is a factor, the project will need to be balanced; that is, the balance between the cost, schedule, and quality of the product will need to be reconsidered. This balancing can take place at several different levels.

THREE LEVELS OF BALANCING A PROJECT

Balancing a project can take place at one of three different levels of authority in an organization, depending on the kind of change needed:

1. *Project.* Balancing at the project level requires making changes that keep the project on track for its original cost, schedule, and quality objectives. Since these three parts of the project equilibrium won't change, the project manager and team should have authority to make these decisions.
2. *Business case.* If the project cannot achieve its cost-schedule-quality goals, then the equilibrium between these three factors must be reexamined. This means that the business case for the project must be reevaluated. Changing any of the goals of the project puts this decision beyond the authority of the project manager and team. To understand why the decision to change the cost-schedule-quality equilibrium has to be made at the business level consider that:
   - Cost goals are related to profitability goals. Raising cost targets for the project means reevaluating the profit goals.
   - Schedules are closely linked to the business case. Projects that deliver late often incur some profit penalty, either through missed opportunities or actual monetary penalties spelled out in the contract.
   - Changing the features and performance level of the product affects the quality—and therefore the value—of the end product.
   - Balancing the project to the business case requires agreement from all the stakeholders, but most of all, from those who will be affected by changes to cost, schedule, or quality.

3. *Enterprise.* When the project and business case balance, but the firm has to choose which projects to pursue, it is then balancing the project at the enterprise level. The enterprise could be a department within a firm, an entire company, or a government agency. This decision is absolutely beyond the power of the project manager and team, and it may even exceed the authority of the sponsor and the functional managers, though they'll be active participants in the decision. Choosing which projects to pursue and how to spread limited resources over multiple projects is primarily a business management decision, even though it requires project management information.

BALANCING AT THE PROJECT LEVEL

There are as many ways to balance projects as there are projects. This chapter presents the best-known alternatives for balancing at the project, business case, and enterprise levels. Because determining the right alternative depends on which balance problem exists, each alternative is listed with its positive and negative impacts and the best application—the best way of applying the technique. Following are a number of ways of balancing the project at the project level.

1. Reestimate the Project

This is the "optimist's choice." This involves checking your original assumptions in the statement of work and the work package estimates. Perhaps your growing knowledge of the project will allow you to reduce your pessimistic estimates. Here are the possible impacts of this kind of checking.

Positive. If certain estimates can be legitimately reduced, the project cost, and perhaps the schedule estimates, will shrink, and the accuracy of your estimates will have increased.

Negative. Unless there is new information to justify better estimates, don't fall prey to wishful thinking.

Best application. Always check your estimates. Make sure your estimating assumptions about productivity, availability of skilled people, and complexity of tasks are consistent and match all available information. While you are making changes, however, it's important not to succumb to pressure and reduce the estimates just to please management or customers. If anything, the second round of estimating should create an even firmer foundation of facts supporting cost, schedule, and resource estimates.

2. Change Task Assignments to Take Advantage of Schedule Float

This is a straightforward resource allocation maneuver, particularly if you're using project management software (see Figure 9.1). It involves moving people to critical path tasks from tasks that are not on the critical path in order to reduce the duration of the critical path. The noncritical tasks—those with schedule flexibility (float)—will get done later.

Positive. The beauty of this trick is that the schedule can be reduced with no change in the total labor cost. If labor or equipment is pulled from a task with sufficient float, that task will just be performed later for the same cost (see tasks 7 and 8 in Figure 9.1).

Negative. The original work package estimates may have had the optimal number of people assigned to the task. By adding people to a task, the duration may be reduced, but the actual labor costs might go up if efficiency is compromised (certain tasks are not performed as efficiently with more people). The noncritical tasks, from which workers were removed, may also suffer a loss of efficiency.

Best application. There are three considerations when moving people from noncritical tasks to critical tasks:

1. They both need the same resource type. (Pulling attorneys off a task to help a bricklayer won't work.)

2. The noncritical task needs enough float to allow it to be delayed without delaying the entire project. Don't forget that shortening tasks on the critical path will take float away from all noncritical tasks. You may find that reducing duration on a few critical path tasks changes the critical path.

3. You must be able to reduce the duration of the critical path tasks by applying more people. (See Tables 7.2 and 7.5 on pages 139 and 142 for examples of tasks that don't decrease in duration by adding people.)

3. Add People to the Project

This is an obvious way to balance a project because it reduces the schedule. Adding people to the project team can either increase the number of tasks that can be done at the same time or increase the number of people working on each task.

Positive. The schedule is reduced because more labor is applied every day of the project.

Negative. Fred Brooks summed up the danger of this alternative in the title of his landmark book, *The Mythical Man-Month.*[1] Pouring more people onto the project may reduce the schedule, but it increases the cost of coordination and communication. Economists refer to this

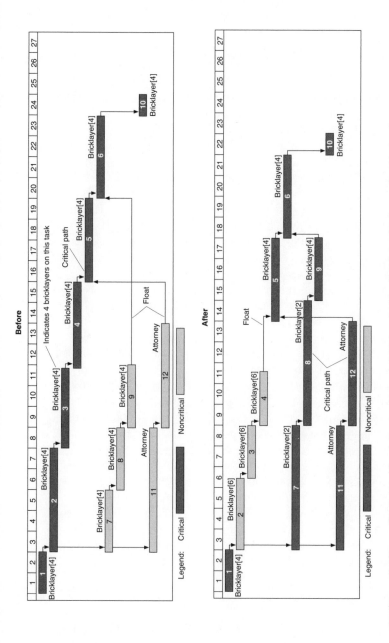

- By taking two bricklayers off tasks 7 and 8 and assigning them to tasks 2, 3, and 4, the original critical path was reduced by four days.
- Since tasks 11 and 12 had only two days float, they became critical.
- As bricklayers were taken from tasks 7 and 8, the tasks increased duration and also became critical.

FIGURE 9.1 *Change task assignments to take advantage of schedule float.*

effect as the *law of diminishing marginal returns.* (As an example, you can refer to the Stellar Performer profile of Adobe Systems in Chapter 8. It demonstrates how each person added to a software project has a diminishing impact on schedule performance.)

You can't just add another warm body to a project; this option requires *qualified* resources. Many project managers have asked for more people only to have the most available people (which usually means the least competent) sent to their projects. Weighing the project down with unskilled workers can create such a drag on productivity that it is almost certain to drive up both cost and schedule.

Best application. Certain work lends itself to piling on, that is, adding more people to get the job done faster. Task independence and product development strategy are both factors to consider when adding people to a project. The greater the independence of the concurrent tasks, the more constant the advantage of adding people.

For instance, a highway department plans on repaving a 100-mile stretch of highway. They could break down the repaving into ten 10-mile subprojects and perform them all at the same time, assuming they had enough qualified contractors to run 10 projects concurrently. (If shortening the schedule were really important and there were enough road paving contractors, they could even break it into twenty 5-mile subprojects.) The independence among all the subprojects makes it possible to overlap them. Trying to coordinate that many people and that much equipment would require extra project management effort, but even if it took 10 times as many supervisors from the highway department to coordinate the project, these costs would remain constant because the duration would be cut by 90 percent. There are other realities to consider on a project like this, however, such as whether all the various contractors will use the same roads, gravel pits, and equipment parking. But these are only resource constraints (resource constraints can be analyzed using the resource-leveling technique described in Chapter 7).

Fred Brooks also points out that a software development schedule is not strictly divisible by the number of people on the project. But developing software products can require huge teams. Likewise, producing a new commercial aircraft requires thousands of engineers. Projects that use knowledge workers can usefully add people to reduce their schedules by following good product development practices such as these:

- The project team organization reflects the product design. The overall project must be broken into teams and/or subprojects the same way the overall product is broken into components or sub-products. Manufacturing companies refer to this organizational style as *integrated product teams* (IPTs), because all of the disciplines required to develop a component of the product are teamed together. (Chapter 13 contains a Stellar Performer profile of Integrated Product Teams.)

- The product is designed from the top down, and the schedule contains design synchronization points. Top-down design means establishing the product's overall design parameters first, then repeatedly breaking the product into components and subcomponents. Scheduled synchronization points are times to focus on component interfaces and reevaluate how the entire product is meeting the overall product design requirements (see Figure 9.2).

- Actual construction of any part of the product begins only after the design for that component has been synchronized and stabilized against the design for interfacing components. Aircraft manufacturers commonly use three-dimensional engineering software that actually models the interaction of different components, eliminating

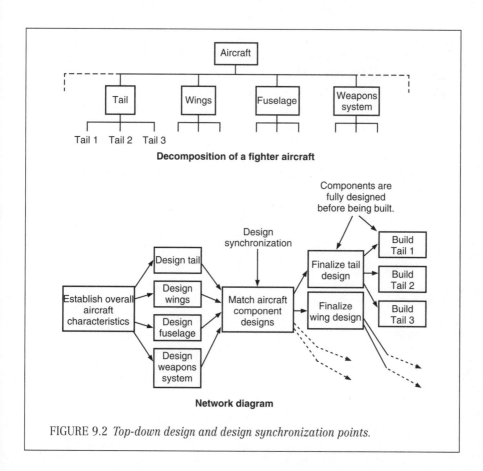

FIGURE 9.2 *Top-down design and design synchronization points.*

the need for physical mock-ups of the aircraft. Figure 9.2 demonstrates how useful a network diagram is for identifying concurrent tasks. These concurrent tasks are opportunities for adding people to the project in order to reduce overall duration.

- Component construction includes unit testing and frequent integration testing. Unit tests refer to testing the functions of individual components as they are built. Frequent integration tests pull together the most up-to-date versions of completed components to make sure they work together. Frequent integration testing has emerged as a required development technique for products with many components because the sheer number of possible interface failures is beyond the ability to test and effectively debug (see Figure 9.3).

Finally, don't forget that by adding people to the project to reduce schedule, you are increasing cost risks. The more people that are idled by unexpected delays, the higher the cost per day of any delay.

4. Increase Productivity by Using Experts from within the Firm

It's no secret that some people are more productive than others. I've seen top computer programmers turn out 10 times as much as the weakest member of a team. Though it may not be at a 10:1 ratio, every industry has people who are just more capable. So why not get as many of them as you can on your project? These high performers have technical competence, problem-solving skills, and positive attitudes. After they've reestimated your project, it will probably meet or beat all the original assumptions about cost and schedule performance.

Positive. Not only will this team deliver the best possible schedule performance, it will also be cost-effective. These high performers might double the output of the average team member, but it's rare that they get paid twice as much for doing it. On top of that, their expertise is likely to produce a better product.

Negative. This can be an inefficient strategy for the firm. Putting all these stars on one project means that they'll probably be doing work that's well below their ability levels—something a junior staff member could do as well, even if not as fast. Another negative is that when other projects begin to suffer, the stars will be reassigned and the stellar project will slowly fall behind schedule.

Best application. Top people are spread around many projects so their ability and expertise can make other people more productive. You'll have a better chance of getting the optimal mix of average and star players when you do two things.

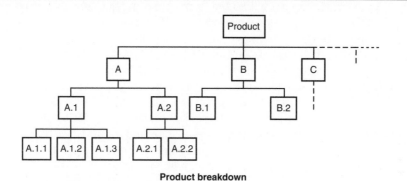

Product breakdown

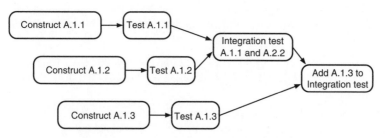

Network diagram showing an incremental approach to integration testing

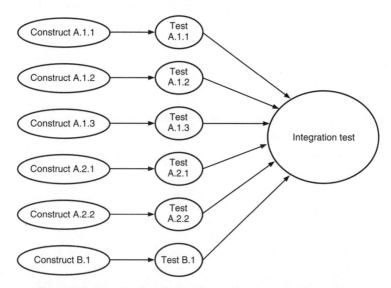

Network diagram showing an all-at-once approach to integration testing

FIGURE 9.3 *Component construction phase includes frequent unit and integration tests.*

First, create experts within the team by putting the same people on related tasks. For instance, when a team of business analysts was working with a hospital to redesign the hospital's methods for keeping records of patients, the project leader assigned one person to be responsible for decisions affecting the maternity ward, another for the pediatric ward, another for the pharmacy, and so on. Even though these assignments didn't necessarily increase their skill level as analysts, each person did become the subject-matter expert for his or her part of the project. This strategy is even more important when there are many people who won't be working full-time on the project, because it keeps specialized knowledge in one place.

Second, using the work breakdown structure, network diagram, and work package estimates, identify the tasks that benefit most from top talent. Here are some indicators that you'll get a big payback from a star:

- *Cost.* The most complex tasks produce the highest returns from top performers. These are the kind of tasks that produce productivity ratios of 10:1.

- *Schedule.* Put the top performers on critical path tasks, where their speed will translate to a shorter overall project schedule.

- *Quality.* Top performers make good technical leads by making major design decisions and spending time discussing work with junior team members.

Most important, involve top performers in project management activities such as risk management, estimating, and effective assignment of personnel.

5. Increase Productivity by Using Experts from Outside the Firm

The same logic for the last alternative applies here, except that this option seeks to pull in the best people from outside the firm. Whether you hire individual people as contract labor or engage a firm to perform specialized tasks, the process is similar: Use the work breakdown structure to identify the best application of their talents and manage them like one of the team.

Positive. Some work is so specialized that it doesn't pay to have qualified people on staff do it. The additional costs incurred by hiring the outside experts will be more than offset by the speed and quality of their work. Just as with the experts from within the firm, assign them the time- or quality-critical tasks to get the most leverage from their work.

Negative. There are two downsides to this option: vendor risk and lost expertise.

1. *Vendor risk.* Bringing an outsider into the project introduces additional uncertainty. Unfortunately, not every expert delivers; he or she may not live up to the promises. By the time you find out your expert isn't productive, you may find, in spite of the added costs, that the project is behind schedule. In addition, locating a qualified vendor or contract employee can be time-consuming; if it takes too much time, it can become a bottleneck in the schedule.

2. *Lost expertise.* Every contract laborer or subcontractor who walks out the door at the end of the project takes some knowledge along—and this problem intensifies if the work is "brain work." In this case, the project manager needs to make sure that the work has been properly recorded and documented.

Best application. Hiring outside experts is useful when it appears that their specialized skills will move the project along faster. You should expect these experts to attend team meetings and participate in product development discussions; don't let them become "islands," working alone and avoiding interaction with long-term employees. Like the inside experts, they should be included in project management and other high-leverage activities. And, before they leave the project, whatever they produce should be tested and documented.

The added productivity that outside resources bring to the project must outweigh the effort to find and hire them. The ideal situation is to have a long-term relationship with a special-services firm whose employees have demonstrated their expertise on past projects.

6. Outsourcing the Entire Project or a Significant Portion of It

This method of balancing a project involves carving out a portion of the project and handing it to an external firm to manage and complete. This option is especially attractive if this portion of the project requires specialized skills not possessed by internal workers.

Positive. This moves a large portion of the work to experts whose skills should result in greater productivity and a shortened schedule.

Negative. This shifting of responsibility creates more risk. The project manager will have less control over the progress of the work and, if the outside specialists prove to be less than competent, it may be too late to "switch horses." Even if it succeeds, an outside firm will leave little of its expertise with your firm at the end of the project.

Best application. Outsourcing is at the high end of the risk/return spectrum. When it works, it can be a miracle of modern business methods; when it doesn't, it can result in real catastrophes. The keys to successful outsourcing are finding qualified vendors and coming to clear agreements before the work begins. These agreements must be built using various tools from this book, including responsibility matrixes, work breakdown structures, network diagrams, and Gantt charts.

 Don't Underestimate the Risks of Outsourcing

The full process for finding and hiring a qualified subcontractor involves many of the techniques in this book—and even more that you won't find here. Finding qualified subcontractors for large projects amounts to a major subproject in itself. Don't underestimate the risks and challenges of outsourcing major projects.

7. Crashing the Schedule

When tasks are compressed on the critical path, the entire project is shortened.[2,3] But compressing task duration can be expensive. Crashing can employ any of the alternatives listed in this chapter to reduce the duration of critical path tasks, but it takes the extra step of producing a *cost/schedule trade-off table,* which is used to analyze the cost of reducing the schedule (see Figure 9.4).

Positive. The table makes it clear which tasks are the cheapest to compress.

Negative. The only potential negative is that the estimates in the table may turn out to be not completely accurate.

Best application. Any time that tasks on the critical path need to be compressed, a crash table points out the path where the payback will be the greatest.

8. Working Overtime

The easiest way to add more labor to a project is not to add more people, but to increase the daily hours of the people already on the project. If a team works 60 hours a week instead of 40, it might accomplish 50 percent more.

Positive. Having the same people work more hours avoids the additional costs of coordination and communication encountered when people are added. Another advantage is that, during overtime hours, whether they come before or after normal working hours, there are fewer distractions in the workplace.

Negative. Overtime costs more. Hourly workers typically earn 50 percent more when working overtime. When salaried workers put in overtime, it may not cost the project more money, but sustained overtime can incur other, intangible costs. In *Peopleware: Productive Projects and Teams,* Tom DeMarco and Timothy Lister not only recognize the intangible cost of sustained overtime (divorce, burnout,

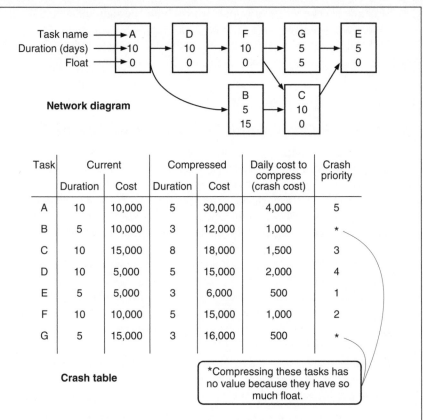

FIGURE 9.4 *Using a crash table to evaluate the cost of compressing the schedule.*

turnover), they also call into question whether *any* overtime on projects involving knowledge workers was effective. They state: "Nobody can really work much more than forty hours [per week], at least not continually and with the intensity required for creative work. . . . Throughout the effort there will be more or less an hour of undertime for every hour of overtime," where *undertime* is described as nonwork activities such as "personal phone calls, bull sessions, and just resting."[4] Adding in overtime assumes that people are as productive during the ninth, tenth, and eleventh hours as they were the first 8 hours of a day. Since this is rarely the case for any type of worker in any industry, the extra pay and intangible costs of overtime may not really buy much in increased output.

Best application. How much overtime is effective is debatable, but one thing is certain: Overtime is perceived by the project team as over and above the normal expected performance. Whether he or she demands overtime or allows people to voluntarily sign up for it, the project manager must demonstrate clearly the ways in which the extra work will benefit the project and the individual team members. The best rule is to apply overtime sparingly and only where it produces big paybacks.

Reducing Product Performance Is Not an Option

As stated in Chapter 2, the two characteristics of product quality are functionality and performance. *Functionality* describes what the product does, while *performance* describes how well the functionality works. Reducing the performance of the product is another way of balancing a project. Time and money can be saved by cutting the testing and quality control tasks and by performing other tasks more quickly and less thoroughly.

Positive. The cost and schedule may very well be reduced because we're spending less effort on the project.

Negative. Philip Crosby titled his book *Quality Is Free* on the premise that the cost of doing things twice is far greater than the cost of doing them right the first time.[5] When performance is cut, costs go up for many reasons, including these:

- Rework (performing the same tasks twice because they weren't done right the first time) during the project will drive the cost higher and delay completion.

- Rework after the project finishes is even more expensive than rework during the project. Any potential development cost savings are wiped out by the high cost of fixing the product.

- Failures due to poor product performance can be staggeringly expensive. Product recalls always bear the expense of contacting the consumers as well as fixing or replacing the product. Product failures such as collapsing bridges and malfunctioning medical equipment can even cost lives.

- Poor product performance causes damage to the reputation of the firm and ultimately reduces the demand for its product. A sad example is the Big Three U.S. car manufacturers, which have been fighting a reputation for poor quality for 20 years. No matter how many surveys demonstrate that American-made automobiles have solved the quality problem, American consumers continue to perceive European and Japanese cars as more reliable.

Best application. Never! Crosby's argument is correct: It is cheaper to do it right than to do it twice. The only legitimate arguments in favor of cutting performance are presented in the next section under Alternative 1, "Reduce the Product Scope."

BALANCING AT THE BUSINESS CASE LEVEL

If, in spite of all attempts to balance a project at the project level, the cost-schedule-quality goals still cannot be achieved, then the equilibrium of these three factors needs to be reexamined. This means that the business case for the project must be reevaluated. Decisions relating to goals are beyond the authority of the project manager and team alone; this reevaluation requires the authorization of all the stakeholders. This section will look at the various ways that the business case for a project can be reevaluated.

1. Reduce the Product Scope

If the goals of the project will take too long to accomplish or cost too much, the first step is to scale down the objectives—the product scope. The result of this alternative will be to reduce the functionality of the end product. Perhaps an aircraft will carry less weight, a software product will have fewer features, or a building will have fewer square feet or less expensive wood paneling. (Remember the difference between product scope and project scope: *Product scope* describes the functionality and performance of the product; *project scope* is all the work required to deliver the product scope.)

Positive. This will save the project while saving both time and money.

Negative. When a product's functionality is reduced, its value is reduced. If the airplane won't carry as much weight, will the customers still want it? If a software product has fewer features, will it stand up to competition? A smaller office building with less expensive wood paneling may not attract high enough rents to justify the project.

Best application. The key to reducing a product's scope without reducing its value is to reevaluate the true requirements for the business case. Many a product has been over budget because it was overbuilt. *Quality* has best been defined as "conformance to requirements." Therefore, reducing product scope so that the requirements are met more accurately actually improves the value of the product, because it is produced more quickly and for a lower cost.

Calculating the cost and schedule savings of reduced functionality begins with the work breakdown structure. Reducing the functionality means that certain tasks can be reduced or eliminated; these tasks need to be found and the estimates reduced accordingly (see Figure 9.5). As always, focusing on critical path tasks is the surest way to reduce a schedule.

If the project remains over budget or over schedule after you have reevaluated the requirements and scaled back the product scope, then it is time to focus on the customer's use of the product. Which requirements are absolutely necessary and which could be modified or elimi-

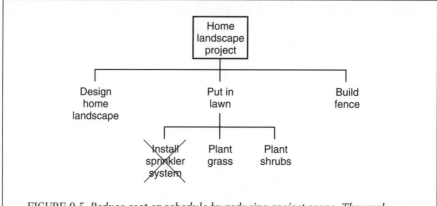

FIGURE 9.5 *Reduce cost or schedule by reducing project scope. The work breakdown structure is the basis for evaluating possible cost and schedule reductions to the home landscape project.*

nated? You can start by prioritizing the requirements, then analyzing the cost-benefit trade-off of each requirement. In particular, expensive requirements that add little benefit need to be identified. Again, the first tool used in evaluating the cost and schedule savings of each requirement is the work breakdown structure.

2. Fixed-Phase Scheduling

During the early days of a product development life cycle, it is difficult to pin down the cost, schedule, or product quality. But some projects, for very important reasons, need to complete by a specific date. When fixed-phase scheduling is employed, the project phases are apportioned from the top down and scheduled according to the required completion date. (See "Phased Estimating" and "Apportioning" in Chapter 8.) At the end of each phase, the scope of the project is reevaluated (functionality is added or removed) to fit the remaining schedule (see Figure 9.6).

Positive. Since functionality can be added as well as removed, the project will meet the schedule with the best possible product because it was consciously rescoped several times. Quality (product performance) will remain high with this method, because quality-oriented tasks won't be sacrificed at the last minute to meet the schedule.

Negative. Not every product lends itself to functionality changes several times during the life cycle. The design for many products is holistic, encompassing all the functions. During construction of a house, for instance, it isn't appropriate to add another bedroom and bathroom just because the project is ahead of schedule or under budget.

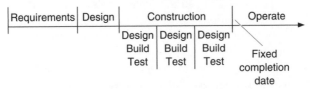

Product development life cycle

- Use apportioning to determine the duration of each phase given the amount of total development time available.
- Break down the construction phase into detailed design–build–test phases. These subphases are used to control scope, because a shippable product is created at the end of every construction subphase.
- At the end of every product development phase, including requirements, design, and all construction subphases, reestimate how much functionality can be built without changing the ship date.
- Be sure the functionality is prioritized, ensuring only low-priority functions are cut during each phase review.
- If everything is ahead of schedule, add another design–build–test phase to add more functionality.

FIGURE 9.6 *Fixed-phase scheduling.*

Best application. Projects whose delivery date is set and whose products can be scaled up or down during development without compromising design lend themselves best to this method. Software (including information systems) is probably the best candidate for fixed-phase estimating, because most software designs are modular. In addition, it's critical that these products meet their delivery date because their market success often depends on beating a competitor to the punch.

Because fixed-phased scheduling does require product scope changes, the project manager must be prepared to present hard choices to the customer and other stakeholders several times during the project.

3. Fast-Tracking

Fast-tracking involves overlapping tasks that are traditionally done in sequence. The best example of this balancing technique is beginning construction on a building before the design is complete. The argument for fast-tracking holds that you don't have to know where all the closets and doorways will be before you start digging the foundation.

Positive. Fast-tracking can decrease the project schedule significantly, sometimes by as much as 40 percent.

Negative. Overlapping design and construction is risky, and this is why the decision to fast-track a project must be made at the business level. All the stakeholders need to understand and accept the risk that if initial design assumptions prove to be mistaken, part of the product will have to be demolished and built again. In the worst cases, the mistakes made in a fast-track environment cannot only slow down the project to the point where there is no schedule advantage, but can also cause the costs to run far over the estimates.

Best application. The fundamental assumptions of fast-tracking are that only 15 to 30 percent of the total design work can provide a stable design framework and that the remainder of design activities can be performed faster than construction activities. For these assumptions to hold true, the product must be capable of modular, top-down design. (This type of design was described in the previous section under alternative 3, "Add People to the Project.")

Overlapping design and construction is becoming more common in software development, but in addition to overlapping these phases they also *repeat* each phase. Instead of increasing risk, this design-build-design-build approach actually lowers risk, because the product is developed incrementally. Because of the incremental development, this doesn't quite qualify as a fast-track example, but it does point up how this technique can be successfully modified.

The bottom line with fast-tracking is that it overlaps tasks that have traditionally been done in sequence. The overlap is the risk. The stellar performer profile of SAFECO Field at the end of this chapter demonstrates how risky it can be.

4. Phased Product Delivery

In a situation where the project can't deliver the complete product by the deadline, there is still the possibility that it might deliver some useful part of it. Information systems composed of several subsystems, for example, will often implement one subsystem at a time. Tenants can move into some floors in a new office building while there is active construction on other floors, and sections of a new freeway are opened as they are completed rather than waiting for the entire freeway to be complete.

Positive. Phased delivery has several benefits:

- Something useful is delivered as soon as possible.

- Often, as in the case of information systems, phased delivery is actually preferred because the changes introduced by the new system happen a little at a time. This longer time frame can reduce the negative impacts to ongoing business operations.

- Feedback on the delivered product is used to improve the products still in development.

- By delivering over a longer period, the size of the project team can be reduced; a smaller team can lead to lower communication and coordination costs. And, since the people are working for a longer time on the project, project-specific expertise grows. These factors should lead to increased productivity in subsequent project phases and to an overall lower cost for the project.

- Phased delivery allows for phased payment. By spreading the cost of the project over a longer time, a larger budget might be more feasible.

Negative. Not all products can be implemented a piece at a time. Phased implementation may also require parallel processes, in which old methods run concurrently with new methods, and this can temporarily lead to higher operating costs.

Best application. Modularized products, whose components can operate independently, can be delivered in phases. In order to determine how to phase a product delivery, you need to look for the core functionality—the part of the product that the other pieces rely on—and implement that first. The same criteria may be used in identifying the second and third most important components. When multiple components are equally good candidates, they can be prioritized according to business requirements.

Although consumer products such as automobiles don't appear to be good candidates for phased delivery ("You'll be getting the wind-shield in January and the bumpers should arrive in early March . . ."), a limited amount of phased delivery is possible for some consumer products. For example, software products can be upgraded cheaply and effectively over time by using the Internet, and current customers can download product updates directly onto their computers from company sites on the World Wide Web.

5. Do It Twice—Quickly and Correctly

This method seems to contradict all the edicts about the cost advantages of doing it right the first time (as in Philip Crosby's *Quality Is Free*). Instead, this alternative suggests that if you are in a hurry, try building a quick-and-dirty short-term solution at first, then go back and build the right product the right way.

Positive. This method gets a product to the customer quickly. The secondary advantage is that what is learned on the first product may improve the second product.

Negative. Crosby is right: It is more expensive to build it twice.

Best application. This is an alternative to use when the demand for the product is intense and urgent—when every day (even every hour!) it isn't there is expensive. The high costs of doing it twice are more than compensated by the reduced costs or increased profits that even an inferior product offers. Military examples abound, such as pontoon bridges that replace concrete bridges destroyed by combat. In the realm of business, a product that is first to market not only gains market share, but may actually provide the revenue stream that keeps the company alive to develop the next product.

6. Change the Profit Requirement

If your project needs to cost less in order to be competitively priced, this method recommends reducing the profit margin. This means reducing the markups on the project and the hourly rates charged for the project employees.

Positive. Costs are reduced while schedule and quality stay constant. Perhaps the lower cost helps the company win a big project. Even if the project isn't as profitable, it may give a good position to the firm in a new marketplace. Or it may be that a long-term, lower-profit engagement gives you the stability to take on other projects with higher returns.

Negative. The project may not bring in enough profit to allow the firm to survive.

Best application. Reducing the profit margin is clearly a strategic decision made by the owners or executives of the firm. This is a viable option when a firm must remain competitive in a difficult market. But deciding whether to go ahead with a project with a reduced profit margin would be considered an enterprise-level decision for the firm bidding the project.

BALANCING AT THE ENTERPRISE LEVEL

Enterprise-level balancing mainly confronts the constraints of insufficient equipment, personnel, and budget. At the enterprise level, the firm decides which projects to pursue, given finite resources. Making these decisions requires accurate estimates of individual project resources, costs, and schedules (see the discussion on program management in Chapter 13).

Choosing between projects is difficult; there will always be important ones that don't make the cut. While it might be tempting to do them all, pursuing too many might be more costly than pursuing too few. When an organization tries to complete 10 projects with resources enough for only 8, it may wind up with 10 projects that are 80 percent complete. In spite of all the effort, it may not finish a single project.

The alternatives that are successful at the enterprise level are variations of the ones applied at the project and business case levels.

1. *Outsourcing* allows you to pursue more projects with the same number of people, if you have enough money to pay the outside firm.

2. *Phased product delivery* means that more projects can be run at the same time, with many small product deliveries rather than a few big ones.

3. *Shifting work to the customer* on several projects will free up enough people to pursue one or two additional projects.

4. *Reducing product scope* on several projects requires cost/benefit trade-off analysis among projects, rather than just among functions on a single product.

5. *Using productivity tools* can be a strategic decision to improve productivity across projects. The proper tools can bring great leaps in productivity increases; this may enable firms to pursue many more projects with the same number of people. For example, process improvement techniques are a form of productivity tool; these techniques allow all projects to learn from their predecessors. (Chapter 13 explores the opportunities for improving project management processes.)

But no matter which alternatives the enterprise chooses, or how successfully they are applied, there will always be more good ideas than time or money allows.

END POINT

Balancing shouldn't wait until the end of the planning phase; it should be a part of every project definition and planning activity. Balancing involves reconsidering the balance between the cost, schedule, and quality of the product.

Though it is usually referred to as "course correction," balancing will continue to be present during project control, as the team responds to the realities of project execution and finds that the original plan must be altered.

It would be a mistake to see project management techniques as a tool set for proving that schedules or cost requirements cannot be met. Rather, they're intended to make sure projects are performed the fastest, cheapest, and best way. Balancing requires stakeholders to face the facts about what is possible and what isn't. When a project is badly out of balance, it will do no good to "fire up the troops" through motivational speeches or threats. People know when a job is impossible. Instead, the project manager's job is to create a vision of what is possible and then to rebalance the project in such a way that the vision can become a reality. Balancing requires thought, strategy, innovation, and honesty.

Stellar Performer: SAFECO Field
Fast-Tracking a Baseball Stadium

Baseball is full of surprises. In 2001, the Seattle Mariners won a record-tying 116 wins in regular-season play. But they were eliminated during the American League playoffs, so the winningest team in baseball didn't make it to the World Series. That up-and-down feeling characterized the building of SAFECO Field, the Mariners state-of-the-art stadium that opened in July of 1999. The stadium's classic design and 11-acre, three-piece retractable roof made it an exciting project for the contractor, joint venture team Hunt-Kiewit. But the biggest challenge was the accelerated schedule.

In August of 1998, the project was plunging forward on a fast-track schedule when J. C. Brummond, project manager for the new baseball complex, took time to explain how the intense schedule was affecting the project.

Prominently displayed in Brummond's office was a simple chart comparing the normal 50-month schedule for a ballpark of this size and the fast-track, 34-month schedule for SAFECO Field. "This chart tells the whole story," said Brummond, a 25-year veteran of the construction industry who has built everything from an island at Prudhoe Bay to bus tunnels in Seattle and freeway bridges in Hawaii. As with most fast-track projects, the speed of construction came with a price. "There are a thousand reasons why the cost of this project is climbing, but they all come back—in whole or in part—to an aggressive schedule," said Brummond. (See Figure 9.7.)

Fast-tracking, the practice of beginning construction before design is complete, is inherently risky because it opens up the possibility of wrong assumptions and subsequent rework. At SAFECO Field, fast-tracking led to many cases where design modifications and detail drawings were released the same day concrete for that part of the structure was poured. Brummond emphasized the unusual situation, "We accepted drawings up until the time of pour. I called it just-in-time design." Amazingly, the project stayed on schedule. But the relentless pace was balanced by predictable, but unavoidable, cost increases.

OVERTIME

From the start, the men and women on the site worked overtime. Ten-hour days were common, and work often continued over weekends. With the average overtime rate at time and a half (50 percent more than the regular wage) it's easy to understand why these costs increased.

INEFFICIENCY OF OVERTIME

The theory of overtime is that one person can accomplish 80 hours of work by working either two 40-hour weeks or by working 12 hours a day, for seven days straight. The reality is different, par-

(Continued)

(Continued)

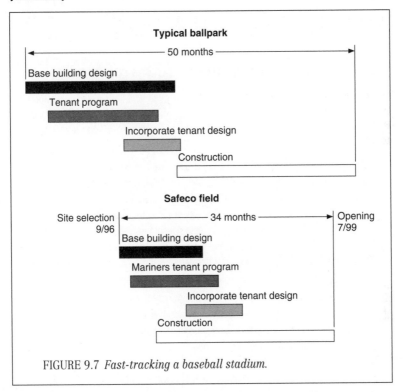

Typical ballpark

50 months

Base building design

Tenant program

Incorporate tenant design

Construction

Safeco field

Site selection
9/96

34 months

Opening
7/99

Base building design

Mariners tenant program

Incorporate tenant design

Construction

FIGURE 9.7 *Fast-tracking a baseball stadium.*

ticularly when it's physical labor. "Bricklayers are a good example," Brummond explained. "Brick-laying is exacting, hard work. You can't speed brickwork with overtime, because you wear out the laborers. The law of diminishing marginal returns applies to everyone on this site. So all the extra overtime helps the schedule, but the overtime hours aren't as productive."

LATE DESIGN PRODUCED MORE CONCURRENT WORK

"Ideally, we would have started with the most complex part of the structure, the area behind home plate," explained Brummond, "and then worked both left and right around the park, meeting in center field." But with design still in progress, construction began in center field instead. Then last-minute changes to the scoreboard design forced construction to begin in right center field and proceed clockwise around the park in one direction only. "There are limits to how many peo-ple you can stack on any part of this park before they start to get in each other's way. If we could have worked two directions at the same time, there would have been many more opportunities for

(Continued)

(Continued)

efficiency. Concrete for instance. We could have had the pouring and finishing crews alternating between the two sides of the stadium, keeping both of them busy and out of each other's way."

SCHEDULE PRESSURE CUT TIME TO PLAN FOR COST SAVINGS

Normally, the engineers and architects have an opportunity to scrub the design for constructibility issues—modifications that make the structure more efficient to build. With the intense schedule pressure, many constructibility issues weren't identified until they had already become obstacles on the job. For example:

- The computer-assisted design optimized every concrete beam in the stadium, designing each one to the minimum size for its structural requirements. While that reduced the total amount of materials (concrete and reinforcing steel) needed to build these beams, it resulted in over 900 beam sizes, some of them only fractions of an inch in difference. "They should have standardized all the beam sizes in the design stage because standard sizes make it more efficient to build the forms," said Brummond. "In this business you focus on labor to cut costs." Again, a fast-track schedule called for building part of the structure before design for other parts was complete— leaving out the time necessary to reevaluate the design for constructibility cost savings.

- The anchor bolts used to tie the structural steel to the cast-in-place concrete structure had a similar problem. Again, the concrete columns, beams, and shear walls were optimized for materials, producing a design where the reinforcing steel was so tightly packed there was barely room for the lag bolts that stick up from the tops of the columns, beams, and slabs. This made it impossible for the craftsmen setting the lag bolts to put them in exactly the right place—a problem that became apparent every time a crane lifted a piece of structural steel to be attached and its holes didn't match the bolts. "So then you have a bunch of steelworkers standing around while the old anchor bolt is cut off and a new one is installed in the right position. We hit this problem over and over throughout the erection of the steel."

NO TIME TO PLAN FOR EFFICIENCY

Part of keeping the costs down on a big construction project is thinking through how all the different subcontractors will work together—for example, which subcontractor needs to deliver materials to an area before another puts up the walls. But on a fast-track project, with everyone working as fast as they can, this type of planning often falls by the wayside, with predictable results. For instance, during the August 1998 tour, a number of 20- and 40-foot copper pipes, four inches in diameter, sat in a hallway outside of rooms that they should have been in. When they were delivered only days before, there had been no hallways or rooms because the walls hadn't been built. It cost extra labor to get the pipes into the right room to be installed.

(Continued)

(Continued)

REWORK

Fast-tracking's most predictable risk is rework, and SAFECO Field saw plenty. Since the schedule demanded that the structure's concrete be poured before the commercial tenants had designed their spaces, holes had to be cut through the concrete for many of the drain lines, water pipes, cables, and other service lines. When a huge air duct was installed after the fire sprinkler lines had been hung from the ceiling, the duct was blocked by some of the sprinkler lines. Brummond pointed this out as just one more example of the cost of building before completing design, then recorded it in a notebook he carried with him constantly. "When they installed it, there was no way the people who put in that sprinkler line could know that vent would come through here. But now they have to move that line."

SPECIAL EQUIPMENT

To speed the schedule, four large tower cranes were placed at the four corners of the ballpark, allowing the exterior structure and the seating structures to be raised at the same time. This strategy cut as much as six months off the schedule, but the tower cranes were significantly more expensive than conventional track-mounted mobile cranes.

Not every innovation was more expensive. Rather than building wooden forms for some of the stairs and other concrete structures in the stands, the construction team decided to pour the concrete over Styrofoam blocks. "The Styrofoam is lighter weight, won't rot, and it takes a guy about five minutes to cut the blocks. It's a lot faster than plywood."

The decision to fast-track a project is always a risky one, and it always comes down to one question: Which is more important, cost or schedule? For the Seattle Mariners, moving to their new stadium immediately following the All-Star break in 1999 was the dominant factor. The construction team, architects, engineers, and the public agency overseeing construction of the ballpark all walked into this fast-track project with their eyes open, aware of the risks. In August 1998, halfway through the construction schedule, the budget for the stadium had been raised from $417 million to $498 million; this was due to many factors, including increased scope and underestimating the original job. But there is no denying that a portion of the budget increase was due to the pace of the work and the inevitable inefficiencies that came with it.

When the stadium opened, on time, in July 1999, the final budget had been revised to $515 million. SAFECO Field has been filled ever since, with fans who love to watch baseball in this beautiful park.

Sources: Interview with J.C. Brummond, Project Manager, Hunt-Kiewit Joint Venture, August 25, 1998; "M's Will Pay Overruns," *Seattle Times*, July 21, 1998, pp. A1, A11.

Stellar Performer: Boeing 767-400ER Program
Integrated Schedule Development

The Boeing Company of Seattle, Washington, is known for its ability to deliver huge, complex projects on time. The challenge of building a new-model commercial aircraft includes optimizing the efforts of thousands of people while building a complex product that requires integrating hundreds of design decisions. To meet these challenges, Boeing's 767-400ER program rigorously applied classic schedule integration techniques.

SETTING THE DELIVERY DATE

Launched in April 1997, the 767-400ER program put together an aggressive schedule to deliver the first airplane to Delta Air Lines in May 2000. But an aggressive schedule isn't worth much if it can't be met. "The program used right-to-left scheduling," explained Fred Black, the manager responsible for program planning and schedule integration. Using parametric estimates from previous derivative programs, the program tied airplane requirements to a high-level schedule. *Right to left* means that they set a delivery date and worked backward to figure out all other project milestones. Once they had a delivery date and a launch customer, the program was under way. "Right-to-left scheduling works only if it's based on a realistic overall estimate, but because we had the performance data from other recent models we knew we would meet our commitment to Delta." The 767-400ER planned on shaving several months off recent airplane development schedules.

TOP DOWN AND BOTTOM UP

With the delivery date set, the program schedule was developed top down and bottom up. Top-down scheduling broke the overall schedule into major phases. Within those phases, *integrated product teams,* cross-functional teams often known as IPTs, decomposed the airplane require-ments into specific *part identification numbers* (PINs). In other words, the entire aircraft was decomposed into 2,600 groups of drawings. A schedule was developed for each PIN, and then the PIN schedules were tied to the major development milestones. Keeping the program-level schedule milestones constant, the resources required to meet the PIN-level schedules were devel-oped from the bottom up, that is, using bottom-up resource estimating.

(Continued)

(Continued)

A REQUIREMENTS-DRIVEN PROGRAM

It's one thing to determine that it will take an army of engineers to deliver on schedule, but how do you integrate the hundreds of design decisions required to optimize the new aircraft? Fred Black described the complexity of the major design reviews that were necessary throughout the program schedule. "The basic requirement of airplane weight is a good example. The aircraft's weight is one of the prime factors affecting range. A target weight determined by the range requirement is established at the beginning of the design effort. Of course, all the components of the aircraft add weight, and the weight of one component often affects the design of another. The weight of the wing impacts the design of the fuselage attach points for the wing. The weight of the landing gear impacts both the fuselage and the wing. The weight of the engines impacts the design of the engine pylon structure. All of the integrated product teams for these areas work together to manage the weight of the airplane to the target weight at periodic reviews throughout the design process. Thus, one of the major contributors to the eventual range of the airplane is managed to that requirement. During design reviews, we constantly refer back to the requirements, because we are a requirements-driven program."

767-400ER MEETS CUSTOMER COMMITMENTS

767-400ER is using classic project management techniques to remain focused on the business requirements of the aircraft. For example:

- The high-level schedule is based on performance data from similar programs. Launch customer Delta Air Lines and other early customers can be confident their airplanes will be delivered when they need them.

- The work breakdown structure for the entire program is a decomposition of the business requirements, ensuring that all the needed work will be performed to deliver the right aircraft.

- Bottom-up resource estimating means taking an honest look at the effort required to meet all the program requirements.

- Cross-functional design reviews bring integrated product teams together to make sure that all of their decisions are driven by the aircraft's business requirements.

Boeing understandably emphasizes the aircraft's new technological advancements, such as a raked wingtip that reduces airplane weight while increasing performance. But behind all the twenty-first-century technology, proven project management techniques kept the program on track, delivering the first airplane to Delta as promised.

Sources: Interview with Fred Black, Manager, Program Plan and Schedule Integration, 767-400ER Program, June 12, 1998; Boeing press release, www.boeing.com/news/releases/1998/news_release_980507.html, www.boeing.com/commercial/767-400ER/background.html.

Controlling the Project

There is a time in the life of every problem when it is big enough to see, yet small enough to solve.

—Mike Leavitt

During the first two phases of a project, as presented in Parts 2 and 3, the focus was on preventing possible problems through careful planning. Now, in Part 4, Chapters 10, 11 and 12, the project is under way, and the focus has shifted to keeping the project on track—controlling the project.

Controlling a project blends the art and science of project management—building a strong, committed team at the same time you are making progress against the plan. Controlling also involves discovering and solving problems while they are still small, measuring progress, and ensuring continued agreement on goals and expectations. The key to these control activities is communication—making sure that the right people have the right information at the right time. Strong communication among all stakeholders is what allows a project to evolve in an ordered way, instead of veering out of control.

Building a High-Performance Project Team

INTRODUCTION

As we have detailed the science of project management in previous chapters, there has been an unspoken assumption: that the people on the project team would work together in harmony to build plans, manage risks, perform tasks, and commit themselves to achieving the clearly stated goals of the project. But that is not always the case.

Despite detailed plans and frequent status meetings, some teams don't work well together. Most of us, at one time or another, experience the frustration of teamwork that is characterized by bickering, unproductive meetings, and a joyless plodding as the projects falls further and further behind. If that challenge isn't enough, consider that project teams are temporary, existing only for the duration of the project—how can we expect the team members to commit to the success of *this* project? It is no secret that the science of project management cannot create successful projects without the committed, cooperative work of a cohesive team.

To discuss this topic thoroughly, we must begin with a basic definition of a *team:* "a group of people working interdependently to produce an outcome for which they hold themselves mutually accountable." Project teams have another characteristic: They will be temporary, formed specifically for the purpose of achieving the goal, after which they will disband.

Our purpose in this chapter is to provide guidelines for building a cohesive project team. It is a large topic, which leads to it being a long chapter. Therefore a brief explanation of the structure of the chapter will make it easier to assimilate all the information. The introduction establishes how project team dynamics contribute to project success. In these first few pages we'll also begin to solve the problem of building a cohesive team by understanding the two major obstacles that all project teams face. Next, to explain the factors that contribute to a high-performance team, we'll use a model, or framework. That framework is initially described at a high level. After that, the remainder of the chapter explores each of the components of the framework in detail.

There have been scores of books written on the topics of leadership and team performance—one chapter cannot attempt to address the breadth of the topic. Therefore, we limit the scope of this chapter to the challenge of forming a cohesive team from a collection of individuals assigned to a project. We will present a framework for building a high-performance project team by describing specific traits the team must possess and the steps a project leader must take to build the team. Despite the fact that one or two disruptive individuals can derail an entire team, we will not address managing individual people or individual performance problems.

 The Importance of Project Team Dynamics

A weak, uncooperative team isn't just *unproductive;* it can make your job a daily grind of frustration and resentment. People burn out, blow up, or quit their jobs because of negative interpersonal dynamics on teams. Conversely, many people cite the strength of a team or their terrific teammates when recounting how they survived a project when everything seemed to go wrong. Of all the topics in this book, this chapter has the greatest potential to change the daily work experience for you and your team.

When a Team Is Not a Team

Accomplishing the work of a project can require the effort of several people without requiring them to work as a cooperative unit. For example, hosting a major conference can require hundreds of people to perform in the right place at exactly the right time, but many of the performers won't interact with each other at any time before, during, or after the conference. Caterers, conference speakers, audio/visual equipment technicians, and trade-show vendors all play a key role, yet each is typically managed directly by the conference management team, with no communication among themselves.

In other cases, the project team does need to meet and talk periodically, but individuals are able to accomplish their own responsibilities *independently* of other team members. To test your own team's cohesion requirement, consider these two variables.[1]

1. Individuals must cooperate in order to complete their tasks.
2. The team has a whole product or service to produce rather than individual components.

To the degree that these are true, your team benefits from all the factors described in this chapter. If these factors don't exist, you'll still need to follow the science of project management—knowing the goals and constraints, tracking progress, and coordinating activities—but cohesion isn't as important. As a project leader, gauging the interdependence of the team members helps you calibrate the degree of effort you should invest in team unity.

KEY CONCEPT · The Challenge of Building Project Teams

Why is it so difficult to get a team to jell? To the novice project manager it can seem mysterious, the result of luck, and certainly unpredictable. But the productivity and joy that come with a high-performance team are too important to rely on luck. In reality, every project team faces two central challenges, two obstacles to becoming a high-performing team.

1. Project teams form to solve complex problems, and they must solve those problems together.
2. Project teams are temporary and so they must *learn to work together.*

Understanding these two challenges reveals why some teams work while others never do. Teams that learn to work together to produce effective decisions with efficiency become increasingly bonded and productive throughout a project. The framework presented in this chapter addresses these two obstacles. Before we present the framework, it is worthwhile to clearly understand the two obstacles our teams face, for by understanding these challenges we are better prepared to overcome them.

A Series of Problems to Solve

Viewing your project as a series of problems to solve may surprise you, but consider these typical activities you find on large and small projects:

- Determining the goals and success criteria for the project
- Making trade-offs between cost, schedule, and scope
- Designing a product, or even a sub-subcomponent of a product
- Setting a time and a place for a milestone celebration event

Each task requires a group of people to arrive at a conclusion. Some of these decisions may be easy to make, others more difficult. But viewed in this way it is clear that projects are filled with problems to solve.

The challenge is multiplied for so-called knowledge workers—anyone from engineers to attorneys to administrators—who *think* for a living rather than use their bodies to perform work. Knowledge workers often tackle complex, abstract problems. Designing an ad campaign, an aircraft wing, or a compensation and benefits plan is actually a series of decisions.

As individual humans we tend to work through problems in a variety of ways. Some of us are linear thinkers, others intuitive. Some study the details, while others focus on the big picture. Some of us are comfortable discussing problems and solutions out loud, forming our views as we speak, but others won't utter a word until they've thoroughly evaluated the information and formed a position. All of these approaches can be effective for us as individuals, but when mixed together in a team they can create chaos that results in frustration and distrust.

As a project leader, your challenge is to harness the problem-solving power of a diverse team. The guidelines and techniques in this chapter will help you build a team that thrives on solving problems and produces truly synergistic results: decisions and products that are superior because they are made by a team with diverse talents and styles.

Temporary Teams

Projects begin and end, and so, therefore, do project teams. Not only are teams temporary, but the trend toward teams that cross functional, corporate, and even national boundaries increases the likelihood that a new project team will be made up of people who haven't worked together previously. Developing trust, respect, effective communication patterns, and the ability to maintain positive relationships despite disagreements takes time. Most important, it takes a conscious effort by the project team leader. This chapter describes specific activities you can take to move a team from a loose collection of individuals to a cohesive unit.

Understanding the Problem Lays the Foundation

The chapter thus far has established why we need to pay attention to the health of the project team and has outlined the challenges we face in building a strong team. Next we present an overall framework for understanding the desirable components of a team. The remainder of the chapter is broken into examining each of those components in greater detail. As you read the chapter, refer to the model in Figure 10.1 to maintain the context of each topic.

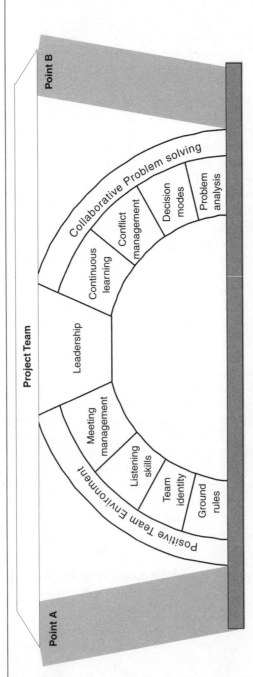

The project team takes the project from point A to point B, spanning the distance just as a bridge spans from one point to another. An arch strengthens the bridge span. The high-performance team arch strengthens the team.

FIGURE 10.1 *High-performance team framework.*

 **A FRAMEWORK FOR BUILDING HIGH-PERFORMANCE TEAMS**

So far we've established the importance of a strong team and the challenges of creating one. But what, exactly, do we mean by a *high-performance team?* In this section we examine the attributes of such a team and present a model that will help us build one.

High-performance teams are more than merely highly productive. A team composed of experienced, capable people can be very productive until those people hit an obstacle or are confronted with an unexpected challenge. This is the point at which the team either shows its strength or reveals its limitations. Teams that successfully persevere tend to have certain characteristics described by the model in Figure 10.1.

As the diagram suggests, we can break the components of a strong project team into three areas that work together in the same way that an arch works to support a bridge. Our teamwork arch shares the same properties as a structural arch:

1. A strong team requires each of the individual components.

2. The strength of the arch lies in the way the pieces work together.

3. Weakness in one component cannot be compensated for by strength in another component.

Envision the goal of your project team as getting from point A to point B. In the model, the project team forms the bridge, spanning from A to B. For simple projects, you could simply grab a handful of people, drop them onto the project, and they'd somehow get from A to B without a lot of special attention to team building. Similarly, you might throw a couple of strong boards across a small ditch to make a simple bridge—quickly and easily. That works fine for simple projects and simple bridges, but if that bridge has to hold up the weight of a complex project, it must be strong. That's the purpose of the arch—to provide the strength and support to a team with a heavy load.

The three primary components in our model—*positive team environment, collaborative problem solving,* and *leadership*—are introduced here with their component parts. Each part is described in detail later in the chapter.

A Positive Team Environment

A positive environment promotes trust and respect among team members and increases performance through more productive work habits. Creating this environment requires four specific elements:

1. *Ground rules that describe the work patterns and values of the team.* Ground rules are explicitly stated expectations about personal behavior that reflect the team's values.

2. *A team identity built on commitment to a shared goal.* This commitment relies on goal and scope clarity, demonstrated support from the project sponsor, and understanding the strengths and contributions of all team members.

3. *The ability to listen.* Problem solving demands an exchange of ideas, which is possible only if team members actually work hard to listen to perspectives that are different from their own.

4. *The ability to effectively manage meetings.* Much team work gets accomplished in meetings (or at least it should!). Just like a project, a meeting needs to begin with goals and a plan, and it must be actively steered toward the goals.

Broken into these elements, we see that a positive environment is not merely an abstract feeling; it is a set of observable skills that a project manager can instill. Further, this positive environment produces two important characteristics of the high-performing team:

1. *Personal ownership of the team goal.* Each team member interprets his or her own success in terms of the team's goal. When team success becomes a matter of personal and professional pride, we've tapped a powerful source of motivation and determination.

2. *Strong interpersonal relationships based on trust and respect.* For many who have worked on high-performance teams, the camaraderie during the project was far more satisfying than the act of achieving the goal. This element is the most essential and most elusive, because it begets itself. Trust builds trust and respect breeds respect. Trust and respect are essential for people working interdependently because they allow us to rely on one another, which is absolutely necessary if the whole is going to be greater than the sum of the parts.

Collaborative Problem-Solving Capability

We have established that project teams solve a series of problems and that they need to learn to work together to solve those problems. Build this collaborative capability by focusing on four team abilities:

1. *Problem-solving skills tied to an accepted problem-solving process.* A team made up of individuals with diverse skills and styles must agree on the process they'll follow for working through problems, both large and small. A commonly accepted problem-solving process enables all team members to flex their styles because each understands and trusts the process.

2. *Understanding and applying multiple decision modes.* Some decisions are made solely by the project leader; other decisions are made by the entire team. These are only two examples of decision

modes. Efficient decision making requires that a team understand the possible decision modes and consciously choose which are appropriate for any decision.

3. *Conflict-resolution skills.* Producing superior decisions demands creativity, which necessarily produces disagreement. Mature teams accept and value the inevitability of conflict. They have the skills to leverage conflict to achieve the best decisions while maintaining strong relationships.

4. *Continuous learning.* When innovation and breakthrough solutions are required, the team's culture must embrace a certain amount of risk taking and have the ability to improve its own performance throughout the project by learning from *both* success and failure.

Each of these capabilities can be developed by the team, though not all are simple. Together they create a truly synergistic result: decisions and products that are superior because they are developed by a team with diverse styles and talents.

Leadership

The keystone of our high-performance framework is the leader who ties the team together as he or she embodies the skills and characteristics found in the two legs of the arch. No team will reach its potential without one or more people consciously attending to the health of the team.

The key focus of the framework is the abilities that the *team* possesses. For that reason, we will limit our discussion on leadership to the actions a leader must take to nurture and establish these capabilities.

Competence Matters

In 1980, the U.S. Olympic hockey team upset the dominant Soviet Union team in the medal rounds of the Winter Olympics and went on to win the gold medal. It was a perfect story of the power of a united, cohesive team, as the much younger, all-amateur U.S. team beat a veteran Soviet team that was the overwhelming favorite. Commenting years later on what became known as the "Miracle on Ice," coach Herb Brooks had this to say: "We could not beat the teams we beat just on talent. If we forgot about the team-building aspect and just relied on talent we wouldn't have been able to do it."

Underdog stories exist in every industry—stories in which the power of a united team produces unexpected, even miraculous, results. Each story is a testament to the themes of this chapter. We must never forget that, though these underdog teams were not made up of acknowledged stars, neither were they made up of novices, incompetents, or those with attitude problems. The high-performance team framework leverages the talents of your team, but if the talents don't exist, don't expect a miracle. Make a realistic assessment of the skills required for the project, and make sure the team either has these skills or can gain them during the project.

Framework Summary

A positive team environment, collaborative problem solving capability, and leadership; these are the three primary components of a high performance team. The model in Figure 10.1 demonstrates how these pieces fit together. In the remainder of the chapter we will explore the skills and capabilities that make up each of these components, beginning with leadership.

LEADERSHIP RESPONSIBILITIES

> What you are stands over you and thunders so, I cannot hear what you say to the contrary.
> —Ralph Waldo Emerson

Leadership is difficult to define but critical to project success. Every topic in this book is a leadership topic, because the actions the project manager takes—or fails to take—influence every stakeholder on the project. In this section of the chapter, we focus on leadership—the keystone of our high-performance team arch—in the context of how a project manager influences the performance of the core team.

We lead through our actions. The ideals and attitudes we carry in our heads mean nothing to our teams because their only experience is our action. The leadership actions that contribute to a high-performance team fall into the five categories discussed in this section.

Attending to the Health of the Team

The first required leadership action is to allocate the time of the leader and the team to building the capabilities described in this chapter. The concept is simple but the action is difficult.

As project leaders, our days are full of status meetings, responding to problems, and completing our own assignments. Our sponsor and customers may demand the tangible products of the science of project management: a WBS, a schedule, or a risk management plan. Our success is measured by being on time and on budget and adhering to specifications. There is no space on our status report to indicate whether our team atmosphere fosters learning and creativity, no measurable statistic on team unity. Virtually no one will ask for your plan to build and maintain a high-performance team—or demand that you devote time and resources to building one.

Faced with these apparent priorities, team building requires personal conviction that team health actually affects the project's result. We demonstrate this conviction by allocating the time of the leader and the team to monitoring and improving the building blocks of team performance.

Maintaining the Strategic Vision

While team members focus on the near-term problems and tasks, the project leader maintains a steady focus on the final outcome of the project and the path toward the goal. This steady focus informs our actions as we engage in day-to-day activities with the team, ensuring that tasks are performed and problems solved in the context of the overall goals of the project. The science of project management makes an obvious contribution to this leadership responsibility as the statement of work, the work breakdown structure, and other planning techniques provide structured methods to understand both the forest and the trees.

Attending to the Team Members

For better or worse, our team members are human beings with feelings, egos, nonwork interests, and career goals beyond the project. Their personal performance will vary according to their motivation, confidence in project leadership, and the respect with which they are treated. Recognize their efforts and accomplishments. Beware of working them to the point of burnout. Treat them with a little more respect than you would want for yourself. When the project demands an above-and-beyond effort, your demonstrated concern for them as human beings will be a deciding factor in whether that effort materializes.

Exhibiting and Demanding Accountability

Successful projects rely on execution. Plans are meaningless if the team does not carry through. Leaders set the tone by keeping their promises and delivering on their responsibilities, and they expect the same of every team member. Holding team members accountable can require some tough conversations and real consequences for nonperformance. It is not the best part of a leader's duties, but we owe it to the team to make sure the efforts of some are not diminished by the nonperformance of others.

STAGES OF TEAM DEVELOPMENT

Forming

The team begins as a collection of individuals. Initial reactions reflect the uncertainty everyone feels at the outset: pride at being selected for the team, excitement about the work ahead, yet a cautious or tentative attachment to the team. At this stage team members act as most people do when introduced into a roomful of strangers: They are polite and avoid conflict, seeking to find common ground and common purpose, and each wants to be accepted as a member of the group.

Leadership Style for Forming Stage. Respond to the uncertainty of the group by providing structure and clear direction. Provide background information to help them understand the goals and purpose of the group. The general desire to avoid conflict means that group decision making may not be comfortable or effective. Establish team expectations using ground rules. (Ground rules are explained later in this chapter.)

Storming

As the team digs in and goes to work, conflict is inevitable. The team hasn't yet learned to trust each other. Greater awareness of the work ahead can cause feelings of anxiety, even a desire to leave the group. Some are impatient to progress. Others are confused about tasks and responsibilities. A sense of thrashing emerges and may produce power struggles. Amidst this seeming chaos, the team is actually gaining clarity about goals and roles. They are starting to make decisions together, albeit somewhat painfully.

Leadership Style for Storming Stage. This stage is rarely fun, but it is natural. Respond to the chaos with structure and clear direction. Recognize early accomplishments. Be willing to engage the group in participative decision making to address their concerns. Facilitate group decisions, demonstrate effective listening, and ensure equitable participation among all team members. Your example will be setting the tone that moves them to the next stage.

Norming

During this stage team members begin to trust each other and trust the group. People can help each other and focus on team goals because their own need for role clarity has been met. They are capable of making team decisions, though they may try to avoid conflict in order to maintain harmony. Ground rules have become accepted and internalized.

Leadership Style for Norming Stage. The strength of the group enables the leader to shift to a facilitative style, giving increasing authority to the team. Don't let the team's new harmony cause them to avoid necessary conflict (learn the value of conflict later in this chapter under "Conflict Management"). Build momentum from the group's unity by reviewing and improving team processes.

Performing

Not all teams reach this stage, but those that do enjoy the power of a united, effective work group. A hallmark of a team in the performing stage is the ease with which it handles changes and obstacles.

Personal relationships are strong, enabling high trust. Team skills for conflict resolution and problem solving enable the group to be highly productive. Team ownership of the goal results in a focus on task accomplishment. Commitment to the team keeps people helping each other, building confidence in the ability of the team.

Leadership Style for Performing Stage. As the team practically manages itself, the leader can focus on removing obstacles and improving team processes. Delegate leadership responsibility to members of the team, particularly as the team self-selects informal leaders. Don't abdicate your leadership role, just share it more widely.

Adjourning

As projects end, teams disband. The satisfaction of accomplishment is tempered by the sadness of leaving the team. Closure rituals enable the team to say good-bye to the project and their team members.

Leadership Style for Adjourning Stage. Facilitate closure by setting up opportunities to review the team's performance. Recognize their successes and opportunities for improvement.

Teams progress through these stages and, at times, move backward into previous stages. Changes to team membership or team goals can cause a team in the forming stage to move back to the storming stage. Throughout all these stages, the team leader adjusts his or her style to address the needs of the group.

Bruce Tuckman originally addressed this topic in *Psychological Bulletin,* vol. 63, no. 6, pp. 384–399, American Psychological Association, 1965.

Personal Energy That Inspires the Team through Example

Teams need leaders. Somebody must put the group in motion, focus the goals, facilitate the plan, and maintain forward momentum. Every project management action described in this book is a visible signal of our personal commitment to create a successful team and to meet the project goal. The energy, attitude, and commitment of the team rarely rise above those of the leader. In the words of Emerson, "What you are stands over you and thunders so I cannot hear what you say to the contrary."

KEY CONCEPT Leadership Styles

What kind of a leadership style makes a project team kick into high gear? Should you be laid-back? Hard-driving? Participative? Autocratic? The options and strategies fill books, yet there is no single best way. There is, however, a well accepted model for team development that should inform whichever leadership strategy we choose. The model articulated in 1967 by Bruce Tuckman, which has been referenced and expanded upon ever since, identifies five stages of team development—stages that every team will pass through as it evolves from a collection of strangers to a cohesive unit to the point at which the team disbands. The stages, and how each informs our leadership style, are summarized in the box on the previous pages. The benefit of understanding these stages is that at each stage of development a team has different requirements of its leader. Understanding these stages enables us to flex our style to the needs of the team.

Leadership Summary

The leadership responsibilities we've described in this section form the keystone of the high-performance team framework. Without leadership the other components of the framework are drastically diminished.

KEY CONCEPT
BUILDING A POSITIVE TEAM ENVIRONMENT

Relationships among team members, the way meetings are conducted, role and goal clarity—all these factors form the daily environment of the team. People can fight a hostile environment and still make progress, but who wants to? We would rather put our energy into accomplishing tasks than wrangling with uncooperative coworkers or spinning our wheels because the goals and roles aren't clear.

Project leaders can influence the daily environment of their project team members. We can set expectations for conduct during meetings and create opportunities for team members to know and trust each other. In short, the project manager can consciously put into place the attributes that contribute to a *positive team environment*. This major component of our high-performance team was described earlier when we introduced the framework and forms the left side of the arch in Figure 10.1. The next four topics describe specific skills and attributes that affect our team environment on a daily basis. Each is relatively simple, yet when any of them are absent it creates a negative drain on the energy of the team. Our goal in the following sections is to understand each attribute and identify actions we can take to build them into our team.

KEY CONCEPT
GROUND RULES

Building a positive environment begins the first time the team gets together. As Tuckman pointed out, during the Forming stage the team wants structure. We meet that team need and begin establishing our team's culture by setting ground rules.

Ground rules are explicitly stated expectations about team behavior and values. Making these expectations explicit accomplishes three things:

1. Team members understand what is expected of them as a member of an interdependent group.
2. The team has an opportunity to form and own its culture;
3. You meet the team's need for structure.

Ground rules can cover a lot of territory, but generally fall into two categories:

1. *Team values.* Ground rules reinforce specific values by identifying behaviors or attitudes that support the value. An example can be found on a project to redesign a firm's compensation plan—the team may want to emphasize the importance of confidentiality.
2. *Meeting behavior.* Setting expected meeting behaviors is a classic application of ground rules. Since we often brainstorm solutions, debate alternatives, assign new work among ourselves, and perform other creative work, it is essential that our behaviors demonstrate respect for each other and, at the same time, make productive use of the time we are together.

Table 10.1 contains examples of ground rules in these two categories.

Though ground rules may seem to state the obvious, such as "listen to and respect other points of view," the reality is that such obviously desirable behaviors don't always exist on teams. Ground rules provide a way for the team's leader to gain agreement on expected behavior, and they serve as a tool for reminding people of what behavior is expected. Post the rules for the first several project team meetings and refer to them during the meeting. Once it is clear that the team has internalized the rules, it may not be necessary to post this list of "obvious rules."

Prime the Pump

 A team will take greater ownership over a set of ground rules that it develops, but starting with a blank sheet of paper can paralyze the group, particularly if many team members aren't familiar with the concept of ground rules. Prime the pump by bringing a starting list of ground rules to the first meeting. People will quickly understand the concept from the suggestions you've made. Then enlist the group to complete your initial set of ground rules.

TEAM IDENTITY

When a colonel in the army was selected to lead a task force that consisted of members from each branch of the military, he knew his suc-

TABLE 10.1 EXAMPLE GROUND RULES

These examples show how ground rules create clear expectations for team member behavior. A team could have many more.

Team Values
- *Confidentiality.* We do not discuss project information with anyone outside the project team or the project steering committee.
- *Team learning.* Be open to new approaches. It's okay to ask questions and to ask for help. Be curious.
- *Respect.* No personal attacks. Don't ridicule ideas or suggestions.
- *Accountability.* Follow through on commitments. Perform on time or alert others when you know you'll miss a deadline.

Meeting Behavior
- *Use active listening.* Ask for clarification. Suspend judgment of the idea until it is understood. No side conversations.
- *Be solution focused.* Don't just criticize, bring new ideas. Attack ideas, not people.
- *Limit distractions.* No cell phones.
- *Begin and end on time.* Arrive before the meeting is scheduled to begin.
- *Challenge the group.* Explore the pros and cons of all ideas. Don't hold back just to avoid conflict.
- *Be prepared.*

cess would be limited if he could not convince the team members to put the goals of the team ahead of the goals of their individual branch. It is a problem common to all temporary teams: to gain each member's commitment to a common goal to which all will hold themselves accountable. A large part of creating this commitment is accomplished through the four elements of building a *team identity* which are described in this section. All work together to build one more component of the positive team environment.

Communicate the Goals and Scope of the Project

Chapter 4 of this book contains a detailed description of determining project goals and scope and recording them in the statement of work. In addition, Chapter 6 describes the work breakdown structure (WBS) technique for creating a detailed description of project scope. Share this information with the project team to give them a tangible description of why this project exists and where it is going. If the team members are assembled before the statement of work or project plan has been completed, their involvement in defining and planning the project will increase their sense of ownership for the goals and plans.

We Learn through Repetition

Announcing the project goals at the first team meeting gives all participants a vision of why the team exists. That is important, because the goal should be the North Star for the team, a reference point that influences all team activity. For the goal to have that level of influence, each team member must learn it deeply and internalize it, something that happens only with repetition. Here are a few simple actions you can take as a project leader to appropriately repeat the goal.

- Write the goal at the top of every meeting agenda. You won't necessarily even have to mention it, but seeing it there at every meeting will be a steady reminder.

- Start with the project goal when introducing the project to any new team member or involving any new stakeholder.

- Reference the goal frequently during early meetings, particularly when making a decision, as in: "Let's remember that our ultimate goal is to have the right products on hand and to decrease excess inventory; therefore . . ." You will be showing the team how the goal is related to all team activity.

 **Establish the Project's Organizational Alignment**

Provide the context for the project within the organization. What relationship does this project have with other projects? How will this project affect strategic goals? If this project shares personnel and other resources with other projects, are there established priorities among these projects? Though as project managers we often consider our own project to be important, we need to be realistic about how it fits into the larger picture. The statement of work and business case will contain some information about the contribution this project has to the organization. Your sponsor will also be a source of information.

The organizational alignment of a project may be complex or abstract. As with the project goal, it may require time and repetition for the team to truly understand. In addition to your own explanation, you may enlist other project stakeholders to visit a project meeting to describe how the project will affect their operation. For example, information technology project teams typically benefit from spending time with the people that will be affected by their systems.

Demonstrate Management Support for the Project

A project sponsor's job is to champion the project manager and the project team. As discussed in Chapter 3, a temporary project team needs the power and authority of a sponsor in order to overcome organizational obstacles. The team members also need to feel that their team is important to the organization—to know that the team is not alone in its pursuit of the project goal. The attention of a sponsor signals that both the project and the team matter.

As a project manager, look for opportunities to invite the sponsor or other involved executives into team activities. When working with your sponsor and executive management, ask them how they would like to participate in the project, particularly to demonstrate support for the team. Here are some classic sponsor activities:

- Attend the kickoff meeting to explain the purpose and importance of the project.
- Continue to attend project team meetings periodically throughout the project, particularly after significant accomplishments, to recognize the team's performance.
- Recognize individual performance with a phone call or visit to the team member.

As a sponsor displays interest in the project, enthusiasm will build within the project team. Early visible involvement by management builds excitement; sustained visible involvement builds commitment.

Actions Speak Louder than Words

Unfortunately, many of us can recall projects where sponsorship consisted of all talk and no action. *Management support* is one of our five project success factors. Teams know when they have management support because they get sufficient resources to accomplish their work and receive timely attention to problems.

Build Team Relationships Based on Understanding Strengths and Diversity

Strong teams rely on positive, productive relationships between team members—relationships the project manager can consciously foster.

A project team with positive, productive relationships does not mean everyone on the team will be personal friends who choose to socialize outside of the work environment. Rather, these relationships recognize that sharing a common goal as colleagues, all will be more successful by treating each other with respect, cooperation, and accountability to the team. These relationships are characterized by several factors that we can work to build.

- The team knows the strengths and contributions of each member. Each of us brings technical expertise, customer knowledge, business savvy, and a range of other talents to the project team. This awareness enables us to increase our reliance on each other.

- We understand our diversity of styles and the benefits and potential risks that exist when we bring together introverts and extroverts, detail-oriented and big-picture thinkers, people who are task oriented and those who are people oriented, and so on.

- We trust our teammates to keep their word and perform as they have promised.

- We see each other as human beings as well as coworkers. Human beings get sick, have honeymoons, celebrate birthdays, become stressed by family and work trade-offs, and generally have a range of emotions and experiences that go beyond the workplace.

These factors, particularly trust, can be difficult to build, but they begin with the team's leader creating opportunities for team members to get to know each other early in the project. Try some of these activities:

- Interview each team member as they come on board to understand the person's background, strengths, and personal goals for the project. Then, at the next team meeting, introduce that person to the rest of the team. Alternatively, you could ask each person to be prepared to introduce themselves, as long as it is clear in advance what you'll be asking them to say at the meeting.

- Bring food to a meeting. Better yet, schedule a working lunch, with the project picking up the tab. Breaking bread together is a strong symbol, and the downtime for eating will provide a bonding opportunity.

- Meet regularly in person, if that is possible. While all meetings should have a purpose and be productive, remember that the act of coming together for a shared purpose builds identity and a sense of belonging to the group.

- If the group is geographically separated, the sooner they get together, the better. A single daylong planning session early in the project will accelerate relationship building far faster than teleconferences or any other electronic media.

These are all simple activities that can be done in the context of other project tasks. Each contributes to people getting to know and understand each other. Of course, there are many project teams whose challenges justify hours or even days spent on activities whose sole purpose is to build stronger working relationships. These examples show the depth and variety available to us.

- Many personality and behavioral assessment tools have been developed to help people understand their own preferences and styles in performing work. The Myers-Briggs Type Indicator is probably the best known of these tools, but there are many more to choose from. Each attempts to help us see ourselves and others, and to understand how our different approaches affect teamwork. As a team leader, we could devote a few hours to using such a tool within our teams.

- Physically challenging team-building events have been designed to focus teams on their interpersonal dynamics. Usually facilitated by experts, these events range from learning to sail a boat to rappelling down a cliff to crossing a rope bridge suspended 40 feet in the air. In particular, these exercises strive to reveal the importance and existence (or lack) of trust among team members. Ideally, the lessons the teams learn from cooperating in these extreme events will carry back to the workplace.

Focusing on team relationships early speeds the growth of the team, but relationships are not static. It is the project leader's job to pay attention to this factor throughout the life of the project and to address relationships that become negative.

Summary of Building Team Identity

Forging a team identity is an organic process that benefits from repetition and attention. As you work to build these elements into your project team, recall Tuckman's stages of team development and adjust your style accordingly. The structure of your early attempts to clarify the goals and scope and provide a strong kickoff to the project will be welcomed when the team is Forming. Likewise, initial attempts to build relationships may be embraced and may seem productive, yet more attention may be necessary as the team reaches the Storming phase. If your investment in team identity pays off, you will find that your team progresses rapidly from Norming to Performing.

TEAM LISTENING SKILLS

When teams form around common challenges and overcome them with creativity and perseverance, strong communication skills are at work. In such a dynamic problem-solving environment, no communication skill is more important than listening, because it is through listening that we gain the value of another person's insight. In addition, effective listening builds trust and demonstrates respect during the give-and-take of creativity. As I work to understand your idea, I show you respect that builds trust and increases the likelihood that you will treat my ideas the same way.

Listening is a personal communication skill. The work of group problem solving requires that every team member have this. Therefore, it is the job of project leaders to model, teach, and coach this skill. Here we highlight some well-known guidelines you and your team can follow. As your team members develop this skill, it will contribute to the overall goal of building a positive team environment.

KEY CONCEPT — Active Listening

The term *active listening* implies that listening to others and actually understanding their intended message requires effort and skill. When you consider some of the naturally occurring obstacles to listening, it is easy to understand why.

- Physical distractions, such as a hot, stuffy conference room, telephones, or a computer screen with an e-mail in-box, can take our attention away from a speaker.

- Knowledge of a subject matter gives us preconceived ideas about what the speaker is saying. Whether we know a lot or a little, our own ideas might crowd out the idea the speaker is trying to transmit.

- The speaker's style or skill in speaking, when it is different from our own, can confuse us. Not everyone is good at clearly describing ideas or speaking concisely. Idioms and jargon of one company or geographical area need to be translated to outsiders.

- Mental noise from other problems we are facing, past experience with the speaker, frustration, or impatience with the meeting distracts us. Our brains are capable of thinking roughly twice as fast as we speak, which often leads to mentally drifting off to other topics at the same time we are listening.

For a summary of active listening tips, see the box on the next page.

Listening during team meetings requires even more skill than listening during one-to-one conversations. Many natural obstacles to listening are typically present during meetings. Obviously, whoever is leading the meeting should also lead the active listening, but that may not be sufficient. An honest dialogue may require several participants to use active listening techniques, such as summarizing or asking clarifying questions, in order to understand just one person's point of view. That makes it all the more important for the entire team to have these skills.

ACTIVE LISTENING TIPS

As you listen to others—whether in a one-on-one discussion or during a meeting—practice these behaviors to maximize your ability to understand their message.

1. Focus yourself *physically.* To the degree possible, eliminate environmental distractions. Provide the speaker an environment conducive to listening.

2. Use nonverbal cues to show you are involved in what the speaker is saying, including nodding your head, making eye contact, and leaning forward.

3. Provide feedback, paraphrasing or summarizing the speaker's statements to ensure that you understand them as the speaker intended.

4. Ask relevant follow-up or clarifying questions.

5. Listen for the *idea* behind the facts and data.

6. Suspend judgment on the speaker's statements. Understand his or her point first. As you ask questions or acknowledge points, remain neutral in your responses. "So, what you are saying is . . ." "From your point of view . . ." Demonstrate that you understand without revealing whether you agree or disagree.

During active listening, here are some behaviors you should work to avoid.

1. Don't try to solve the problem or give advice until it is asked for. Analyzing a problem with questions shifts the focus from the speaker to *your* hypothesis. "Have you tried . . . ?" "What happened before . . ." "Are you sure that is the issue?" You may be able to help the speaker solve a problem, but first you need to listen.

2. Don't judge what you are hearing, either positive or negative. Particularly don't share a judgment, as in, "That's not logical."

3. Don't shift the attention to yourself. This happens when we try to relate to the speaker, but end up talking about our own experiences, ideas, or emotions.

4. Finally, be aware of resistance and defensiveness by the speaker. Probing too deeply or playing psychiatrist may not be welcome.

These simple guidelines can get you started. As with any skill, your ability to listen will improve with practice.

For a thorough reference on the skills and value of listening, see Erik Van Slyke's *Listening to Conflict: Finding Constructive Solutions to Workplace Conflict,* American Management Association, 1999

 **The Most Important Skill:**
Suspending Judgment

The physical activities listed above help us engage our bodies and demonstrate our attention, but listening truly takes place only when we suspend judgment on what we are hearing before we respond.

For example, someone makes the following statement: "The best vacation is Phoenix in the summer."

Does the voice in your head respond, "Hah! The temperature in Phoenix averages over a hundred degrees a day in the summer—it's a terrible place to vacation!" Or does the voice say, "Phoenix in the summer? I don't understand. I'd better listen closely."

If the voice in your head sounds more like the latter, you have just suspended judgment in an effort to understand. If your voice responds more like the former statement, you made a judgment before you heard all the facts. When you present a new idea to your team or a team member, which response would you like from them?

Suspending judgment is a personal discipline that requires conscious practice. By applying this skill, we are choosing to delay forming an opinion or response to what the speaker is saying. Instead, we practice the active listening behaviors until we have established that we do understand.

This skill has additional value when the speaker is having difficulty articulating his or her idea. Whether because it is a sensitive subject, because the speaker is uncomfortable speaking in front of the group, or because the speaker lacks the language skills, if we don't work at it, we won't understand. When people with positions of authority practice this skill, it is even more powerful. Our patience and respect will demonstrate that we value the speaker's contribution. Demonstrating our respect reinforces the positive atmosphere we are trying to establish for our team.

Suspending Judgment Does Not Require Agreement

Once you have clearly understood the speaker, you are free to disagree. You have established, via summarizing or paraphrasing, that you understand the person's point. That was respectful. Now make your judgment and form your response.

Teach Your Team to Listen

CONCEPT

Effective listening is a habit that your entire team needs to develop. You can speed this development through several actions early in the project.

- Be aware of the skill level of the team. That will tell you how quickly and how formally you need to address the skill.

- Plan time to teach the skills. Over the course of the project, it is appropriate to spend some time attending to the team's effectiveness. Show a video, pass out and discuss a good article (or this chapter), or bring in a professional trainer to instruct the team.

- As the project leader, you can demonstrate effective listening, which teaches by example.
- Look for effective listening behaviors within the team. Point them out as you debrief a team meeting, emphasizing how active listening contributed to a better discussion.
- Add "active listening" as a desired behavior to your ground rules. Use the ground rules as a reminder during meetings if discussions start to degenerate into arguments.

Teaching the team to listen pays off rapidly. It is not a difficult skill, but it does take practice and a conscious attempt to improve.

Listening Is a Team-Building Activity

Our project teams come together temporarily to solve a series of problems. As the group learns to work together and struggles to find new solutions, they are likely to disagree time and time again. Though such disagreement is a sign of a healthy dialogue, not everyone is used to or comfortable with this type of disagreement or conflict. The listening skills we have described here enable the people to use respectful conversations as they discuss ideas, maintaining relationships while pursuing the best solution. To the degree that a team leader can teach these skills, it can help the team move more quickly through Tuckman's Storming phase.

Finally, listening skills have a special role in the high-performance team framework: All of the other capabilities depend on team members being able to listen effectively.

MEETING MANAGEMENT

Much teamwork is accomplished in meetings. We gather and distribute information, coordinate activities, uncover new problems, assign tasks, and make decisions. Meetings also reinforce team identity, as we gather to make progress on common goals. Productive meetings demonstrate all the characteristics of a high-performance team and produce a result that is beyond what any team members working individually could achieve. *Meeting management* is the last of our four topics that address the high-performance component of a positive team environment.

Unfortunately, we have all attended ineffective meetings that produced nothing but boredom and frustration. As the team's leader, we set the guidelines for running project meetings, whether we lead the meeting or somebody else does. The box that follows highlights commonly accepted guidelines for running effective meetings. During the meeting itself, every component of the high-performance team framework is in play, and weakness in any component will show up as behavior that detracts from the value of the meeting.

Meeting Structure and Stages of Team Development

The formality and structure of team meetings necessarily changes during the life of the project team. During the Forming stage, the team will welcome the structure provided by agendas, action items, and meeting minutes. As the team Storms, it is likely to become more challenging to run a meeting that stays on task—all the more reason to use these meeting management tools. Once the Forming stage begins, the benefits of structured meetings will start to appear as team members adopt effective meeting habits. Now you can begin to share the leadership of the meetings, a pleasure that will increase as the team reaches the Performing stage.

EFFECTIVE MEETING GUIDELINES

Meetings are held to accomplish work. Whether that is to coordinate tasks, distribute information, make decisions, or explore ideas, we expect specific accomplishments through attending the meeting. The guidelines here provide structure to make our meetings more efficient and productive. These guidelines are targeted to address meetings of anywhere from two to twenty people. When the group grows beyond that size, the dynamics change significantly, and some of these guidelines no longer make sense.

Before the Meeting

1. Send a meeting invitation specifying the purpose, planned start and finish times, and location of the meeting. Let everyone know in advance who else will be there.

2. Send out an agenda stating the purpose of the meeting and listing the major topics to be discussed. Assign a time frame and a topic leader for every topic. Frame each topic as specifically as possible, using a goal, so people know the objective of the discussion. "Goal: Agree on laptop performance requirements" is much clearer than simply "laptops." A strong agenda enables people to prepare for the meeting.

During the Meeting

1. Start on time. Reward promptness.

2. Review the process you expect to follow. If necessary, set ground rules and determine how decisions will be made (i.e., consensus, voting, or autocratic).

3. Have a recorder track decisions and the key points leading to the decisions. These will become the meeting minutes. Meeting minutes are not a transcript of the meeting, but a recap of the decisions made and their rationale.

---

4. Use the agenda to structure the meeting. If a topic appears to be too big to resolve within the time allocated, particularly if the entire group is not needed for resolution, develop an action item and handle it outside the meeting.

5. Drive topics to resolution. Summarize comments and bring the group to a decision.

6. During discussions, someone must monitor the group and control involvement. If you are seeking a group consensus, the meeting leader or facilitator must encourage fair participation.

Ending the Meeting

1. Summarize the meeting by reviewing the decisions and action items.

2. Be clear about the next meeting date.

3. Briefly wrap up each meeting with an evaluation of the meeting process. A simple method is to run a quick Plus-Delta exercise. On a chart put the headings + (*positive*) and Δ (*change*). Have meeting participants make two lists: what really worked about the meeting (the pluses) and what they would like to see changed (deltas).

4. End on time or get the group's permission to end later.

After the Meeting

Send out meeting minutes. The sooner these are issued, the more likely people will be to read and respond to them.

Following these simple guidelines demonstrates respect for your team by making all your meetings as productive as possible.

SUMMARY OF BUILDING A POSITIVE TEAM ENVIRONMENT

We want the people on our teams to hold themselves mutually accountable to a common goal. The team members want to trust each other and to be treated with respect. They also want to accomplish something, to know their energy and talents are producing results. Ground rules, listening skills, meeting management, and the actions that build team identity all work together to create a positive team environment, as shown on the left side of the arch in our high-performance team model (see Figure 10.1). As the team's leader, it is your job to put each of these pieces in place.

KEY CONCEPT — COLLABORATIVE PROBLEM SOLVING

There is ample evidence that decisions made by a group are superior to decisions made by a single manager or executive in isolation. A group can bring more background, information, and creativity to a problem. In addition, if the group that made the decision is responsible for its implementation, its members are likely to be more committed to making it work.

The advantages are clear, but not always easy to achieve. Even a project that has established a positive team environment can get bogged down in consensus or spend endless meetings flogging a dead horse. The components of *collaborative problem solving* enable a project team to harness the strength of the group to generate *creativity and productivity.*

It is easier to understand this collaborative problem-solving capability if we break it into four team competencies: problem analysis, conflict management, continuous learning, and the ability to use multiple decision modes. In practice, these skills are interwoven so tightly they appear as one, and if any of these elements are missing, the effectiveness of the others is diminished. The remainder of this chapter explores each of these topics, which together comprise the right side of the high performance team arch in Figure 10.1.

PROBLEM ANALYSIS

As individuals we vary in our approach and ability when it comes to analyzing problems. When we come together as a team, this variation becomes both a strength and a weakness. My ability to maintain a view of the big picture and see how the big pieces fit together is complemented by your attention to detail. Another team member's creativity brings a fresh perspective, encouraging us to look beyond the same old solutions. The risk, however, is that I may grow impatient with irrelevant details and unrealistic options, and a detail-oriented team member may lose commitment to our decisions because he or she perceives the team as jumping ahead, skipping the hard work in favor of quick solutions. As individuals with different styles, each of us can become frustrated and begin to disengage from the team because the group is not following a process that we personally consider practical or effective.

Minimizing the risks and maximizing the advantages of analyzing problems as a team requires an acknowledged problem-solving process and skill with problem analysis methods. As with all the topics in this chapter, entire books have explored these subjects. Our purpose here is to provide an understanding of the skills the team requires.

 Acknowledged Problem Analysis Method: Diverge and Converge

If you accuse me of jumping to a conclusion, it is not a compliment. The phrase suggests that I have not sufficiently understood the problem before I made a decision. It reflects the reality that problem analysis should be viewed as shown in Figure 10.2, diverging to gather facts and perceptions, then drawing conclusions to converge on a solution. Your accusation also reflects our different approaches to problem analysis—what you perceive as "jumping" may just be a different path of understanding the facts and options.

As a team, we all benefit when there is an acknowledged method of problem analysis, for three reasons:

1. We want to be sure the team is using sound problem analysis methods. Much study and practical experience has produced a field of generally accepted principles and techniques. Using these techniques will improve the quality of our decisions and, ultimately, our projects.

2. Having an acknowledged process provides a commonly accepted view of the correct steps for working through a problem. This reduces the frustration that results from being individuals with different styles and improves the group's unity and focus on each step.

3. An acknowledged process also provides a common language to describe the experience, which allows the team to improve the process. It enables us to talk about what we are doing. For example, "We agree we have developed a clear problem statement," or, "We need to stay in the alternatives-generation step longer."

There is certainly debate over the right steps to follow to solve a problem. The steps provided in the box that follows reflect generally accepted stages of analyzing a problem. You'll scale your use of this process depending on the complexity of the problem. For instance, you may follow these steps several times within a single meeting to

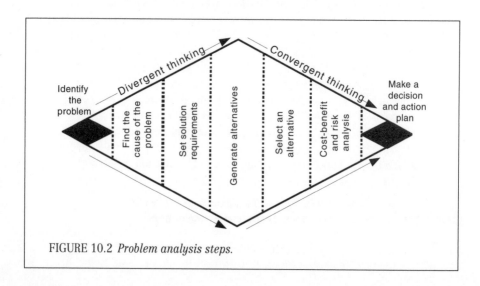

FIGURE 10.2 *Problem analysis steps.*

address small problems. For a major problem, the process may take weeks or even months and will be reflected in the tasks of your work breakdown structure. Whether your team uses this one or invents its own, as a project leader you can make sure the team has an acknowledged problem analysis process.

PROBLEM ANALYSIS STEPS

1. *Identify the problem.* The team agrees on the problem, the severity of the problem, and the desired state. The way the problem is defined will influence the subsequent analysis, so a clear understanding of the problem by the entire team is important.

2. *Find the true source of the problem.* Root-cause analysis ensures we dig deeper than the symptoms to uncover the real problem. Many forms of investigation may be required to determine the root cause, including interviewing stakeholders, gathering past performance data, and conducting tests.

3. *Set solution requirements.* These requirements describe our ideal state after the problem has been solved. They'll be used to compare among possible alternative solutions. Here is an example of a useful format for phrasing solution requirements.

The problem will be solved when:

We know _____

We have _____

We can _____

We are _____

4. *Generate possible alternative solutions to the problem.* We can't sufficiently emphasize the importance of this step. Finding breakthrough solutions is possible only when we devote time and energy to generating many potential solutions. During this step we must accept that many useless ideas will be generated in the process of finding some new useful ones. The team realizes there is inefficiency in creativity, enabling everyone to be more patient and focused on this step.

5. *Select an alternative.* Ideally, we've created several reasonable alternatives by this stage. Now we use the solution requirements to screen and prioritize the alternatives. There may be an obvious solution now, but if not, quantitative and qualitative comparison techniques help us sift through the options and select one.

6. *Perform risk and cost-benefit analysis on the selected option.* Risk analysis ensures that we have considered the disadvantages as well as the strengths of this option. Cost-benefit analysis checks to make sure the solution won't cost more than the problem. Based on the more detailed analysis of this step, the team may decide to consider another alternative that might be cheaper or have fewer risks.

7. *Make a decision and action plan.* Put the actions and responsibilities to carry out the decision in meeting minutes or into the project plan. Organize and file the results of the problem analysis in case you need to revisit the problem again in the future.

Problem Analysis Is a Discipline

Just as project management is a discipline made up of accepted techniques and processes, problem analysis has its own body of knowledge that is captured primarily in the quality management literature. The simple seven-step framework laid out in the box may be adequate for simple problems, but if your team is grappling with complex problems, you could benefit from exploring this field further.

As with other team skills we've described in this chapter, monitor the problem analysis skills of your team to determine if they would benefit from additional training. The presence or absence of these skills will have a tremendous effect on the team's collaborative problem-solving ability.

DECISION MODES

Groups have a variety of options available to them as they make decisions. Consensus, though often touted as the best mode, is only one. Teams can also decide by majority vote, delegate the decision to an expert or a subgroup, or allow the leader to make the decision after discussion. There are even times when the best decision is made by a leader without involving the group.

Given these choices, understanding the decision modes available and deciding when each is appropriate is an essential part of a team's collaborative problem-solving capability.

A team functions best when members know which decision mode they are applying to any problem and why. If part of my team expects a consensus decision, yet I intend to make the decision myself after listening to the team, people will become confused, disappointed, or resentful. As a leader, I need to understand the implications of choosing one decision mode over another. The following list describes common modes for making decisions and offers the strengths and weaknesses of each.

- *Consensus.* The entire team participates in the decision together, including understanding the problem and creating alternatives. Performed correctly, consensus is a powerful way to leverage the capability of a group, because it builds a solution using ideas from the entire team.

  Advantages. The decisions made through consensus can be far superior, and because they are involved in making the decision, the commitment of the team to the decision is very high.

  Disadvantages. The consensus process can take a lot of time, particularly if the team doesn't have the requisite skills. (See the box on Consensus Guidelines later in this section.) Also, there is a physical limit to the number of people who can realistically be involved in a consensus decision. For a group much larger than 15 people, the pace becomes glacial.

Consensus is a good choice for complex decisions with far-reaching consequences, where the quality of the decision and the commitment from the group outweigh the need for a speedy decision. A team in the Performing stage is likely to use consensus more frequently, both because they seek the best solution and because their consensus skills are mature enough to provide a reasonably quick decision.

- *Voting.* This method is completely democratic. It assumes the options are well understood, and a simple majority vote makes the decision.

  Advantages: It is quick and can include many people.

  Disadvantages: If the options are complex, it is less likely that they are well understood. Further, if there are more than two options, it can take multiple rounds of voting to identify a clear majority. Voting risks low commitment to the solution by the losing side.

  Best application. Voting is appropriate for well-understood options, particularly when there is a large group involved. Before using this technique, make sure that opposition to the decision by the losing side can't derail implementation. Voting is sometimes used as the fallback decision mode when a consensus process is bogged down and the time for the decision has arrived.

- *Delegating.* Allow one or a few of the team to make the decision because they are perceived to have the necessary information and expertise.

  Advantages: It simplifies the decision process because it requires fewer people.

  Disadvantages: The decision maker(s) must have the trust of the entire group, and they have the knowledge and ability to work independently of the group.

  Best application. Delegating works well when specialized knowledge is required and the decision makers are strong individual performers capable of managing themselves.

- *Autocratic.* The project manager makes the decision. The variable in this mode is the degree that the team is asked to contribute to the decision.

  Advantages: One person can make a decision faster than a group, particularly when that person is well informed. Often, the group leader has a perspective or responsibility that is different than the rest of the group's, which also makes it appropriate for the leader to make the final decision.

Disadvantages: A speedy, uninformed decision may be disastrous. Team commitment to the decision will depend on team commitment to the project manager. If the project leader always makes autocratic decisions and the team often disagrees with those decisions, trust in the leader and commitment to the team will disintegrate.

Ironically, strong teams need leaders who will make autocratic decisions. "Decisive" is an oft-cited characteristic of a good project leader. It's necessary when a choice must be made but there is insufficient information for the team to reach a consensus. At other times, the impact of the decision is small, so the time required for consensus building isn't justified. But the most important autocratic decisions are often those that have the biggest impact. The image of General Eisenhower setting the date for the Normandy invasion is one of a participative, yet still autocratic decision. Whether the team is Forming or Performing, asking for input to help make a decision is practical in order to make an *informed* decision, but the leader is the one who must make the call. The responsibility of leadership cannot always be shared with the team.

As the team leader, you can make the rest of the team conscious of the mode being used for any decision. For example, "The selection of our vendor will have such broad consequences that we will make this decision by consensus." Or, in the case of an autocratic decision, "I want each of you to give me your ideas and concerns about the layout for our new office space. I do value your views and I will take them into account as I make the decision."

Decision Modes Reflect the Team's Maturity

Clearly, the decision modes of the team will reflect the leadership style of the project manager, which in turn is influenced by the development stage of the team. For example, arriving at a consensus for a complex problem may be too difficult for the team early in the project when they are still forming. During the Storming phase, the team is likely to challenge a leader who is not using participative decision styles. This need to change leadership styles during the project increases the need for the project leader to be clear about which decision mode is being pursued from problem to problem. Further, the team's ability to participate in choosing decision styles relies on the entire team's awareness of the factors that cause each mode to be appropriate.

GUIDELINES FOR BUILDING A CONSENSUS DECISION

Building decisions through consensus can produce superior decisions, because we leverage the knowledge and skills of the team. Consensus is not the same as unanimity, where every participant agrees that the decision is the best choice. Rather, we reach a consensus when every participant can agree that the decision process was fair, that their perspective was heard and understood, and that each of them can support implementation of the decision.

Here are five leadership tips for reaching consensus in meetings:

1. *Follow a structured problem-solving process.* Begin with a clear understanding of the problem or decision to be made. Use the structure to create focus at each step of the process.

2. *Manage group participation.* Encourage people to use active listening skills. Ensure a balance of power—don't allow the most vocal to dominate or the least vocal to not participate. Use a method to ensure each person has been heard at each step of the process.

3. *Embrace conflict as a sign of creative thinking.* People should avoid changing positions just to avoid conflict. Examine differences of opinion thoroughly.

4. *Build consensus.* Seek alternatives that satisfy the goals of all members. Try to find ways to integrate multiple viewpoints.

5. *Know how you'll make the final decision.* Identify an alternative decision method in advance in case the team deadlocks.

The key to consensus is ensuring balanced participation and creating a decision everyone will support in implementation. To arrive at the final decision, Kristin Arnold offers the "Five L" scale.[2] Once it seems the group has come to a decision, the leader asks everyone to rank the decision on the Five L scale: You *loathe* it. You will *lament* it, complaining about the decision after the meeting. You can *live* with it. You *like* it. You *love* it! If there are people who will either loathe or lament the decision, then you aren't finished.

CONFLICT MANAGEMENT

Conflict is an inevitable result of group problem solving. In any project where two or more people need to make decisions, there will eventually be disagreement—which is why conflict management skills are absolutely necessary to build the collaborative problem-solving capability of a team.

Though it isn't always comfortable, high-performance teams actually use conflict to solve problems. They know conflict is a natural, valuable source of energy for the group. It's often a product of legitimate differences of opinion that must be resolved in order to move forward on a project. Working through these differences involves real learning and often results in significant breakthroughs.

There are two risks in any decision where conflict exists: First, the wrong decision may be reached, particularly if conflict affects the problem-solving process. Second, relationships may be damaged as the issue is resolved. The terms *win-win* and *win-lose* refer to the ability for positive relationships to be maintained while achieving the best decision. In situations where both sides will have to work together after the conflict is resolved—the reality for project teams—it is essential to both maintain the relationship *and* get a good decision.

Employing conflict to a team's advantage takes trust, respect, and lots of practice. Our own experiences with conflict can affect how we respond to it in team situations. Successful conflict resolution requires recognizing the common responses to conflict and understanding the techniques that allow you to make productive use of the conflict itself. The following list describes four common but *usually unproductive* approaches to conflict.[3] The team leader and team members should understand what these behaviors are and why they are unproductive. Then keep on the lookout for these approaches and head them off.

1. *Withdrawing from the conflict.* Avoid both the issues and the people associated with the conflict. This strategy relies on the belief that it is easier to avoid conflict than to work through it. If the issue is real, this approach just delays the inevitable and increases the tension as schedule pressure adds to the situation.

2. *Smoothing over the conflict.* Focus on the positive relationships and de-emphasize the areas of conflict. Smoothing prioritizes relationships over resolving disagreements, a short-term solution at best.

3. *Forcing resolution to the conflict.* Attempt to overpower others into accepting a position or solution without regard to the relationships within the group. Forcing behaviors include physical force, such as raising one's voice, ridiculing an idea, and the pure use of organizational authority, "I'm the boss, so do it my way." Though forcing does result in a decision, there may be very low commitment to the decision by those who perceive that it was forced on them. Clearly, forcing exhibits a lack of respect for other team members and threatens the positive relationships required in a high-performance team.

4. *Compromising, accepting a no-win solution.* Accept that neither side will get what they want. Each side accepts less than they want, with the consolation that they got as much as the other party. Though this strategy attempts to respect both parties, compromise is considered lose-lose because the solution doesn't satisfy anyone and the disappointment can cause resentment.

There are times when each of these strategies can be the right choice. We may apply the old wisdom "Choose your battles" when we avoid or smooth over a conflict because the issue at stake just isn't worth the emotional energy required to confront the problem, or the relationship has been under a lot of strain. Likewise, there is a time for compromise, for accepting that no commonly acceptable solution exists and at least a compromise allows the team to make a decision and move on. The rationale for forcing a decision does not apply often, particularly on teams where respect for each other is important.

Understanding these responses to conflict allows team members to recognize when someone is choosing an unproductive method to handle conflict. When the symptoms become evident, you need to switch to a better approach, known as *confronting conflict,* or simply, *problem solving.*

Confronting Conflict

KEY CONCEPT   Viewing conflict—disagreement among team members—as a source of *positive* creative energy doesn't make it fun or easy. The project team and the project manager should be on the lookout for conflict and steer its energy into productive problem solving by applying these guidelines.[4]

- *Prevent the conflict.* Even though we acknowledge that conflict will arise, we can avoid the stress of many conflicts by attending to the components of a high-performance team. Ground rules, effective listening, good meeting management, and a clear problem-solving process all contribute to a smoothly functioning team.

- *Acknowledge the conflict.* Point out the disagreement and recognize the emotions that are surfacing. Describing the conflict helps focus on the problem rather than on the people with whom we disagree. "We seem to disagree on the amount of memory these computers will need, and everyone is getting pretty excited about it."

- *Frame the conflict in reference to the project.* Make it clear how the decision being considered will ripple through other decisions. Understanding the context of the decision within the project also reveals the urgency to solve the problem: Can we wait for more information, or do we need to make a decision now?

- *Focus on interests, not positions.* Early life experience may have taught us that stubbornness wins arguments. That is a forcing response. Rather than digging in and defending positions, each side of the conflict should be explicit about their interest, goals, and requirements for the outcome. This focus reveals all that we have in common, a starting point for building a mutually satisfying solution.

- *Trade places.* Attempt to describe the situation from the other person's perspective. Understand that person's reluctance to embrace your proposal. Listen as he or she describes your perspective to you.

- *Separate identifying and selecting alternatives.* As described in the problem-solving method earlier, keep the group focused on identifying possible solutions first. Use clear ground rules that encourage generating many ideas, not evaluating them. As in brainstorming, this tactic leads to new thinking by combining ideas and allowing either side to offer unorthodox options to expand the thinking of the group.

- *Agree on process, if not outcome.* If the logjam continues, with no mutually agreeable solution appearing and no way for either side to accept the other's position, shift the focus to creating a process for deciding that both sides can accept. For example, can we find a third party everyone trusts to make the decision?

These guidelines are designed to maintain trust and respect within teams while working through disagreements. They work because everyone on the team shares the same overall project goal. On the other hand, these guidelines are not necessarily the right rules to follow for negotiating in an adversarial setting.

Conflict Management Requires Skill

Conflict management is not a natural talent for many people. Life and job experience may not have taught you the skills for confronting a conflict. If this is not your strength, enlist support from outside the project. Strong disagreement that polarizes the group or erupts into emotional arguments justifies involvement from a seasoned facilitator.

Conflict management is not just for project leaders; it is a team skill. If your team breaks down when facing disagreement, then it is time to focus on building this skill. This is one topic that the project leader probably shouldn't try to teach to the team. Unless you have been trained in this area, avoid the do-it-yourself approach. Most large organizations have human resources or organizational development professionals who are educated in conflict management. Invest in this skill early in the project to reduce Storming and speed the transition from Norming to Performing.

CONTINUOUS LEARNING

Pioneering, innovating, and delivering breakthrough solutions means taking risks and learning from mistakes. Continuous learning means that we recognize the need for the team to learn and improve throughout the project. The final component of our collaborative capability contains both the culture and habits that promote continuous learning throughout the project.

KEY CONCEPT **Create a Continuous Learning Culture**

High-performance teams learn rapidly, but only if the project's culture makes it safe. No one has more influence on this factor than the project leader. Do we punish every failure? Do we quickly dismiss new or uncommon ideas? Are we willing to question our own perceptions in order to fully understand an opposing point of view? Do we recognize ineffective habits—our own as well as the team's—and consciously change them? Our daily actions set the tone for the team. The box that follows offers insights to the kinds of actions we can take every day to show we value team learning.

PROJECT MANAGERS CAN SPEED UP TEAM LEARNING

Project leaders who recognize the need for the team to learn, change, and improve throughout the project can follow these guidelines to encourage the team to both take risks and learn from mistakes.

- *Be accessible.* Creativity and curiosity are difficult to schedule. Planning to be available makes it clear that others' opinions are welcomed and valued and makes interaction possible.

- *Ask for input.* Develop a team habit of asking for and sharing information. Frequently ask team members for their input, observations, and opinions. You'll be surprised at how many people withhold critical information or informed opinions until they are directly asked for their input. Somebody else trained them not to share; now it's your turn to help them create a new habit.

- *Recognize the need to learn.* Characterize the project as an organizational challenge—how will we work together to overcome the problem?—rather than attack it as a purely technical challenge.

- *Serve as a model.* Admit to your own mistakes. That sends the signal that errors and concerns can be discussed without fear of punishment.

- *Enlist full participation.* Emphasize that the challenge is difficult and requires active participation from every member. Nonparticipants may be afraid of making mistakes, but their fear doesn't help the team.

- *Eliminate fear.* Fear of losing face or losing respect for saying the wrong thing or asking for help is an obstacle to sharing ideas or learning from others. Ground rules should establish the value of curiosity, team learning, and honesty.

- *Recognize success.* Learning can happen in small increments. Use frequent, informal opportunities to recognize what has been learned. Conscious awareness of learning builds momentum and confidence.

Recognizing the value of team learning puts an added burden on the team leader at the outset of the project. Following these guidelines instills learning values and habits in the team, thus accelerating their growth and making your job a little easier.

Source: Amy Edmondson, et al., "Speeding Up Team Learning," *Harvard Business Review,* October 2001.

Continuous Learning Habits

It may seem as though the habits that contribute most to continuous learning have been previously discussed: setting ground rules, routine self-assessments, and following active listening and consensus decision-making guidelines to promote honest discussion. But teams can do all of these things and not reach their potential. John Redding, author of *The Radical Team Handbook,* notes that routine self-assessment by project teams is fairly common. What differs, he notes, is whether the assessments lead to new or deeper understanding of the problems the team is facing.[5] Likewise, many teams use ground rules to set norms without developing the habits that create original solutions. What makes the difference?

Ground rules and self-assessments are designed to reinforce desired behaviors, so if you want outside-the-box thinking, ask for it! The following list describes the behaviors you can ask for with ground rules. As the project moves forward, when you debrief a meeting's effectiveness or run a periodic lessons-learned session, be able to cite specific examples of these actions.

Actively identify and question assumptions. Assumptions constrain our thinking, often unconsciously. When we define assumptions as "a premise not supported by objective evidence or concrete information," we may find we are using more assumptions than facts to drive our thinking.[6] If you can't find facts to support an assumption, then be willing to question the assumption, and be cautious about letting it drive decisions.

Strive for honesty over conformance. As discussed earlier in the chapter, some people avoid conflict in order to maintain harmony. That leads to suppressing bad news or new information that contradicts our plans. If the real problems are discussed in the hall *after* the meeting, it's a danger sign that people are avoiding the truth.

Make learning a conscious goal on an ongoing basis. When debriefing a meeting, ask these questions: What did we learn? What do we need to learn? What information could improve our understanding? As another example, Redding suggests that, when discussing an issue, team members should begin by asking questions rather than presenting solutions.[7]

Be disciplined in creativity. That may sound illogical, but finding the best answer for a complex problem often means viewing it from many perspectives and exploring many options. Employ techniques that force the team to dig deeper to uncover the root of a problem or cause more potential solutions to be produced. Brainstorming is a well-known example of disciplined creativity, but many other techniques exist. Finding specific techniques to promote idea generation and providing the time for creativity are signals to the team that new ideas and thorough analysis are valuable.

Question the project's goal, scope, and plan. These are the foundations of all activity for the team. They were set early in the project. Progress is likely to shed new light on the assumptions and facts that drove the original business case. Periodically question the premise for the project. To paraphrase common wisdom, if you are climbing a ladder and find it is leaning against the wrong wall, quit climbing and move the ladder!

Peter Senge's landmark book, *The Fifth Discipline,* introduced corporate America to the idea of a learning organization. In this book and its companion, *The Fifth Discipline Fieldbook,* Senge and others describe how a wide array of methods produce a culture that values curiosity, truth, and original thinking.[8] As a project leader, you can use these and other sources to educate your team on both the values and behaviors that promote continuous learning.

Continuous Learning Unleashes Team Potential

Continuous learning values and behaviors tie our high-performance framework together in several ways. All of the previous components of both a positive team environment and collaborative problem solving must be in place for the continuous learning behaviors to function. Adding this final capability lifts the team out of the ruts of seeing problems and options in the same old way, thus releasing the true creativity of your united group.

SUMMARY OF COLLABORATIVE PROBLEM SOLVING

Project teams cause change and deliver unique results, solving problems every step of the way. A mature high-performance team combines the four components described in this section to move through these problems with both efficiency and effectiveness: Using a structured approach to *problem solving* provides focus and a common language. The ability to switch among *decision modes* leverages the strength of group decisions while maintaining momentum. *Conflict management* skills enable individuals to bring contrasting perspectives to build better ideas and maintain team relationships. Finally, the culture and habits of *continuous learning* promote the creativity necessary to discover the best solutions.

As these skills increase, the benefits of a positive team environment are magnified. Commitment, unity, and perseverance combine with creativity and continuous learning to maximize the strengths of all team members. The team is more likely to meet its goal, and the journey is more exciting and satisfying.

JOB SATISFACTION

We have framed our discussion of high-performance teams by focusing on the productivity benefits such teams produce. Productivity is important to our project-driven organizations because it brings down the total cost of delivering a project. But high-performance teams have another benefit, one that is harder to grasp but perhaps of even greater importance. When we work with people whom we trust and respect, when our individual efforts are multiplied by our teammates, when we overcome huge challenges and deliver to the best of our potential, we have pride and joy in the work we perform.

The satisfaction of delivering a project on time, on budget, and with a superior product is brief. Our daily work lives are filled far more with the journey to the goal than with the momentary enjoyment that comes from meeting the goal. When we devote our energy to building high-performance teams, we give our teammates and ourselves one of the greatest gifts available in the workplace: a job we can enjoy.

END POINT

This chapter has emphasized that project team members are challenged to work interdependently to solve many problems. These problems can be simple or complex, but every project is, essentially, a series of decisions to make and problems to solve. The greater our team's need to work interdependently, the more we need to trust each other and the more we need the skills to work together. Since project teams are temporary, each project team must *learn* to work together.

The topic of team leadership is large and covers far more than we can address in this single chapter.[9] For that reason, we have limited our scope to presenting a framework of specific skills and attributes that are necessary in a high-performing team.

The high-performance team framework identifies the factors that must be present for a team to reach its synergistic potential: to deliver more as a team than the individuals working alone ever could. A project manager helps the team establish a positive environment for daily interaction by setting ground rules for team behaviors, ensuring the team uses good listening skills, practicing good meeting management, and building team identity. To enable the team to face problem after problem together, the project manager works to improve its collaborative capability, including teaching the team problem solving and conflict-resolution skills.

Leadership is the keystone of a high-performance team. Among the many important characteristics of a good leader, this chapter recognizes several as essential for leading a project team:

- Maintaining a strategic vision and keeping it attached to the tactical plan
- Developing a culture that promotes learning during the project
- Giving attention to individual team members to keep them bonded to the project
- Consciously attending to the factors identified in the high-performance team framework
- The ability to flex leadership style to the needs of the team

The leadership actions and team factors described in this chapter take energy and effort. Though project managers are routinely asked for cost and schedule status, we are rarely asked for an update on the health of the team. That makes it easy to stay focused on task execution rather than team process. Investing in building a high-performance team requires the conviction that a cohesive team with mature problem-solving skills does make a difference to the team's productivity.

Finally, we have addressed another benefit of applying the concepts in this chapter. A high-performance team gives us more than high productivity; it gives us the joy and satisfaction that is possible when we reach our potential.

Communication

INTRODUCTION

Although it's been said before, it is worth repeating: *Every technique in every chapter of this book can be used every day of the project.* Figure 2.2, on page 21, showed the continuing relationships among the techniques of defining, planning, and controlling a project. The primary difference in controlling, as opposed to defining or planning, is that controlling refers to the project management oversight required to actually execute approved projects. Project control adds techniques for project communication and for measuring progress.

KEY CONCEPT — PROJECT COMMUNICATION

Communication ranks high among the factors leading to the success of a project. Specifically, what is required is *constant, effective communication among everyone involved in the project.*

Projects are made up of people getting things done. Getting the right things done in the right way requires communication among all the stakeholders. As project managers, we spend a great deal of our time communicating. This includes setting and getting agreement on goals, coordinating people, discovering and solving problems, and managing expectations. (We've addressed these topics throughout this book.) What this means is that from the statement of work through risk management and detailed planning, every project management technique is a method of communicating.

This chapter presents several project-oriented techniques for ensuring that the right people have the right information to make the necessary decisions and carry them out. You will recognize some of these techniques from previous chapters:

- Communicating within the team
- Communicating with management and customers
- Change management
- Closeout reporting

Communication is a vital skill for project managers. Project managers need to be able to write and speak well, lead meetings effectively, and resolve conflicts constructively. They also need to listen well, so that they really understand what's being said. Some of these topics are addressed in this chapter; others are addressed in Chapter 10; but to truly teach these essential communication skills is beyond the scope of this book. This chapter describes the communication *responsibilities* of a project manager without going into depth on communication skills. In addition, the downloadable forms found at the end of this chapter emphasize that structuring our communication on projects leads to greater consistency and effectiveness.

COMMUNICATING WITHIN THE PROJECT TEAM

Project team members have four major communication needs:

1. *Responsibility.* Each team member needs to know exactly what part of the project he or she is responsible for.

2. *Coordination.* As team members carry out their work, they rely on each other. Coordination information enables them to work together efficiently.

3. *Status.* Meeting the goal requires tracking progress along the way to identify problems and take corrective action. The team members must be kept up to speed on the status of the project.

4. *Authorization.* Team members need to know about all the decisions made by customers, sponsors, and management that relate to the project and its business environment. Team members need to know these decisions to keep all project decisions synchronized.

Each technique in this section addresses two or more of these communication needs.

ENLISTING COOPERATION

Marlene Kissler

It is rare for a project of any size not to rely on at least one person or group outside your department or even your company. Even in a minor role, these external players have the potential to loom large if they fall behind schedule. So be proactive in making them a successful part of your project. Even in the best of circumstances, with support from management, a competent contact person, and clearly defined specifications, things can go wrong. It seems as if this should be a simple relationship: All you need to do is make a phone call to introduce yourself, briefly explain your project and what she needs to do, and give her the name of the contact within your group. Then you can tell her the major project milestones, invite her to call any time she has questions or concerns, and ring off.

But if you only do that, it's likely that you'll find out a few weeks later that nothing has been done—that this "minor" component of your project may limp along behind schedule for the rest of the project, perhaps eventually affecting your critical path. The component may have to be minutely tested for every function. In short, that small but now significant portion of the project has become a disaster. Why?

To answer this, you need to consider the situation from the contact person's point of view: Perhaps, on the day you called, she was distracted by another problem and didn't catch everything you said; then later on, when she looked at what she did write down, it didn't make any sense. To her, you were just a disembodied voice full of your own self-importance, and this rubbed her the wrong way. She may have felt that your assignment had been thanklessly dumped on her; perhaps her supervisor "volunteered" her without reducing her existing workload. She never called the contact you gave her because she didn't know where to begin and didn't want to appear foolish. And, because your project never came up in status meetings with her supervisor, the whole thing was easy to shuffle to the bottom of her things-to-do list.

The lesson here is that when working with people outside your group, your department, or even your company, you need to overcome any tendency to assume too much and minimize contact; in actuality, these are the people who need interpersonal contact the most.

Here are some tips to help you avoid the pitfalls described in this scenario:

1. Make personal contact. Whenever possible, arrange a face-to-face meeting with contact people. Don't interact solely over the phone or by memo unless you work in different countries. Establish some rapport face-to-face.

2. Start with a short warm-up visit; this should be no more than a brief introductory meeting at a mutually convenient time. Send a friendly memo with a succinct overview of your project prior to the meeting. Don't blindside them with a cold call, filled with details they can't absorb. Instead, give them some more documentation and some time to prepare for the in-depth follow-up meeting. Allow them ample time to review it and bring their questions.

3. Ask for their help. Don't assume that they are already on board psychologically. The tone of your initial meeting should be "Will you help me?" not "You will do this." Ask if they can meet the projected schedule. Give them an honest opportunity to say no. And make sure they have a realistic workload and support from their manager.

4. Personally introduce them to their contacts and technical resources in your company or department. Walk them to the office of each person they will need to work with or get information from and introduce them. Sit in on high-level meetings if necessary. Make sure your group is accessible and helpful.

5. Provide an in-depth explanation in person, including documentation they can refer to later. Either personally review the project at the required level of detail with them or make sure the right person does. Don't force them to ask for everything.

6. Invite them to all meetings. That includes the kickoff meeting as well as all status and impromptu meetings. Treat them like full team members. Even though they may not choose to attend everything, give them the option.

7. Include them in the information loop. Make sure they are on all relevant distribution lists. They need to know project status, design changes, and schedule adjustments just as much as the other stakeholders.

8. Do milestone check-ins. The early ones are the most important. Personally review the deliverables. Be sure to catch miscommunications up front. Be explicit in your feedback about what has been done right and what needs improvement. Once you're comfortable that the contact people are on track, you can then do high-level check-ins.

9. Include them in all acknowledgment meetings and accomplishment write-ups. Everyone likes to have his or her name associated with a successful project. Make the acknowledgments appropriate to their level of contribution.

10. Write them personal thank-you notes. Acknowledge that their contributions required effort above and beyond their regular assignments (if this was the case).

11. Write a memo to their supervisor specifically describing their contributions. Be honest, fair, and timely with your report.

But why bother with all this time-consuming personal contact? Here are several reasons.

The first is that it will ensure the success of your project. If you don't use your "soft" management skills, all the "hard" skills in the world won't get your project completed. Because people get the work done, people skills are what will encourage them to do it right.

The second reason relates to your product or service. Every component and every person on your project is important, and this includes interfaces with projects and people outside your project. If it fails in any area, your project and others will be negatively impacted, perhaps in ways you may not even be aware of until serious damage has been done.

The third reason to pay special attention to personal contact has to do with your career and your reputation. A good project manager wants to be known as a person with whom people want to work. Yes, there may have been a few successful projects that left dead bodies and bad feelings in their wake, but you need to consider all the projects that will follow the present one; in short, you need to consider your career. It's never worthwhile to stay on bad terms with people you have worked with; you may need them for your next project; they may get transferred to your department, or you might get transferred to theirs. One of you may end up as the other's boss. You never know.

In addition, the people you work with have coworkers, spouses, friends, and acquaintances in the industry. The bigger the impact you've had on them—positively or negatively—the more likely your name will come up—positively or negatively. If people feel that you dealt with them fairly and helped them to do a good job (or at least to avoid failure), your good reputation will follow you.

Marlene Kissler earned her MBA at the University of Washington. She has been a project manager and system manager for Fortune 500 companies.

Making Task Assignments Clear

Projects and project managers need clear direction if they are to succeed; this is why developing the statement of work is so worthwhile. Team members also need clear direction. Fortunately, all the work that's gone into project planning tells them just what they need to know. Every work package is like a miniproject, with timelines, dependencies, and deliverables. Whether you are assigning work to an individual performer or to a vendor, these basic rules should be observed:

- Explain the deliverables. Be sure they know exactly what they are supposed to deliver, including any completion criteria that will be used to judge it.

- Be clear about the level of effort expected and the due dates. The network diagram is a good tool to explain how their pieces fit into the whole project.

- If you know of any obstacles they can expect or special information they'll need, make sure they know it, too. Set them up for success.

- Hand out work assignments personally, allowing plenty of time for questions and discussion. These meetings should be considered an investment in team performance: The better you prepare them, the better they'll perform.

We can't overemphasize the importance of clear task assignments, but it doesn't have to be difficult. The downloadable task assignment form at the end of the chapter covers the basic information a team member needs.

Individual Status Meetings

Plan on spending time with every member of the team on a regular basis. Remember, your job is to make them more productive, and you can't do that if you don't understand what they're working on—and what problems they're struggling with. The project status meeting just doesn't allow for this level of interaction. The project manager must take responsibility for setting up these meetings. Even though a manager might say, "I have an open-door policy; my team doesn't have to wait for a special meeting; they can find me any time they want," this would be true only if the manager was always at his or her desk. In reality, project managers spend a lot of time in meetings and can be difficult to find. If you make team members seek you out, they may wait until their problems have grown too big to solve easily; the same problems might have been nipped early on if a meeting had been held sooner.

Put the Meetings on the Calendar

Many project managers intend to spend a lot of time with team members, but as the project goes on they are just too busy. The best bet is to put time for every team member on your weekly calendar. That way you've planned in advance to be available.

The Kickoff Meeting: Start the Project with a Bang

In football, the kickoff represents a clear, decisive start. Everyone knows the game is under way. Projects can start the same way. The kickoff meeting brings all the stakeholders together to look each other in the eye and commit to reaching the goals.

A kickoff meeting usually marks the beginning of the execution phase of a project. By this time, the statement of work and project plan have been approved and the team is assembled. It's an opportunity to celebrate initiation of the project. Here's a format for a kickoff meeting:

- The sponsor leads the meeting and takes the opportunity to explain the project's purpose and connection to the overall business.
- The customers are introduced; they offer an explanation of the project's importance to their business.
- The project manager is introduced and enthusiastically endorsed by the sponsor.
- Project team members are introduced, if there are not too many. Vendors and contractors also need to be introduced.
- The coffee mugs, T-shirts, or other project memorabilia are passed out. This is a good time to do this, rather than at the end of the project, because they can help in creating a sense of unity and team spirit.
- Celebrate. Everyone needs to get to know each other and communicate their enthusiasm for the project.

On big projects there are usually too many team members to introduce at the kickoff meeting. So have kickoff meetings for teams within the project, too. The hour or two spent on each of these meetings is an investment in team cohesion and performance. It will pay off.

Project Status Meetings

Keeping a project on track requires regularly scheduled meetings to both share information and make decisions. A good project status meeting meets a lot of communication needs within the project team. Status meetings give the project manager an opportunity to:

- Increase team cohesion; status meetings are often the only time the entire team gets together.

- Keep the team informed about project developments from sources external to the team, such as from the sponsor, the customer, or management.

- Identify potential problems or share solutions to common problems.

- Ensure that the team understands the progress of the project and works together to determine any necessary changes to the project plan.

- *Make sure that the entire team shares the responsibility of meeting all the project objectives!*

Project status meetings rely on a participative management style. They build on the team's involvement in planning the project; the manager should encourage the same kind of involvement to keep it on track. This attitude is based on the philosophy that involvement leads to ownership, and ownership leads to greater commitment and accountability. In addition to the basic rules for running an effective meeting that were covered in Chapter 10, the following guidelines are useful for running a project status meeting:

- Be prepared. In addition to your agenda, everyone attending the meeting needs to have an open task report (OTR) *before* the meeting begins. (Table 11.1 shows an open task report.) An OTR is a subset of the project plan listing any tasks that should have been completed but weren't, plus the tasks scheduled for the next two reporting periods.[1] (A *reporting period* is defined as the period between status meetings. If you have a status meeting every week, then a reporting period is one week.)

- Include the part-time team members who have been working on project tasks or who will be working on them during the next two reporting periods.

- Use the meeting to disseminate decisions made by management or customers. Be sure to pass on any positive feedback from these stakeholders.

- Using the open task report, get the status of every task that should have been started or completed since the last status meeting.

- Take advantage of the fact that the entire team is available to consider what action needs to be taken on any problems. If special action needs to be taken, be sure that you *write it down*. Either add a task to the project plan or an action to the issues log. Every action should have a due date and a person responsible for its completion. (A downloadable issue log is included at the end of this chapter.)

TABLE 11.1 OPEN TASK REPORT (OTR)

OTR for a 10/14 Status Meeting

ID	Task Name	Responsibility	Plan Start	Actual Start	Plan Finish	Actual Finish
7	Task G	Lee	10/5	10/5	10/12	
8	Task H	Chris	10/8		10/14	
12	Task I	Lee	10/17		10/25	
15	Task O	Lee	10/20		11/2	
22	Task V	Chris	10/25		11/7	

The OTR acts as an agenda for progress reporting and near-term planning.

The OTR includes tasks that are incomplete but scheduled for completion and tasks in the next two reporting periods.

- Don't try to solve problems that are too big for the meeting or that don't include everyone present. If a problem takes more than five minutes to resolve, assign it as an action item.
- Review the readiness for future tasks on the OTR. Are the right people assigned? Are there any known obstacles to performing the tasks as planned?
- Review project logs, including issues logs (see Table 11.2) and the risk log. Are the issues and risks being resolved, or do they need to be escalated to higher management?

When team members participate in managing the project, they are more likely to take responsibility for its success. This participation changes the project manager from an enforcer to an enabler, and the team from individual performers to team members. If a member is behind on his or her work, peer pressure is more effective at boosting this individual's output than management pressure. A project manager at one software company takes it one step further: "We rotate leadership of the weekly status meeting. Everyone has a sense of ownership over the project."

With voice mail, faxes, e-mail, and Internet communication available, it may seem old-fashioned to bring people together around a conference table every week. Struggling with a busy schedule might tempt us to replace project status meetings with virtual meetings via e-mail or voice mail. But don't be fooled: Humans are complex animals, and communication happens in many ways. For example, reluctant bearers of bad news may first use their body language to report their feelings; a discouraged demeanor should signal the project manager to probe deeper. In addition, problem solving and team building

TABLE 11.2 ISSUES LOG

An *issue* is a problem or obstacle the project team doesn't have the power to resolve. Every issue is recorded and tracked with some basic information:

Issue ID—Unique identifier, probably a number, assigned as each issue is identified.
Status—An issue is either open or closed. Keeping closed issues in the log is one form of project history.
Description—What is the issue and what is the impact if it is not resolved?
Assigned to—The project team member (or project manager) responsible for pursuing resolution.
Date identified—Date the issue was originally added to the log.
Last action/current status—The date of the last action, a description of the action, and the current status of the issue. Leave all the action/status lines in the log as a record of how the action was pursued.

become more natural when people can look each other in the eye or slap each other on the back. Successful project managers recognize the benefits of face-to-face communication, balance it with the need to be efficient, and run their meetings so that they are a good use of everyone's time.

Long-Distance Status Meetings Benefit from Formality

Project teams that are geographically dispersed don't get the benefit of informal communication of the kind that happens in the break room or hallway. Conference calls and videoconferencing bring people together, but they need an additional level of formality to make sure all the issues are raised and everyone is heard. The open task report provides the structure for keeping all parties on track and ensuring that all the details are discussed.

Use the Fast Foundation in Project Management Templates

At the end of this chapter you'll find some basic downloadable templates for planning a meeting and reporting status. In addition, you could use the basic action plan found at the end of Chapter 8 for communication on small projects.

Set Communication Expectations

Managing expectations is a repetitive theme in project management, and it applies equally to project communication. The communication plan described in Chapter 4 outlined the communication channels and responsibilities for project participants. Putting the communication structure in place by setting up the schedule for meetings and status reports, establishing the location of issue logs (see Table 11.2), and publishing change management procedures makes it easier for people to know both what to expect and what is expected of them.

The Project Kickoff Checklist

A strong beginning to the project creates positive momentum. The downloadable project kickoff checklist, at the end of this chapter, will help.

COMMUNICATING WITH MANAGEMENT AND CUSTOMERS

"Successful projects meet stakeholder expectations." This mantra for project managers bears repeating, with this addendum: Of all the stakeholders to satisfy, customers and management top the list. The communication plan should detail the strategy not only for *informing* these stakeholders, but for *actively managing their expectations* as well.

Recall from Chapter 4 that when formulating the communication plan, the project manager needs to ask certain questions about relaying information to management and customers.

- Who needs information and why?
- What type of information will they need, in what detail, and how frequently?
- When you communicate with customers and management, what will your goal be and which medium will best accomplish that?

Answering these questions will help you to manage the expectations of these important stakeholders as well as obtain timely decisions from them.

Confronting the Facts

The best way to communicate difficulties to customers and managers is simply to present them with facts. When projects are late or over budget, the sooner the problem is acknowledged the easier it will be to solve. Putting off the bad news is rarely good for you or your project. The impact of the bad news is likely to grow and damage your credibility.

CONTROL DOCUMENTS

KEY CONCEPT

In Chapter 6, we described intermediate deliverables as essential products produced during the project that may not be part of the final product. These intermediate products vary from industry to industry—software development requires a list of product functions and features, while residential construction requires a list of the carpets, kitchen appliances, and other materials selected by the homeowner. Design documents such as blueprints are another example. Intermediate products such as these are both a record of decisions and a basis for action. Plumbers, electricians, and carpenters, for instance, carry out the engineering decisions represented on a blueprint. Therefore, it is critical that these documents be kept accurate and up-to-date, because they represent the series of decisions that lead up to the final product. They are called *control documents* because they are tools to maintain control over the product and project.

THE CHANGE MANAGEMENT PROCESS

KEY CONCEPT

Every kind of project faces changes. During a kitchen remodel, the customers might change their minds about appliances, or a certain type of window might be unavailable. During a software development project, the competition might release a product with some exciting new features, forcing the development team to add these features as well. The specific change management process you follow should fit the size and complexity of your project; you will need to pay special attention to the number and diversity of your stakeholders. But every change process is based on the same fundamental model shown in Figure 11.1. Downloadable forms for requesting a change and tracking changes throughout the project are found at the end of this chapter.

There are two parts to the change management process: the steps leading up to the initial approval of a product and the process for controlling changes to that product. As Figure 11.1 shows, once the stakeholders accept a product, it becomes "controlled" and any subsequent changes must pass through the change management process.

Change management planning—establishing how the process of change will take place—occurs during the project definition stage. You will need to select the members of the change board and decide how often meetings will be held. The intermediate products that will be

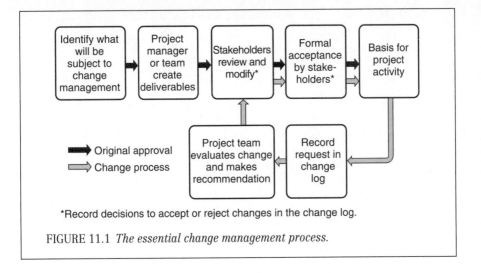

FIGURE 11.1 *The essential change management process.*

subject to change management need to be identified and a configuration management structure created. (*Configuration management* means controlling the different versions of the product. It is explained later in this section.)

Figure 11.1 describes the eight basic components common to every change management process:

1. *Identification of deliverables.* Identify all the project deliverables that will be subject to change management. The list will include everything that all stakeholders must approve, including requirements descriptions, design documents, and, of course, the statement of work.

2. *Creation of the intermediate deliverables.* The project manager and team develop these intermediate deliverables as they execute the project. As each of these deliverables is created, it becomes a candidate for stakeholder approval.

3. *Stakeholder evaluation/modification.* Once the product is created, various stakeholders will evaluate it and may request modifications. This step, along with continued development of the product, is repeated until the appropriate stakeholders are satisfied with the documents.

4. *Formal acceptance.* Stakeholders formally accept the product, producing a record of who approved the product and the approval date. At this point, the record becomes a control document; it is now a basis for action, and project team members will begin to execute the decisions represented by the product. These approved products are now subject to configuration management.

5. *The recording of change requests.* As ideas for change come in from the stakeholders, a designated team member records all change requests in a change log, noting their source, the date, and a description of the change. Each change request will have a unique identifier, usually a number, so that it can be tracked and referenced.

6. *Evaluation of requests and recommendation.* On a regular basis, the project manager or a designated team member will evaluate all potential changes for their impact on cost, schedule, and product quality and make a recommendation to accept or reject the change. Both the evaluation and the recommendation are recorded in the change log.

7. *Ongoing stakeholder evaluation/modification.* Stakeholders consider the proposed change to the control documents and the recommendation from the project manager. There are three possible outcomes to this evaluation: (1) The change is accepted as recommended or with minor modifications; (2) if the request has merit, but the decision maker(s) need(s) additional information, the request may be sent back to the project team with specific questions (this step may be repeated until the request is accepted or denied); (3) the request is denied and the reasons for denial are recorded in the change log. No matter what the outcome, the status of the request is updated in the change log and the originator is notified of the result.

8. *Formal acceptance.* When stakeholders formally accept the change, this acceptance will be recorded in the change log, including who approved the change, the date of the approval, and the impact. The change may also produce an update to the project plan in the form of added, changed, or deleted activities. If the change affects a control document, the document is updated and the new version becomes the basis for action.

Change Thresholds and Change Boards

KEY CONCEPT

While everyone admits the value of change management, we also want to avoid any drag it might add to decision making. Including all stakeholders in every decision just isn't necessary. Therefore, to balance the need for change management against the desire for flexibility and quick decisions, the project manager needs to separate changes into different categories, depending on how deeply they affect the project. These categories, called *change thresholds,* are as follows:

- The lowest threshold is for changes that the project team can approve. These changes typically don't affect the cost, the project schedule, or the way in which the customer will use the product. However, they can include design changes that make the product work better or last longer. Even though the team or project manager has the authority to approve these changes, they will still need to be documented.

- The second threshold, which involves changes that *will* affect cost, schedule, or functionality, requires more formal approval. This is the domain of the *change board.* Change boards meet on a regularly scheduled basis and consist of people representing the views of all stakeholders.

- Even though a change board may be authorized to approve cost and schedule changes, it is usually for a limited amount only. Above that designated amount, higher-level executives from the customer and project organizations must be involved. This is because these changes are usually large enough to threaten the business case for the project, fundamentally altering its profitability and market value.

Let's look more closely at who makes up a change board:

1. *Representatives from the project team.* These representatives offer the most expertise on the proposed change to the product and its effect on cost, schedule, and functionality. Though the project manager often plays this role, it is also appropriate for other team members to represent the project team.

2. *The customer's representative.* This board member must not only approve changes to the cost and schedule, but must also understand how the change affects the product's usefulness.

3. *Representatives from groups with related products.* For instance, the change board for a redesign of a truck fender may include engineers responsible for other parts of the truck's cab. They will want to identify any changes that might alter the way their parts work.

4. *Representatives from functional management.* Management participates on change boards to represent company policy. If the project team for the fender redesign should recommend a change that would result in using a new vendor, the company's procurement representatives would have a say in this decision.

The larger the project, the more change management thresholds will exist—along with more change boards. Large programs have change boards operating at many levels. While this adds complexity, it is an appropriate strategy for controlling project decisions and pushing decision-making authority down as far as possible.

Don't Let the Change Management Process Be Subverted

Stakeholders make decisions throughout the project. They choose the size, speed, color, and strength of the product. They agree on the cost-schedule-quality equilibrium. They divide the work and accept responsibilities. But the fastest way for a project to degenerate into a confusing mass of expensive rework is to allow these decisions to be changed randomly and without record. The formal change management process guards against this anarchy of sudden decision changes. Even though it adds bureaucracy and overhead to the project, it remains one of the project manager's strongest tools, both for self-preservation and for managing expectations.

CONFIGURATION MANAGEMENT

When the fifth revision is made to the blueprints, the electricians and plumbers may still be working from the third version, and the roofers from the first version. At this point, someone is bound to notice that the chimney and the fireplace are on different sides of the house. Configuration management prevents disasters like these by limiting the changes to control documents and other project deliverables. It is a subset of change management, which focuses specifically on how to implement approved changes. It keeps everyone in a project reading from the same sheet of music.

What Products Are Subject to Configuration Management?

It is unlikely that a driveway or building foundation, once completed, will be lost or a second one will be mistakenly installed. But when products are less tangible, these kinds of mistakes are more likely to happen. The items that should be subject to configuration management come from a wide variety of sources (and many are every bit as tangible as a driveway). So, what should be subject to configuration management? The answer is: any product that might have multiple versions during the project. This list includes many possible candidates.

- Control documents are obvious candidates for configuration management because they are the basis for project action. In addition, they are easily changed, since many of them are stored electronically as computer files. (Because they are easily changed, this increases the possibility that the change will be performed without the knowledge of other groups in the project.)

- Any products produced by computer and stored on electronic files, including computer programs, word processing documents, drawings, and so on, are candidates.

- Prototypes or product mock-ups may be revised and upgraded many times during a project. A test lab may contain models of many ideas, some of which are actively being pursued, while others may have been long since discarded. Configuration management prevents these discarded prototypes from being confused with the latest models.

- Test environments are set up to simulate real-life product behavior. These can be costly to create and might lead to incorrect test results if changes were randomly introduced.

How Is Configuration Management Accomplished?

Configuration management is practiced most robustly in the manufacturing of complex products, such as automobiles and aircraft. Each revision or upgrade to a component of the product is formally controlled by the product's configuration management process. The fundamental process for configuration management is the same at any level of complexity: Identify the items that will be controlled, set up the control structure, and assign responsibility for control. Let's look at the steps involved in this process.

Step One: Identify Items/Products

There are two sets of items to control: the end products and the intermediate deliverables. Both types of products need to be identified by using the work breakdown structure. (As we mentioned earlier, the control documents are obvious candidates for configuration management.)

Step Two: Establish the Control Structure

A number of questions must be answered in order to design the configuration management structure.

- How will access to the controlled item be restricted? If an engineering drawing is stored electronically on a computer file or on paper in a filing cabinet, how will you control who can update it?

- Do you need a record of the changes? At the end of the project, will it be useful to compare the first approved version of a design document to the final version? Will it be valuable to know not only the changes made along the way, but also the reasons for the changes? If the answer is yes, the next question is, how much are you willing to spend? If you need a record of the changes, the change log might be sufficient—or you may need a log for every controlled item. If, on the other hand, you don't need a record of the changes, or if the final product is the only one that matters, this will simplify your control structures (because each outdated version can be discarded or deleted).

- How will everyone know if they have the most recent version? This can be accomplished with version numbers or revision dates in electronic documents and files. Tangible products will require labels.

Step Three: Assign Configuration Management Responsibility

Somebody, preferably not the project manager, needs to be responsible for implementing and administering the structure. This is an administrative chore that doesn't require the project manager's authority or broad knowledge of the project; it can be accomplished effectively by team members. Everyone on the team needs to respect the controls and follow the rules, but unless the responsibility is specifically assigned, the controls may not be fully implemented or their value fully realized.

CHANGE MANAGEMENT GUIDELINES ARE ESSENTIAL FOR MANAGING EXPECTATIONS

TiP

While you are carrying out all these change management guidelines, don't forget that the ultimate goal of change management is to maintain realistic expectations. Too often, the project manager and customer will sign off on every $1,000 change, never considering that all the changes together are adding $100,000 to the project. Change management is more than recording the cost-schedule-quality impact of each potential change; its purpose is to keep the overall cost-schedule-quality equilibrium realistic and desirable.

KEY CONCEPT — CLOSEOUT REPORTING

The most neglected project management activity is closing out the project. The reporting and accounting tasks associated with the closeout just aren't as exciting as developing the product, and on many projects they are completely ignored. This is unfortunate, because these activities can bring a very high return to the project manager's firm. A simple, downloadable project closure form is found at the end of this chapter.

The end of a project may coincide with delivery of a final product or may simply be the end of a product development phase. In either case, the deliverables from project closeout serve two purposes: They finalize the project in the eyes of the stakeholders, and they present a learning opportunity. The customer's formal acceptance of the product, the reconciling of project accounts, closing out the change logs and issues logs—all these things bring the project to crisp completion. In addition, producing a lessons-learned report and organizing the project documentation present opportunities for process improvement or, in the case of the project manager, personal improvement.

The real proof that the project is finished comes from the customer. Formal acceptance of the finished product, or acknowledgment of phase completion, signifies that the work is complete. The project manager must plan for customer acceptance from the beginning. You need to be clear what form it will take and the work required to get it. The acceptance process may be lengthy, including extensive testing and evaluation that begin long before the final signature is given. To ensure that it goes smoothly, the customer's acceptance process should be on your work breakdown structure and in the project plan.

Some closeout activities may be classified as *transition tasks*. These include:

- Notifying all project participants of the new status of a project and whom to contact in the future. This is accomplished with a *project turnover memo.*

- Giving product improvement ideas that weren't used on the project to the team supporting the product. Some good ideas become even better when implemented in subsequent versions.

- Detailing any open tasks or unresolved issues by means of an updated project plan. Pass this on to the person taking responsibility for the next phase, and you'll make his or her job easier.

Finally, take the opportunity for organizational and personal improvement. Poll project participants—team, customers, vendors, management—on the effectiveness of the project management process. What was done well? What should be done differently next time? How could you improve communication, estimating, risk management, or change control?

When you document the results, be sure to both distribute them and store a copy where it can easily be found when you start your next project.

END POINT

It's no mystery that good communication is cited as a factor common to all successful projects. When people work together to accomplish a unique goal, they need to coordinate their activities, agree on responsibilities, and reevaluate the cost-schedule-quality equilibrium. Consciously setting up the mechanisms that enable communication—status meetings, reports, change management—puts the project on a strong foundation. The project control checklist found at the end of this chapter is an aid for keeping track of the many responsibilities of a project manager.

Project communication structures make it easier for people to interact, but they are not enough to bring about good communication. Project managers need to set the tone for project communication. They accomplish this by:

- *The discipline they display in using the communication channels.* For instance, if the project manager routinely circumvents the change management process, it quickly loses its authority in the eyes of all stakeholders. Similarly, if the project manager produces accurate, timely, and useful status reports, it is easier to hold all stakeholders accountable to their reporting responsibilities.

- *The attitude that they display when interacting with any stakeholder.* Is the project manager combative? Honest? Free with information? Judgmental? Assertive? Communication is the foundation of relationships. The project manager's attitude and style will color all relationships on the project. Consciously choose to lead by example in every action you take.

Along with the structures to enable communication, a project manager needs strong communication skills. Negotiating, listening, conflict resolution, writing, and many more skills affect our ability to work with the many people we encounter on every project. Even though these skills are not specifically addressed in this book (because they are not unique to project management), they are essential skills for project managers.

FAST FOUNDATION IN PROJECT MANAGEMENT

Project control can feel like juggling. The templates and checklist you find on the next several pages provide the basis for a structured, systematic approach to staying in control of the project.

1. The *kickoff checklist* is a guide for putting all the pieces in place as you put the project in motion.

2. Use the *task assignment* to make sure each team member clearly understands his or her responsibility.

3. The *meeting agenda* is structured to help you prepare for a meeting and take useful meeting minutes.

4. A *status report* for your management should be brief and focused to help the audience read it quickly and identify any necessary action. This template will get you started.

5. Evaluate your project and your project management style with the *control checklist* on a regular basis. These are the activities that keep the project on track from beginning to end.

6. Keeping track of problems that need to be resolved can be done using the *issues log*. The format ensures that someone is taking responsibility for every issue.

7. The *change log* and *change request* provide structure to keep track of the many proposed and accepted changes on the project.

8. When the project is finished, the *project closure report* summarizes the outcome of the project and compares the original goal with what actually happened.

Every one of these templates is available for download at www.versatilecompany.com/forms. Use these documents as the foundation of your own project management standards.

Stellar Performer: Lockheed Martin
Making Aviation History

Rod Pipinich

The F-35 Joint Strike Fighter (JSF) Program is the most significant aircraft development program ever undertaken at the Lockheed Martin Aeronautics Company. The F-35 is a stealthy, supersonic multirole fighter that will be produced in three variants: a conventional takeoff and landing aircraft (CTOL) for the U.S. Air Force; a carrier-based variant (CV) for the U.S. Navy; and a short takeoff and vertical landing (STOVL) aircraft for the U.S. Marine Corps, U.S. Air Force, Royal Air Force, and the Royal Navy. The F-35 will replace such aircraft as the Navy's F/A-18, the USAF's F-16, and the Marines' AV-8B Harrier. Production potential for both domestic and international sales could be as many as 6,000 airplanes.

The team assembled for the system design and development phase, as well as well as subsequent production and support, includes Northrop Grumman Corporation, BAE Systems, international partner countries, two security-cooperation participants, and a variety of subcontractors. To keep the aircraft affordable and to maximize the available expertise, the F-35 has been broken down into systems, many of which are being developed by team members and subcontractors, leaving Lockheed Martin to focus on its core competencies of airframe development, systems integration, and final assembly.

Lockheed Martin's effective execution of program and project management skills is essential to coordinate all of the requirements of the customers with the capabilities of the contractors and subcontractors across international boundaries and within security constraints while forging new ground in technology.

UNPRECEDENTED LEVEL OF SUBCONTRACTING

One example of the complexity and challenge facing Lockheed Martin involves the F-35 hydraulic system, which has been subcontracted in its entirety to Eaton Fluid Systems in Jackson, Mississippi. This subcontracting of a complete hydraulic system is a first for both Lockheed Martin and Eaton. With previous development efforts, Lockheed Martin has developed the systems concurrently with the airframe and then subcontracted the various components to multiple subcontractors.

In this case, Eaton has assumed responsibility not only for the design, but for specifying and acquiring all components such as pumps, reservoirs, accumulators, utility actuators, valves, and filter manifolds, and designing a production operation to deliver a complete hydraulic system at a rate of approximately one per day when the F-35 is in full production. Lockheed Martin's concurrent finalizing of the design of the F-35 airframe added dynamic requirements changes from multiple sources to create an extraordinary level of complexity of design and development of the hydraulic system.

(Continued)

(Continued)

VIRTUAL TEAM ESTABLISHED

Effective program and project management skills were considered essential to reduce risk, meet design and integration milestones, and keep a lid on costs, all critical objectives to the F-35 JSF Program. However, it is impossible to design a workable hydraulic system or any key system independent of the airframe, so one of the first tasks completed involved establishing a virtual project team.

Eaton collocated 13 engineers at Lockheed Martin to form an innovative and collaborative project environment. Eaton and other team members actively work side by side with Lockheed Martin engineers, sharing cubicles in some cases, and making the most of formal and informal communication channels. The transparency of Eaton–Lockheed Martin boundaries enabled minor changes to be made easily and major changes to be easily elevated for more thorough reviews. Eaton also collocated management team members, including one director, to help streamline the decision-making process.

Eaton had access to Lockheed Martin's information systems, JSF Data Library, CATIA CAD/CAM product life cycle management system, and other engineering and configuration management tools used by Lockheed Martin. As the designs for both the airframe and the hydraulic system progressed, Eaton was responsible for achieving project milestones and participating in Lockheed Martin F-35 design reviews.

VISUALIZING THE PROJECT VALUE STREAM

Although project progress was managed using work breakdown structures and other traditional project tools, individual team members had difficulty visualizing all of the interactions across contractors, subcontractors, and customer representatives. Part of the difficulty arose from the complete immersion of the Eaton engineers into an initially unfamiliar environment using unique systems and protocols. As the design of both the system and the airframe matured, near the time of the completion of the CTOL F-35 design but prior to the beginning of the STOVL F-35 design, the team decided to pursue ways to better understand the system design process and use continuous improvement tools to find ways to enhance the design process.

The team decided to conduct a joint value stream mapping event of the design process used by Eaton, Lockheed Martin, and subtier suppliers. The team selected value stream mapping because of the tool's effectiveness in visually depicting complex information flow and to identify which activities in the process add value and which activities do not add value. The tool is also consistent with Lockheed's philosophy that improvement is continuous and that there is no end to the process of reducing waste of all kinds. Several team members were eager to apply the tool to the design process after having used value stream mapping with great success on other projects and in production operations.

(Continued)

(Continued)

The team met off-site for two days to complete the value stream map with the objective of improving the information flow through project activities such as requirements definition, PDR, CDR, design freeze, issuing drawings and specifications, and system change management. During the event, the team identified current inputs, outputs, and supporting documentation for each step of the design process. The team then focused on identifying waste in the process and brainstorming ways to reduce or eliminate waste throughout the value stream.

At the conclusion of the two-day event, the team had developed an action plan to adopt a smoother-flowing design/development process, including improved design interfaces and communication enhancements to better utilize design resources and achieve a timely completion of systems design in support of program objectives. The off-site venue also provided a brief reprieve from an intense design process and brought the team closer together by helping team members better understand one another's roles in the overall design process.

AIRCRAFT #1 ENTERS PRODUCTION

Effective project management execution and the establishment of the virtual team contributed to Eaton's success in meeting the challenge and completing the CTOL hydraulic system on time and within budget. The team met their specific objective of freezing a complete design and entering the system models into the JSF data library, which enabled Eaton's subtier suppliers to become authorized to begin building hardware for Aircraft #1, the first preproduction F-35, which entered production in June 2004.

The positive effect of collocated individuals on the day-to-day interactions became evident in the team's informal, unplanned communication and collaboration required to complete the project. In addition to enhancing project management, the improved information flow resulting from the value stream mapping activity has positioned the virtual team favorably to begin design work for the next and most complex version of the F-35, the STOVL version that will provide the U.S. Marine Corps, U.S. Air Force, Royal Air Force, and the Royal Navy with short takeoff and vertical landing capability.

Rod Pipinich is a principal at Lockheed Martin.

Downloadable Task Assignment*

Task Name:

Task WBS #

Task assigned to

Assigned date

Task description

Completion criteria

Planned start date

Planned finish date:

Planned labor costs

    Labor hours

    Labor rate $0.00

    Total labor cost $0.00

Planned nonlabor costs

Predecessor tasks

Downloadable Issues Log*

Project name

Project manager

Last updated

Issue ID	WBS	Date Found	Assigned To	Description	Status	Closeout Date

Description of Fields:

Issue ID: A unique identifier.

WBS: WBS number of the task(s) related to this risk.

Date found: Date issue became known. mm/dd/yy.

Assigned: Person who is assigned to resolve this issue.

Description: What is the problem or what action needs to be taken?

Status: Ongoing log of changes to issue, in order from most recent to oldest. Format: mm/dd/yy – action/update.

Closeout date: When did the issue get resolved?

Downloadable Meeting Agenda*

Meeting date: **Meeting time:**   **Location:**

Meeting leader:

Meeting purpose:

Project purpose:

Participant Names   **Attended?**

Agenda Item	Who's Responsible	Time Allotted
Description		
Discussion		
Resolution		
Description		
Discussion		
Resolution		
Description		
Discussion		
Resolution		
Description		
Discussion		
Resolution		
Description		
Discussion		
Resolution		

Downloadable Status Report*

Status date: **Project manager:**   **Sponsor:**

Status period   From: To:

Cost performance [cost variance] % under/over budget
        Planned cost to date
        Actual cost to date
        Approved project cost baseline
        Estimated cost at completion

Schedule performance [schedule variance] % ahead/behind schedule
        Attach a tier 1 Gantt chart with baseline and current schedule

Issues requiring management attention

Changes to scope, schedule, cost during this period

Major problems encountered and planned action to resolve

Issues identified this period and required action

Major accomplishments in the past week

Major accomplishments scheduled for next week

Downloadable Kickoff Checklist*

Stakeholder Participation
- ❑ The project sponsor has clearly communicated the project goal to the project team.
- ❑ The project goal is understood and accepted by the project team.
- ❑ The project team understands how the project fits into the overall goals of the organization.
- ❑ Team members understand their specific assignments and how they fit into the overall project.
- ❑ Part-time team members and support organizations within the firm understand their contribution to the project and have agreed to fulfill this role.
- ❑ Key vendors/suppliers understand the project and their roles.
- ❑ Functional managers who contribute personnel to the project understand the work required from their personnel and have committed to support these people in fulfilling their project duties.
- ❑ The customer is represented and has agreed to a regular plan for communication.

Project Process
- ❑ The project plan has a baseline budget and schedule.
- ❑ The project plan shows specific tasks and responsibilities and is easily accessible to all project team members.
- ❑ There is an accepted process for team members to record progress against their task assignments.
- ❑ There is a change management process in place.
- ❑ An issue log has been established and it is easily accessible to all project team members.
- ❑ A configuration management plan has established the location of all project documents, naming conventions, and version control.
- ❑ Management has agreed to format and frequency for status reports.
- ❑ There is a schedule established for project team meetings.

Project Team
- ❑ The team has established ground rules for team behaviors.
- ❑ All team members understand the contributions of other team members.
- ❑ All team members understand the experience and skills other team members bring to the project.
- ❑ There are activities planned to build relationships within the team, including improving communication among team members.

Downloadable Change Request*

Change name: **Date submitted:**

Change request number:

Requested by:

Submitted by:

Detailed Description of Change

Impact Analysis

      Schedule

      Cost

      Related affects to
      other projects or
      parts of this project

Decision and Rationale

Approval: _____

Approved by:

Approval date:

Downloadable Change Log*

Project name

Project manager

Last updated

Change ID	Date Submitted	Requested by	Description	Cost/Schedule Impact	Status

Description of fields:

Change ID: A unique identifier.
Date Submitted: Date change request was submitted in writing (mm/dd/yy).
Requested by: Person who is requesting the change.
Description: Describe the change being requested.
Impact: Describe the impact to cost or schedule.
Status: *Approved* or *Pending* or *Rejected* and date.

Downloadable Closure Report*

Project name

Project manager

Sponsor

Project Goal

Project Objectives and Results

Objectives from Statement of Work	Results

Scope Comparison
  Additional scope

  Decreased scope

Cost Performance

Cost categories	Approved	Actual
Internal labor hours		
External costs		
Labor (consultants, contract labor)		
Equipment, hardware, or software		
List other costs such as travel and training		
Explanation of cost variance		

Schedule Performance

	Approved	Actual
Project completion date		
Explanation of schedule variance		

Major Obstacles Encountered

Lessons Learned that are Relevant to Other Projects

Downloadable Control Checklist*

Project name: **Project manager:**

Use this evaluation on an ongoing basis throughout the project.

Stakeholder Participation

❑ The project sponsor is fully aware of the state of the project, including revised schedule and budget estimates.

❑ The customer is fully aware of the state of the project, including revised schedule and budget estimates.

❑ The project team is fully aware of the state of the project, including revised schedule and budget estimates.

❑ Team members understand their specific assignments and how they fit into the overall project.

❑ Part-time team members and support organizations within the firm understand their contribution to the project. These expectations are clearly communicated both well in advance and again just prior to their involvement in order to give them the opportunity to plan to meet these expectations.

❑ The responsibility matrix is accurate and all stakeholders understand their commitment.

❑ All stakeholders who need to be informed of project progress have adequate access to project information.

Project Process

❑ The project plan is routinely updated to reflect the near-term action plan.

❑ Progress against the baseline budget and schedule is recorded and understood by the team.

❑ The baseline budget and schedule continue to be realistic.

❑ An issue log has been established and it is being used to track issues.

❑ Continuous risk management activities reveal new risks, which are evaluated and assigned to team members.

❑ Known risks are monitored and, where possible, mitigation strategies are followed to reduce the probability or impact.

❑ The project team meets on a regular basis to discuss accomplishments, plan for near-term activities, and share new information about the project.

Project Team

- ☐ The team has established ground rules for team behaviors and follows them.
- ☐ The team understands and has internalized the project goal.
- ☐ Team members practice active listening skills.
- ☐ Team members actively attempt to adjust their communication or problem-solving styles to accommodate other members of the team whose styles are different.
- ☐ Good meeting management practices are followed, including sending out agendas in advance and documenting decisions and action items in the meeting minutes.
- ☐ The team has an articulated problem-solving process and displays good problem-analysis skills.
- ☐ The team is able to use multiple decision modes, including effectively reaching consensus.
- ☐ The team demonstrates the ability to work through conflict, reaching better decisions and maintaining positive relationships.

Project Leadership

- ☐ I lead by example, showing a positive attitude and commitment to the project goal.
- ☐ I am accessible to team members so they can easily discuss problems or concerns with me.
- ☐ I hold myself and others accountable to project responsibilities.
- ☐ I consciously work to develop a positive team environment.
- ☐ I consciously work to develop collaborative problem-solving skills among the team.
- ☐ I treat all team members and stakeholders with respect.

Measuring Progress

INTRODUCTION

True or false? It becomes increasingly important to track progress as the deadline nears to see how close the project will be to finishing on time and on budget.

False! This is a pretty easy question to answer if you've read the previous chapters. By the end of the project it doesn't matter how close you are because you have almost no ability to change your cost and schedule performance. The key to *finishing* on time and on budget is to *start out* that way and stay on track throughout the project.

When projects start with challenging schedules, if they fall behind, even by a little, they spend the rest of the project trying to catch up. Other projects, however, seem to have a self-correcting process built into them; if they fall behind a little, the problem is quickly identified and dealt with immediately. The best project managers find problems early and solve them without overtime. They make the project look easy.

Progress measurements are the tools we use to identify problems when they are small—when there is still time to catch up. Since cost and schedule progress comprise two-thirds of the cost-schedule-quality equilibrium, they are the primary focus of progress measurement.

KEY CONCEPT — MEASURING SCHEDULE PERFORMANCE

Each work package in the plan is a measurable unit of progress. Each has start and finish dates. The smaller the work packages, the more progress points you can refer to, and therefore the more accurate your schedule progress will be. (Work package size guidelines are covered in Chapter 6.) The following story highlights the importance of breaking down a project into small, measurable units.

A software project manager responsible for a major release of a flagship product was trying to ascertain the schedule status. Several of the development managers had broken their work down into only a few tasks that were six months long. All were reporting that they were "on schedule" four and a half months into their work. The project manager's gut feeling was that the developers really had no idea where they were. She also felt that they were not likely to recognize a schedule problem for at least three more weeks—and that they wouldn't admit to it even at that point. To get the truth, she sat down with each development manager and said, "We've got six weeks until your deadline. Can you give me a week-by-week description of the work you have left to do?" During these meetings, three of the four managers had to admit they were dangerously behind schedule. Although they were 75 percent through the project schedule, the managers were able to finish their portion on time by turning all their developers onto this project.

This near-disaster illustrates the importance of questioning schedule status when the work is not broken down into small, detailed tasks.

The primary tool for illustrating a schedule is also good for displaying schedule status. Figure 12.1 is a Gantt chart showing schedule progress.

Notice that the focus here is on *displaying* schedule status. You will use project status meetings, as described in Chapter 11, for capturing actual task completion status. The real truth about schedule status is often elusive because it is hard to pin down what proportion of a project is really complete. The following tips are commonsense ways to get the most accurate picture possible of a project's progress.

Use the 0-50-100 Rule

A project manager should always be suspicious of work package status that is reported in detailed increments, such as 12 percent, 35 percent, or 87 percent, unless there is empirical basis for this amount of detail. When possible, use the 0-50-100 rule for recording schedule completion of tasks that span no more than two reporting periods.

- 0 percent complete: The task has not begun.
- 50 percent complete: The task has been started but not finished.
- 100 percent complete: The task is complete.

Using this method, as long as the work packages are small, no task will have 50 percent completion for two status meetings in a row

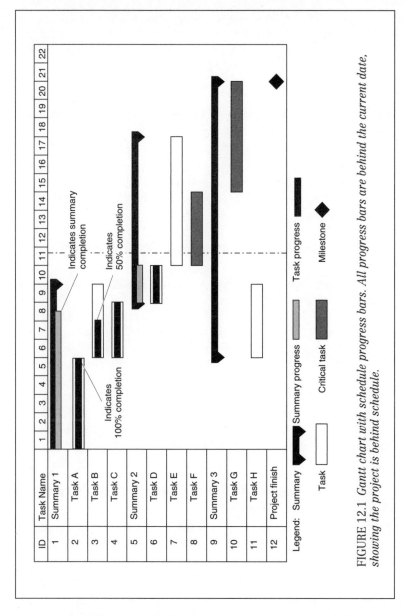

FIGURE 12.1 *Gantt chart with schedule progress bars. All progress bars are behind the current date, showing the project is behind schedule.*

(because the maximum time to complete each task is no more than two reporting periods).

Take Completion Criteria Seriously

Every work package is supposed to have completion criteria (see Chapter 6) and should not be considered 100 percent complete until it meets these criteria. You need to be rigid about this—if tasks are consistently allowed to register as complete before all the final details are taken care of, the project might fall far behind, even though the official status reports it as being on schedule.

Schedule Performance Measures Accomplishment

Schedule completion measures accomplishment, not effort expended. Just because you've used up 50 percent of your labor budget doesn't mean you've accomplished 50 percent of the project. Schedule status is a measure of whether you've accomplished as much to date as you had planned to.

The Dangers of Management by Exception

Management by exception is a seductive method for keeping the project on schedule that, in many cases, can actually increase schedule problems. Management by exception focuses on keeping critical path tasks on schedule while ignoring noncritical tasks that fall behind their scheduled start or end dates. Although it may be true that tasks that have float can continue to be delayed until they run out of float and become critical, these delays can lead to a resource crisis at the end of the project—which is the worst time to try to get extra work accomplished. The people poured onto the project at the end will have had little or no experience with the project. In addition, you will have increased your schedule risk, because a late completion of any one of the critical tasks can delay the project finish.

 Measuring Progress When There Are Many Similar Tasks

There is a way to measure schedule progress if your project contains many similar tasks. To begin, consider what these three projects have in common:

1. Driving hundreds of piles into marshy soil to form the foundation for a huge building
2. Creating thousands of engineering drawings to produce a next-generation fighter aircraft
3. Converting hundreds of computer programs originally written for one brand of hardware to run on another manufacturer's hardware

In each case, the portion of the total number of piles, engineering drawings, or computer programs completed can produce a useful schedule status. Figure 12.2 shows an example of a simple graph that displays this type of status. This graph can be generated by simple spreadsheet programs or project management software. These graphs can be extremely useful, but they can be misleading because they don't differentiate between easy and difficult tasks. For example, if all the easy piles were driven first, or if all the easy drawings were created first, the projects might initially show progress ahead of schedule, only to fall behind later when the time comes to handle the difficult piles and drawings.

KEY CONCEPT — MEASURING COST PERFORMANCE

Measuring costs accurately is critical as a project progresses because cost measures productivity. Every work package has cost estimates for labor, equipment, and materials. As each one is executed, be sure to capture the actual costs; comparing planned and actual costs will tell you whether the project is progressing as planned (see Table 12.1).

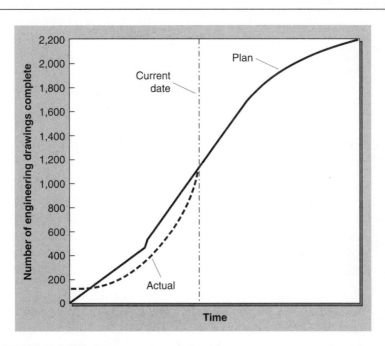

FIGURE 12.2 *Simple progress completion chart.*

TABLE 12.1 TRACK ACTUAL COSTS FOR EACH WORK PACKAGE

Task Name	Planned			Actual		
	Labor	Equipment	Materials	Labor	Equipment	Materials
Task n	40 hrs.	$1000	$1500	50 hrs.	$1200	$1500
Task p	30 hrs.	$200	$100	25 hrs.	$200	$150
Task r	60 hrs.	0	0	55 hrs.	0	0

How to Get Cooperation in Reporting Labor Hours

If project management is new to your firm, you may encounter plenty of resistance to tracking actual labor hours on tasks. Engineers, programmers, scientists, and other knowledge workers often complain bitterly about the lost productive hours they must spend each week just writing down their labor for specific tasks (even though experience has shown that this rarely takes more than five minutes a day). Here are two approaches for overcoming their resistance. These methods concentrate on winning their cooperation rather than forcing their compliance:

1. Point out that there is a legitimate need to track actual labor hours. Being able to compare planned and actual labor provides early warning on cost problems—and will improve estimates on future projects. Help them to understand that they will benefit from both of these factors.

2. Make it easy for them to report by using the largest increments possible for reporting actual hours. For instance, a department in a software company that was introducing project management chose to estimate and report labor in increments of five hours. As long as the work packages were kept small, it was easy to report actual labor at every project status meeting. This might not have been quite as accurate as planning and reporting in hourly increments, but it was a great leap forward compared to what they did before (which was nothing).

Problems Associated with Graphing Cost Performance

Graphing cost performance usually compares the projected expense over time to actual expenses (see Figure 12.3). That's useful information, but this kind of graph has some potential drawbacks:

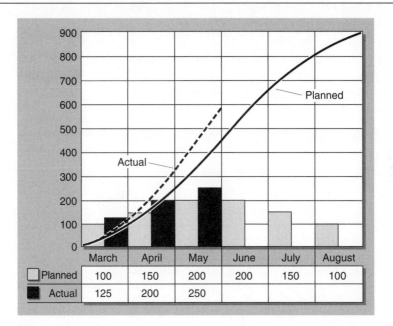

	March	April	May	June	July	August
☐ Planned	100	150	200	200	150	100
■ Actual	125	200	250			

FIGURE 12.3 *Planned versus actual cost over time. During the first three months, the project spent money faster than forecasted, but that isn't necessarily an indication the project will be over budget—it might be ahead of schedule.*

- *The rate at which money is being spent doesn't indicate whether the work is getting done.* For example, the project in Figure 12.3 could show higher-than-planned expenditures because it is ahead of schedule.

- *Accounting lag times can make cost information arrive months late.* This kind of delay means that a project's cost performance might appear to be excellent all the way through the project—but after completion the bills just keep coming in.

KEY CONCEPT — EARNED VALUE REPORTING

Comparing planned cash flow with actual cash flow has its uses, but it doesn't tell you whether the project will be over or under budget. To get the true picture of cost performance, the planned and actual costs for all completed tasks need to be compared. This is accomplished with a technique called *earned value reporting*. Earned value reporting uses cost data to give more accurate cost and schedule reports. It does this by combining cost and schedule status to provide a complete picture of the project. For example, projects can be ahead

311

of schedule (good), but over budget (bad). Or they can be ahead of schedule (good), and under budget (good). Altogether, there are five possible combinations when you include "on schedule and on budget" (see Figure 12.4). As this diagram shows, project managers who track only cost or only schedule are getting only half the picture and won't really know if their project is in trouble.

Calculating the Cost Variance Using Earned Value

Tracking cost with earned value introduces some new terms:

- *Planned cost:* The planned (budgeted) cost of any or all tasks.
- *Budgeted cost of work performed* (BCWP): The planned (budgeted) cost of tasks that are complete. This is the actual earned value of the project to date, because it is the value of the work that has been completed.
- *Actual cost of work performed* (ACWP): The actual cost of tasks that have been completed.
- *Cost variance* (CV): The cost variance is the difference between planned and actual costs for completed work. CV = BCWP – ACWP.

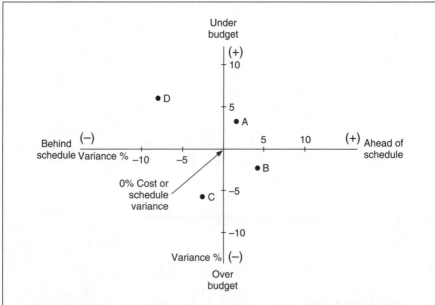

FIGURE 12.4 *Cost and schedule performance chart. Graphing the cost and schedule variance of Projects A, B, C, and D quickly identifies which needs the most immediate attention.*

- *Cost variance percent* (CV%): The cost variance divided by the planned cost. A positive CV% is good; it means the work was performed under budget. A negative CV% is bad, because it means the work was over budget. CV% = CV/BCWP.

- *Cost performance index* (CPI): Earned value (BCWP) divided by actual cost (CPI > 1.0 = under budget; CPI < 1.0 = over budget).

- *Budget at completion* (BAC): The budget at the end of the project. This represents the approved budget for the project.

- *Estimate at completion* (EAC): This is a reestimate of the total project budget. The original budget is multiplied by the ACWP and divided by BCWP. It's a way of saying that if the current cost performance trends continue, the final cost can be predicted.

- *Estimate to complete* (ETC): The budget amount needed to finish the project, based on the current CPI. ETC = EAC – AC.

- *Variance at Completion* (VAC): The estimated difference, at the end of the project, between the budget and actual cost of the project. VAC = BAC – EAC.

Figure 12.5 shows an example of using earned value both to measure cost performance to date and to recalculate the budget.

DANGER! Terminology Is Changing

Not long ago, only the U.S. Department of Defense (DoD) used earned value to manage projects. Now the practice has spread to large and small commercial firms as well as the civilian agencies of the federal government. Through increased use, the terminology is beginning to change. Although international standards organizations still promote use of the preceding terms, the Project Management Institute (PMI), based in the United States, recommends substituting the following terms:

- *Planned value* (PV) replaces *budgeted cost of work scheduled* (BCWS).

- *Earned value* (EV) replaces *budgeted cost of work performed* (BCWP).

- *Actual cost* (AC) replaces *actual cost of work performed* (ACWP).

Firms that want to be aligned with PMI terminology and individuals studying for one of PMI's certification exams should take special note of these terms.

DANGER! Use the Cost Variance to Identify Problems Early

Recalculating the estimated cost at completion using earned value implies the current trends will continue. But be careful not to assume

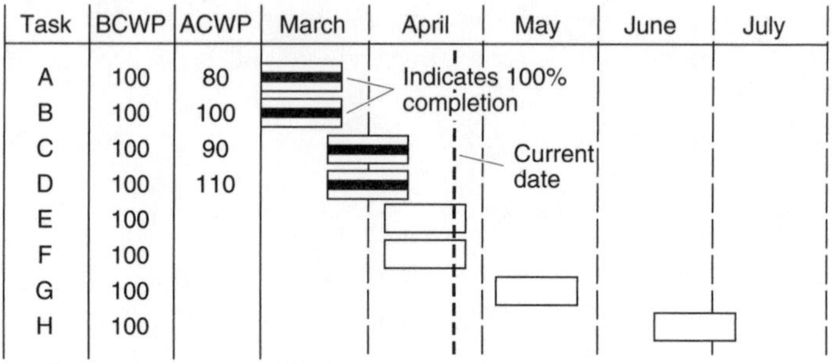

Task	BCWP	ACWP	March	April	May	June	July
A	100	80		Indicates 100% completion			
B	100	100					
C	100	90		Current date			
D	100	110					
E	100						
F	100						
G	100						
H	100						

As of April 30: total ACWP = 380, total BCWP = 400, total BCWS = 600

$$SV\% = \frac{BCWP - BCWS}{BCWS} \qquad CV\% = \frac{BCWP - ACWP}{BCWP}$$

$$SV\% = \frac{400 - 600}{600} \qquad CV\% = \frac{400 - 380}{400}$$

SV% = −.33 or 33% behind schedule   CV% = .05 or 5% under budget

New estimate at completion = original estimate × (ACWP/BCWP)

$$EAC = 800 \times (380/400)$$

$$EAC = 760$$

FIGURE 12.5 *Measuring cost and schedule performance with earned value.*

that just because you are over budget now that you will be granted more budget. Instead, the cost variance should be used as a warning flag to help you identify problems early, when there is still time to get back on track.

Calculating Schedule Variance Using Earned Value

Is the project on schedule? This is a question that all the stakeholders want answered. But it can be difficult to measure the degree to which a project is ahead or behind schedule. What if the majority of tasks are on schedule, but a few are ahead of schedule and others are behind? What is an accurate description of this project's schedule status? In this kind of situation, earned value calculations can help measure schedule variance just as they help in measuring cost variance. Calculating schedule variance uses some of the same concepts as the cost variance calculation. (Substitute PMI terminology here as well). These are:

- *Budgeted cost of work performed* (BCWP): The planned (budgeted) cost of tasks that are complete.

- *Budgeted cost of work scheduled* (BCWS): The planned (budgeted) cost of work that should have been completed to date.

- *Schedule variance* (SV): The schedule variance is the difference between the value of the work that was planned for completion and the value of the work that was actually completed. It uses *cost* values to measure *schedule* performance. SV = BCWP – BCWS. (The example in Figure 12.5 demonstrates how schedule variance works.)

- *Schedule variance percent* (SV%): The schedule variance divided by the planned cost to date. A positive SV% is good; it means more work has been performed to date than originally planned. A negative SV% is bad, because it means less work has been completed than the plan called for. SV% = SV/BCWS.

- *Schedule performance index* (SPI): BCWP divided by BCWS (SPI > 1.0 = ahead of schedule; SPI < 1.0 = behind schedule).

Using the cost figures as the basis for schedule measurement is useful because it takes into account the number and size of tasks that are behind schedule. That means if 10 concurrent tasks, each worth $10,000, are all one week behind schedule, the schedule variance will be larger than if only one of those tasks is one week behind schedule.

Graphing Earned Value

There is no more accurate presentation of a project's cost and schedule performance than earned value charts. Not only do they show the cost and schedule status at any given date, but they also indicate performance trends. Figure 12.6 shows an earned value chart.

An executive with 10, or even 100, projects under his or her control can use the kind of graph shown in Figure 12.4 to pinpoint the cost and schedule performance of each one. This will help to determine which project demands the most attention.

 Earned Value Relies on Disciplined Project Management

The example in Figure 12.5 shows how simple it can be to use earned value metrics to report progress. Unfortunately, many firms trying to apply earned value practices find it much more confusing. If you've read the previous chapters in this book and are practicing the discipline as it is described here, earned value metrics are practically free. In other words, if you have a detailed plan and capture actual perfor-

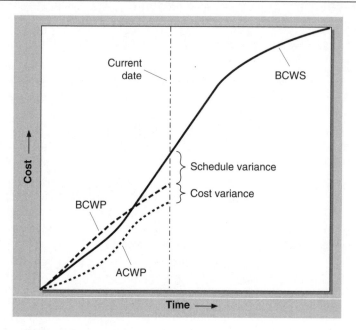

FIGURE 12.6 *Earned value curves. This project is under budget and behind schedule.*

mance data, the earned value calculations become easy. What follows here are some hard-won insights on applying the earned value reporting methods on projects.

The Work Breakdown Structure Is Critical

The secret to making earned value work is in the work breakdown structure (WBS). Each task on the WBS must be a discrete task that meets these criteria:

- It must have defined start and finish dates.
- The task must produce a tangible outcome whose completion can be objectively assessed.
- Costs must be assigned to the task, even if they are only labor costs.

If you've applied the guidelines in Chapter 6, your WBS will probably enable easy earned value reporting. The problem occurs when the WBS contains one of these mistakes:

WBS tasks should rarely represent an ongoing activity. There will always be some tasks that are planned as *level of effort* (LOE) tasks, meaning that a function within the project requires some basic staffing level that runs throughout the project. Project management is an example of an LOE task—we expect a certain amount of labor cost each week to be spent on project management, and the total duration of this activity is dictated by the length of the project. A construction project that hires security services to monitor the site is also an example of a task where a weekly cost can be estimated, and the task duration depends on the project's duration. But these should be the exception within the WBS. The problem arises when a category of tasks is lumped together under a heading such as "Engineering." Rather than breaking all the engineering work into separate discrete tasks, the manager simply assigns people to the task for a period of time. The result is a WBS task like this: " 'Engineering' will last four months, and we'll assign eight engineers." That produces a couple of problems:

- With this task description we can't track cost or schedule variance—as long as the task begins on time and doesn't use more than eight engineers, there is no cost or schedule variance.
- LOE tasks produce the illusion that the task is on schedule and on budget until the day that it doesn't finish on time—then every day after that we watch the costs and schedule variances increase.
- An LOE task that is understaffed actually sends the message that it is under budget because fewer people are working on the task than originally called for. Of course, since there is no objective way to track incremental schedule progress, the news might look very good until the day the task is supposed to be complete yet isn't.

Keep the lowest level tasks small. The size of work packages plays a big role in calculating cost and schedule variance accurately. When it comes to assessing schedule progress at the task level, you really know only two things: whether the task has started and whether it is finished. In between we are guessing if we report incremental progress. The simple method of assigning 50 percent of the BCWP to a task once it has begun and 100 percent of the BCWP when it is complete results in very accurate schedule variance calculations if the work packages are small. If the work packages are large, the variance is likely to be skewed, both positively and negatively, from week to week.

Data Isn't Information

What does a CPI of 0.95 really mean? If my SPI is 1.1 what should I do? Although we've defined the basic terms of earned value analysis, we still need to make sense of the numbers in the context of our project.

Trends are more useful than snapshots. A CPI of 0.95 means the project is over budget. But if the CPI a month ago was 0.90, it means we may have figured out the problem behind the cost overrun. A major value of these metrics are their predictive capability—forecasting the total cost or schedule variance for the entire project based on variance early in the project. Focusing on trends tells us whether our management strategies are working. The graphing techniques shown in Figures 12.4 and 12.6 can show earned value data over time. (The graph in Figure 12.4 could be drawn for a single project, with each week's variance represented as a single point—connecting the dots tells a story.)

Schedule variance doesn't tell the whole story. Don't forget the importance of the critical path as you track schedule. Projects with many concurrent tasks benefit from tracking schedule variance, because with many tasks being simultaneously performed, many are bound to be ahead while others will be late. In this scenario, however, many noncritical tasks could be ahead of schedule while critical path tasks are falling behind—providing a positive schedule variance and false confidence. If critical path tasks are late, sooner or later the entire project will be held up. *Watch both the schedule variance and the critical path.*

Size Increases Complexity for Earned Value

The projects that benefit most from earned value will have the greatest challenges implementing it. The larger the project, the more difficult it is to understand all the parts and to stay on top of cost and schedule variance. That's why these practices were invented—to manage huge defense programs. Putting the infrastructure in place to generate honest data on a routine basis is a formidable task on a major project or program—but the alternative is even worse.

Escalation Thresholds

While the project team has the authority to solve certain problems, others need to be escalated to higher management or may even demand the direct attention of senior management. The determining factors for who handles a problem or approves a solution are its cost and schedule impacts. Escalation thresholds represent preset variances that signal the severity of a problem; these thresholds are set during the planning process. The communication plan developed early in the project and described in Chapter 4 contains a description of the cost and schedule escalation thresholds (see Figure 12.7).

Thresholds accomplish several important functions:

- Change management thresholds separate the types of changes the project team can approve from those the change board must approve (see Chapter 11).

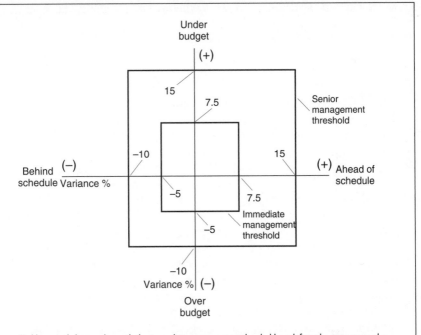

- Problems and changes beneath the immediate management threshold are left to the team to resolve.
- Any problem that can potentially cause a −10 percent cost or schedule variance will be immediately escalated to senior management.
- Changes that result in extremely positive variances will also be quickly escalated.
- Both midlevel and senior management will monitor the project on a routine basis while it is below their escalation thresholds, but they are less likely to actively intervene.

FIGURE 12.7 *Escalation thresholds.*

- Problem-resolution thresholds bring the proper level of attention to specific problems. When a problem is encountered that threatens project cost and schedule goals, it needs to be identified and raised to the proper level immediately, skipping the normal project status process. Any single problem that is big enough to cross an escalation threshold is big enough to demand immediate attention; passing the problem from one level of management to the next using the normal status process of weekly or monthly status meetings would take much too long. The threshold shows exactly who needs to be involved in solving the problem.

- Overall project progress thresholds signal upper management it is time to become actively involved in the project. The project may have fallen behind a little at a time, and the trend may have been apparent over several status periods, but at a certain point in this decline the escalation threshold will be crossed. This is the signal that management must intervene to solve the problems or set new cost and schedule goals.

KEY CONCEPT — COST AND SCHEDULE BASELINES

A baseline is a comparison point. Cost and schedule baselines represent the original project plan as approved by the stakeholders. Ideally, a project should never vary from its original plan, so a comparison between actual performance and the baseline would show no variance. But in reality this zero variance never happens. Even though everything may not happen according to the plan, however, many projects do meet original cost and schedule goals. Keeping the baseline cost and schedule goals visible is one way of holding the focus on the original goals, even when changes start to happen. Earned value reporting, as shown in Figure 12.6, is one way of keeping this vital information visible, because it emphasizes variance from the baseline. A Gantt chart may be used to focus on schedule variance alone (see Figure 12.8).

The baseline is more than just a starting point; it also represents the accepted cost-schedule-quality equilibrium on the project. The project team is committed to meeting the baseline and should assume it will continue to be held to the baseline, unless otherwise directed by the project manager. Consider the following example.

The BoxBetter project had been stuck about two weeks behind schedule for a month. The project manager had tried several ways to catch up, but none of them were working. At this point, Terry and Madison, who spent about a quarter of their time on the project, gave up on bringing the schedule up-to-date and decided to turn their attention to other projects. Although the schedule for BoxBetter called for them to complete a task prior to the next status meeting, neither of them worked on the task. At the meeting, Terry and Madison were chagrined to learn that the other project team members had done extra duty to bring the project back on schedule. Their task was now the only one that was late—and others were waiting for them to complete it. In this case, Terry and Madison had mistakenly assumed that the baseline for the project had changed.

Changing the baseline, however, is a big deal because it represents a new cost-schedule-quality equilibrium. This new equilibrium requires approval from all the stakeholders. If the justification for the change is good enough, meeting the new baseline might even be considered a success. Other times, however, it simply represents accepting a new reality. If all the evidence suggests that the project will miss the original cost and schedule goals, then it probably makes sense to change them. Maintaining unrealistic goals is rarely motivating. At the

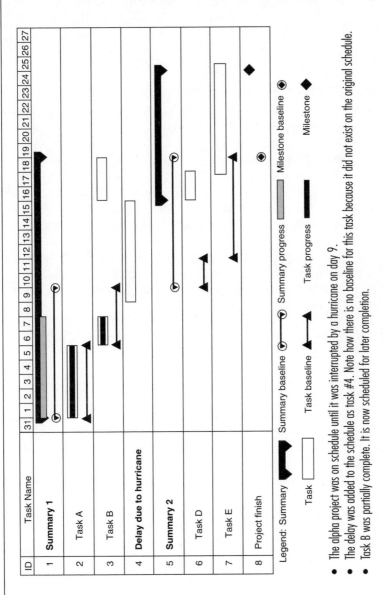

FIGURE 12.8 *Compare the baseline schedule to the current schedule.*

same time, however, the baseline must be changed cautiously and honestly, because it affects motivation if the baseline is changed over and over again. The new baseline should be as realistic as possible, reflecting the level of performance that led to the baseline change.

END POINT

It's surprising how many projects never really know their status until they get close to the deadline, when they have no hope of finishing on time or on budget. There's no mystery to measuring progress accurately; all you need is a detailed project plan with cost and schedule estimates for each work package. But it does require disciplined, systematic attention to the details. It is this attention to the details that enables the project manager and team to spot the problems early, when they are still small and there are still good options for solving them.

The financial analysts on Wall Street wouldn't stand for companies releasing quarterly or annual results based on gut feelings; they demand hard data to show quantifiable results. It's time every project was held to the same standard.

PART 5

Putting the Discipline to Work

In a rapidly changing business environment, projects are the means by which companies develop new products and services. Part 5 looks at the ways in which project management techniques are being adopted by a growing number of organizations. Chapter 13 describes how the tools presented in this book can be leveraged by organizations as well as project managers. And finally, Chapter 14 looks at the kind of problems that project managers are likely to face—and the best tools and techniques to deal with them.

Enterprise Project Management

INTRODUCTION

Project management techniques have been practiced for more than 50 years on projects around the world, but until the 1990s, they focused primarily on individual projects. With few exceptions, projects have been treated as organizational anomalies—each one was looked on as so unique that there seemed to be little value in changing organizational practices or policies to accommodate the special needs of managing them. Even the giant construction and engineering firms that worked exclusively on projects simply hired good project managers for each individual project instead of developing a corporate approach to managing projects.

A dramatic change has taken place since the mid-1990s. As companies restructure to strengthen their competitiveness, projects have become the focus, whether they are developing new products or delivering better service. Project-focused companies can't be dependent on heroes to pull off a miracle each time; the heroes get tired and there just aren't enough of them. These firms need a new paradigm. The frontier in modern project management is to take the lessons learned at the project level and apply them to the enterprise—whether the enterprise is a department or an entire corporation.

This chapter explores the most current questions and practices for institutionalizing the use of project management principles—what is becoming known as *enterprise project management* (EPM). Unlike the concepts in previous chapters, many of these new practices have not been proven over decades, but instead are emerging as new trends.

We will explore these trends and present the common wisdom for accomplishing the shift to EPM.

Reading This Chapter

This chapter is designed to introduce enterprise project management—to describe what it is and the path for getting there. Let's begin by providing a path through the chapter, which is broken into five major parts:

1. It begins by defining what is meant by EPM and introduces the model showing how all the elements of EPM work together (Figure 13.1).

2. Next we explain the three tiers of EPM, describing what function each tier serves.

3. In the third section we explore each of the four structural components that enable EPM, one by one. For each component we offer a description of what that component is and some tips for putting it in place. This section represents the 'nuts and bolts' of EPM, so it is the largest of the five parts in the chapter.

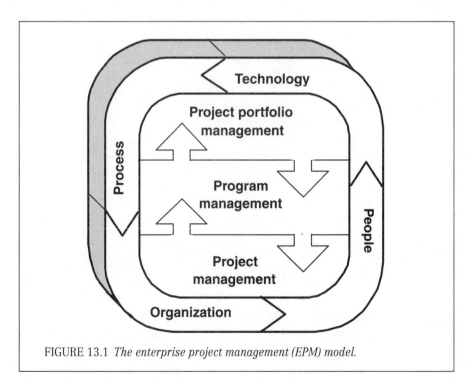

FIGURE 13.1 *The enterprise project management (EPM) model.*

4. The fourth part is devoted to understanding how the decision to align projects with strategy may also require that an organization change its structure to optimize project performance.

5. We end with general guidelines for making the shift to EPM.

The Benefits of Formalizing Project Management

Consider again the five project success factors:

1. *Agreement among the project team, customer, and management on the goals of the project*

2. *A plan that shows an overall path and clear responsibilities, which is used to measure progress during the project*

3. *Constant, effective communication between everyone involved in the project*

4. *A controlled scope*

5. *Management support*

When all these factors are present in a project, the likelihood of success markedly increases. In fact, it would make excellent sense for a firm to institutionalize these factors in order to achieve them consistently. Indeed, a survey performed by the pci group of Troy, Michigan, determined that firms that have implemented the components of enterprise project management have significantly better rates of completing projects on time and on budget.[1]

Firms like General Electric, which have embraced the notion of Six Sigma quality (only three defects per million products), view project management as one of the necessary components to achieving that level of process predictability. These organizations have discovered that the lessons of the quality movement apply to projects and project management. They have learned that consistent, defined processes are a launching pad for improving productivity and profitability.

In recognition of this trend, in 2003, the Project Management Institute released a framework for assessing the degree to which an organization had standardized practices for managing projects and programs, including project selection. PMI calls this framework the Organizational Project Management Maturity Model, or OPM3 for short. Although the EPM movement is still young, OPM3 has begun the process of creating a common language for understanding it.

DEFINING ENTERPRISE PROJECT MANAGEMENT

Enterprise project management (EPM) is the conscious integration of processes, technology, organization structure, and people in order to align strategy with the execution of projects. Figure 13.1 illustrates all the components of EPM. The structural components of EPM enable the three tiers of management that is possible when EPM exists. We will describe the model briefly here, then delve into each element in greater detail later in the chapter.

The three tiers of management in the EPM model form the link between project resources and organizational strategy. At the lowest level, *project management* focuses on the efficient execution of selected projects, the subject of all previous chapters. The next tier, *program and multiproject management,* serves to coordinate projects and the resources that all projects share—particularly the people. The highest tier, *project portfolio management,* connects the selection of projects and programs to the strategic goals of the organization.

The enabling components of the EPM model all work together (see Figure 13.1). Standardized *processes* are the accepted methods for managing projects and for management activities at the program and project portfolio levels. *Technology* consists of the information and telecommunication technology that enables people to follow the processes. A project management office, or PMO, is an *organization structure* with specific responsibility for implementing and maintaining the other elements of EPM. Finally, the *people* in the model are the people who both manage and work on projects. The skills of the people must be adequate to use the technology, follow the processes, and perform project work.

As we introduce the components of EPM we must also confront the term *enterprise* and be clear about where EPM can apply. In practice, an enterprise can range from an entire business to a department or product group. Small and midsize businesses that are project-driven, such as engineering or consulting firms, can include their entire operation within the scope of EPM. In large corporations or government agencies, an EPM initiative more often falls within specific departments, because the complexity of EPM increases dramatically when it is applied to loosely related groups. Factors for drawing practical EPM boundaries are covered later in this chapter.

Enterprise Project Management Is an Enterprise Commitment

It should be obvious from this brief introduction that EPM won't cause a ripple in your organization; it will cause a tidal wave. The shift to EPM requires far more than new software, training, or a project management methodology—although those are the tangible evidence of the shift. Gaining the benefits of EPM will require the cooperation of every person in the organization that touches projects. It is an enterprisewide discipline that requires commitment from top to bottom. This chapter contains many guidelines for making the shift to EPM—none is more important than full commitment from the top.

THREE TIERS OF MANAGEMENT WITHIN EPM

A major challenge of managing an organization filled with projects is the very nature of projects themselves. Each project is temporary and unique—some are quick, others stretch over years; some are routine, while others require special skills. As projects begin and end and staffing requirements go up and down, the kind of efficiency possible in managing a repetitive operation seems nearly impossible. The three tiers of EPM are a response to this challenge.

Project management comprises the practices used to define, plan, and control a single project. These have been described in detail throughout the rest of this book. The other two tiers are explained here in greater detail.

Program Management

Keeping track of all current and potential projects causes confusion for many firms, particularly when they are spreading the same people across many projects. Program and multiproject management respond by providing visibility and coordination across projects. It should be noted that the term *program* has two separate, yet commonly accepted definitions. One definition refers to all the projects that support a related goal—such as capturing and performing a contract to design, build, and operate a telecommunications network. This is consistent with the Project Management Institute's definition of a program. A program in this sense contains functions that extend beyond the scope of EPM, with supplier management and operations management as only two examples. The other commonly used definition of *program* is simply the oversight of multiple projects within an organization. In this case, all the projects are related because they share broad organizational goals and draw on the same resources. Using either definition, program management strives to remove the chaos posed by many related projects with the following activities:

- *Deploying limited resources—particularly personnel—among many projects.* Among IT projects there are often tasks requiring a database analyst (DBA), yet many of these projects don't need one full-time. An energy company must assess and respond to the environmental impacts of its hydroelectric dams, and therefore has a staff of scientists, each with their own specialty, that all work on a variety of projects. In fact, most people working on internal projects for their employers are spread across many projects—and they also have operational duties to balance. Whether it's people with special skills, equipment, or even suppliers, the availability of project resources constrain the project schedule. The flip side of this challenge is that we also want all of our resources in steady use, with neither too much nor too little to do. In Chapter 7 we explored the techniques and rationale behind resource leveling on a single project. The problem is more complex and every bit as important when we are spreading resources across many projects. Matching limited resources to many projects must be done based on the priorities set by the project portfolio management tier. Without this linkage, a firm does not really have enterprise project management.

- *Tracking relationships among projects.* When several projects are launched to support an initiative they are likely to be interdependent, with the product of one providing a necessary input to another. Likewise, projects with unrelated goals may actually both affect the same part of an organization. Managing these kinds of relationships among projects is typically outside a project manager's control, yet these add complexity and risk to the project. Program management specifically attends to the interactions and overlaps that occur among projects.

- *Managing projects or tasks that add value across projects yet are onerous to any one.* For example, selecting a supplier of equipment or services that will be used on many projects. The work associated with the selection could substantially increase the cost of any one project, and the results of the selection process will benefit many projects and create consistency among projects. Additionally, the choice will reflect the requirements of many projects rather than just one. This is one more way the program management tier strives to make the project management tier efficient.

The functions of program management are typically performed by a *project* or *program management office* (PMO). The various forms and responsibilities of the PMO are described later in this chapter, where we will see that PMO responsibilities typically extend beyond the program management activities described here.

Project Portfolio Management

Improving the management of each project has its rewards, but a consistent project management framework isn't complete unless it includes processes for managing the project portfolio. Like a portfolio of stock and bond investments, managing a portfolio of project investments requires a systematic approach to selecting, monitoring, and canceling projects. This makes portfolio management the link between the limited resources of the firm and its strategic objectives.

Portfolio Management Is the Link to Strategic Planning and Budgeting

"When is the last time you canceled a project that was ahead of schedule, under budget, and on track to deliver the promised product?" Caine O'Brien, who represents ProSight, a leading portfolio management application, challenged a group of project management professionals with this question. Why would we cancel such a project? Because a firm has limited resources. If that seemingly successful project would not deliver a better return on investment than another project, then it should be canceled and its resources redirected. Only projects that best enable a company to fulfill its mission, vision, and goals should be in the project portfolio.

What are the mission, vision, and goals of the department, company, or agency? These questions are answered in the strategic plan of the organization. Whatever direction the firm wants to move in, it will accomplish the goals through projects. Portfolio management balances the vision of strategic plans with the realities of limited resources. The components of portfolio management link project approval gates to the strategic and operational plans of the firm, as well as to its budgeting process. Here's a look at these components:

- *Authority.* Project portfolio management relies on a single body with the authority to initiate, cancel, and continue projects. The broader the spectrum of projects this body oversees, the greater will be the formal authority of its members. This steering group needs to make decisions, not just recommendations. They must be the same people who determine the annual budget of the organization, because decisions to pursue projects are decisions to spend money.

- *Budgeting guidelines.* Budget cycles rarely coincide with project cycles, but organizational budgets fund projects. Portfolio management contains estimating guidelines to facilitate consistency when evaluating potential projects, particularly when cost and schedule estimates are difficult to forecast accurately. As the organization matures, past project data is increasingly incorporated in the estimating process; this further improves the accuracy of the estimates. Budgeting guidelines also spell out how to account for projects that span budget cycles.

- *Strategic and operational goals.* Portfolio management uses strategic and operational goals to prioritize projects. A single body overseeing all projects is more efficient when it comes to making the hard decisions about which projects to pursue.

- *Discipline.* Portfolio management must be a proactive process. This means meeting on a regular basis and creating clear standards for proposing, approving, and reviewing projects.

- *Accurate project information.* In order to choose among projects, portfolio management requires four kinds of information from all sectors of the organization: estimates for proposed projects, cost and schedule status of projects that are under way, projections of resource availability, and past performance data that can be used to generate future project estimates. Without accurate information, the oversight body is steering blind.

- *Phase gates.* Project evaluation balances cost, schedule, risk, and benefits. As described in Chapter 8 under the topic of phased estimating, our understanding of these project attributes is likely to change as we move from the initial project proposal through the phases of the project. Phase gates are standard review points where the business case is updated and commitment to the project is reconsidered. Classic points for phase gates are the initial selection of a project, then between the requirements and design phases, and finally between design and construction. Standard phase gates prevent runaway projects and encourage cancellation of projects when budget estimates shoot up or projected benefits suddenly drop.

Project portfolio management relies on information from the program management tier for decision making and then passes those decisions to the program management tier to guide resource deployment.

Project Portfolio Management Is Part of Strategic Planning

Strategic goals drive project portfolio management. The methods and discipline of setting these goals is far beyond the discipline of project management. We must also recognize that when we apply the term *portfolio management* to strategic planning, that portfolio will include far more than projects; it contains the budgets for all the operations of the firm. True portfolio management happens above the EPM level.

The Three Tiers Work Together

Project, program, and portfolio management combine to align every resource on every project with the goals of the enterprise. Project execution is improved as resources are more consistently and realistically available. Management decisions to favor one project over another are based more on facts than assumptions. Consistent reporting and oversight identify projects that are straying from their cost and schedule goals. We see how these tiers make the entire project delivery system more effective. Now let's examine what enables these tiers to operate.

THE FOUR COMPONENTS OF EPM

The three tiers of EPM that we just discussed can operate only when the four components are in place—processes, people, technology, and organization. In the model in Figure 13.1, these components form the structure of EPM. All four work together, so if your firm is moving toward EPM, include all four in your vision. In the following sections, we will examine each of the components to understand what contribution it makes to effective project delivery. We will also introduce some guidelines to consider as you develop each component.

 ## The EPM Structure Is Not the Goal

Enterprise project management means aligning your project resources to accomplish your organizational goals as efficiently as possible. The four components of EPM are the means for reaching the goal, but they are not themselves the goal. As we examine each of the four components in greater detail in the following sections below, bear in mind that our organizations do not exist to fund EPM tools or processes—nor even to accomplish projects. It works the other way around. The tools, people, processes, and organization that form EPM within a firm exist to support the projects. The projects exist to support the goals of the firm. This warning may seem obvious, but too many organizations lose sight of this primary goal as they develop the infrastructure that enables EPM.

ESTABLISH CONSISTENT EPM PROCESSES

Good project managers have a system—a method of understanding and organizing projects that they bring to every assignment. This method is distilled from their successes and failures, from all the lessons they've learned in the past. Bring two or three seasoned project managers together from the same firm and they'll compare their approaches and techniques in an effort to learn from the others' experiences. While this kind of informal sharing can benefit the individual managers, it doesn't really help their firm. Their knowledge and experience stay with each of them, and if they leave the firm, their knowledge leaves with them. Enterprise project management creates a framework for the firm to build expertise in project management—which carries the added benefit of building better project managers. This portion of the chapter describes the *process* component of EPM, describing the contribution of defined EPM processes and guidelines for putting them in place.

Consistent process is necessary at the program and portfolio levels for EPM to function, but the most essential processes—which have also been the most difficult to define—have been those at the project level. Despite the abundance of project management methodologies available, many firms struggle to build practical guidelines for managing projects, so we will examine this level in detail first.

Using common status reports and risk assessments are obvious examples of consistent project management practices, but consistent practices are more than just standard formats for project management deliverables. In this part of the chapter we'll also see that clear responsibilities and decision points also make up a process description.

The Project Life Cycle Defines the Project Process

All process improvement efforts begin by establishing the boundaries of the process, then move on to breaking the process down into smaller units in an attempt to improve the whole by improving the individual parts. When it comes to project management, the "process" is the project life cycle. Therefore, the creation of consistent project management practices begins by defining the phases in the life cycle of a project, then determining the most appropriate practices for each phase.

Create Standard Deliverables and Approvals for Each Project Phase

Just as every work package on a work breakdown structure has a deliverable and completion criteria, every phase of a project life cycle has deliverables and approval processes. The approvals constitute the boundaries between project phases (the approval gates). The deliverables represent the various activities described in this book, such as a statement of work, communication plan, risk log, or change management process. Table 13.1 lists potential standard deliverables by project phase. The downloadable forms included in previous chapters are a starting point for creating standard deliverables.

Creating a standard for the content and format of all these project management deliverables will make them easier to produce and easier to read. For example, project managers can avoid the struggle of creating a new statement of work by using a template with an outline of all the required content. Status reports, which use a standard template, create consistency among all projects; not only does this consistency make it easier for management to understand the report, it also presents a unified look to customers. Similarly, guidelines for work

TABLE 13.1 POTENTIAL STANDARD DELIVERABLES BY PROJECT PHASE

Definition

- Charter
- Statement of work
- Responsibility matrix
- Communication plan
- Order-of-magnitude estimating guidelines

Plan

- Risk profiles
- Risk log
- Risk management plan
- Work breakdown structure
- Guidelines for task size
- Network diagram (PERT)
- Gantt chart
- Cost-estimating worksheet

Execution

- Status reports for different audiences
- Cost and schedule tracking charts
- Meeting agendas, including open task reports
- Cost-tracking guidelines
- Issues log
- Change request form
- Change log

Closeout

- Postproject review agenda and guidelines
- Postproject review report
- Client satisfaction assessment
- Project history file guidelines
- Project summary report

package size can build more consistency in estimating and tracking progress.

 **Defining Practices Requires Assigning Responsibility and Authority**

Authority shapes processes and cultures. One of the most important tasks in organizing for projects is to establish the authority that will govern the projects. At the portfolio level, we must know who will have the authority to approve or cancel a project. At the program level, we ask who will assign or remove people from project teams.

Assigning authority at the project level begins by defining the roles of project manager and sponsor. Other roles that will exist on every project must also be included. A standard organization chart showing the management roles for every project will be helpful. (Figure 13.2 is one example of how standard project roles might be defined.) An organization chart, which shows the standard management structure, should demonstrate where the authority lies and the escalation path to follow when referring decisions to higher management. It should also answer some basic questions:

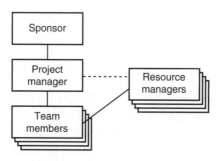

Project manager: Responsible for cost, schedule, and quality objectives. Authority to make decisions that don't change those objectives. Directly supervises members of project team once they are assigned.

Sponsor: Has final accountability for project objectives. Responsible to select project manager, issue charter, review and approve statement of work and project plan. Directly supervises the project manager and monitors the project on a detail level. Approves changes to cost, schedule, and quality objectives.

Resource managers: Functional managers supplying people or resources to the project. Cooperates with project manager to select project team. Resource managers monitor their staff for availability and guard against overallocation for people on multiple projects.

FIGURE 13.2 *Standard management structure and roles.*

- Who will the project manager report to? What responsibility to the project will this person or group have?

- What does it mean to sponsor a project? A sponsor, by definition, provides authority and management support to the project team. But, because terms like *authority* and *management support* can be vague and subject to different interpretations, they need to be defined more clearly.

- What responsibility, if any, will functional management have for a project?

In addition to a standard organization chart, these roles should be clarified by describing the way that each role is responsible for the project management deliverables. Does the group or individual filling a particular role create, review, or approve the deliverables? Answering this question, which connects the decision-making roles to the project management deliverables, will add accountability to the process.

Validate the Authority Structure in the Statement of Work

Even as we are looking for similarities in projects in order to establish common authority structures, it's important to remember that each project is unique and that some just won't fit the mold. No matter what authority structure you come up with, you will need to validate the structure for each project in the statement of work with an organization chart or description of the escalation path.

Separate Project Management Practices from Development Practices

Recall the distinction made throughout this book between a project life cycle and a development life cycle: The *project life cycle* reflects the activity required to *manage* the work (such as building a detailed plan or communicating status), whereas the *development life cycle* contains the actual description of how to *perform* the work (such as standards for design documents or testing procedures). This distinction should be maintained when establishing project management practices. An effective organization will have standards for both project management and product development, but it also recognizes that different kinds of projects exist, so a universal, one-methodology-for-all projects approach isn't practical. Allow the standards for establishing requirements, designing the product, building it, and so on to be developed independently of the standards for managing the project. True, both product and project methodologies should mesh, but they'll both work better if they are designed to be separate but complementary.

**Different Kinds of Projects Deserve
Different Project Management Practices**

Why does a company have to develop project management standards? Why can't it just buy a set from a project management consulting firm or use the downloadable forms in this book? Or better yet, why can't we all agree on a single best way to manage projects? The obvious answer is that not every project has the same management requirements. The differences between projects make it impossible to use a one-size-fits-all approach. There may be several different types of projects within an organization and each type will require different management standards. The downloadable forms in this book are meant to provide a starting point for a firm's project management standards, but they'll have to be customized to reach their full potential.

Before creating project management standards for each type of project, company managers will need to step back and determine how many kinds of projects exist within the organization. They will look for the kind of complexity that requires different tools or management techniques. Here are two major factors that separate projects into different categories:

1. *Approvals.* If different types of projects have different approval processes, they will require different standards for passing their approval gates. Cost is often a factor in formalizing approvals; so are the organizational boundaries spanned by projects. For instance, low-cost projects usually require less oversight than large, expensive projects, and projects that stay within a department will have a simpler approval process, particularly compared to projects serving customers outside the firm.

2. *Common risk factors.* Projects that share certain risk factors, especially organizational or management risk factors, benefit from consistent project management standards. Here are some examples: projects that serve many customers instead of a single one that is easily identified; projects with large or geographically dispersed teams; projects employing subcontractors to perform portions of the work; and projects with similar technical challenges or that deliver similar products.

For example, one department came up with three project types:

1. *Small:* Projects requiring less than 100 labor hours.

2. *Internal:* Projects in which the department had complete control of the people and decisions.

3. *External:* Projects in which the department was delivering a service outside its boundaries—and therefore required a good deal more coordination and communication.

For each project type, department staff devised templates and guidelines for creating a statement of work, project plans, status reports, and other project management deliverables. Since each type of project was progressively more complex to manage (small projects were easier to manage than external projects), each set of standards was progressively more thorough. That added much more structure to the larger projects with external customers, but the simplest projects weren't weighted down with excessive management requirements.

Use History to Help Develop Standards

Since the one-size-fits-all strategy doesn't work, the question arises, "What is the best way to develop standards that fit the organization and project type?" You can start answering this question by asking other questions, such as, "What have been the key factors that determined success and failure in past projects?" The lessons learned from these successes and failures in previous projects will aid in determining the standards to set for each deliverable.

Here's an example of how this process can work: The managers in an information systems department were in the process of developing project management standards for their projects. Upon interviewing their most experienced and respected project managers and customers, they discovered that the single most important success factor was the ability to get clear, speedy decisions from a strong customer. Conversely, the most common cause of failure was an inability to obtain quick decisions from the customer; in these cases, there were often multiple customers spread across several states.

As a result of this analysis, both the statement of work and the approval process in the definition phase now place special emphasis on determining the customer's decision-making structure.

Roles, Practices, and Standards Establish a Consistent Approach to Project Management

We have been discussing the ways to establish consistent project management practices, including identifying project types, setting project life cycles, defining standard deliverables, and clarifying decision-making roles. (Figure 13.2 and Table 13.1 demonstrate some of the results of these practices.) This framework provides a common approach for managing every project and, most important, establishes the basis for process improvement. Project managers will know what is expected of them, and they will be able to add lessons from their projects to the project management standards. These two factors will increase the performance of all project managers.

TECHNOLOGY ENABLES EPM PROCESSES

The science of project management is the foundation for the art of leadership—a theme that's been stressed in every chapter. The science of project management relies heavily on our ability to assemble and maintain accurate information. In the case of enterprise project management it is even more important. EPM requires a broader scope within an organization, and the only way to manage that broader scope is with accurate, up-to-date information.

In the previous section we looked at the process component of EPM. In this section we'll describe how technology contributes to our EPM goals. In addition, we'll provide guidelines for achieving successful implementation of EPM technology.

EPM Technology Capability

EPM has a broad scope, which includes successfully managing individual projects, understanding relationships among projects, and selecting and monitoring projects based on their fit with strategic goals. The following list categorizes eight common capabilities of EPM technology as they relate to the discipline of project management.

1. *Project management.* From the work breakdown structure to the resource-leveled project schedule, individual projects need a detailed plan that integrates cost, schedule, scope, and resource constraints and can be used to measure progress against these goals. The diagrams found in Chapters 6, 7, 8, and 12 (and repeated in the appendix) show example output from software used at the project level.

2. *Team communication and collaboration.* Organizing project documentation, tracking issues and risks, and reporting individual progress against assignments are all necessary within projects. Internet- and network-based technology enables teams to consistently and efficiently share this information, whether team members share office space or are spread around the world.

3. *Visibility of interproject dependencies.* When projects share personnel, or when one project is waiting for another project to reach a key milestone, coordination of multiple projects requires visibility of their relationships. Systems that store all project information in a common database provide an integrated view of all projects.

4. *Visibility of resource use across all projects.* As people are assigned to projects, we try to avoid overloading some people and underassigning others. The complexity of this problem grows when people work part-time on many projects. The capability to see availability or overallocation of personnel across many projects has become one of the driving factors for implementing EPM technology.

5. *Project portfolio summary.* Managers responsible for many projects benefit when they are able to see accurate summary status for all their projects. Figure 13.3 shows how an executive could organize all projects within his or her span of control, with access to detailed project information, by selecting any project. Again, this is typically the product of a system that stores all project information in a common database.

6. *Project status reporting.* Project status consists of both hard data, such as cost performance, and verbal descriptions of project events (both the good and the bad). EPM technology enables both types of information to be merged in a consistent format so that management gets a common, reliable view of progress across all projects.

7. *Cost accounting.* Aligning resources and goals is pretty theoretical if we can't capture and analyze costs. Costs are typically incurred at the project level, but useful cost analysis includes categorizing costs that span projects. The fundamental task of recording time (labor) spent on projects is increasingly fulfilled by EPM technology.

8. *Interfaces to complementary systems.* EPM doesn't cover every business process. The ability of the EPM system to interface with accounting and portfolio management systems decreases the work required to keep project accounting—particularly timekeeping for individual project team members—synchronized with the overall accounting system.

Most of the Solution Already Exists

Many off-the-shelf software packages are designed for enterprise project management—both managing projects and summarizing information above the project level—and they do their job well. They are available in a range of costs, capabilities, and architectures. Or you can keep it simple with a system you build yourself (very simple!). Either way, choosing your tool and implementing it successfully should follow the common wisdom of any information system implementation. The guidelines in the next section provide a high-level framework for implementing your EPM solution with minimum pain and maximum value.

Guidelines for EPM Technology Implementation

EPM applications may still be relatively new, but there are decades of experience to guide information system implementations. The guidelines in this section won't take you into detailed analysis or application configuration techniques—those tend to be system-specific. Rather, these are general guidelines that apply to an EPM implementation of any size.

Category and Project Name	Approved Budget $	$ Cost Variance	% Cost Variance	% Complete	% Schedule Variance	M J J A S O N D J
Proposed	9,850,000	0				
Region Expansion	9,850,000	0	0	0	0	
Auto	319,000	1,962				
LAN Upgrade	89,000	(2315)	+1%	77%	+2%	
ARM Calculator ★	230,000	4,277	-18%	8%	-1%	
Home Mortgage	377,500	245				
Branch 23 Remodel	245,000	1,255	-2%	33%	+3%	
Branch 33 Security	37,500	(1,010)	+3%	90%	-5%	
AIPA Training	95,000	0	0%	70%	0%	
Financial Services	1,957,000	8,265				
Credit Card ★	677,000	24,300	-9%	44%	-3%	
IRRP Extension ★	1,215,000	(16,440)	+2%	68%	-14%	
Utility Web	65,000	405	-2%	25%	+1%	

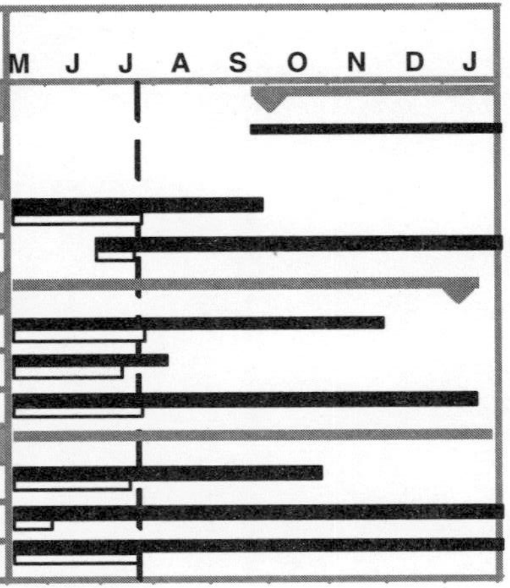

An example of the way EPM technology enables a bank executive to view summary information about all active and proposed projects. The summary schedule bars show the baseline schedule and the percent complete against the baseline. The first column identifies projects with a significant cost or schedule variance. (Cost variance and schedule variance are described in Chapter 12.) EPM technology typically allows an executive broad flexibility in creating such summary information.

FIGURE 13.3 *Project portfolio information.*

Treat It Like a Project

An EPM technology implementation benefits from the same project success factors we've been discussing throughout the book. Apply all of the lessons from previous chapters in this book and your probability of success should increase.

The EPM Project Team Needs a Broad Skill Set

Build the EPM team to include these key skills and knowledge areas.

- *Users.* High user involvement in system design is always a success factor. In the case of EPM, users will be project managers, team members, functional managers (also referred to as *resource managers* to imply that they are the long-term supervisors of many project team members in a matrix environment), and the executives who oversee and sponsor projects. The perspective of these users is critically important to designing the way project information will be entered, stored, and retrieved.

- *Sponsor.* Every project needs a sponsor. A strong sponsor is an essential ally when it comes to convincing reluctant users that this new way is a better way.

- *Business analyst.* The team needs the ability to understand, design, and communicate processes, both as they currently are and as they will be. The skills to facilitate a team through this analysis are often found in a business or systems analyst.

- *Project management expertise.* The team will be making decisions about the best way to manage and oversee projects, but they don't need to reinvent any wheels. There is enough EPM and project management expertise around that the team should benefit from the common wisdom that has emerged from similar experiences.

- *Tool or technology expertise.* Making the most of your technology choice requires an intimate knowledge of the technology. Somebody on your team should understand all of its capabilities and limitations.

- *IT expertise.* There are no stand-alone systems anymore. Your EPM technology will operate within your IT infrastructure. The team must include people with the knowledge to integrate the new system's security and data interchange requirements with the existing environment.

The skills and knowledge of your project team will affect the quality of the decisions made as the new system is designed and configured. It must be said that an EPM technology implementation is not an ideal do-it-yourself job. There are firms that specialize in these technologies and in making the implementations go as smoothly as possible.

They've learned how the technology really works, which process decisions will come back to haunt you, and the best strategies for winning cooperation from all the stakeholders. True, their advice is not free, but you are buying hard-won experience. Implementing EPM technology is challenging under the best circumstances, and making it a learn-as-you-go initiative dramatically increases the risks. As we can see from the preceding list, the ideal team includes the experienced expert, the passionate change leader, and those who will live with the results on a daily basis.

Begin with a Vision of the Future

Before any kind of implementation strategy is developed, break free from the current practices your organization is using and imagine what's possible using EPM technology. Remember, you aren't just trying to automate current processes; you are trying to manage and deliver projects in the best way possible. If new technology changes what is possible, then imagining a new way of working is the right place to start.

As you envision the possible, the breadth of your team's skills pays off. The project management expert offers the concepts and practices that have worked in other firms balanced by the users who are firmly rooted in the reality of their projects. The technology expert contributes with examples of what has been done before. This initial stage is akin to asking a freight company back in 1910 how it might change if it switched from horse-drawn wagons to automobiles. It's not enough to ask open-ended questions such as "What would make your business better?" Unless we give the freight haulers a ride in an automobile they might never envision the dramatic possibilities. Our EPM options will be the same.

Address the three management tiers of EPM and ask what could improve performance at each of these levels. The results of this stage represent the high-level vision, or business requirements, the system will strive to achieve. This vision energizes the team, transforming the project from a technology implementation to an organizational change.

Accounting Systems Have Requirements, Too

Most firms have had accounting systems long before any attempts to use EPM technology. The accounting system may be replaced as part of the new technology implementation, or the new EPM technology may be required to talk to the old system. Either way, accounting systems have well-defined rules that won't change to accommodate the EPM system. If you plan to integrate accounting into the final EPM system, start with the accounting requirements and work your way to project management rather than the other way around.

Risk Management Is Always a Project Success Factor

EPM projects have certain predictable risks—as well as the usual unpredictable ones! Some predictable risks are listed here. If they exist on your project, you'll need to include a mitigation strategy.

- *Skills to perform the new processes.* Do the people who will be using the EPM system understand the project management theory that forms its foundation? Without this knowledge, any training on the new tool is likely to be ineffectual; the users will struggle with new terminology and concepts while trying to learn the technology.

- *Existing systems.* Prior to EPM technology many firms used inconsistent tools for managing projects across the organization. You don't want the people who have other tools in place to experience a big setback on their projects when the new system goes live. That does not build enthusiasm and adoption.

- *Aversion to change.* Is the enthusiasm for EPM widespread or coming only from an intense core? How many people will resist the change? Something as minor as changing time-reporting can generate enormous resistance.

- *Reorganization or change in authority.* If the switch to EPM technology enables a dramatic change in the way projects are managed, it may also precipitate changes to authority structures within the organization. Those changes always create upheaval and may threaten some people who perceive the change as a threat to their own authority or status.

We'll explore other risks related to EPM implementations in general at the end of the chapter.

Revisit Your Processes

In the previous section we described the importance of having standard processes for all three tiers of EPM. The technology will enable those processes, so make sure they are realistic at a detailed level. That typically means watching what's actually happening on project teams—how people *really* get assigned to teams, perform work, and report status. If there is a big disconnect between our ideal EPM processes and the way people actually work, we need to figure out what we can practically achieve.

It's worth emphasizing that we can have project and program management processes in place without sophisticated EPM software. The difference is that these processes end up being high-level guidelines—insufficient for capturing details of cost or resource availability. The capability that EPM technology offers demands a detailed understanding of current and proposed practices. The end result of this step is a detailed design for how you'll use the technology in your unique environment.

Off-the-Shelf Technology Must Be Configured

EPM technology is designed around proven EPM concepts. Although those concepts may apply universally, your organization is unique. When you purchase an EPM software application, it must be configured as well as installed. Installation means loading the software and making sure it runs on your network. Configuration means setting all the variables within the system to reflect the way that you want to manage projects. A simple example is found in Figure 13.3, which shows what an executive might see looking at all the projects under his or her span of control. The projects are grouped by categories— categories that were chosen and entered into the technology as part of the configuration. The more powerful the tool, the more configuration options you have.

Configuration should be distinguished from customization. As powerful as EPM tools can be, you may still find some functionality that is important to your organization but not included in the tool. In that case, you'll develop some unique interface or add-on to the EPM tool. That is customization.

Use a Phased Deployment Strategy

There's no question that the transition to the EPM tool will cause disruption. We also know that using the tool is the best way to shake out the design and configuration decisions. For both these reasons, using a phased deployment strategy keeps the risks smaller and the project moving ahead. (Phased deployment was described in Chapter 9 under the heading "Phased Product Delivery.")

There are two dimensions of phased deployment available: *functionality* and *audience*. Phasing the functionality means asking people to use only basic features of the EPM tool during the initial rollout. That directly addresses the risks associated with the reluctance to change or the skills necessary to use the tool. Keeping the initial functionality simpler will reduce the learning curve for users. Later functionality deployment will be easier as it builds on existing practices. Phasing the audience starts with a small group for testing the tool and configuration, then rolls it out to other groups once it is stable.

A pilot deployment often blends both dimensions of phased deployment. The goal of this phase is to test the viability of the product and the processes, to make sure the vision, the tool, and reality sync up. Real project teams use real project data, with functional managers and executives practicing their use of the new tool. The ideal pilot audience has routine projects, good project management skills, and is receptive to the new tool. There are three general results we should expect of the pilot:

1. Revisit the vision established at the outset. Evaluate whether the requirements laid out in that vision are going to be met and whether we should add to or change the vision based on experience with the tool. Rather than viewing additional requirements as scope creep, view them as learning by doing, or *prototyping*—it will be cheaper and easier to adjust our vision during the pilot stage than after the EPM technology is deployed across many groups.

2. Validate that work processes make sense and that the tool is working as intended. Some things are just a lot harder to do on a daily basis than expected. The people using the product will have a lot to say about what worked well and what didn't. Based on their experience, you'll probably make some adjustments to the processes or the way the technology has been configured.

3. Check that all the data is moving as intended, particularly if your EPM system exchanges data with other systems.

If the pilot produced a lot of changes, it probably makes sense to extend the pilot. However, once the team is confident in the work processes and the tool, you can expand the audience for the tool in phases. The benefit of incremental deployment to new users is to ensure that the EPM team can respond to the new users' needs for coaching, training, or other support. Depending on the size of your organization and its enthusiasm for EPM, this iterative deployment may last a few months to a few years.

EPM Technology Is Ready

Technology has been a driving force behind the growth of project management. Prior to the advent of PCs, few projects could afford the software that simply calculated a critical path schedule or produced reports showing personnel assignments within a project. Many people believed in the project management theory but just didn't have the tools to put it into practice. Now it is the reverse. With every passing year, technology designed for project management increases in power and capability. Reliable products now exist to perform every capability described in this chapter. We are no longer waiting for technology that enables firms to efficiently put EPM theory into practice; the obstacle has now become our ability as an organization to change. We will discuss this obstacle further at the end of this chapter.

THE PEOPLE WHO DELIVER PROJECTS

In our focus on the processes and technology of EPM, we dare not lose sight of the reality that the purpose of our organization is to deliver projects, and those projects are delivered by people. In nearly every field, no matter what the maturity of the firm's tools and processes, when difficult projects loom, management turns to its proven leaders to bring these projects home successfully. In short, the best projects are performed by the best people.

The best projects are performed by the best people. That might seem to argue against our focus on standardized tools and processes—just hire better people! However, when we examine these challenging projects that are delivered successfully, we find that the best project leaders consistently use the best practices. Listening to stories of project success is how we derived the five project success factors referenced throughout this book. In fact, successful project leaders are usually the greatest advocates for institutionalizing the project management discipline because that has been the source of their own effectiveness.

The best people use the best practices. If we believe that, the question becomes, how do we get more people to use the best practices? Our tools and processes represent the practices we want our project leaders to use, so institutionalizing these practices through our EPM initiative is the best way to develop the project leaders of the future. Training is certainly part of answer, because we want people to be able to understand and use the best practices of the firm. But beyond classroom training, our people will improve their project management ability through experience using our EPM tools and methods. Through day-to-day practice, they will reach the level of "unconscious competence"—doing it right without thinking about it—because project management has become a habit.

Institutionalizing the best project management practices creates an environment that teaches and reinforces project management skills to our project managers. But what about our other EPM stakeholders—the team, the sponsors, and the functional managers? Their situation is similar, only with a smaller learning curve. These stakeholders all have key roles to play if we are to have effective EPM. They need to be aware of how they fit into the big picture and know how to make their contribution. That's why training for these stakeholders typically includes a description of the goals and value of EPM and the overall EPM structure for the firm as well as the details of how they will be expected to perform.

EPM Serves the People

It is not a question of whether people or processes make the difference—people, processes, and tools work together. When our EPM components are all present and effective, the contributions of every person bring a greater reward to the enterprise.

SUPPORT PROJECT MANAGEMENT: THE PROJECT OFFICE

An undeniable reality of organizational behavior is *entropy;* this means that, if left to themselves, policies and processes will decompose and return to their natural state. It follows, then, that if nobody is responsible for project management practices, including portfolio management, the whole idea will likely fade away and be chalked up as one more management fad. The last component of our enterprise project management model, therefore, establishes responsibility for the continued support of the standards, practices, and technology that define project management for the organization. This role is increasingly known as the *project office.*

This section is broken into two parts: The first describes the forms of authority found in project offices, and the second part describes the possible duties a project office may fulfill.

◆DANGER!▶ Project Office Goes by Many Different Names

The forms of project office are new and evolving, and the names for the different models are by no means standard. The names, however, are not as important as the concepts. If you focus on how the responsibilities and authority are handled in each model, the different names will assume less importance.

K E Y CONCEPT The Spectrum of Project Office Models

Like any good idea, the concept of the project office may be implemented in a variety of ways. The two factors that govern a project office role are *responsibilities* and *authority.* This section describes the most common models for the project office in terms of responsibility, authority, and best application. (Table 13.2 is a matrix showing the spectrum of project office incarnations and their associated responsibilities.)

Center of Excellence

The primary purpose of a center of excellence is to maintain the project management standards and promote their use in an organization. Although the staff is often called on to support project managers in a consultative capacity, they don't have a direct role in making project decisions. Instead, their authority in the organization comes almost entirely from their expertise in project management skills; this means that, in addition to their knowledge, they must also be skilled change agents, persuasively offering counsel to personnel at all levels of the organization.

TABLE 13.2 PROJECT OFFICE FORMS AND RESPONSIBILITIES

	Low	Authority to influence projects			High
		Forms of the Project Office			
Responsibility	Center of excellence	Project support office	Project management office	Program management office	Accountable project office
Maintain standards	●	●	●	●	●
Maintain history	●	●	●	●	●
Organize training	○	○	○	○	○
Mentoring and consulting support	○	●	●	●	●
Schedule and budget analysis		●	●	●	●
EPM technology		●	●	●	●
Multiproject coordination		●	●	●	●
Project oversight		○	○	●	●
Make project management decisions				●	●
Supervise project managers			○		●
Meeting project objectives			○	○	●
Career growth for project managers	○	○	●	○	●
Supply project managers to the organization			○		●
Participate in project portfolio management	○	○	○	●	●

Legend: ● = Full responsibility
○ = Partial responsibility
Blank = No responsibility

Project Support Office

In addition to maintaining and promoting project management standards and practices, the project support office (PSO) actively supports a variety of projects by handling the mechanical chores such as building and updating the project plan and budget. Staffed by planning analysts, the PSO can be compared to bookkeepers who are responsible for maintaining accurate accounts while having no responsibility for profit and loss decisions. Planning analysts often grow into project managers, which means that adding more project managers to the firm's talent pool is another benefit of project support offices.

Project Management Office

A project management office (PMO) can supply schedule and budget support in the same way as the PSO. The major difference is that a PMO will supply project managers to projects all over the organization. A PMO thus becomes a long-term home in the organization for people who want to make a career out of project management. And, because it is populated by project managers, the PMO has the capacity to enforce project management standards. Although PMOs are responsible for managing the salaries and the career growth of their project managers, they are not responsible for project success or failure. That responsibility stays with the organization to whom the project manager is loaned. On the other hand, if the firm develops a series of failed projects, the PMO would share the blame, because it is the source of the firm's project management expertise.

Program Management Office

Programs are a series of related projects. For instance, when Boeing develops a new model aircraft, the effort—from customer support through procurement—is organized into a program. Programs have many similarities to projects; the most obvious are that they produce a unique product and that they have a beginning and an end. (The primary difference is that programs are so large and last so long that they develop some ongoing operations within them.) The role of the program management office is to supply project management expertise to the entire program, thus linking all the projects together. A large program management office will contain teams that perform many of the project management functions, such as schedule, budget, and risk management. Like a project support office, a program management office is not directly responsible for meeting schedules and budgets; its role is mainly to put good project management practices in place and support them. Unlike a project support office, the program management office does participate in program decision making, usually having an equal seat at the table with the other program leaders. (Figure 13.4 shows how the organizational structure of a program

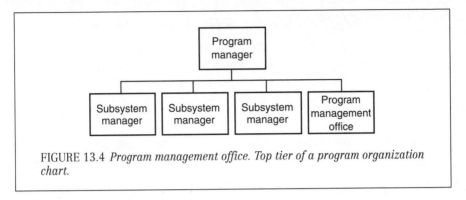

FIGURE 13.4 *Program management office. Top tier of a program organization chart.*

includes the program management office.) Finally, unlike any other form of project office, the program management office has a life span—it will be dismantled when the program is over.

Accountable Project Office

The accountable project office is the oldest, but in some ways the most radical, incarnation of the project office models. Although it is commonly referred to simply as "the project office," we call it the *accountable* project office to distinguish it from the other forms of project office in this chapter. This traditional model is accountable because it bears complete responsibility for meeting quality, cost, and schedule objectives of the projects assigned to it. Like the project management office, it is a long-term home for project managers, providing them a career path and administrative management. Its staff includes both project managers and project support personnel. The degree of influence wielded by the accountable project office depends on two factors:

1. *The degree to which the organizational structure favors projects.* When the accountable project office oversees a project-oriented organization, it sits at the top of the authority structure. More commonly, however, this office is responsible for cross-functional projects, resulting in a classic matrix organization. (Figure 13.5 in the next section shows an information technology project office that will lead matrixed projects and that will have total oversight for other projects.)

2. *The degree to which the organization embraces consistent project management practices.* This most powerful form of project office is often given more authority over projects at the same time that the organization is resisting implementation of the EPM components described in this chapter. This paradox results from the outdated notion that project management is an individual skill set rather than an organizational ability. However, in firms that embrace project management as a discipline, the dual role of executing projects and maintaining the project management process makes the accountable project office extremely influential.

KEY CONCEPT **Possible Project Office Responsibilities**

There is a large range of responsibilities that a project office can assume. (The first column of Table 13.2 lists a range of possible responsibilities.) Let's look at the possible range and what is involved in performing each of these various responsibilities:

Maintaining Project Management Standards

This includes documenting, promoting, and updating the best practices for project management. For example, a project office might make standards available via intranets or attend postproject reviews to look for improvements in the current standards.

Maintaining Project History

The collective experience of the enterprise is far more useful when it is maintained and organized for future retrieval. A project office can provide the structure and guidelines for storing and retrieving project history.

Organizing Training

Project office personnel may establish training objectives for project managers and teams and administer a training program to accomplish these objectives. The training program may be developed and delivered by the project office or brought in from an outside vendor. Given the range of skills required to manage a project, a project management training curriculum can be complex to build and administer. Because of this, many project offices share this responsibility with a functional training department.

Mentoring and Consulting Support

Because the acknowledged experts in project management techniques are in the project office, projects across the organization will look to this office for hands-on support of their project managers. Project office personnel will participate in planning sessions, phase reviews, and turnaround efforts. Even though the project office may simply be acting as a consultant and not running the project, there are still some activities, such as performing a risk assessment, where the expertise of project office personnel might make them the natural leaders. The advantage of this advisory role is that the expertise of the project office can be leveraged across many projects, without the burden of the day-to-day duties of project leadership.

Schedule Analysis and Budget Analysis

Perhaps the most common role of a project office is that of supplying planning analysts to assist project managers; these analysts help to build and maintain the detailed project cost and schedule information. They are well versed in the science of project management, and the project manager relies on them for accurate information and even recommendations. This, however, is where their responsibility ends; analysts do not make project management decisions.

Enterprise Project Management Technology

If the firm chooses to implement EPM technology, every form of project office will participate in this to some degree. At the lowest level of involvement, the center of excellence will determine the system requirements and design, but will have no role in collecting or consolidating project information. Both the project support office and project management office models will assist in development and operation of the system. In fact, the need for such information is often the catalyst for forming a PSO or PMO. The program management office and accountable project office will each have complete authority over generation and consolidation of project information within their respective spans of control.

Multiproject Coordination

The program management functions of cross-project resource leveling and monitoring relationships among projects will be practiced by every form of the project office except the center of excellence. These activities must be performed routinely with the cooperation of all the project managers and functional managers. If they perform this function well, it leads to the project office having greater influence within the organization.

Project Oversight

Creating and consolidating a consistent view of project status so that management can usefully monitor all projects is a responsibility of many forms of the project office. If state-of-the-art EPM technology is in place, this job is simplified, but the project office is still responsible for making it happen. In addition, the project office will usually participate in analyzing the information, using its expertise to identify a problem before it becomes a crisis.

Making Project Management Decisions

Here is where the strong line of authority and responsibility is drawn. Only the program management office and accountable project office will participate in managing a project.

Supervising Project Managers in Their Project Responsibilities

Only the accountable project office is actively involved in supervising project managers as they perform their jobs. A program management office can raise alarms if it sees problems and can use its influence with the program manager to bring about changes on particular projects, but project managers do not report to this office. A good PMO will also be proactive in mentoring its project managers, even though the project reporting structure doesn't include them.

Meeting Quality, Cost, and Schedule Objectives

Accountability for project success lies directly with the accountable project office. However, the roles of both the project management office and the program management office also bind them tightly to project success or failure. A string of project failures will bring scrutiny to a project management office, and a program management office will share much of the glory or blame for the end result of a program.

Career Growth for Project Managers

To some degree, all forms of the project office are responsible for the career growth and opportunities of project managers within the firm. At the very least, the training programs will provide a path to gain skills in project management. In addition, any of the models that employ planning analysts provide a potential source for future project managers. However, only the project management office and accountable project office models have complete responsibility for developing project managers and creating opportunities for them.

Supply Project Managers to the Organization

Only two of the models provide an ongoing source for people with the ability to manage projects and a place for project managers to call home between projects: the project management office and the accountable project office.

Participate in Project Portfolio Management

Each form of project office can have different levels of influence on project portfolio management, ranging from no involvement to an equal seat at the table. At the very least, staff from a project office may participate because their expert opinions and judgments carry weight. The PSO or PMO that consolidates and presents project information can add to its expert authority with the value of its data. And finally, just as they participate in managing projects, the program management office and accountable project office are likely to have an equal vote in decisions to initiate or cancel projects.

All Forms of the Project Office Have Value

It would be a mistake to consider the various forms of project offices as a progression that all firms should follow. This would suggest that a center of excellence is just the beginning and that the natural and correct evolution will always lead to the accountable project office with responsibility for managing all projects. This is the mistake of the fervent disciple—that if some is good, more is necessarily better. Instead, the project office should reflect the organizational structure and the location of projects within the firm. For instance, a Fortune 500 corporation that has been steadily increasing its project management focus for two decades uses both the weakest and the strongest models. It has a center of excellence located within its corporate information technology (IT) group to maintain corporate best practices and organize training. In addition, within the separate business units of the corporation, some IT directors have created an accountable project office responsible for managing all IT projects. The accountable project office at the business unit relies on the standards and training from the center of excellence and even uses them for consulting support on occasion. This firm has succeeded in matching the strength of each model to different needs within the corporation.

Scale the PMO to the Projects

Our discussion of PMOs so far implies full-time staffing to accomplish the many responsibilities of even a center of excellence–style PMO. Organizations with many complex projects probably do need to have people assigned full-time to handle PMO activities. But smaller organizations with smaller projects can accomplish the same activities with less formality. For example, a department with 10 project managers overseeing about 50 projects assigned all the project managers the task of creating their own standards and tools to accomplish project management, program management, and project portfolio management. These project leaders worked as a team, supported by the various functional managers to whom they reported. Without a spot on the organization chart, they were still able to act as a virtual PMO.

The mere presence of a project office, in any of its forms, is a commitment to improving project management. The most successful project offices serve as both experts in the science of project management and evangelists—untiring advocates of its value.

ORGANIZE FOR PROJECT MANAGEMENT

In the drive to build a more effective project delivery capability, another factor emerges that influences the complexity and value of the

EPM components we've examined so far. The firm's organization structure can have a huge impact on the efficiency of communication and decision making at the three tiers of EPM. The investment in EPM technology, for example, may reveal that assigning people to cross-functional project teams creates chaotic communication channels between the functional managers, project managers, and team members. Likewise, there may be agreement that a PMO needs to exist, but absolute disagreement on where the PMO should report. Re-creating the organization structure to favor enterprise project management isn't always necessary, but we should at least understand the factors that work for and against EPM effectiveness.

Projects, by their very nature, make any organization structure inefficient. Since projects are unique and temporary, they can run counter to an organization chart designed to support ongoing operations. Therefore, leveraging the value of project management begins with optimizing the organizational style—for both projects and operations.

KEY CONCEPT — Optimizing the Organizational Style

The three organizational models (as listed in Chapter 2)—function-driven, matrix, and project-oriented—include a wide spectrum of organizational styles. Every firm has projects and operations, and favoring one usually comes at the expense of the other. Figure 13.5 illustrates just a few of the many possible options. It would be wrong to suggest all firms should become completely project-oriented. Following are six factors that influence which organizational style is the best fit for a given company, in order of importance.

Projects versus Operations
Organizations that spend a majority of their budgets (or earn a majority of their revenues) on projects are better served by a more project-oriented structure.

Function Spanning
Functions are usually organized around technical specialties or knowledge, such as engineering, accounting, or marketing. If projects tend to include multiple functions, this will increase the cost of communication and coordination in a function-driven environment. The more frequently this happens, the *more a project-oriented style* will increase efficiency.

Size
Generally, the larger the projects, the more it makes sense to organize around them. And if a large proportion of costs and revenue come

Example 1

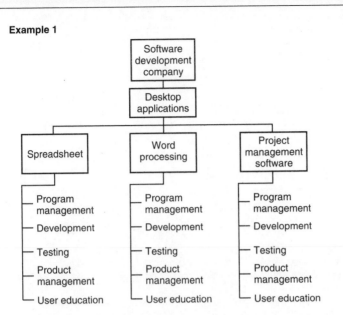

Product-oriented units are a form of project-oriented organization. Since the units are focused on developing new releases, most of their work is project-oriented. Though the products are compatible, they operate independently, a factor which also supports a project-oriented structure.

Example 2

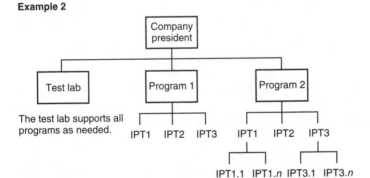

The test lab supports all programs as needed.

Programs are broken into integrated product teams. Each IPT is a cross-functional team responsible for producing a part of the product.

The company has organized around its two major programs—a very project-oriented structure. However, the test lab is still a functional organization because it is too expensive to create a test lab for each program.

FIGURE 13.5 *Examples of organizational structures.*

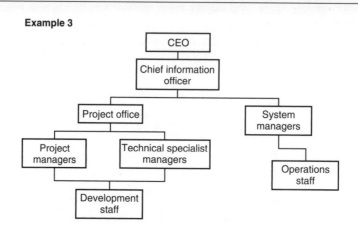

Example 3

The **project office** is responsible for new development.
System managers are responsible for operating established systems.
Operations staff have the necessary technical specialty skills required to support their systems.
Development staff are assigned to one or more projects at a time. They report directly to project managers for project work.
Technical specialist managers are responsible for long-term administration of development staff. They represent different technical specialties such as database administration and testing, as well as maintaining best practices with their specialty.
The CIO, along with the project office and system managers, performs portfolio management.

FIGURE 13.5 *(Continued)*

from projects, this argument becomes even stronger. In other words, a firm with a majority of its revenue coming from a few large projects should be more project-oriented than a firm with a majority of its revenue coming from many small projects. A number of size factors are worth considering:

- *Duration.* How long do projects last? If the length of average projects is at least as long as a budgeting cycle (usually a year), the projects will have a bigger impact on the budget process. This should push the organization toward organizing around projects.

- *Team commitment.* Are people assigned to one project on a full-time basis, or do they spread their time between projects and operations? When typical projects require full-time teams, this is a strong indicator in favor of a project-oriented structure.

- *Budget proportion.* When a project makes up a large portion of the organization's budget, it demands more attention. You can better understand the impact of a project on a firm by focusing on budget proportion instead of dollar amounts. For example, a million-dollar project may not rate the attention of a Fortune 500 executive, but it could be the difference between survival and bankruptcy for a small start-up. Another factor represented by budget proportion is the number of people on the project team. How many people are required per project will also influence how much project orientation is appropriate.

Similarity of Projects

Projects are unique (by definition), but in some firms there is a great deal of similarity among the projects. The greater the similarities, the greater the opportunity to manage projects in the same way as ongoing operations. Therefore, it is more likely that a firm like this will be function-driven. And if projects tend to be small, the tendency toward function-driven organization is amplified. This similarity factor has two components:

- *The actual work from one project to the next is similar.* For instance, an information systems department included a wide variety of projects, but all the projects for Year 2000 compliance had a lot in common: The tasks were the same and only the size of the systems varied. When a single manager was assigned to oversee all Year 2000 projects, she leveraged their similarities to make a large number of projects look like an ongoing operation that lasted for 18 months.

- *The projects produce unrelated products.* The more independent the products, the more project-oriented the structure needs to be. For example, a construction firm may be building a bridge in Hawaii, a stadium in Phoenix, and a canal in Costa Rica. These are three completely independent products and, therefore, three completely independent organizations. Product-focused organizations also provide examples of this factor; for instance, each of Microsoft's desktop applications groups supports a specific product (see Figure 13.5).[2]

Complexity of the Work

Companies rely on their experience to build up a knowledge base that gives them a competitive advantage. It's easier to build up expertise in a function-driven structure, because the expertise tends to grow within a function, and people organize their careers around the function. In the project-oriented structure, knowledge transfer from past to future projects is slower and requires more conscious effort to document—something most companies ignore. In a purely project-oriented structure, technical innovations might end up dying when the project is over. This factor highlights the challenge of choosing an organizational structure, because the short-term benefits of favoring projects can have the long-term disadvantage of losing institutional knowledge.

Predictability of Projects

The temporary nature of projects makes it harder for organizations to match people and projects. If this is combined with an inability to predict the volume of project work, it will be doubly difficult to forecast how many people they'll require. In companies like this, it becomes more important for their organizational structure to reflect this challenge by becoming more project-oriented. But as firms increase their control over the size and number of projects they manage in any budget cycle, there is less of a need to be project-oriented. Figure 13.5 contains three examples of how these factors will influence the degree to which a firm's organizational style will favor projects or ongoing operations.

 Allow Groups within the Firm to Organize around Projects Separately

The size and complexity of modern organizations defy easy decisions about organizational styles. In a large company or government agency, all forms may be appropriate, including the project-oriented form, so the proper question becomes, "*Where* should they become project-oriented?" Thus, the first decision for organizing for project management is defining the organizational boundaries of the change.

The aforementioned six organizational indicators can help define the practical limits of a project-oriented emphasis. For example, there were proponents of project management in two project-oriented sectors of a large health care organization: facilities and information technology (IT). Even though IT projects often required the support of facilities, the differences between their projects were so great that it made sense for both of them to establish their own project management practices and standards. But it also made sense for them to share ideas and work together so that each would gain from the experience of the other.

Any organizational style has strengths and weaknesses. The key is being willing to look for the risks and realizing that the best answer will require elements from both ends of the spectrum. For instance, when an aerospace company reorganized around its major aircraft programs, it embraced a project-oriented style and managed each program independently, even though the programs used common technologies. At the same time, however, company executives realized that the short-term gain of focusing on programs carried the downside risk of losing lessons learned from one program to the next. Even though a single program might last for years, the question arose: How would they transfer knowledge gained from one program to the next if each was being managed independently? This emerged as a particularly big risk because of the costs of developing the leading-edge technology required on modern aircraft. To counter this disadvantage, the company established support organizations responsible for maintaining and transferring the unique technical knowledge gained on each program. Since these support organizations exist to maintain and improve best practices, they are organized around the functional disciplines of the company.

Choosing the locations within a firm around which to reorganize projects lays the foundation for all decisions in the path toward organizing for project management.

Functional Organizations Still Have Projects

Organizing for projects doesn't require a complete reorganization to a project-oriented structure. A company or department that is primarily driven by ongoing operations and structured around functional disciplines can still set consistent project management practices in an effort to make the project portion of its work more effective. In fact, it makes good sense for operations-oriented firms to set project management standards, because projects are unusual to them and therefore pose greater management challenges. The bottom line is, if an organization has projects, it will benefit from a consistent approach to managing them.

Recognizing that individual departments can shift toward a project focus without requiring an entire company or agency to embrace the change enables the change to happen incrementally—and this slower rate reduces the risks associated with organizational change.

MANAGING THE CHANGE TO ENTERPRISE PROJECT MANAGEMENT

There are few corporate projects with higher risk than those that attempt to change organizational structure and culture. The business landscape is littered with failed implementations of the latest business fads. Long-term employees are cynical about such changes, having watched the corporate commitment to each new idea surge and falter until things eventually returned to business as usual. Considering all this, we need to ask, "Why should the change to project management be any different?" This final section performs basic risk management by identifying some of the pitfalls on the road to harnessing the potential of project management for the organization.

Long-Term Change Requires Leadership Commitment

Getting the cynics off the sidelines and into the game requires strong action by the firm's leadership team. Nothing speaks louder than authority and funding to demonstrate a commitment to real organizational change.

The change process should begin by recognizing the process itself as a project, with specific goals, identified stakeholders, and an accountable project manager. Both the amount of the budget and, especially, the number and caliber of people assigned to the team send a clear message. This team should answer to the highest possible level of management, and management support must be shown by a charter and by visible involvement in the project.

Management support is one of our five project success factors. In the case of EPM, that support must be visible throughout the initial implementation and endure until the new practices become good habits.

Discipline Is Not Optional

During the initial implementation of the new EPM practices, senior management can demonstrate their commitment by basing decisions and actions on the new project management deliverables. Management will add teeth to project approval gates by withholding funding or staff to teams that don't produce viable plans or a sufficient statement of work. Hold regular project reviews and ask the key questions that force project teams to use the discipline. Allowing teams or departments to bypass these requirements sends a clear signal that the new process is optional and might just go away if it's ignored long enough. While this type of management support may sound obvious, it isn't easy to accomplish. It takes discipline and commitment—and that's exactly what it will communicate.

Recognize the Power of Authority and Rewards

The speed of change will be in direct proportion to the authority of the project office. The center of excellence model has all the authority of an Old Testament prophet; that is, truth may be on their side, but they are fighting established traditions. At the other end of the authority spectrum, an accountable project office responsible for implementing projects is the only model that can enforce every aspect of the process. That doesn't mean the powerful version of the project office is the only one that will work, but you need to realize that the pace of acceptance will be slower with the other models. In fact, this slower pace might be acceptable, as long as the commitment to see it through doesn't waver.

In the long term, an organizational culture must evolve that respects and develops project managers. To achieve this, the career path must be well defined and well rewarded. As long as functional managers maintain a higher job code or salary grade, they will appear to be valued more than project managers. One way that companies are effecting change is by requiring some proof of project management competence; this proof might be a degree or certification from a college or professional association that qualifies the graduates to lead projects above a specific dollar value. The companies then match this responsibility with appropriate compensation. Actions speak louder than words, and nothing speaks louder about what's valued than what gets rewarded.

The Solution Must Fit the Problem

By now, it should be clear that the one-size-fits-all concept doesn't work when moving toward enterprise project management. That's why the process for change described in this chapter repeatedly emphasizes that understanding the nature of the firm's projects must act as the basis for designing the process. To review:

- The EPM standards and practices should reflect the various project types that exist within the organization. The expectations for managing different kinds of projects will reflect their different complexities.

- Deliverables such as the statement of work and risk management plan are developed based on the past success and failure factors for projects.

- All EPM technology is configured to support the firm's EPM goals. The technology is the *enabler,* not the purpose.

- EPM technology implementations will be as smooth or as rough as the underlying processes. The up-front analysis to nail down just exactly how the system will work and who will have authority is an investment that pays off during the pilot and deployment phases.

- The model for a project office is determined by the projects it will serve and the degree to which the organizational structure favors projects.

- EPM can vary in form and formality depending on the projects that exist within the firm, a difference that can extend to the organization structure. Different parts of a company or agency often have very different project management challenges and can benefit from different organizational structures.

If organizing for project management were easy, it would already be done. In making the new process fit the organization, it's necessary to listen to the dictates of common sense and the lessons learned from experience.

One of the best lessons comes from the many willing but cautious faces evident when a firm begins the process of organizing for project management. These are the project leaders who understand the value of better project management but aren't sure they can afford it. These people are already 110 percent busy, and they don't need more paperwork unless it is going to dramatically improve their lives. Respect their caution. As you develop standards and approval processes, err on the side of simplicity. When the minimum works, it creates success that can be built on later.

Most of all, you need to remember that projects are not ongoing operations—and they never will be. Operating as smoothly as a fine watch may be a legitimate goal for ongoing operations, because much of what they do is repetitive, but it's counter to the very nature of projects. Every project is unique, formed to solve a specific problem or capture an opportunity. This should lead to a more focused, more efficient project team. Organizing for project management should magnify that benefit, not reduce it by piling on unproductive bureaucracy.

KEY CONCEPT — EPM Leaders Are Subject-Matter Experts

Good project managers know more than just project management. As established in Chapter 2 (Figure 2.1), project managers have a degree of technical competence as well as other management skills. If an information technology (IT) project manager needs to understand something about computers, software, and networks, then it follows that the people leading the EPM implementation ought to understand project management. These people will be making a lot of decisions about the best ways to manage projects, programs, and the project portfolio. Those decisions demand good judgment—something that is developed through experience.

The EPM leaders best suited to creating a vision for the organization have already established good project management practices on their own projects. They also have the project management skills and experience to weigh the promises of EPM technology vendors against the reality of the firm's project challenges.

Another key skill of effective project managers is that of change agent. No matter how much formal authority EPM leaders are given, they will need strong influencing skills to gain the cooperation needed across the firm.

Assigning EPM leadership to a project management novice carries the same risks as handing over your accounting department to your best engineer. Pure intelligence, general management skills, and hard work won't make up for the intuition that comes from hands-on experience.

Process Change Relies on Cultural Change

Making the change to consistent project management, even in very large organizations, could theoretically be accomplished in a few months. In this scenario, the right team analyzes the organization, recommends the proper changes, and implements standards. Training follows to bring everyone up to speed. Change happens.

Why is it that the change often takes years to accomplish? Perhaps the most commonly ignored risk factor in the change process is the realization that people have to both understand and believe in the change. No matter how much authority is behind it, if project teams or project leaders resist the change, it will be a slow, torturous journey. Recognizing the risk of this kind of resistance, let's look at some options for reducing it.

Some firms are beginning to include change management specialists in the team that sets up the project office. This isn't change management in the sense of controlling scope or cost, but organizational change management, which includes "people issues." So right from the start these specialists focus on the issues that create resistance, incorporating organizational development techniques to smooth the transition.

Abraham Lincoln is credited with saying that we'll catch more flies with honey than with vinegar. That means that the change agents—the people in the project office—must be able to sell persuasively instead of simply trying to enforce change. Too many project office staff alienate their stakeholders, and even their sponsors, by demanding rigid adherence to the new processes. They justify a totalitarian management style by the need for immediate change, while insisting that "we're only doing what's best for the organization." Unfortunately, authoritative enforcement of standards ultimately demands more energy, as the role of the project office changes from mentoring to policing. This method often leads to total rejection of the new idea. Instead, project office staff and leadership should be evangelists—fervent believers, experienced practitioners, and tireless supporters of the new techniques. They need to realize that their mission is to change hearts and minds, and that their job is as much about selling as it is about schedule and budget analysis. If they are abrasive, condescending, or inflexible, they will close any open minds and poison their own message.

In implementing project management in his unit at Boeing, Steve Weidner has paid close attention to winning support from stakeholders. "Experiment, learn from users what adds value and what does not. . . . It was amazing to see how much resistance came down when we changed from pilots—which inferred the system was a done deal—to experiments, which left the users with the ability to influence their own destiny."[3] It should be obvious that people who are involved in making decisions are more likely to take ownership of the result.

Evolution versus Revolution

Even enthusiastic supporters can become cautious when the effort to change is overwhelming. It's necessary to remember that the people who will be learning the new process also have full-time jobs that can't be put on hold while they go to training or experiment with software tools. Change must be broken into increments that they can assimilate while they keep up with their workload.

Help Them Help You

Helping people succeed is another way of bringing down resistance. Having project office staff available to coach project teams speeds the learning curve. Strive for early wins to build momentum on projects. Coaches from the project office can facilitate a project planning workshop for the entire team, guiding them past the common pitfalls that might otherwise drain their enthusiasm. Make project office involvement a regular part of the project, guiding early status meetings to build good habits.

Skilled training helps, too. The best training promotes the new process and shows people what they'll be asked to do. Training should also allow people to experiment with new techniques or tools so that mistakes will be made in class rather than on actual projects. Finally, good training will allow people an opportunity to question the process, to argue a bit over its value, and to understand how adopting it will make them more successful.

Managing the Change Is Risk Management

The many benefits of embracing project management must be factored against the risks that come with organizational change. As we discussed in Chapter 5, success in risk management begins with recognizing the problem. Once we accept that the success of our project management processes relies on the people who will use them, we can also accept the need to win those people to our side through common sense, persistence, and leadership.

END POINT

The frontier of modern project management—and possibly the future survival of your organization—is dependent on the transfer of solid project management practices from individual projects to the organization. It is a transition that holds huge potential for magnifying productivity, but it carries with it the risks associated with organizational change.

The term emerging to describe the cohesive management of all projects and resources is *enterprise project management* (EPM), which is the conscious integration of processes, technology, organization structure, and people in order to align company strategy with the execution of projects. EPM recognizes the need to manage all the projects at three different levels:

1. The *project* tier represents the tools and methods for managing individual projects.

2. The *project portfolio* tier is responsible for the selection of projects and prioritization of resource deployment across projects.

3. The *program* tier operates between the other two, overseeing the relationships between projects, assembling the information necessary for portfolio decisions, and coordinating the deployment of resources across projects.

To enable these three levels of management, four components form the structure of EPM:

1. *Processes* are described for each tier of management, describing what should be done and who should do it.

2. EPM *technology* enables the processes—putting the application of project management theory in practical reach of the people performing the work.

3. The *people* who select, manage, and work on projects have the skills and knowledge to use the tools and processes.

4. A *project office* has responsibility for the EPM structure. Without some entity taking responsibility for EPM, it cannot endure. In addition to the project office, the organization may restructure lines of authority to streamline the communications and decisions taking place at the three levels of EPM.

As firms strive to implement enterprise project management certain guidelines are emerging.

- Recognize that organizing for project management is much more than developing standards and rolling out software tools. Rather, it is a cultural shift, which requires a change in values at organizational and personal levels. To make the change successfully requires close attention to the human element. Common sense and experience have taught us to listen to the stakeholders and realize that the wrong messenger can spoil the message.

- There is no one-size-fits-all solution. Project management has proven its effectiveness, but it's not the answer to every problem. Many departments within a company or agency can make the change, but each one should change in a way that is appropriate to its projects. A fundamental advantage of projects is that each is created to solve a specific problem, but this advantage will be lost if an organization tries to make every project the same.

- Treat the change as a project. Apply every lesson described in the other chapters of this book. Every one of the five project success factors will improve the odds for the EPM initiative—particularly management support!

The project management tool set has been in development for more than 50 years, driven by the belief that rational decisions based on accurate information will lead us to higher levels of productivity. Applying that tool set at the enterprise level not only has the potential for still greater productivity gains, but also helps to build the foundation for developing the next generation of project managers.

Stellar Performers:
Boeing and Lockheed Martin
Integrated Product Teams

Developing complex new products—whether they are automobiles, jet fighters, software applications, or commercial airliners—requires the cooperation of a wide range of specialists. From concept through delivery, staff from marketing, engineering, production, and a wide variety of other departments contribute their unique expertise. Traditionally, this has caused problems, as the leaders of these development efforts had to fight entrenched organizational "silos." Cooperation between different engineering disciplines was often low, as each group viewed the new product from its own perspective, leading to combative design phases and blown schedules.

To solve this problem, established industries are embracing a radical restructuring of their organizations, a process known as *integrated product teams* (IPTs). IPTs have swept away organizational structures that focus on functional specialties and replaced them with structures that emphasize the product being developed. (See Figure 13.6.) The Department of Defense, a leader in the movement toward IPTs, defines them as "cross-functional teams that are formed for the specific purpose of delivering a product."[1]

Each IPT contains the necessary disciplines to completely develop and deliver a product, which both empowers the team and increases accountability. Some of America's largest companies provide excellent examples of the shift toward integrated product teams.

When the Boeing Company developed its revolutionary 777 in the early 1990s, and new-generation 737s later in the decade, it used integrated product teams to speed development and optimize design. Each IPT had representatives from multiple engineering disciplines, manufacturing, procurement, customer support, finance, and in some cases, even airlines. With all disciplines working together on the same team, design for each part of the aircraft was optimized from all perspectives, including ease of manufacturing and maintenance.[2]

Lockheed Martin Tactical Aircraft Systems (LMTAS), the Fort Worth, Texas, producer of F-16 fighter aircraft, chose to reorganize around integrated product teams as part of its bid to build the new Joint Strike Fighter (JSF). As part of this effort, the firm has installed a new *integrated cost and schedule* (ICAS) accounting system to plan and manage this massive program. ICAS plans and tracks program costs and schedules at the lowest level of the work breakdown structure, then allows both cost and schedule status to be rolled up all the way to the program level. Using a WBS as the basis for accounting aids in early detection of cost and schedule problems, because costs are attributed to specific program components. Joint Strike Fighter, the first program to fully implement ICAS, reports lower administration costs and more timely program performance reports. LMTAS also participates in building the F-22 jet fighter. ICAS has enabled F-22 program managers to model potential scope, schedule, and pricing changes in less than a day—compared to several weeks in the past. That kind of modeling leads to better program management decisions.[3]

(Continued)

(Continued)

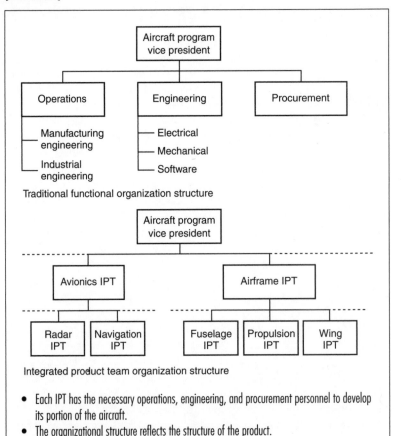

Traditional functional organization structure

Integrated product team organization structure

- Each IPT has the necessary operations, engineering, and procurement personnel to develop its portion of the aircraft.
- The organizational structure reflects the structure of the product.

FIGURE 13.6 *Integrated product teams change organizational structure.*

The transition to integrated product teams is just one more example of the way companies are transforming themselves to take advantage of project management techniques, bringing their product development efforts to a higher level of efficiency and quality.

1. *Department of Defense Guide to Integrated Product and Process Development*, Chapter 1, 1996 (http://www.acq.osd.mil/te/survey/exec_sum.html).
2. Speech by Boeing Commercial Aircraft President Ron Woodard, June 1997 (http://www.boeing.com/new/speeches/archive/value.html).
3. Becky Jacobs, *Earned Value Management Designed for IPD Teams, LMTAS Integrated Cost & Schedule (ICAS-EVMS)*, Lockheed Martin Corporation, 1997; *Integrated Cost and Scheduling Will Enhance Affordability of Lockheed Martin Fighters*, LMTAS press release, November 17, 1997.

14

Application Is the Art: Solving Common Project Problems

INTRODUCTION

The science of project management gives us the ability to calculate
schedules, calculate budgets, forecast resource requirements, measure
performance, estimate risk probabilities, and much more. Project
management software is increasingly available to make the number
crunching easier and to distribute the information faster. But computers don't manage projects, and estimates don't magically come true.
The tools and techniques described in this book form a powerful tool
set, but, as with any tools, they require a skilled hand to deliver a
completed project. This chapter describes how this tool set will help
you overcome problems that crop up on projects of any size, in any
industry.

Each problem or challenge is accompanied by a strategy for using
the tools we've discussed throughout this book. Many of the problems
will sound familiar, and the proposed solutions may give you new
insights. But don't stop with the answers you read here. The art of
project management is applying the science to achieve your goals.
With this chapter as a starting point, you can begin practicing the
art of project management on the problems confronting your own
projects.

RESPONSIBILITY BEYOND YOUR AUTHORITY

When projects span organizational boundaries, you can suddenly find
yourself relying on people over whom you have no authority. They

work for neither you nor your sponsor. How will you enlist them as accountable, enthusiastic team members you can count on?

- *Charter.* Ask your sponsor to publish a charter for all the stake-holders. Make sure that it strongly designates your authority on this project.

- *Statement of work.* Explain the reason behind the project, and give them the background necessary to understand its importance to the organization.

- *Communication plan.* Involve them in setting up your primary means of communication. If they are outside your organization, you'll probably need a formal means of keeping them up-to-date. Make sure that this is a two-way medium so you'll know that they are up-to-date and involved.

- *Small work packages with strong completion criteria.* Make assignments easy to understand and track. Involve them in estimating the cost and duration of tasks and in defining completion criteria. The more they are involved in developing the plan, the more ownership and commitment they'll feel.

- *Network diagram.* Show them how they fit into the project; emphasize the importance of their input and the probable impact on the project if they fall behind on their schedule. If they have tasks with a lot of float, you can let them set their own schedule, but be sure to let them know that you expect them to meet the planned start and finish dates.

- *Project status meetings with an open task report.* Give them updates on the project even during times when they aren't actively involved. Invite them to status meetings when their tasks are near enough to appear on the open task report. Hold them accountable to the schedule and to the rest of the project team.

- *Sponsor.* Develop a strong relationship with your sponsor by keeping him or her informed of your plans and your progress. You may need the sponsor's help in overcoming organizational obstacles.

DISASTER RECOVERY

In this scenario, a project is off the rails in a big way. After missing several major schedule milestones, the project manager is removed. You are assigned to turn this project around. What do you do?

- *Statement of work.* Start at the beginning with this project. What are its goals? Prioritize the remaining scope and clarify the penalties for missing the deadline or running over budget.

- *Project plan.* Using the work breakdown structure and critical path analysis, figure out the best possible schedule scenario, assuming infinite resources. This will give you the absolute shortest possible schedule. Next, negotiate for more resources, more time, or less scope (or all three) based on your plan. You can use your critical path schedule to show management which resources you will need to get the project done as fast as possible. If you do get more people, you shouldn't expect them to be productive immediately; you will need to allow for some learning time. There will be a lot of pressure on you to come up with a schedule that shows you will meet the deadline. At this point, you need to resist this pressure and remember that an unrealistic schedule will benefit nobody. Because there is already recognition that this project wasn't being managed correctly, you are likely to get management to agree to a realistic schedule if you present your facts confidently. In a situation like this, the project team needs a leader with a firm resolve to stick to the discipline.

- *Work package estimates.* Use the actual performance so far to create realistic estimates, and include the team in the estimating process. You'll be dealing with an exhausted, frustrated team—don't alienate team members by ignoring their experience as you create the plan.

- *Project status meetings.* Frequent status meetings focused on completing near-term tasks will keep you on top of progress and allow you to solve problems early. Use the open task report to keep your meetings brief and productive. Graph the progress on the plan so it's plain to everyone, especially the team, that there is tangible progress. Celebrate the small victories.

REDUCING THE TIME TO MARKET

Speed counts in your industry. The pace of change demands that your next release of a current product have a development time 20 percent less than that of the previous release. Between now and the deadline, you have to take your product through requirements, design, and construction, while building in the maximum functionality.

- *Statement of work.* Fast, focused performance demands a solid foundation. Getting agreement on authority, decision structures, and responsibilities among the participating groups will ensure that you don't waste time fighting organizational battles during the project.

- *Fixed-phase estimating.* Since you'll be working through the entire product development life cycle, there's no point in generating a detailed schedule from start to finish. Instead, choose several review points where you can reevaluate the functions of the product against the available resources and deadline. These review points constitute phase-end milestones. You can determine the duration of these phases using performance data from previous development efforts. You will need to stick to these review dates; for the team to meet the deadline, it must meet every phase-end milestone.

- *Project plan.* Develop a detailed plan for every phase. Using a network diagram, identify all possible concurrent tasks. The concurrent tasks are the opportunities for performing more work at the same time; these are the places where adding people to the project can compress the schedule. You can use this technique to determine the largest number of people who can work on the project productively. (Don't forget the resource-leveling guidelines, though.) Just remember that compressing the schedule by adding people may result in higher project costs.

- *Completion criteria.* Build quality checks into the project every step of the way. Although it may be tempting to skip some of the early quality-related activities in order to save time, you need to stay the course. It really is faster to do it right the first time.

- *Project status meetings.* Be clear about responsibilities and track schedule progress rigorously. Create a culture of schedule accountability by having strong completion criteria, and show clearly that falling behind, even by a little bit, is not acceptable. Build enthusiasm and a positive attitude by celebrating victories all along the way.

WHEN THE CUSTOMER DELAYS THE PROJECT

Based on a good statement of work and solid project plan, you and your team are making steady progress and are right on schedule. At this point, however, you start encountering delays that are the fault of the *customer.* How can you stick to the schedule when the customer is causing the holdup?

- *Network diagram.* First look for other activities that the team can shift its attention to. The network diagram will show you what other tasks you can be pursuing while you are waiting for the customer. The network is also the tool for assessing the impact of the delay. Is the customer working on a critical path task? If not, how much float is there? Use the network to demonstrate the customer's impact on the schedule.

- *Change management.* Determine the cost and schedule impacts of the delay. Even if the customer isn't on the critical path, there may be costs associated with changing your plan. Document the reason for the delay as well as the cost and schedule impacts, and bring it to the customer's attention without delay. You can show the unexpected delay on the project plan by adding a task to the work breakdown structure called "Delay due to _____"; insert the delay in the network diagram, too. If the delay idles any of your team members, you can start assigning their hours to the delay task. Even though you need to keep a positive attitude when working with the client to stay on schedule, these actions will send a clear message that the cause of the delay is well understood by all stakeholders.

THE IMPOSSIBLE DREAM

You've been handed a deadline and budget that are impossible. When you tried to tell the managers that it was not realistic, they started talking about "can-do attitudes." How will you handle this situation?

- *Statement of work.* Be extremely clear about the project's purpose, scope, and deliverables. Make sure that the scope and deliverables are really necessary to accomplish the purpose. Learn all the schedule and cost penalties.

- *Project plan.* Putting on your best can-do attitude, develop at least three options for what can be done. You must be able to demonstrate the trade-offs available to the managers. Then, recommend the option that seems to match their cost-schedule-quality priorities. Figure out the maximum number of people you can usefully apply to the project, using the network diagram and resource spreadsheet. Then look for the schedule adjustments that will bring the greatest cost reductions. Finally, use a crash table to analyze the most cost-effective tasks to compress.

- *Risk management.* Because this project will have risks that affect both cost and/or schedule, you will need to perform risk assessments at both the high level and the detail level to find your danger points. You can then take appropriate steps to mitigate the risk, including frequent monitoring and watching for new risks.

- *Status reports.* If you are attempting to meet a schedule that you believe is impossible, don't give up on changing your stakeholders' expectations. Let them know with every status report how diligently the team is striving to meet the goals and what the actual progress is. Raise the alarm frequently that if early progress is an indicator, actual cost and schedule performance won't match the plan. They may not believe you the first time, but as the evidence builds that this is a well-managed project that was underestimated, they will be forced to come to terms with reality.

FIGHTING FIRES

Your projects are always quick, high-intensity, and have little lead time. While the definition and planning activities sound great in theory, there just isn't any time for them.

- *Organizing for project management.* Rather than making the excuse that your projects are too fast or too fluid for these project management techniques, remember that a systematic method for using all of them will increase your ability to respond quickly to any situation. Fire departments—the folks who literally fight fires for a living—don't wing it. When their fire bell rings, they know all the right questions to ask to define the project, identify the risks, and make a plan. They don't call them project managers, but they have a designated leader whose job it is to monitor, coordinate, and communicate. So take a tip from the real firefighters: Get organized before the fire starts.

MANAGING VOLUNTEERS

You are leading a project for a volunteer organization. No one disputes your leadership, but you must accomplish all the goals without having any authority over anyone on the team. What's the secret?

- *Statement of work.* Build enthusiasm and a common vision by focusing on the purpose and deliverables. Sharing the purpose engages team members emotionally, and focusing on the deliverables will keep the scope limited. (Controlling the scope is particularly important for a volunteer project around which it may be difficult to rally the team to spend extra hours.)

- *Small tasks with strong completion criteria.* Make it easy for each person to succeed by giving everyone clear direction and little latitude for straying from the task.

- *Project plan.* You must be extremely organized and very aware of the critical path and the float. People may procrastinate early in the project if they don't perceive any urgency. Volunteers are often very busy people, so you will need to do some resource analysis. Without it, you may end up with a few people trying to accomplish everything at once.

- *Communication plan.* Develop a method of staying in touch with everyone without a lot of effort or frequent meetings. They will want to spend their limited volunteer time getting things done, not attending meetings.

- *Status meetings.* Frequent status checks will keep you in touch with progress, but periodic status meetings provide opportunities to energize the group, build relationships, and make project decisions. Celebrate the progress. Use good meeting management techniques to ensure that these are productive meetings that people will want to attend.

Manage Professionals Like Volunteers

In a way, you are managing volunteers. Peter Drucker likens managing professionals to managing volunteers, because they both want the same thing, that is, interesting, meaningful work that is a good use of their time.[1] Ask yourself, if you viewed every project you lead as a volunteer project, would it change your management style? Would your team be more enthusiastic? Would you be more enthusiastic?

ACHIEVING THE FIVE PROJECT SUCCESS FACTORS

Once again, let's take a look at the five factors that make a successful project:

1. *Agreement among the project team, customer, and management on the goals of the project*
2. *A plan that shows an overall path and clear responsibilities, which is also used to measure progress during the project*
3. *Constant, effective communication between everyone involved in the project*
4. *A controlled scope*
5. *Management support*

Clear goals, strong communication, realistic schedules supported by detailed plans. It's no wonder these have proven to be the ingredients of a successful project. None of these will happen accidentally. You will achieve them only by systematically applying the techniques of project management.

END POINT

The art of project management is applying the science to achieve success. When you are armed with the basic tool set of techniques to define, plan, and control projects, you have the components of every successful project. This is a tool set, however, that is sharpened through use.

Practicing the art of project management begins not only with understanding the science of project management, but also by believing that it works. Learning the science is not terribly difficult. I sincerely hope that this book has revealed the techniques in a way that makes them simple and easy to understand. Unfortunately, no book can ever make them easy to apply.

Project management is hard work. It requires persistence, dedication, and a thick skin. You will encounter opposition from people who consider project definition and planning a waste of time. They will test your conviction, particularly if the cynic is your boss or customer. You must hold true to the discipline through any opposition. This will ultimately bring you success and the reputation of being a professional project manager.

The Detailed Planning Model

I n Chapters 6 to 8 we explored a six-step model for developing a detailed project plan. The example for this model, the home landscape project, was spread over these three chapters. To make it easier to see the steps of planning, the home landscape project example is repeated here, beginning with the detailed planning model in Figure A.1 and following the stages through to completion (Figures A.2 through A.6).

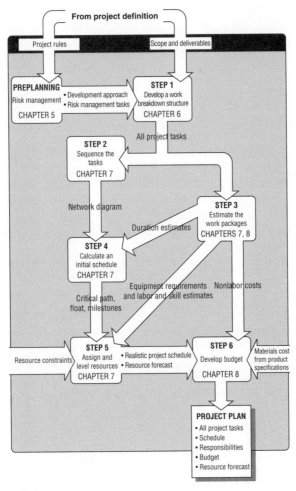

FIGURE A.1 *Detailed planning model.*

ID	Task Name	Predecessors	Duration	Labor Hours	Resource
1	Design home landscape		5 days	80 hrs.	Homeowner [0.5], Teens [1.5]*
2	Put in lawn				
3	Acquire lawn materials	1	2 days	64 hrs.	Homeowner, Teens [3]
4	Install sprinkler system				
5	Identify sprinkler locations	1	1 day	Fixed fee, 8 hrs.	Contractor, homeowner
6	Dig trenches	5, 11	2 days	Fixed fee	Contractor
7	Install pipe and hardware	6	3 days	Fixed fee	Contractor
8	Cover sprinkler system	7	1 day	Fixed fee	Contractor
9	Plant grass				
10	Remove debris		4 days	256 hrs.	Teens [3], Youth group [5]
11	Prepare soil	10, 3	4 days	96 hrs.	Teens [3], rototiller
12	Plant lawn seed	8	1 day	16 hrs.	Teens [2]
13	Plant shrubs	10, 1	6 days	96 hrs.	Teens [2]
14	Build fence				
15	Acquire fence material	1	2 days	16 hrs.	Homeowner
16	Install fence				
17	Mark fence line	1	1 day	32 hrs.	Homeowner, Teens [3]
18	Install posts	17, 15	5 days	80 hrs.	Teens [2]
19	Install fencing and gates	18	6 days	144 hrs.	Teens [3]
20	Paint/stain fence and gates	19	3 days	72 hrs.	Teens [3]

*On task 1, both the homeowner and teens are working 4 hours per day.

FIGURE A.2 *Develop a work breakdown structure, sequence the tasks, and estimate the work packages.*

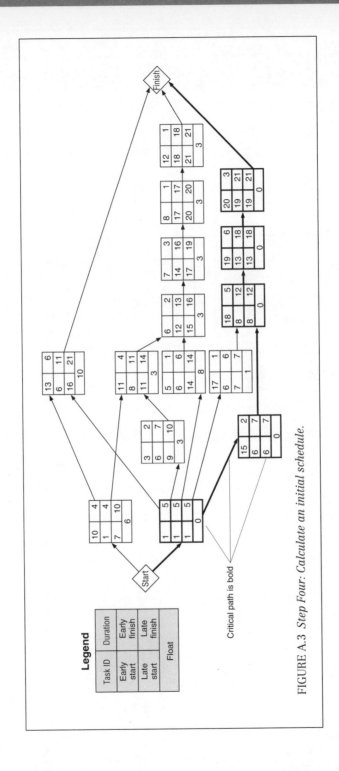

FIGURE A.3 *Step Four: Calculate an initial schedule.*

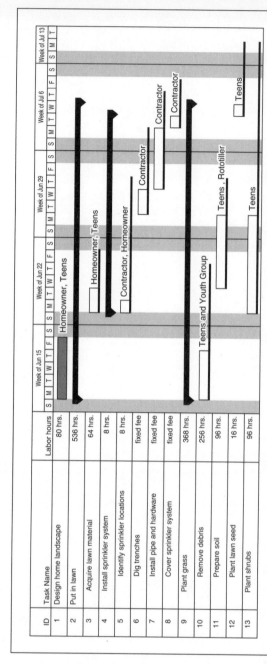

FIGURE A.4A *Gantt chart with resource spreadsheet for home landscape project*

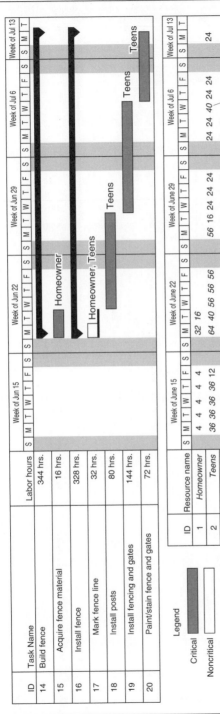

ID	Task Name	Labor hours
14	Build fence	344 hrs.
15	Acquire fence material	16 hrs.
16	Install fence	328 hrs.
17	Mark fence line	32 hrs.
18	Install posts	80 hrs.
19	Install fencing and gates	144 hrs.
20	Paint/stain fence and gates	72 hrs.

Legend
- Critical
- Noncritical
- Float
- Summary

ID	Resource name
1	*Homeowner*
2	*Teens*
3	Contractor
4	Youth group
5	Rototiller

Hours per day

- The resource spreadsheet shows the labor hours per day for each resource. Overallocated resources are in italics.
- The family has three teenagers working on the project, for a total of 24 hours each day. (3 teens @ 8 hours).
- There is only one homeowner, who is available for 8 hours a day.
- Given this initial schedule, with all tasks beginning on their early start dates, both the homeowner and teens are overscheduled during much of the project.

FIGURE A.4B

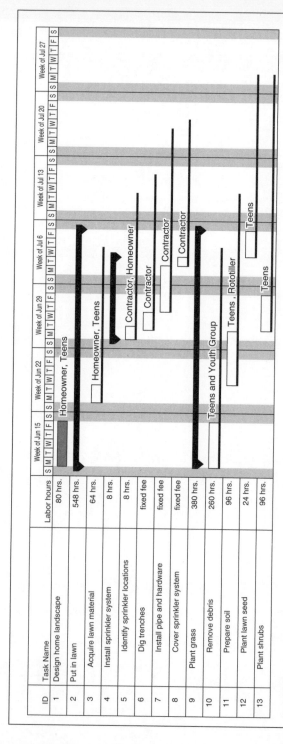

FIGURE A.5A *Step Five: Assign and level resources*

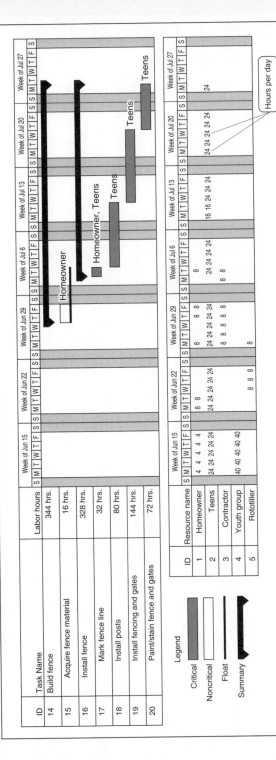

ID	Task Name	Labor hours
14	Build fence	344 hrs.
15	Acquire fence material	16 hrs.
16	Install fence	328 hrs.
17	Mark fence line	32 hrs.
18	Install posts	80 hrs.
19	Install fencing and gates	144 hrs.
20	Paint/stain fence and gates	72 hrs.

Legend

Critical
Noncritical
Float
Summary

The leveled schedule has eliminated the task overlaps, which caused unrealistic work hours for the teens and homeowner.

- *Task 5*—Delayed 5 days to level homeowner while keeping the sprinkler contractor on schedule.
- *Task 10*—Reduced teens to 4 hours per day (each) so they can participate in design home landscape at the same time. (Design home landscape also calls for each teen to work 4 hours per day.) Added on additional day for the youth group to work on the task. This changed the task duration from 4 to 5 days and the total labor from 256 hours to 260 hours.
- *Task 12*—Changed the task from two teens for one day (16 hours labor) to one teen for 3 days (24 hours labor). One teen working on the task alone won't be as efficient, but now the other two teens can work on task 18 at the same time.
- Tasks 13, 15, and 17—Delayed these tasks to level the project and their successor tasks were delayed as well.
- The new schedule is 10 workdays longer, but neither the teens nor the homeowner are overallocated on any day.

FIGURE A.5B

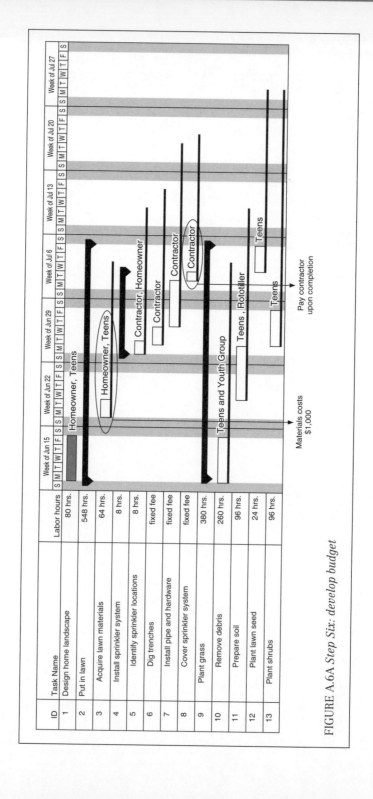

FIGURE A.6A *Step Six: develop budget*

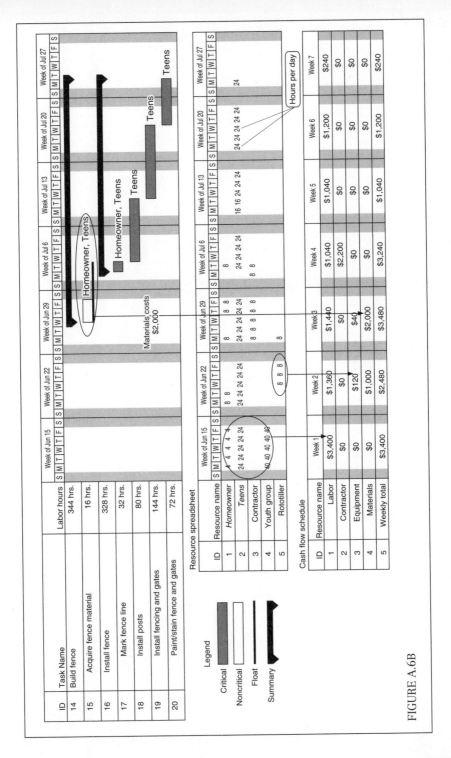

FIGURE A.6B

CHAPTER 1

1. Atul Gawande, "The Mop Up," *New Yorker* (January 12, 2004).
2. Project Management Institute and PMI web site (www.pmi.org).
3. Jeanette Cabanis, "Envisioning the Next Century," *PM Network* (September 1997).
4. Thomas A. Stewart, "Planning a Career in a World Without Managers," *Fortune* (March 20, 1995).
5. *PM Network* (September 1997), p. 31.
6. Bossidy, Larry, et al., *Execution: The Discipline of Getting Things Done* (New York: Crown Business, 2002), p. 8.
7. Robert Cooper, "Stage Gate™ New Product Development Processes: A Game Plan from Idea to Launch," in *The Portable MBA in Project Management,* ed. Eric Verzuh (New York: John Wiley & Sons), 2003, chap. 11.

CHAPTER 2

1. Philip B. Crosby, *Quality Is Free* (New York: McGraw-Hill, 1979).

CHAPTER 3

1. Robert Miller and Stephen Heiman, *Strategic Selling* (New York: Warner Books, 1985).

CHAPTER 4

1. Project Management Institute, *A Guide to the Project Management Body of Knowledge* (Newtown Square, PA: PMI, 1996), p. 167.

CHAPTER 5

1. Software Engineering Institute, *Continuous Risk Management Guidebook* (Pittsburgh, PA: SEI, 1996), pp. 439–442, 471–500.
2. Ibid., p. 32.
3. Ibid., pp. 439–442, 471–500.
4. R. Max Wideman, ed., *Project and Program Risk Management* (Newtown Square, PA: Project Management Institute, 1992).

CHAPTER 6

1. Michael A. Cusumano, "How Microsoft Makes Large Teams Work Like Small Teams," *Sloan Management Review* (Fall 1997), p. 13.
2. Steve McConnell, *Rapid Development: Taming Wild Software Schedules* (Redmond, WA: Microsoft Press, 1996), p. 72.
3. Stephen R. Covey, *The Seven Habits of Highly Effective People: Restoring the Character Ethic* (New York: Fireside, 1989).

CHAPTER 8

1. Project Management Institute, *Project Management Body of Knowledge* (*PMBOK*), (Newtown Square, PA: PMI, 1987).

CHAPTER 9

1. Fred Brooks, *The Mythical Man-Month* (Reading, MA: Addison-Wesley, 1995).
2. Project Management Institute, *A Guide to the Project Management Body of Knowledge* (Newtown Square, PA: PMI, 1996), pp. 68, 162.
3. Harold Kerzner, *Project Management: A Systems Approach to Planning, Scheduling and Controlling,* 4th ed., 1992), p. 684–688.
4. Tom DeMarco and Timothy Lister, *Peopleware: Productive Projects and Teams* (New York: Dorset House, 1987), pp. 15–16.
5. Philip B. Crosby, *Quality Is Free* (New York: McGraw-Hill, 1979).

CHAPTER 10

1. David P. Hanna, *Designing Organizations for High Performance* (New York: Prentice Hall, 1988).
2. Kristin Arnold, "Making Team Decisions," in *The Pfeiffer Book of Successful Team-Building Tools,* ed. Elaine Biech (San Francisco: Jossey Bass/Pfeiffer, 2001), p. 157.
3. The responses to conflict have been written about widely. The original reference on this topic is R. R. Blake and J. S. Mouton, *The Managerial Grid* (Houston: Gulf Publishing, 1964).
4. Roger Fisher et al., *Getting to Yes: Negotiating Agreement without Giving In* (New York: Penguin Books, 1991). To some degree, all the guidelines for working through conflict are expressed in this useful book. In particular, guideline #4 comes directly from chapter 3.

5. John C. Redding, *The Radical Team Handbook* (San Francisco: Jossey-Bass Business & Management Series, 2000), pp. 64–65.
6. Ibid., pp. 89–90.
7. Ibid., p. 103.
8. Peter Senge, *The Fifth Discipline: The Art and Practice of the Learning Organization* (New York: Doubleday, 1990). Also *The Fifth Discipline Fieldbook: Strategies and Tools for Building a Learning Organization* (New York: Doubleday, 1994).
9. An excellent reference on the topic of high-performance teams is Peter R. Scholtes, Brian L. Joiner, and Barbara J. Streibel, *The Team Handbook* (Madison, WI: Oriel Inc., 1996).

CHAPTER 11

1. Fred Magness, *Fundamentals of Project Management* (Washington: Qualitech Systems, Inc., 1990).

CHAPTER 13

1. Denis Couture, "Enterprise Product Management," in *The Portable MBA in Project Management,* ed. Eric Verzuh (New York: John Wiley & Sons), p. 349.
2. Michael A. Cusumano and Richard W. Selby, *Microsoft Secrets: How the World's Most Powerful Software Company Creates Technology, Shapes Markets, and Manages People* (New York: The Free Press, 1995), p. 49.
3. Greg Hutchins, "PM@Work," *PM Network* (March 1998), p. 13.

CHAPTER 14

1. Peter F. Drucker, "Management's New Paradigms," *Forbes* (October 5, 1998), pp. 152–177.